NOTES

NOTES

TENTH EDITION — 1974-1975

International Directory of Little Magazines & Small Presses

Len Fulton, Editor/Publisher

Associates:
James Boyer May
Gerald England
Ellen Ferber
Vivienne Finch

ISBN. No. 0 - 913218 - 13 - 8 Paper
ISBN. No. 0 - 913218 - 14 - 6 Cloth

© 1974 by Len Fulton. Published annually by Dustbooks, PO Box 1056, Paradise, California 95969. $4.95/copy; $15.00/4 yr subscription; $7.95/cloth; $25.00/4 yr subscription. Dustbooks also publishes SMALL PRESS REVIEW, DIRECTORY OF SMALL MAGAZINE/PRESS EDITORS AND PUBLISHERS, SMALL PRESS RECORD OF BOOKS, BRITISH DIRECTORY OF LITTLE MAGAZINE AND SMALL PRESSES, and chapbooks of poetry and prose. Dustbooks: Publisher, Len Fulton; Associates: James Boyer May, Ellen Ferber; UK: Gerald England, Vivienne Finch, 56 Blakes Lane, New Malden KT3 6NX.

This Tenth Directory is dedicated to one of the finest poets the world will ever know:

BILL WANTLING, 1933-1974

With great Sadness, Love, and Admiration

We are the less for his going, and the more for his having been.

"A little magazine should suggest, not conclude... should stimulate to thinking rather than dictate thought... I have none of the qualifications of the editor; that's why I think the Little Review *is in good hands."*

— Margaret Anderson
The Little Review, Feb., 1915

PEOPLESHIP

The little magazines and small presses are proud users of the notion that the word is free, raw material. From those early days in this century — the days of Margaret Anderson's *Little Review,* Harriet Monroe's *Poetry,* Alfred Kreymborg's *Glebe* — the notion has possessed a more or less literary frame, though there was always politics and other matter too, as with, for example, *The Masses.* Monroe and Anderson, in fact, planted certain basic ingredients in the movement which still remain: an absolute sensitivity to new poetic forms, and to new, young poets (as in the case of Monroe); and a passionate thirst for fresh culture and thought in general (as in the case of Anderson). Kreymborg too brought something basic: a spirit of fearlessness. After *Glebe* in 1913 he started *Others* (1915), *Broom* (1921), and *The American Caravan* (1927).

The vision is always dissenting and unpopular in political and aesthetic ways. The reach exceeds at virtually every moment the grasp. It has been estimated that since 1912 the large commercial publishers have discovered and sponsored fewer than 20% of the world's writers — the small magazines and presses the rest. The so-called "schools" — imagism, dadaism, surrealism in the early part of the century; the Beats, Concrete Poetry more recently — were all born and nourished through this medium. It is a movement which began in the second decade of this century, flourished through the Twenties and continued into the Thirites, when it took on a more political cast as you might expect. The Forties and early Fifties saw the movement eclipsed, but restoration of its force began again in the mid-Fifties.

A kind of *peopleship* then seemed to seize the day sometime in the early Sixties — perhaps it was Savio naming the University of California, Berkeley, "odious," and calling for bodies to be put upon the wheels and gears to stop the impersonal machine. The streets then came alive, and before long the entire world seemed engulfed in one way or another in an activist re-turn of the people to their strength of tribal spirit. To nothing has this spirit been more indigenous than small-press publishing. The underground newspapers, of course, starting in 1963, flashed and flourished until more than a hundred existed in the United States alone. But it has been the more sluggish publishing, *literary* publishing, which has come more strictly out of the tribal energy, and which has continued to last and build as a fresh movement on into the Seventies.

The small press of the Sixties was characterized by certain dramatic thrusts: the "Mimeo Revolution" (which peaked in 1965), Concrete Poetry (which had started in the early Fifties in Europe and Brazil), and word-plastics experimenters. There was a phenomenal rise in the use of offset printing which freed up technical matters for the flow of an "intermedium" art — the tendency of the genres to overlap each other. There were certain regional effects, generalists, "deep imagists," aesthetic realists, linguistic realists (Immanentists), and so on. In the early century the prime nodes of activity had been Chicago, New York, Paris — the great urban cultural centers. Through the Fifties, Sixties, and into the Seventies, however, an incredible geographic dispersal has occurred. Though New York, San Francisco and London remain as kind of anchoring centers, the small presses are found everywhere there are *people.* What the Sixties introduced to the movement was *do-it-yourselfism,* and a diminution of reliance on, and trust in, the great demon-god ships of world corporate enterprise. You could transport an old Multi-1250 or an A.B. Dick 320 into your cellar, up to your cabin for that matter, or out to the farm. Poets have learned to set type, cut paper, run presses. That poetry known as "Concrete" may have precipitated the last sustained critical/intellectual argument — and that was feeble enough when you look back and consider the heat generated by dadaism, imagism, or surrealism. The passions — and the poetry — are more nearly personal. The aesthete, the *critic,* have become disconnected, isolated. In a do-it-yourself culture the aesthetic tolerance widens, the practical how-to aspects have greater value, and literary "stardom" becomes a useless, almost antithetical phenomenon. Few artists do not covet greatness, of course. But, that assumed always, the *atmosphere* in which this driving force finds itself makes all the difference, whether it will be isolated and angry, or whether it will be participatory, *working.* And the present working atmosphere of small-press publishing rests on a sense of community.

The small press movement has continued into the Seventies, broadening its grasp and its hold both in quality and quantity. In the past ten years something over one thousand small magazines and presses started up in the United States alone, contrasted with, as a decade, the period 1930-1940 in which some two hundred efforts can be counted. This Directory carries more than 450 listings from the United Kingdom, more than double the figure for a mere five years ago. It is probably not quite fair to compare the Sixties and Thirties in *quality* of production, however, because the technological advances in printing have been immense.

In the Thirties most small mags were produced by the process known as "letterpress" (lead) and hence limited in graphic scope and freedom of design. Since the late Fifties there has been increasing and often experimental production with *offset* (photo-chemical) equipment, and now, as the knowledge and equipment become more refined, small press products have taken on an edge of beauty unknown forty years ago. Today more than 70% of the small presses use offset printing, compared to 17% in 1960.

The force has now turned with the decade to cover more and more of the ground the Sixties had only begun to illuminate: the women's movement, the aesthetics of how-to, ecology, prisoners, Native Americans, Blacks, Chicanos, communal living. Entire magazines, issue upon issue, are now devoted to material only touched upon earlier. Poetry, of course, is still the mainstay (and the small press is poetry's) but there is increasing space given to prose, both fiction and non-fiction, and to graphic and experimental design. Poetry *is* the province of the small press. Soon so will be short fiction; and one day, given the vagaries of an economy the large publisher is less and less able to contend with, longer fiction as well.

LISTINGS INCLUDE: Name of magazine and/or press, name of editor(s), address, type of material used, additional comments by editors including recent contributors, frequency (x/yr), one-year subscription price, single copy price, founding year, average no. of pages, page size, circulation, production method (mi, mim – mimeo; lo, of, off – offset/litho; lp – letterpress), length of reporting time of submissions, payment rates, ad rates, discount schedules, back issue prices, no. of issues/titles published in 1973, expected in 1974. Certain special abbreviations apply to listings from the United Kingdom: px=postage is extra; pf=postage is free; pp= pages; p=pence.

Each listing is keyed to certain categories, some self explanatory; others are acronyms for the following organizations: COSMEP=Committee of Small Magazine Editors and Publishers; CCLM=Coordinating Council of Literary Magazines; COSMEPA=Committee of Small Magazine Editors and Publishers, Australasia; UPS=Underground Press Service, which is now changed to APS – Alternative Press Service; ALP=Association of Little Presses (UK); ALMS=Association of Little Magazines (UK); NESPA=New England Small Press Association. Whew.

AB INTRA, Hellric Publications, **Dolores Stewart,** Hellric House, 39 Eliot St., Jamaica Plain, MA 02130. Poetry. *Poetry only. Behind schedule, some, but reading mss.* Irreg; $2.50/4 issues; 75 cents/ea; 75 cents/sample; 1972; 26p; 8½x11; 500 circ; lo. Reports 2 wks to 1 mo. Pays copies only; 5 + sub. No outside ads. Discounts: only on orders for 20 copies or subscriptions 50%. Back issues: 75 cents. Pub'd 1 issue 1973, expects 4 in 1974. Independent.

Aberdeen Arts & Entertainments Guide (see Z MAGAZINE)

ABBEY, White Urp Press, **David Greisman, poetry & circ.,** 5011-2 Green Mountain Circle, Columbia, MD 21044, **Peter Blush, fiction,** 55 Tudor Court, Pointe Claire, Que., Canada. Poetry, fiction, articles, art, photos, interviews, criticism, reviews, letters, parts-of-novels, longpoems, plays. *We prefer longer or shorter prose or verse written in English or Cockney that bore or cheaply thrill our readers who should have known better than to come to us in the first place. Some recent contributors: Andrew Darlington, Michael Joseph Phillips, Steve Sneyd, Lyn Lifshin, Ann Menebroker, Vera Bergstrom, J. Wm. Myers, O. Howard Winn, Mark Mac-Mackin, Mark Levinson.* 4-10/yr; sub. free; free/ea; free sample; 1969; 15p; 8½x 11; 200 circ; mi. Reports 2 yr. Pays copies only. Ads: $7/pg; $3/½; class/wd. 1 cent per. Discounts: you want it, you pay postage. Back issues: 75 cents/ea. Pub'd 8 issues 1973, expects 7 in 1974; expects 1 book in 1974.

Aberdeen Peoples Press (see also INSIDE OUT MAGAZINE), 10 Rubislaw Den South, Aberdeen UK.

ABERDEEN UNIVERSITY REVIEW Aberdeen University Press Ltd., **E.E. Morison,** Dept of Mathematics, King's College, High St., Aberdeen AB9 2UB, UK. Articles, poetry, criticism. 2/yr; £1.50; 75p; 1913; 96pp; 15x24.5cm; 1250 circ. Reports 1 mo. No pay.

ABRAXAS, Abraxas Press, **Warren Woessner,** 2322 Rugby Row, Madison, WI 53705. Poetry, criticism, reviews, graphics. *After* Abraxas 10, *we will no longer consider unsolicited poetry manuscripts.* Abraxas *will be devoted entirely to criticism reviews and graphics. The press will also do occasional single-poet pamphlets.* 1-2/yr; $2/2issues; $1/ea; $1/sample; 1968; 44p; 8½x7; 300 circ. Reports: 2-3 wks. Pays: copies only. Discounts: 40%. Pub'd 1 issue 1973, expects 2 issues 1974. COSMEP, CCLM.

ABYSS, **Gerard Dombrowski,** PO Box C, Somerville, MA 02143. Poetry, fiction, articles, art, photos, cartoons, interviews, satire, criticism, reviews, music, letters. *Completely new policy-look at an issue before submitting.* Q; $4/yr; $1/ea; 75 cents/sample; 1966; 40p; 8½x11; 500 circ; of. Reports 6 wks. Pays copies only. COSMEP, CCLM.

Action Community Pressworks, 1021 H Street, Arcata, CA 95521.

THE ACTIVIST, Activist Publishing Company, Box 163, Oberlin, OH 44074.

ADAM INTERNATIONAL REVIEW, **Miron Grindea,** 28 Emperors Gate, London SW7, UK. Poetry, fiction, art, music, plays. *Anglo-French quarterly. Also publish Adam Poets, concertina booklets devoted to the work of hitherto unpublished authors.* 75p each. £3 per year.

THE ADVOCATE (newspaper), Advocate Publications, Inc., **Dick Michaels,** Box 74695, Los Angeles, CA 90004. News articles, interviews, reviews. Biweekly; $7.50/yr; 50 cents ea; 50 cents/sample; 1967; 48p; full tab; 50,000 circ; lo. Ads: Full page on request. Back issues: $1. Published 26 issues in 1973, expects 26 in 1974. COSMEP, Gay.

AFRICA DIGEST, Africa Publications Trust, **Jane Symonds,** 48 Grafton Way, London W1P 5LB, UK. Articles, news items. Bi-monthly; £3/sub; 50p/ea; pf/sample; 2,000 circ; lp. Discounts: 10% sub. agencies. *Book reviews of publication African affairs.* African Digest *is a press and news digest. Useful for reference.*

THE AGNI REVIEW, Agni Press, **Askold Melnyczuk,** P.O. Box 663, Cranford, NJ 07016. *Recent contributors: Ira Sadoff, Russell Edson, Anselm Hollo, Heather McHugh, Robert Bly, Greg Kuzma, Stuart Dischell and Alvin Greenberg. We are interested in doing one or two chapbooks or full length books of poetry. Inquire first. We would like to see more fiction.* 2/yr; $2/yr; $1/ea; $1/sample; 1972; 50p; 5½x8½; 500 circ; lo. Reports 3 wks. Pays 3 copies. Ads: $50/pg; $25/½. Pub'd 1 issue 1973, expects 2 issues, 1 book in 1974.

AISLING: a quarterly of Irish & American Poetry, **Paul Shuttleworth,** 2526–42nd Avenue, San Francisco, California 94116. Poetry, interviews, criticism, reviews. Aisling *publishes poems of clarity, honesty, vision. Poetry does not have to be Irish in nature. We do not use "St. Patrick's Day verse." Recent contributors: James Liddy/Dave Kelly/ Sydney Bernard-Smith/Daniel Halpern/ James J. McAuley/ Adrianne Marcus/ William Dickey/ Sean Lucy/ James Simmons/ Michael Casey/ Knute Skinner/ Norman H. Russell/Tom McKeown.* Quarterly; $4/yr; $1/ea; $1/sample; 1973; 28p; 8½x11; 300 circ; lo. Reports 2 wks. Pays 2 copies plus sub. Ads: Full pg $25, ½ pg $15. Discounts: 50% off for orders of 20 or more. Pub'd 2 issues in 1973, expects 3 in 1974; 0 books, 1973, expects 1 in 1974. COSMEP, Irish.

AKROS, Akros Publications, **Duncan Glen,** 14 Parklands Ave., Penwortham, Preston, Lancs., UK. *Mainly Scottish poetry and criticism. Contributors include Hugh MacDiarmid, Edwin Morgan, Robert Garioch, Alexander Scott, George Bruce, Alan Jackson, David Black, Duncan Glen, Sydney Goodsir Smith, Donald Campbell, Maurice Lindsay, John Herdman, Tom McGrath, J.K. Annand. Articles, poetry,* interviews, criticism, letters, longpoems. 3/yr; £1 ($4)/sub; 30p/ea; 1965; 64 pp; 9x7inches; 800 circ; lp. Reports: a few days. Pays: £3/page. Ads: £14/page £8/½page. Discounts: 25% below 4; 33% above 4. Back issues: Nos.1-9/$22from Krauss. ALP.

AKWESASNE NOTES, c/o Mohawk Nation, PO Box 435, Rooseveltown, NY 13683.

THE ALASKA REVIEW, Alaska Methodist Univ., Anchorage, AK 99504.

Albion Village Press, **Iain Sinclair,** 28 Albion Drive, London E8 4ET, UK. Poetry, fiction, art, photos, interviews, criticism, letters, longpoems.

Alchemist Publishing, **Bil Paul,** 231 Dorland St., San Francisco, CA 94114. Primarily *printing photo-essay books of my own material but do consider others' work if in 'real' vein.* ½yr. or so; 1972; lo. Discounts: 40% off to bookstores. Pub'd one book in 1973, expects one in 1974. COSMEP.

ALGOL: A Magazine About Science Fiction, Andrew Porter, PO Box 4175, New York, NY 10017. Articles, art, photos, cartoons, interviews, criticism, reviews, letters. Algol is published for the science fiction reader interested in the behind-the-scenes workings of the science fiction field. It regularly publishes articles and letters by award winning authors exploring their own writing and that of others. Algol has been nominated for the Hugo Award by the World Science Fiction Convention. Regular columns by Richard Lupoff (books) and Ted White. Other recent contributors include Ursula K. LeGuin, John Brunner, Alfred Bester, Ray Bradbury, Robert Silverberg, JG Ballard, Barry Malzberg, James Blish. 2/yr; $5/6 issues; $1/ea; $1/sample; 1963; 54p; 8½x11; 4,000+ circ; lo. Reports 2-3 wks. Pays ½-1 cent/wd. Ads: $60/pg, $40/½pg, 10 cents/wd. Discounts: 40% to bookstores, min. 10 copies. Booksellers entitled to free classified ad, 25% discount on display advertising. Back issues: none available. Pub'd 2 issues 1973, expects 2 in 1974. Foreign Agents: England: Ethel Lindsay, Courage House, 6 Langley Ave., Surbiton Surrey KT6 6QL, UK. Europe: Waldemar Kumming, 8 Munchen 2, Herzogspitalstrasse 5, Postscheckkonto Munchen 1478 14-802, W.Germany. Australasia: Mervyn Binns, Space Age Books Ltd., 317 Swanston St., Melbourne Vict. 3000, Australia. Canada serviced directly from New York, Canadians should remit in Canadian cheques or currency. COSMEP, Fantasy Amateur Press Assn.

Alice James Books, 138 Mt. Auburn St., Cambridge, MA 02138. Alice James Books *is publishing its first two volumes of poetry -* US: Women *by Marjorie Fletcher, and* The Trans-Siberian Railway *by Cornelia Veenendaal. They will be followed by two volumes every spring and fall. Alice James Books is a cooperative, with an emphasis on publishing poetry by women. Books by other members of* Alice James - *Patricia Cumming, Jean Pedrick, Lee Rudolph, Ron Schreiber, Betsy Sholl - arescheduled for publication over the next two years.* Individual bks. $3 ($4.25 signed by author). First series subscriptions $18 ($25 signed).

THE ALIEN CRITIC, PO Box 11408, Portland, OR 97211.

ALL IN, **Nina Steane,** 31 Headlands, Kettering, Northants, UK. Poetry, criticism, longpoems. *Nos.5-25 include Thom Gunn, Ted Hughes, Brian Patten, George Mc-*

Beth. 2/yr; £1/sub; 25p/ea; 1958; 1pp; 17x25; off. Reports 1-2 wks. Pays copies (unless commissioned). Ads: free (sep. sheet). Discounts: 50%.

All This & Less Publishers, **Thomas Michael Fisher, Richard Blair,** St. Andrews, Laurinburg, NC 28352. *We did our first book in 1974:* Zen Poems *by David Wade, and issued a cassette tape:* Hugh Fox at St. Andrews-Black Mountain Festival. *More books are on the way, and we're open to submissions. Also to tape submissions for more of them. What we want is ideas from out there on mediums and possibilities – an assembled anthology, for instance, things like that.* All This & Less *is a cooperative undertaken by Tom Fisher and Richard Blair, and each of the editors is a separate publisher of his own magazine – Tom edits* Star-Web Paper, *Richard edits* August. Maybe 3 more books in 74, along with tapes and whatever you might come up with. *August* can be reached at 17 Robin Hood Lane, Chatham, NJ 07928, or through *Star-Web Paper.* COSMEP.

ALL-TIME FAVORITE POETRY, J. Mark Press, **Barbara Fischer,** Box 2057-M, North Babylon, NY 11703. Poetry. *Send 1 or 2 poems, 3-16 lines. Aesthetic, contemporary poetry that interacts with the reader. (No vulgarity, profanity, devoutly religious, or light or humorous. Don't imitate or try to be outlandishly different. Be yourself. Enclose return env. Send one submission to this editor and wait for reply. After ten years, we find we've published scores of today's popular poets. Being partial to everything we accept, we'd have to list 5,000 names to be fair, so we won't give any. We suggest you study a sample. Any of our titles will present a clear picture of what we look for.* Q; $5.95/soft; $8.95/cloth; $3.95/sample; 1963; 50p; 8½x5½; 3M circ; lo. Reports promptly. Pays: 2-10 cents/line. Ads: commercial $5,000 runs 4 issues/pg; poets' books: $5 per 30 wds./classified/wd. Discounts: quoted on request. Back Issues: $50/ea clothbound prior to 1973. Most numbers completely sold out. Pub'd 4 issues, 2 books 1973, expects 20 issues, 10 books in 1974. COSMEP, Suffolk city legislature, Cultural affairs.

The Ally Press, **Paul Feroe, Neil Klotz,** c/o CPS, 1452 Pennsylvania St., Denver, CO 80203. Poetry, fiction, articles, art, photos, interviews, satire, criticism, reviews, parts-of-novels, longpoems, plays. *The Ally Press is now concentrating on publishing small poetry books and pamphlets with essays or stories of pacifist-anarchist-vegetarian leanings. Past publications include* Sucking-Stones Magazine *featuring Robert Bly and Englishman Martin Booth. Future efforts will include Ronald Sampson's* The Anarchist Basis of Pacifism *and a new collection of poems by Booth.*  75 cents/sample; 1973; 50p; lo. Reports 1 mo. Pays copies only. Discounts: 20% disc. trade, 40% classroom. Back issues: 75 cents. Pub'd 1 issue 1973, expects 2-3 books in 1974. COSMEP.

ALOES BOOKS, E.M. Press, **Allen Fisher, Richard Miller, Jim Pennington,** 18 Hayes Court, New Park Road, London SW2 4EX, UK. Poetry, fiction, art, cartoons, photos, interviews, criticism, music, longpoems, collages. *Recent contributors: William Burroughs, Eric Mottram, Jeff Nuttall, Paul Matthews, Ted Berrigan, Alan Anson, Dick Miller, Allen Fisher, Ulli McCarthy, Bill Griffiths, Stefan Themerson, Lee Harwood. 50% shift towards Process-system material.* 30p/sample; 1970; 30pp; A4/A5; 200+ circ; lp; off; mim. Reports 1 mo. No ads. Discounts: trade 33 1/3%. COSMEP, ALP, B.A.A.

ALTERNATIVE LONDON, **Nicholas Saunders,** 65 Edith Grove, London SW10, UK. *This is an information book about alternatives in London. Format is brief article followed by critically descriptive listings. Illustrated by line drawings. Subjects: food bargains, money, communes, law, drugs, homosexuals, sex, crafts, buying guide, etc.* 1/yr; 40p pf/ea; 1970; 384pp; 7x4½"; 50,000 circ; off. No ads. Alternative information.

ALTERNATIVE PINK PAGES, **Stephen Wall, Philomena Horan,** PO Box 8, Surry Hills, Australia 2010. Directory. *Directory of alternatives in Sydney, Adelaide, New Zealand. 3000 items of info.* 2/yr; $2.80/yr; $1.40/ea; 1972; 144pp; 10x8; 10M circ; lo. Discounts: 30%. Pub'd 2 issues 1973.

THE ALTERNATIVE PRESS, **Ken & Ann Mikolowski,** 4339 Avery, Detroit, MI 48208. Poetry, art. *No.6 includes Ted Berrigan, Alice Notley, Bill Berkson, Philip Guston, Jim Gustafson, Jerome Rothenberg, Robert Creeley, Carol Steen, Deborah Richardson, Roy Castleberry, Faye Kicknosway.* Tri-Q; $10/yr; $2.50/ea; 1969; 12pp; page size varies; 500 circ; lp. Reports: erratic. Pays copies only. Pub'd 1 issue 1973, expects 3 issues, 1 book in 1974. COSMEP, CCLM.

ALTERNATIVES: Perspectives on Society and Environment, **Robert Paehlke,** c/o Trent Univ., Peterborough, Ontario, Canada. Articles, art, photos, cartoons, interviews, reviews. *Articles may be in any of social sciences, humanities, or law so long as they relate to pollution, conservation, resources or wilderness. Articles may be up to 6-7000 words. Journalistic coverage of environmental issues is also welcome up to perhaps 3000 words. We are also very much interested in art, particularly line drawings or other readily reproducible items.* Q; $3/yr individual; $5/yr institution; 75 cents/ea; free sample; 1971; 44pp; 8½x11; 1500+ circ; lo. Reports 3 mos. No ads. No pay. Discounts: 10 copies or more to same address at 50 cents per copy. Back issues: from $1 to $3 depending on issue (list available). Pub'd 4 issues 1973, expects 4 in 1974. Food/Ecology.

Am Here Books, Plan D'Essert, 1867 Ollon, Vaud, Switzerland.

AMAZON QUARTERLY, Laurel Akers, Gina Roberson, Audre Lorde, 554 Valle Vista, Oakland, CA 94610. Poetry, fiction, articles, art, photos, interviews, criticism, reviews, music, letters, parts-of-novels, longpoems, collages, plays. We welcome contributions by women who are exploring new patterns in their lives and art. We print no work by men nor any work with a heterosexual bias. Currently we are paying $50 for one outstanding contribution per issue — but this will be more soon. We especially are looking for in-depth essays exploring political and philosophical lesbian-feminist outlooks. Recent contributors have been Judy Grahn, Robin Morgan, Adrienne Rich, Audre Lorde, Fran Winant, Jane Rule (to list the "better knowns"). Q; $4/yr; $1/ea; $1/sample; $6/instit; 1972; 72pp; 7x8; 4M circ; lo. Reports 2-3 mos. Pays: as above. Ads: $100/p; $50/½; no class/wd. Discounts: all bulk (5 copies or more) 75 cents per issue; Special Plain Sealed Wrapper rate — $5 (also all outside U.S.). Back issues: none; most are out of print. Pub'd 4 issues 1973, expects 4 in 1974. COSMEP, Women, Gay.

AMBIT, **Martin Bax,** 17 Priory Gardens, London N6 5QY, UK. Poetry, fiction, art, photos, longpoems. *Always looking for material which excites and interests and suggest contributors read the magazine before they submit, which many seem not to do.* Q; £1/sub; 25p/ea; 30p/sample; 1959; 50-60pp; 9 5/8x7 1/8; 1500 circ; off; lp. Reports 3 mos. Pay: varies; £1 +/page. Ads: £20/page. Discounts: discussable. Back issues: last 12 numbers 25p/ea; earlier numbers £1/ea. ALP.

AMERICAN ARTS PAMPHLETS SERIES, American Arts Documentation Centre, **Mick Gidley,** American Arts Documentation Centre, Queens Bldg., Univ. of Exeter, Exeter EX4 4QH, UK. Articles, interviews, criticism. *The American Arts Pamphlets Series is an irregular series publishing specially commissioned items on the arts in America. Titles include "A Chronological Checklist of the Periodical Publications of Sylvia Plath"; "A Selected Bibliography of Black Literature"; "The Harlem Renaissance" and "A Catalogue of American Paintings in British Public Collections."* 1970; 25pp; 1300 circ; lp. No ads. Discounts: 33% bookshops. The Arts in America.

AMERICAN COLLECTOR, Real Resources Group, **John F. Maloney,** Box A, Reno, NV 89506. Articles, photos, cartoons, interviews, satire. *We use stories of 500 to 2200 words on antiques and collecting, providing information on current prices, availability, fakes, investment potential and history. All collectibles covered in depth, some with color illustrations. Colorful, up-beat and informative coverage of the current collecting scene. Recent features included an expose of the worldwide phony Wells Fargo buckle fraud — as well as other phony non-antique buckles. Another explored the strange comic book collecting boom.* Monthly; $4/yr; 50 cents/ea; sample free; 1970; 40pp; tabloid; 60M circ; lo. Reports 2 wks. Pays: $1.20/inch; $5/b&w art. Ads: $280/p; $195/½; $3/25 wds. Discounts: agency 15%. Back issues: 50 cents. Pub'd 12 issues in 1973.

AMERICAN IMAGO, Wayne State Univ. Press, **Harry Slochower,** 46 East 73 St., New York, NY 10021. *Critical articles on the application of psychoanalysis to the humanities (Art, Philosophy, Culture).* Q; $10/yr; 1939; 100pp; 1500 circ; lp. Reports about 1 mo. No pay. No ads. Back issues: consult Kraus Reprint Corp. Pub'd 4 issues 1973, expects 4-6 books in 1974.

American Mosaic FFCE (see PHOENIX FIRES)

AMERICAN POET, Prairie Poet Books, **Stella Craft Tremble,** Box 35, Charleston, IL 61920. Poetry. *Rather prim.* Q; $4/yr; $1.50/ea; no sample; 1960; 32pp; 5½x 8½; of. Reports 1 wk. No pay. No ads. Discounts: 25%. Back issues: none. Pub'd 4 issues, 30 books 1973, expects 40 books (prbk) in 1974. COSMEP.

AMERICAN POETRY REVIEW, 401 S. Broad St., Philadelphia, PA 19147.

AMERICAN QUARTERLY, **Dr. Bruce Kuklick,** Box 1, Logan Hall CN, Univ. of Pennsylvania, Philadelphia, PA 19174. *Official journal of the American Studies Association. Interdisciplinary articles dealing with all aspects of American life, including history, literature, religion, art, music, politics, folklore, customs, beliefs, popular culture, women's studies, and black studies. Review copies accepted. Scholarly, critical, bibliographical, and pedagogical articles considered.* 5/yr; $15/year regular; $7.50/yr student; $3/ea; 1949; 120pp; 4½x7 5/16"; 5M circ; lo. Reports up to 5 mos. Ads: $150/p; $80/½.

AMERICAN SCENES, J. Mark Press, **Barbara Fischer,** Box 2057-M, North Babylon, NY 11703. Poetry. *Send 1 or 2 poems, 3-16 lines. Aesthetic, contemporary poetry that interacts with the reader. (No vulgarity, profanity, devoutly religious, or light or humorous). Don't imitate or try to be outlandishly different. Be yourself. Enclose return env. Send one submission to this editor and wait for reply. After ten years, we find we've published scores of today's popular poets. Being partial to everything we accept, we'd have to list 5000 names to be fair, so we won't give any. We suggest you study a sample. Any of our titles will present a clear picture of what we look for.* Q; $5.95/soft; $8.95/cloth; $3.95/sample; 1963; 50pp; 8½x5½; 3M circ; lo. Reports promptly. Pays: 2-10 cents/line. Ads: commercial $5,000/p, runs 4 issues; poets' books: $5 per 30 wds. Discounts: quoted on request.

Back issues: $50/ea clothbound prior to 1973; most numbers completely sold out. Pub'd 4 issues, 2 books 1973, expects 20 issues, 10 books in 1974. COSMEP, Suffolk City Legislature, Cultural affairs.

THE AMERICAN SCHOLAR, 1811 Q St., N.W., Washington, DC 20009.

Amnesty International Publications, 53 Theobalds Road, London WC1X 8SP, UK. *We do not solicit manuscripts. Our publications are produced internally and vary in length from short reports to 200+ page books.* 1973; off.

AMPERS& MAGAZINE, Clingstone Press, **John R. Mackay, ed. & pub., Tawdry Millbank, Joyce James, Jack Dawes, assoc. eds.,** 816 S. Hancock St., Philadelphia, PA 19147. Fiction, art, satire. *Some poetry, photography, non-fiction, cartoons, & exquisite pornography. Ampers& is a magazine of literature & satire & is 97% fact-free. For slow readers — each word is chosen carefully. We attempt to publish the best imaginative work now being done in words & graphics. In fiction we look for elegant narrations in the bizarre & mundane. The poetry we accept says something worthwhile & is worth reading twice. Exquisite pornography considered. Experiments in art & photography welcomed. Nonfiction: surprise us. Prose may be 500-5000 words. Looking for lammercracks — fast, five-line satirical poems with surprise endings — on any subject. Recently published: Lynn Rosen, Tim Rumsey, Rockwell Williams, Susan Dailey, Jerry Bumpus, Benjamin Franklin, Herman Melville, Olive Palmer, Mowsle Barton. Address all submissions to: Odo Fernback, Head Examiner. SASE must accompany mss. Come with us. We go all the way.* Q; $2.50/yr; 75 cents/ea; 50 cents/sample; 1971; 24pp; 8x9¾; 3M circ; lo. Reports usually 1 wk. Pays: $5-$25 (lammercracks $3.50/ea). Ads: $50/p; $35/½; $1/line class/wd. Discounts: negotiable. Back issues: Vol.I, No.1=75 cents. Pub'd 4 issues 1973, expects 4 in 1974. Verbal alchemy.

Ampleforth Press, St. Oswald's House, Ampleforth College, York, UK. *Attached to school and monastery of Ampleforth. First book is Alexander Pushkin's "An Amateur Peasant Girl." Limited to 300 copies on H.M.P. illustrated with line drawings and bound in full leather blocked in gold. Cost £4.90 pf. All profits go to the Ampleforth Appeal.* 1973.

Ananda Publications, Alleghany Star Rt., Nevada City, CA 95959. *All books by Swami Kriyananda. Letters from Truth Seekers. Books:* Eastern Thoughts Western Thoughts, The Road Ahead, Letters from India. COSMEP.

ANARCHY, 29 Grosvenor Ave., London N5, UK. Anarchy.

AND, Writers Forum, **John Rowan, Bob Cobbing,** 262 Randolph Ave., London W9, UK. Poetry, art, concrete. *Publishes work by members and those closely associated with* Writers Forum. *Six issues in 20 years.* Irreg; price/ea varies; 1954; 40pp; page size varies; 500 circ; mim; off. Pays copies. Discounts: 33% trade. ALMS.

Andarth Interrelated Projects (see ONE)

AND IT IS DIVINE, **Paul Starr,** PO Box 6495, 511 16th St., Denver, CO 80206. Poetry, fiction, articles, art, photos, interviews, reviews, letters, longpoems. Monthly; $10/yr; $1/ea; free sample; 1972; 50-60pp; 8½x11; 25M circ; lo. Reports 1 mo. Pays: $50-$100. Ads: prices on request. Back issues: bound volume of 12 issues for $5. Pub'd 12 issues, 1 book 1973, expects 7 issues, 2 books in 1974.

Angel Hair Books, **Lewis Warsh, Anne Waldman,** Box 257, Peter Stuyvesant Sta., NYC 10009. Poetry, fiction, parts-of-novels, longpoems. *Recent books by Bill Berkson, Alice Notley, Tom Veitch, Edwin Denby, David Rosenberg, Peter Schjeldahl, Joe Brainard.*

ANGEL HOUR, Angel Publications, **Doris Warren Spearman,** 392 Viewpark Circle, San Jose, CA 95136. Poetry. *Poetry to 16 lines.* 4/yr; $4/yr; 60 cents/ea; 50 cents/ sample; 1964; 22pp; 8½x11; 500 circ; mi. Reports 1 mo. Pays: 1 cent per poem. Discounts: $3/yr to universities, libraries.

ANGLO-SOVIET JOURNAL, Society for Cultural Relations with the U.S.S.R., **M. Hookham,** 320 Brixton Road, London SW9 6AB, UK. 30p/ea; 1940; 48pp; lp.

ANGLO WELSH REVIEW, Dock Leaves Press, **Roland Mathias,** Deffrobani, Maescelyn, Brecon, UK. Articles, poetry, art, criticism, music, letters, longpoems. *Only quality material – any length. Preferably with some Welsh connexion (writer born/ lived in Wales, writes about Wales or Welsh affairs, all in English).* 3/yr; £1.50/sub; 60p/ea; 1949; 250pp; 8x5"; 1500 circ; lp. Reports 3 mos. Pays by arrangement. Ads: £25/page. Back issues: per Wm. Davis & Sons, Cannon House, Folkstone, Kent. ALP.

ANIMALS' DEFENDER & ANTI-VIVISECTION NEWS, National Anti-Vivisection Society, **Jon Evans,** 51 Harley St., London W1N 1DD, UK. *First-rate articles dealing with the humane treatment of animals in regard to necessary reform, legislative and otherwise, occasionally accepted. Length 1000-1500 words.* 6/yr; 8p/ea; Pays: £3.15/1,000 words.

ANN ARBOR REVIEW, **Fred Wolven, Chris McLelland, assoc. ed.,** Washtenaw Community College, Ann Arbor, MI 48106. Fiction, poetry, articles, art, photos, interviews, criticism, reviews, plays, concrete art. 3/yr; $4.50/yr; $1.50/ea; $1.50/ sample; 1967; 98pp; 5x7; 1M circ; lo;lp. Reports 1 wk to 1 mo. Pays copies only. Discounts: individually arranged. Back issues: $1.50 per copy. Pub'd 3 issues 1973. COSMEP, CCLM.

ANTAEUS, The Ecco Press, 1 West 30th St., New York, NY 10001.

Anthology Film Archives (see BULLETIN FOR FILM AND VIDEO INFORMATION)

ANTI-APARTHEID NEWS, Anti-Apartheid Movement, **Christabel Gurney,** 89 Charlotte St., London W1P 2DQ, UK. 10/yr; 75p/sub; 5p/ea; free sample; 1965; 12pp; 17x12"; 7500 circ; off. No pay. Ads: £2/col. inch. Third World.

THE ANTIGONISH REVIEW, **R.J. MacSween,** St. Francis Xavier Univ., Antigonish, Nova Scotia, Canada. Poetry, fiction, articles, reviews. Q; $5/yr; $1.50/ea; sample available; 1970; 110pp; 600 circ; lo. Reports 1 mo. Pays copies only. Discounts: $1 out of $5 for retailer, etc. Pub'd 1 book 1973, expects 4 in 1974. COSMEP.

THE ANTIOCH REVIEW, **Lawrence Grauman, Jr.,** PO Box 148, Yellow Springs, OH 45387. Poetry, fiction, articles, photos, satire, criticism. Q; $6/yr; $2/ea; 1940; 176pp; 9x6; 6M circ; lp. Reports 6-8 wks. Pays: $8-$10/p. Ads: $150/p; $80/½. Discounts: 20% agency. Pub'd 3 issues 1973, expects 4 in 1974. COSMEP, CCLM.

Anvil Press (Liverpool) (see PROFILE, Raven Books)

Anvil Press Poetry, **Peter Jay,** 69 King George St., London SE10 8PX, UK. Poetry. 1968; off; lp. Reports vary. Pays: royalty. ALP.

APALACHEE QUARTERLY, Dixie Dung Beetle Press, **David M. Morrill**, PO Box 20106, Tallahassee, FL 32304. Poetry, fiction, articles, art, interviews, satire, criticism, parts-of-novels. *We encourage younger writers, particularly those from the South. Manuscripts should not exceed 18 pages.* 3/yr; $3.75/yr; $1/ea; $1/sample; 1972; 44pp; 10½x7½; 500 circ; lo. Reports 6 wks. Pays: 4 copies. Ads: $50/p; $30 per ½ page. Back issues: $1 all available back issues. Pub'd 2 issues 1973, expects 3 in 1974. COSMEP.

APHRA, **Elizabeth Fisher, Gerry Sachs, Leah Zahler**, Box 893, Ansonia Sta., New York, NY 10023. Poetry, fiction, articles, art, photos, interviews, criticism, reviews, parts-of-novels, collages, plays, concrete art. *We prefer to be queried on non-fiction – articles, interviews, criticism, etc. Recent contributors include Margaret Atwood, Susan Griffin, Eva Hesse, Erica Jong, Nelly Kaplan, Juli Loesch, Audre Lorde, Dacia Maraini, Marisol, Jane Mayhull, Kate Millett, Louise Nevelson, Tillie Olsen, Marge Piercy, Adrienne Rich, Alix Katis Shulman, Yvonne!* Q; $4.50/yr; $1.25/ea; 1969; 72pp; 6¾x8½; 5M circ; lo. Reports 1-3 mos. Pays: understudy; 10-40 copies. No ads. Discounts: 30%/orders of fewer than 50 copies; 40%/orders of 50 or more copies. Back issues: $1.50 except for rare issues. Pub'd 4 issues 1973. COSMEP, CCLM, Women.

THE APOLLO, Northwoods Press, **Brenda Bailey**, PO Box 24, Bigfork, MN 56628. Poetry, fiction, articles, art, photos, interviews, criticism, reviews, longpoems, collages, plays. 3/yr; $5/yr; $2/ea; $2/sample; 1973; 40pp; 5½x8½; 250 circ; lo. Reports up to 8 wks. No pay. Ads: $25/p; $15/½; 10 cents class/wd. Discounts: 20%. Back issues: $2. Pub'd 3 issues, 16 books 1973, expects 3 issues, 23 books in 1974.

April Dawn Publishing Co., PO Box 4433, Falls Church, VA 22044. Fiction. COSMEP.

AQUARIAN AGENT, Astrology Services Int., Inc., **Henry Weingarten**, 127 Madison Ave., New York, NY 10016. Articles. *All astrology related material.* 6/yr; $9/2 yrs; 75 cents/ea; free sample; 40pp; 8x10½; 1800 circ; lo. Pay varies, usually copies only. Ads: $150/p; $100/½. Discounts: book ads – 20%; same ad 3 times, 4th one insertion free. Back issues: $5 per volume (Vol.1,2,3 available). Pub'd 6 issues 1973, expects 4 in 1974; 2 books 1973, expects 6 in 1974. Astrology.

AQUARIUS, **Eddie S. Linden**, Flat 3, 116 Sutherland Ave., London W9, UK. Articles, poetry, fiction, criticism. *John Heath-stubbs, W.S. Graham, Norman McCaig, George Barker, Iain Chricton Smith, Kathleen Raine, Elizabeth Jennings, Dinah Livingstone, Norman Nicholson, David Wright, Derek Mahon, George Macbeth.* 4/yr; £1.20/sub; 35p/ea; 1969; 100pp; 8x6½"; 1500 circ; off. Reports 6 mos. Pays: for special issues only. Ads: £10/page. Discounts: 33%. Back issues: £1/ea.

The Aquila Publishing Co. Ltd., **J.C.R. Green, A. Green, Michael Edwards**, 18 Atherstone Close, Shirley, Solihull, Warks. B90 1AU, UK. Poetry, criticism, longpoems, concrete. *We publish books and pamphlets of all sizes, including the* Phaethon Press *pamphlets.* off; lp. Reports vary. Pay: on negotiation. Trade discounts: orders over £3=35%; under £3=25%; under £1=20%; all pf. Postage must be included for private orders. 32 books published in 1973. COSMEP, ALMS, ALP, Ecology, Occult, Poetry, Criticism. (see also *PROSPICE*).

Arbitrary Closet Press (see SCREEN DOOR REVIEW)

Arc Publications, **Anthony Ward**, 11 Byron Road, Gillingham, Kent, UK. Poetry, longpoems, concrete. *Length of poem rarely exceeds 24 pages. Any style considered as long as in the opinion of the editor of high standard; and able to accomodate. Recent contributors (1) D.M. Thomas,* The Shaft, *illus. by Alan Davies, 25p;*

(II) Lifelines *by Alexis Lykiard, 20p; (III)* Reclaimed Land *by Paul Brown, 15p; (IV)* A Folio of English Concrete Poetry; *Cobbing, Cox, Edmonds, Furnival, Houedard,* 25 cards + 16pp notes, 75p. Up to 6/yr; 15-75p/ea; 1969; 24pp; size varies; 250-750 circ; off. Reports up to 1 mo. Discounts: 33% (5 copies or more). COSMEP, ALP.

ARCANA, Cokaygne Press, **John Nicholson,** 1 Jesus Terrace, New Square, Cambridge, UK. Articles, news items, interviews, criticism, letters. *The purpose of* Arcana *is to link current research into astro-archaeology with present day politics and cosmology. It is as it were the political magazine of occult sciences. Requires: articles based on original research or with good factual content.* 4/yr; 65p/ea; 1972; 70pp; 10x7"; 2,000 circ; off. Reports 10 days. Pays by arrangement. Ads: £30/p; £15/½page; £10/¼page. Discounts: 20% years booking. Back issues: No.1=£1; No.2=35p; No.3=35p; Nos.4,5=65p. Occult.

ARCANUM, Cypher Press, **James Goodard,** Plovers Barrow, School Road, Nomansland, Salisbury, Wilts, UK. *Poetry, s.f., personal, submissions on request only.* 50 circ; mim. No pay. No ads accepted.

THE ARCHER: A Verse Quarterly, Camas Press, PO Box 9488, North Hollywood, CA 91609.

ARENA, BCM/Seahorse, London WC1V 6XX, UK. Irreg; $9.60/sub. Women.

ARENA: A LITERARY MAGAZINE, The Handcraft Press, **Noel Farr Hoggard,** PO Box 6188, Te Aro, Wellington, New Zealand. *New Zealand writers only. Short stories, poems, essays, excerpts from works in progress. News-Notes and Publications Received. Some recent contributors are: Phyllis Gant, Isobel Williams, Olive Winchester, William E. Morris, Alistair Paterson, Robert Thompson, Stephen Oliver, Gary Langford, Helen Shaw, E.M. Bennett, John Summers, Leo Thompson, Hilda Phillips, Len Chambers, Raymond Watchman, D.S. Long, Eric Beach.* Irreg; 30 cents/ea(NZ); 30 cents/sample(NZ); 1943; 28pp; 8½x5¼"; 600 circ; lp. Reports 3 mos. No pay; copies only. Ads: (NZ): $14/p; $7.50/½; $4/¼. No discounts. Back issues: few back issues; those available at published price. Pub'd 1 issue in 1973 (illness here); expects none in 1974. COSMEP.

Arete Ink (see GOOD NEWS)

ARGOSY, Fleetway House, Farringdon St., London EC4A 4AD, UK. Fiction. *Only the very highest standard of fiction is accepted. Short stories of 1500-7000 words or full length and short complete novels.* Monthly; 25p/ea; 1926.

Ariel Press, **Mary Mackey,** PO Box 9183, Berkeley, CA 94709. Poetry, fiction. *We publish books of women's poetry and act as a clearing house for the distribution of women's poetry and literary magazines in Northern California. Most recently published* Split Ends *(poetry) $1.95. Write for list of works available by such poets as Alta, Susan Griffin, Lynda Koolish, Mary Mackey, etc.* Pub'd 1 book in 1973, expects 1 in 1974. COSMEP, Women.

ARION, A Journal of Humanities and The Classics, **William Arrowsmith, D.S. Carne-Ross,** *Arion,* Boston Univ., 270 Bay State Rd., Boston, MA 02215. Criticism. *Literary criticism of Greek & Latin literature. 10-40 typewritten pages. Concern for* language *and* style. *Recent contributors: Janet Lembke, Guy Davenport, Norman Austin, Kenneth Quinn.* Q; $6/yr; $1.75/ea; 1962; 128pp; 4¾x8½"; 1M circ; lo. Reports 3 mos. No pay. Ads: exchange (limited). Discounts: 20% to agent. Back issues: $1.75/copy. Pub'd 1 issue 1973, expects 3 in 1974. COSMEP.

ARIZONA QUARTERLY, **Albert Frank Gegenheimer,** *The Arizona Quarterly,* The Univ. of Arizona, Tucson, AZ 85721 Poetry, fiction, articles, criticism, reviews. Q; $2/yr; 50 cents/ea; free sample; 1945; 96pp; 6x9. Reports 2-4 wks. Pays copies only. No ads. Discounts: agent/1 yr $1, 3 yrs $3. COSMEP.

THE ARK RIVER REVIEW, **Jonathan Katz, A.G. Sobin,** **Arthur Vogelsang,** 519 Montgomery Ave., Haverford, PA 19041. Poetry, fiction, longpoems. *We work with three editors but with a system which does not require a concensus – thus we hope to be open to a very wide range of material. We would prefer to take a chance with something really new than print something 'highly competent' but usual . . . this is especially true of fiction. (Conventional fiction stands little chance). We're running an annual awards program that grants prizes up to $50 for the best three stories and poems printed during any volume. We like to print a minimum of two pages of poems/poet. And you will pleasantly be surprised at our good taste! One issue each year is a special three-poet issue.* Q; $2/yr; 75 cents/ea; 75 cents/sample; 1971; 52pp; 4x5½; 800 circ; lo. Reports 4 wks. Pays fiction: $3/page ($20 min.) + 2 copies; poetry: 20 cents/line ($5 min.) + 2 copies. Discounts: we get 50 cents and they get a quarter. Back issues: first volume available to libraries only at $10. Pub'd 4 issues 1973, expects 4 in 1974. COSMEP.

ART AND ARCHAEOLOGY NEWSLETTER, **Otto F. Reiss,** 243 E. 39th St., New York, NY 10016. Articles, photos. *Interested in articles, with photos, by students who participated in an archaeological excavation, (such as those sponsored by Brit. Council for Archaeology). Very interested in travelers' reports, with photos, who (without excavating) have trekked to some of the more inaccessible ancient ruins. There are many of these in Turkey, also Italy & Greece. Would pay $25.* Q; $3.50/yr; $1/ea; 80 cents in 8 cent stamps/sample; 1965; 20p; 8½x5½; 1100 circ; lo. Reports 3 wks. Pays $15 to $20. Ads: $50/p; $30/½. Discounts: 20% trade, agent. Back issues: they vary from 75 cents to $3 according to quantity of stock on hand. COSMEP, CCLM.

ART & LITERARY DIGEST, Canada Publishing Co., **Roy Cadwell,** Tweed, Ont., Canada. Poetry, fiction, articles, art, photos, interviews, reviews. *We like well-written articles or stories of an educational nature, how-to-do, humor, and almost anything that makes a person better informed or feeling better as a result of reading what we publish. Articles on how to achieve peace in individuals, the community and the nation are appreciated.* 4/yr; $2/yr; 50 cents/ea; 1967; 4pp; 8½x11; 2M circ; lp. Reports 1 mo. Pays 1 cent/wd. Ads: $35/p; $20/½; 10 cents/wd class/wd. Back issues: $1.

Artes Graficas Soler (see L'ESPRIT CREATEUR)

ARTS ALIVE MERSEYSIDE, Merseyside Arts Association, **The Director, Merseyside Arts Association,** 6 Bluecoat Chambers, School Lane, Liverpool L1 3BX, England, UK. Articles, poetry, art, cartoons, photos, satire, news items, interviews, criticism, music, letters, concrete. Monthly; free/single copy; 1969; 12pp; A4; 50,000 circ; off. Reports 1 wk. Pay: negotiable. Ads: £2.50/single col. inch. Discounts: 10% run of 3.

Arts Council of Great Britain & Northern Ireland, 105 Piccadilly, London W1V OAU, UK.

Arts Council of Northern Ireland Publications, Bedford House, Bedford St., Belfast BT2 7FX, UK.

ARTS IN SOCIETY, **Edward L. Kamarck**, Univ. of Wisconsin-Extension, Rm. 728 Lowell Hall, 610 Langdon, Madison, WI 53706. Poetry, articles, art, reviews, music. *In general* Arts in Society *deals with four areas: the teaching and learning of the arts, aesthetics and philosophy; social analysis; and significant examples of creative expression in a medium which may be served by the printing process. Articles should be around 3000 words.* Tri-annual; $7.50/yr; $2.50/ea; no sample; 1958; 120pp; 6x9; 5M circ; lo. Reports 6 wks. Pays: honorarium. Ads: $150/p; $85/½; no class/wd. Discounts: 15% disc. for bulk orders of 15 or more copies; bookstore disc. 33%; no disc. rates for institutions. Back issues: $3.50. Pub'd 3 issues 1973; expects none in 1974. COSMEP, CCLM, Art.

Ashland Poetry Press, Box 171, Ashland College, Ashland, OH 44805

Ashley Books, Inc., **Billie Young, Gwen Costa, Paul Korea**, Box 768, Port Washington, NY 11050. Fiction. *Hard cover books:* Aiming for the Jugular in New Orleans; The Cookout Conspiracy; Mao, A Young Man From the Yangtze Valley. Lo. Reports fast as possible. Discounts: 1-5 copies 33 1/3%; 5 copies or more 40% off. Pub'd 10 books 1973, expects 15 books in 1974. COSMEP, Women.

ASPECT, **Edward J. Hogan, Gail Braatelien, Pat Hollopeter, Ellen Schwartz**, 66 Rogers Ave., Somerville, MA 02144. Poetry, fiction, articles, art, photos, cartoons, interviews, satire, criticism, reviews, music, letters, parts-of-novels, longpoems, collages, plays. *Open to all comers. If you've done it, and you like it, send it to* Aspect. *We are not looking for any special kind of poetry or political, critical, or other viewpoint. We try to read work on its own terms. We try to publish work by beginning writers as well as those more experienced.* 6/yr; $5/yr; 75 cents/ea; 50 cents/sample; 1969; 44pp; 5½x8½; 150 circ; lo. Reports 30–60 days. Pays 2 copies. Ads: no display; 2 cents per word class/wd. Discounts: 20%. Back issues: 75 cents. Pub'd 6 issues 1973, expects 6 in 1974. COSMEP, CCLM, NESPA.

ASSEMBLING, **Henry Korn, Richard Kostelanetz**, Box 1967, Brooklyn, NY 11202. Poetry, fiction, articles, art, photos, cartoons, interviews, satire, criticism, reviews, music, letters, any idea that prints. Assembling *is collaborative. Contributors print 1M copies of up to four 8½x11 pages of anything they wish at their own expense. Contribution is by invitation. An invitation will be sent to anyone whose work demonstrates a commitment to 'alternate' style or substance. Those wishing invitations are invited to send manuscripts. Editors of* Assembling *are really compilers – they are not interested in institution.* 1/yr; $2.50/yr; 1970; 200pp; 8½x11; 1M circ; mi; of; lp. Reports 1 mo. Pays copies only. "Fourth number out and still going strong."

Association of Working Press   (see CHICAGO JOURNALISM REVIEW)

ASTRAL PROJECTION   (see THE SUN)

Astrology Services International Inc.   (see AQUARIAN AGENT)

ATHANOR, **Douglas Calhoun, George Butterick, contrib. ed.**, PO Box 582, Clarkson, NY 14430. *Biased: power words, lightning. Olson, Creeley, Eigner, Corso, Ginsberg, Ferlinghetti, McAdams, McNaughton, Glover, Baker.* 2/yr; $6/4 issues; $1.50/ea; $1.50/ea; $1.50/sample; 1971; 72pp; 7x8½; 600 circ; lo. Reports 2 wks plus. Pays copies only. No ads. No discount. Back issues: 1-4 @ $17.50. Pub'd 2 issues in 1973.

ATHENE, Society for Education Through Art, **Don Pavey**, JASC House, 30 Wayside, East Sheen, London SW14 7LN, UK. Articles, poetry, art, photos, news items, criticism, collages, concrete. *An international platform for new ideas in the arts and education.* Published by the Society for Education through Art (SEA), its official aim is to further the recognition of art as an essential part of education through which the potential of every child and adult can be realised. Was first promoted by a pioneering group of artists, Eric Gill, Henry Moore, Herbert Read, Clive Bell and others. Recent contributors range from Henry Moore on Space & Environment, de Bono on Creative Thinking, and a research worker on Visual Ability, to an East End of London teacher on Pornography in the classroom, and a school child on Tweeny Boppers. Includes contributions from abroad – Moscow, Belgrade, Rome, Japan, etc. in recent issues. 2/yr; 50p/ea; 1939; 32pp; A4; 4000 circ; off. Reports about 1 wk. Ads: £75/page. Back issues: on application. Visual Art/Education.

Athol Publications (see FATE)

Atlanta Cooperative News Project (see THE GREAT SPECKLED BIRD)

Atlantis Editions, **Richard O'Connell**, 4910 North 12th St., Philadelphia, PA 19141. Poetry. *Poetry of the highest quality. No biases.* Lp. Expects 3 or 4 books in 1974. COSMEP.

ATLATL Press (see ROCKY MOUNTAIN REVIEW)

Augur Publishing Co. (see THE EUGENE AUGUR)

AUM MAGAZINE, **Sri Chinmoy**, 85-45 149th St., Jamaica, NY 11435. Poetry, music, plays, essays, lectures. *A monthly journal of Spiritual Philosophy and Yoga. The magazine contains only the writings of Sri Chinmoy.* Monthly; $5/yr; 50 cents each; 27pp; 5x8; 800 circ; lo. No ads. Discounts: 40% to trade. Pub'd 12 issues 1973, expects 12 in 1974. Yoga.

AUNT HARRIET'S FLAIR FOR WRITING REVIEW, Honeysuckle Publishing Company, **Roy Griffin, Ebenezer Juarez, James Whitaker**, 309 A East 38th, Austin, TX 78705. *Fiction and longpoem limit: 40 pages. Any style as long as it "works." We wince, cringe, and/or get goosepimples reading explicit sentimentality, science fiction, politics, academicism, fad exploitation, and the like. Charles Bukowski.* 4/yr; $3.50/yr; 95 cents/ea; 50 cents/sample; free if request on bookstore stationery; $6.50/2 yrs; $9.50/3 yrs; 1974; 75pp; 5½x8½; circ unknown at present. Reports 3-4 wks. Pays: from copies only to $25 depending on significance and our finances. Ads: to be determined, please inquire later. Discounts: 5-19 copies=65 cents/ea; 20 plus=60 cents/ea; prisons=50 cents/ea. Expects 3 issues, 2 books in 1974. COSMEP.

AURORA: PRISM OF FEMINISM, Aurora Press, **Lynne Farrow, Marcia Danab**, 24 De Baun Ave., Suffern, NY 10901. Poetry, fiction, articles, art, photos, cartoons, letters, parts-of-novels. *Articles 2000 words or more. We especially need art & photos and fiction about women. Recent contributors: Dorothy Tennov, Rebecca Moon.* Q; $4/yr; $1/ea; $1/sample; 1970; 48pp; 8½x11; 2M circ; lo. Reports vary. Pays copies only. Discounts: 20%. Back issues: $1. Expects 4 issues in 1974. Women.

THE AUTHOR, Society of Authors, **Richard Findlater**, 84 Drayton Gardens, London SW10 9SD, UK. *The main journal of professional writers in Britain. NB. No unsolicited material. Contributions only by invitation.* 4/yr; £1/sub; 25p/ea; 1890; 45pp; 4500 circ. Ads: £25/page; £14/½; £8/¼.

Axis Arts, **Ian Taylor, Rosi Mycroft,** 102 Bishopthorpe Road, York., UK. 1973.

B.B. Books (see also GLOBAL TAPESTRY JOURNAL, PM NEWSLETTER), **Dave Cunliffe,** 1 Spring Bank, Salesbury, Blackburn, Lancs. BB1 9EU, UK. Poetry, fiction, art, photos, cartoons, parts-of-novels, longpoems. *Contemporary poetry. Creative prose. Have published books concerned with Buddhism, vegetarianism & art. Poetry collections by David Gitin, Maggie Finn & Ryokwan presently planned.* Reports as soon as possible. Pays copies - number by arrangement. ALP, Poetry & Counter-culture.

B & H Books, Fur Line Press, 330 Paloma Ave., San Rafael, CA 94901.

BABY JOHN, **James Evans,** 5406 Latona Ave., N.E., Seattle, WA 98105. Poetry, fiction, articles, art, criticism, reviews, music, letters, longpoems. *We publish good poetry and good comment on poetry. We have been offered little quality fiction. We'd publish it if we could get it. No restrictions on length or style. BABY JOHN No.5 (Nov. 1972) included: Douglas Blazek, Joan Colby, Kirby Congdon, Judson Crews, Lyn Lifshin, David Lunde, Joyce Odam, John Burnett Payne. We published nothing in 1973; but an excellent 6th issue is now abuilding.* Irreg; $3/4 issues; 50 cents ea; 1970; 36p; 8½x11; 250 circ; lo. Reports 3 to 6 wks. Pays one prize of $5 for the best work of the issue, otherwise copies only. Ads: exchange w/other small presses. Discounts: 40% for bookstores; others inquire. Back issues: same prices, except No.1 & No.4 are sold out. COSMEP.

BACHY, Papa Bach Bookstore, **John Harris, poetry, Bob Mehlman, prose, Pat Washington, art, Gary DeGalla, photography,** 11317 Santa Monica Blvd., Los Angeles, CA 90025. Poetry, fiction, articles, art, photos, cartoons, interviews, satire, criticism, reviews, music, letters, parts-of-novels, longpoems, collages, plays, concrete art. *Black & white art & photos only – no color reproduction. No length limit, but shorter pieces have a better chance of publication. Bachy is dedicated to the discovery of previously unpublished artist of worth. A major portion of our pages is reserved for relatively unknown contributors. We publish all kinds of material – except sentimental, academic, or mataphysical – bullshit. Some contributors: Charles Bukowski, Jack Hirschman, Greg Kuzma, Henry H. Roth, William Pillin, William Matthews.* Semi-annual; $3.50/yr; $2/ea; $2/sample; 1972; 144pp; 5½x8½"; 800 circ; lo. Reports 8 wks. Pays: $2/page. Back issues: no.1 & No.2 = $2/ea. Pub'd 1 issue 1973.

BACONIANA, **Commander Martin Pares, Noel Fermor,** Canonbury Towers, Islington, London N1, UK. Articles, poetry, letters. Annual; £1/ea; 1885; 100pp. Reports 2-3 wks.

The Baleen Press, **Ramona Weeks, Joy Harvey,** Box 13448, Phoenix, AZ 85002. Poetry, art, photos, plays. *Recent contributors: Anne Pitkin, Patricia Cumming, Malcolm Glass, Richard Grossman, Richard Shelton, Margaret Hodge, Joe M. Ferguson, Jr., A. McMiller. No unsolicited manuscripts.* One vol./4 issues; $5/yr; $1.50/ea; sample to libraries, dealers; 1958-61; revived 1969; 32pp; 5½x8½; 200 circ; lo. No submissions please! Ads: $106/pg. Discounts: 20% sub. agency, 20% single trade, 40% 2–10 trade, 50% 11 copies & up. Back issues: $1.50. Pub'd 3 issues 1973; 2 books 1973, expects 2 in 1974. COSMEP, CCLM, Women, Chicano, American Indian.

BALL STATE UNIVERSITY FORUM, **Frances Mayhew Rippy, Merrill Rippy,** Ball State Univ., Muncie, IN 47306. Poetry, fiction, articles, interviews, satire, criticism, parts-of-novels, longpoems, one act plays. *An eclectic journal, publishing articles of general interest in any field, esp. literature, language, education, history,* *social sciences;* also short stories, poetry, one-act plays. Q; $3/yr; $1/ea; free sample; 80p; 10x6½; 1500 circ; lp. Reports 3 mos. Pays 10 copies. Ads: $50/pg; $30/½pg. COSMEP, CCLM.

Balls Press (see SCROTUM)

BALTHUS: Fantasy Literature & Folk-Lore, Spectre Press, **Jon M. Harvey,** 18 Cefn Road, Mynachdy, Cardiff, CF4 3HS, UK. Articles, poetry, fiction, art, satire, interviews, criticism, longpoems. *The magazine is basically comprised of equal proportions of fact (articles, criticism, etc.) and fiction (prose and poetry). Apart from this balance of material, the literature is fairly fluid in status. Subject matter of the material is described adequately by the subtitle — no s.f. or anything gruesome accepted; just plain ol' fantasy and/or folk-lore. Recent contributors: Bruton Connors, Eddy C. Bertin, Andrew Darlington, Gordon Larkin.* Irreg; 75p ($2) /sub; 25p (70 cents)/ea; 25p (70 cents)/sample; 1970; 40pp; 9x7"; 500 circ; lo. Reports 1 mo. Pays copy only. No ads. Discounts: bulk: 6-35 copies, 25%; over 35 copies. 33%; classroom and other recognizable institutions: 33% for up to 35 copies: 50% for over 35 copies. Back issues: 20p (60 cents) for issue 1 & 2; 25p (70 cents) for issue 4. Fantasy.

Bandage Publications, 1411 Divisadero, No. 2, San Francisco, CA 94115.

George Banta Co. (see THE MODERN LANGUAGE JOURNAL)

BARDIC ECHOES, Bardic Echoes Brochures, **Clarence L. Weaver,** 1036 Emerald Ave., NE, Grand Rapids, MI 49503. Poetry. *40 lines or less, any style, strong impact but not smutty. Cornel Lengyel, Gordon Browning, Gaye Giammarino, William S. Day, James Magorian, D.L. Rudy, Max S. Barker, Leonard Opalov, Albert Tallman, E. Nel Snyder, Thane Gower, Asoka Weerasinghe, Robert F. Ambacher, Alice Mackenzie Swaim, P.C. Niblette.* Q; $2/yr; 50 cents/ea; 50 cents/sample; 1960; 24pp; 5½x8½; 500 circ; lo. Reports: 1-2 mos. Pays: copies only. Adsno. No discounts. Back issues: none. Pub'd 4 issues 1973, expects 4 in 1974; one book 1973, expects none in 1974. COSMEP, CCLM.

Barlenmir House, 2180 Bolton St., New York, NY 10462.

Barn Dream Press, 8 Thayer Street, Boston, MA 02118.

BARTLEBY'S REVIEW, **Albert Stainton, Rita Tomasallo Stainton,** Box 332, Machias, ME 04654. Poetry, articles, photos, interviews, reviews. 2/yr; $1.75/yr; $1/ea; 50 cents/sample; 1972; 49pp; 5½x8; 500 circ; lo;lp. Reports:2-8 wks. Pays: copies only. Ads: negotiable. Discounts: by arrangement. Back issues: issues 1 & 2 are $2/ea. Pub'd 2 issues 1973, expects 2 in 1974. NESPA.

The Basilisk Press, **David Lunde,** PO Box 71, Fredonia, NY 14063. Poetry. *We are overstocked until 1975.* 3-4/yr; $1.95/ea; 1970; 64pp; 5½x8½; 600 circ; lo. Reports 3-6 mos. Pays copies only. Discounts: bookstores 40% on 5 or more; colleges 20% in bulk. Back issues: 3/$5. COSMEP, General.

*BASTARD ANGEL,***Harold Norse,** PO Box 3449, San Francisco, CA 94119. Poetry, fiction, art, photos, reviews, letters, parts-of-novels, longpoems, collages, concrete art. *Bias for Beat-Surrealist style but also publish other styles, if impressive to editor. Not interested in conventional/academic/traditional. Originality & individuality always welcome. Contributors include: Anais Nin, William S. Burroughs, Allen Ginsberg, Lawrence Ferlinghetti, Michael McClure, Julian & Judith Beck,*

Lawrence Lipton, Bob Kaufman, Nanos Valaoritis, Andrei Codrescu, Jack Kerouac, Paul Bowles, Harold Norse, Gerard Malanga. Irreg; $8/yr ($12/yr libraries); $2/ea; no sample; 1972; 52-64pp; 8½x11; 1M circ; of. Reports 2-6 mos. Pays: copies only. Ads: $100/page, $50/½. Discounts: trade 40%; no other disc. Back issues: $15 per copy for No. 1. None pub'd 1973, expects 2 in 1974. COSMEP, Literary/Arts.

Battley Bros. (see NEW INTERNATIONALIST)

Beacon Press, 25 Beacon Street, Boston, MA 02108.

Beau Geste Press/Libro Accion Libre (see also SCHMUCK ANTHOLOGICAL), **Felipe Ehrenberg, David Mayor,** Jose de Teresa 52, Mexico 20 D.F., Mexico and Langford Court South, Cullompton, Devon EX15 1SQ, UK. Articles, poetry, fiction, art, cartoons, photos, satire, news items, interviews, criticism, music, letters, collages, concrete. *Look out the window or send for our catalogue.* 2/mo; price/ea varies; sample for review; 1971; no. pages and size varies; 60-2,000 circ; mim; lp; off; screen. Reports immediately. Pays by arrangement. Discounts: usual trade & to collectors. Back issues: on application. COSMEP, ALP, Women, Ecology, Third World, Black, Gay, SF.

Beaver Kosmos (Press) (see IMAGO)

BEDFORDSHIRE MAGAZINE, **James Dyer,** 6 Rogate Road, Luton LU2 8HR, UK.*Articles of Bedfordshire interest up to 1500 words. Illustrations – line and half-tone photographs.* 4/yr; 12½p/ea; 1947. Pays: £1.05/1,000 words; Illus. 75p.

BEDSITTER ANNUALS, **Olive Rhodes Teugels,** 6 Clapham Mansions, Nightingale Lane, London SW4 9AQ, UK. Articles, poetry, fiction, criticism. 2/yr; 60p($2)/yr (14 International Reply coupons): £6($14)/life sub. (140 Inter. Reply coupons); 40p($1)/ea ($8 Inter. Reply coupons): 1959; 100+pp; 8x6½"; 800 circ. Reports: all stories etc. must be submitted as comp. entries. Ads: 5p/word. Back issues are kept solely to send out to new subscribers.

The Bellevue Press, Gil Williams, Deborah Hollander Williams, 60 Schubert Street, Binghamton, NY 13905. Poetry, art, photos, essays, belles-lettres. We prefer to publish only work which has never appeared in any prior format or place, works which have been written for us. Works should be for short booklets or broadsides, small groups of poems which have a common unity, a suite, a sonnet group, a sequence. Recently published include: Frederic Will, Gil Williams, David Mitchell, Laura M. White, Jack Dann, Al Glover. We publish chapbooks, broadsides, and poetry and art postcards. Soon to be published include: Robert Kelly, Allan Block, Anselm Hollo, Joseph Theroux, and others. Catalogue available on written request. 1972; lp. Reports within 6 wks. Pays: $5 for postcard poems; copies and some royalties. Discounts: 20% off on single copies to anyone except library orders which are billed for the retail price without postage, 40% to anyone including libraries with orders of 5 or more items. Pub'd 2 books 1973, expects 6 in 1974. **COSMEP, NESPA.**

BELOIT POETRY JOURNAL, **Robert Glauber, David M. Stocking, Marion K. Stocking,** Box 2, Beloit, WI 53511. Poetry, reviews, longpoems. *We publish the best of the poems submitted. No biases as to length, form, subject, or school.* Occasional chapbooks, such as recent issue of work of Kaoru Maruyama. Q: $3/yr; 75 cents/ea; 50 cents/sample; $7.50/3 yrs; 1950; 40pp; 5½x8½; 1200 circ; lo. Reports immediately to 4 mos. Pays: 3 copies. Ads: $50/pg. Discounts: by arrangement. Back issues: 1950-1973 file (less 7 o.p.) $76.50.

Belvedere Publications (see HUMOROUS HOTCHPOTCH)

BERKELEY BARB, **Jim Schreiber,** PO Box 1247, Berkeley, CA 94701. Poetry, articles, art, photos, cartoons, interviews, satire, criticism, reviews, music, letters, longpoems, collages. Wkly; $10/yr; 25 cents/ea; 1965; 48pp; 11x7½"; 21M circ; lo. Ads: $370/p; $160/½; class/wd $1 a line of 27 characters. Discounts: 13 cents to distributors; if over 600 copies, 10 cents a copy. Back issues: 35 cents, if last 8 issues; others vary, some issues not for sale. Pub'd 52 issues 1973, expects 52 in 1974. APS, Intergalactic World Brain, Liberation News Service, New York News Service, Zodiac New Service, Earth New Service.

BERKELEY POETS' COOPERATIVE, Berkeley Poets' Workshop & Press, PO Box 459, Berkeley, CA 94701. Poetry, fiction, art, photos, reviews, parts-of-novels, longpoems, plays. *Although we accept some contributions via mail, most of the work published in our magazine has been presented and discussed at one of the workshops we sponsor. We feel that the high quality of the magazine is due, in part, to the stimulating and democratic atmosphere of the workshops.* 2/yr;$2.25/ yr; $1.25/ea; 1970; 68pp; 7x9; 2500 circ; lo. Reports up to 6 mos. Pays: 2 copies. No ads. Discounts: 45% trade. Back issues: No.1/$5; No.2/$5; No.3/$2.50; No.4/ $2; No.5/$1.50. Pub'd 2 issues, 1 book 1973, expects 2 issues, 1 book in 1974. COSMEP, CCLM.

THE BERKELEY SAMISDAT REVIEW, Samisdat Associates, **Merrit Clifton, ed., John Coppock, poetry, Tom Suddick, fic. ed., Robin Michelle Clifton, reviews,** 1150 Spruce St., Berkeley, CA 94707. Poetry, fiction, art, satire, parts-of-novels, longpoems. *Fiction is our emphasis; our heavy interest hardhitting, speculative, often surreal and/or satirical material reminiscent of Mikail Bulgakov, Franz Kafka, or any of the great Soviet satirists of the 1920s. Our only bias, however, is against bad writing; we'll always find space for work of top literary caliber. Recent contributors include Kay Valentine, L.W. Michaelson, Ray Pitts, Scott Sanders, Linda Kraemer, D.G.H. Schramm, Herbert R. Coursen Jr., Miriam Sagan, Jan Zaleski, Janice Hays, Katherine Gibson, Hal Shows, Geoffrey S. Geiger, Bill Swanson, Lynda Shearin, Tom McCarty, Ron Vinyard, Robert Burdette Sweet, Jon Ilgen, Archibald Henderson, Dennis Shelley, Jayne Beilke, Nils Peterson, Jo Anne Churchill, Denise K. Taylor, Glenn H. Perelson, the editors, and some two dozen others.* 4/yr*; $2/yr*; 75 cents/ea; 50 cents/sample; 1973; 80pp; 8½x5½; 500 circ; lo. Reports 3 wks. Pays: Comps; copies only. Ads: $18/page; $9/½; no class. Discounts: 40% off to classrooms, other purchasers of more than ten of any one issue. Distributors get from 20% to 40% depending on what kind of job they do. Back issues: 1st is out of print. 2nd: $1; 3rd: 50 cents; 4th: 50 cents; 5th: 50 cents. Subsequent issues are 75 cents owing to expanded format. *Pub'd 5 issues plus combo with *The Reed* in 1973; expects 4 issues and 3 books in 1974. (*does not include various specially produced and priced combination issues with other small magazines.)

BEST IN POETRY, J. Mark Press, **Barbara Fischer,** Box 2057-M, North Babylon, New York 11703. Poetry. *Send 1 or 2 poems, 3-16 lines. Aesthetic, contemporary poetry that interacts with the reader. (No vulgarity, profanity, devoutly religious, or light or humorous.) Don't imitate or try to be outlandishly different. Be yourself. Enclose return envelope. Send one submission to this editor and wait for reply. After ten years, we find we've published scores of today's popular poets. Being partial to everything we accept, we'd have to list 5,000 names to be fair, so we won't give any. We suggest you study a sample. Any of our titles will present a clear picture of what we look for.* Q; $5.95/soft; $8.95/cloth; $3.95/sample; 1963; 50pp; 8½x5½; 3M circ; lo. Reports promptly. Pays: 2-10 cts/line. For ads, discounts, back issues, etc. see *ALL-TIME FAVORITE POETRY.*

25

BEST POETS OF THE 20th CENTURY, Winston-Paramount Books, **B. Winston Paramount,** 110-M Cooper St., Drawer-J, Babylon Village, NY 11702. Poetry, reviews. *Aesthetic, sensitive poetry. Send 1 or 2 poems, 3-16 lines, enclose return envelope. Our quarterly sub-titled editions are:* Man & Environment, People & Places, Nature & Introspection, Life & Reflections. *We want sincerity. No vulgarity or profanity, devoutly religious, personal pondering or suffering. We suggest you study a sample.*Q; $5.95/soft; $8.95/cloth; $3.95/sample; 1973; 50p; 8½x5½; 3M circ; lo. Reports within 3 wks. Pays 50 cents to 75 cents per poem. Discounts: on request. Pub'd 1 issue 1973, expects 4 in 1974.

Bettiscombe Press, Bettiscombe, Bridport, Dorset, UK.

BEYOND BAROQUE,Beyond Baroque Foundation Publications, **George Drury Smith, James Krusoe, Alexandra Garrett,**1639 W. Washington Blvd., Venice, CA 90291. Poetry, fiction, articles, art, photos, parts-of-novels, longpoems, collages, concrete art. *Avant-garde, experimental prose and poetry, related graphics. (Note:* Beyond Baroque *is part of* Beyond Baroque Foundation Publications *which publishes 8 to 10 issues per year. Subscription rates include all publications, among them the frequent* Newletters *(q.v.) and a number of chapbooks a year.* 2/yr; $5/yr; $2.50/ea; 1968; 80pp; 8½x11; 1000 circ; electro-serichrome. Reports 2-6 wks. Pays: copies only. No ads. Discounts: 40% trade, 20% agent. Back issues: price varies. Pub'd 2 issues 1973. COSMEP, CCLM.

Beyond Baroque Foundation Publications (see BEYOND BAROQUE, NEWLETTERS)

BIBLIOTHECK, The Library, The University, Stirling, UK.

Alison Bielski, **Alison Bielski,** Cottage Studio, Itton Common, Chepstow, Mon. NP6 6BX, UK. Poetry, art, longpoems, collages, concrete. *Emphasis on layout of shaped poetry which traditional publishers will not take because of time involved in setting up. I also use two presses, one local in Chepstow, one in Bristol.* 2/yr; 1972; 5x6½"; off; lp. Discounts: 33% trade. ALP.

*BIG BOULEVARD,***William Robson,** 5585 Orange Ave., Long Beach, CA 90805. Poetry, fiction, articles, photos, interviews, criticism. BB *is beginning as a poet's and writer's showcase of very small circulation, directed to the better poets, writers and publishing houses. One or more poets or writers will be featured each issue usually with a self-interview.* Ron Koertge, Linda King, F.A. Nettelbeck, John Harris, John Bennett, Chas. Stetler, Gerald Locklin, Chas. Potts, Lyn Lifshin *and* Ann Menebroker *are among contributors.* 12/yr; $10/yr; $1/ea; 1973; 13pp; 8½x11. Reports 1 mo. Pays: copies only. COSMEP.

Big Deal Press (see CHERNOZEM)

BIG SKY, Big Sky Books, **Bill Berkson,** Box 272, Bolinas, CA 94924. Poetry, fiction, art, photos, cartoons, interviews, letters, parts-of-novels, longpoems, collages, plays. *Recent contributors:* Robert Creeley, Philip Whalen, Tom Clark, Joanne Kygen, Bill Berkson, Anne Waldman, Fielding Dawson, Johnny Stanton, Philip Guston, Clark Coolidge, Alice Notley, Hilton Obenzinger, Allen Ginsberg, Ted Berrigan, Edwin Denby, Rudy Burkhardt, Ron Padgett, Curtis Faville, Tom Veitch, Alex Katz, Joe Brainard. 4/yr; $5/yr; $1.50/ea; 1972; 80pp; 7x10; 800 circ; lo. Reports immediately. Pays: copies only. No ads. Discounts: 40% to bkstrs. Pub'd 3 issues 1973, expects 4 in 1974; one book 1973, expects 5 in 1974. COSMEP, CCLM

Bing America Publications, **D.K. Gast,** 1555 Murray Avenue, El Cajon, CA 92020. *"How-To" media for the Aware. So far we have re-issued Ross H. Gast's 1933 farm-home movement classic,* Vegetables in the California Garden, *59p; $1.25 and* Food from Your Soil, A Practical Guide for the Backyard Gardener and Semi-Rural Home Owner, *108pp; $2. Discounts on quantity orders. Please query before submitting manuscripts.*

Birmingham Poetry Centre (see MUSE)

Birth Press, **Tuli Kupferberg,** 381 E 10th Street, New York, NY 10009.

BITMAN (occasionally Bitwoman or Bithuman), Bit Publications, **Donald Winterton, Clive Love, Benedicta Blossom, Rattles Chudzhinsky,** c/o 146 Great Western Road, London W11, UK. Articles, poetry, fiction, art, cartoons, photos, satire, news items, interviews, criticism, music, letters, longpoems, plays, collages, concrete. *Hot from the energy centre of the Alternative Society. Jammed-packed with useful information and visions. A regular bible and survival manual for active deviants.* 6/yr; £1/sub; 25p, px/ea; 1968; 50pp; 13x8"; 1,000 circ; mim. Reports: inconsistent. No pay. No ads accepted. Back issues: 25p px; No.3 not available. Alternative Press Syndicate.

BITTERROOT, **Menke Katz,** PO Box 51, Blythebourne Station, Brooklyn, NY 11219. Poetry. *We publish the very best regardless of styles etc.* Q; $4/yr; $1.50/each; No sample; 1962; 50pp; lo. Reports immediately. Pays: one copy. Ads: $50/page, $25/½. Discounts: yes. Back issues: $1.50. Pub'd 4 issues 1973.

BITTERSWEET, **Ellen Massey, teacher adv.,** Lebanon High School, Lebanon, MO 65536. Poetry, fiction, articles, art, photos, interviews, music, letters. *This is a student written and published quarterly on Ozark folklore, traditions, heritage and land. We include a variety of styles and use articles anything from one page to 10-15. There are how-to articles, history, memoirs, fictionalized accounts based on experience and other features about the region. We use mostly staff work, but will consider work from others, especially personal experience of years ago.* Q; $6/year; $2/ea; 1973; 64pp; 8½x11; 1M circ; lo. Reports 1 mo. Pays: copies only. Ads: none. No discounts. Back issues: $2. Pub'd 2 issues 1973, expect 4 in 1974. Folklore–regional of Ozarks.

BkMk Press, **Dan Jaffe,** Johnson County Library, 8700 West 63 Street, Shawnee Mission, KS 66202. Poetry, photos. *1972-73 = 16 "half-books," photo-covered, 20 page, poetry. 1973-74 = anthology Kansas City area poets; anthology, photos, children's poetry (by children): Future plans=collection of short stories, other forms of good writing. Editorial biases best seen in type of material, styles published. Some writers: John Knoepfle, Dave Etter, David Ray, Dan Jaffe and Glen Anderson (poetry, collages), Michael Novak, Robert Killoren, Milton Smith, George Cuomo, David Perkins, Peter Simpson, Kenneth Lauter, Sylvia Wheeler, Robert Slater, others.* Often; $12/yr; $1/ea; 1972; half-books; 20pp; 6x9; lo; library rates. Reports 6 mos. Pays: royalty 20%. Discounts: sub., classroom, other at 25% (over 10 copies purchased).

BLACK ACADEMY REVIEW, 3296 Main St., Buffalo, NY 14214.

BLACK & RED, Box 9546, Detroit, MI 48202. Articles, Lo. Pub'd 5 books 1973, expects 5 in 1974.

Black Books Bulletin, 7848-50 S. Ellis Ave., Chicago, IL 60619.

BLACK BOX, 3725 Jocelyn St., N.W., Washington, DC 20015.

THE BLACK COLLEGIAN, **Preston J. Edwards,** 3217 Melpomene Ave., New Orleans, LA 70125. Articles, art, photos, cartoons, interviews, reviews, parts-of-novels. *2500 words maximum, popular style.* Bimonthly; $2.50/yr; 50 cents/ea; free sample; 1970; 56pp; 8½x11; 25M circ; lo. Reports 1 mo. Ads: $1,000/p; $650/½; $35/inch class/wd. Back issues: 75 cents. Pub'd 5 issues 1973, expects 6 in 1974. Black.

Black Dragon Books, **Robert W. Starfire,** 99 Sanchez St., San Francisco, CA 94114. Fiction. *Short Story Collections. Short books to 80 pages. Our style is eclectic. No bias. Open to any manuscript.* 2 books/yr; 1972; lp. Reports 2 mos. Will pay up to $200. Discounts: 40%. Pub'd 2 books 1973, expects 2 in 1974. Chicano, Food/Ecology, Fiction.

BLACK GRAPHICS INTERNATIONAL, PO Box 732, Detroit, MI 48206.

BLACK LIBERATOR, **AX Cambridge,** 67 Helix Road, London SW2, UK. Articles, poetry, cartoons, photos, news items, interviews, criticism, letters. *Marxist-Leninist. Recent contributors: Ly Van Sau (PRG South Vietnam), Cheddi Jagan (PPP Guyana), Chris Searle.* 4/yr; £2/sub; 25p/ea; 1971; 75pp; A4; 3000 circ. Discount: 33% bookshops. Third World, Black.

BLACK MARIA, **Sue Bodenstein, Francine Krasno, Barbara Peart,** 815 W. Wrightwood Ave., Chicago, IL 60614. Poetry, fiction, articles, art, photos, cartoons, interviews, reviews, parts-of-novels, plays, concrete art. *Black Maria is a feminist quarterly that's been publishing since 1972. All material should be pro-women without being rhetorical. All authors published are women. We like articles (essays, historical essays, interviews, book reviews) that are non-academic but well written and incisive. Some recent contributors have been Rochelle Holt, Sharon Spencer, Natalie Petesch, and Leonora Carrington. We prefer non-fiction and fiction to poetry. We tend to publish a few poems by one or two authors in each issue. Photos and graphics welcome.* Q; $3.50/yr; $1.10/ea; $1.10/sample; Vol.II, Nos.1&2/$2; 1972; 64pp; 6x9; 1M circ; lo. Reports 1-4 mos. Pays copies only. Pub'd 2 issues 1973, expects 4 in 1974. COSMEP, Women.

Black Orpheus Press, 322 New Mark Esplanade, Rockville, MD 20850.

BLACK PANTHER, PO Box 841, Emeryville Branch, Oakland, CA 94608.

THE BLACK POSITION, Broadside Press, 12651 Old Mill Pl., Detroit, MI 48238.

Black River Writers, PO Box 1591, East St. Louis, IL 62205. *The first LP recording of a much-talked about poet:* Eugene B. Redmond *reciting poems of* love & struggle: Bloodlinks And Sacred Places, *$4.00. Recorded live May 10, 1973 in Sacramento, California.*

Black Rose Books (see also *OUR GENERATION),* 3934 Rue St. Urbain, Montreal 131, Que., Canada. *Publishes radical left libertarian material of an analytical and/ or muck-raking variety. It has published 14 books since founding in 1970 — 5 of them in 1973 — 3 are out of print and will not be re-printed. We give regular trade discounts to stores, and jobbers. Four titles are planned for 1974.*

BLACK SCHOLAR, Box 31245, Sausalito, CA 94965.

Black Sparrow Press (see SPARROW)

BLACK WOLF, Crow Mountain Pressworks, **G. Sutton Breiding,** 2240 Bush St., San Francisco, CA 94115. Wolf *is published mainly as the editor's mouthpiece, for friends, kinfolk, and interested parties. A 10 cent stamp will get you a sample. No outside submissions solicited. Circulation to be kept at about 50 persons, unless interest demands more copies & longer page number. Very limited financially.* Irreg; 10 cents/sample; 1974; 4pp; 8½x11; 50 circ. Discounts: would love to trade. Back issues: same as sample when available. No issues pub'd 1973.

THE BLACKBIRD CIRCLE, The Blackbird Press, Inc., **Dean Deter, Robert Conley,** Box 233, Cazenovia, NY 13035. Poetry. *No preconceptions about style or form. Our tone is informal, and we like to give young poets a first hearing as well as see what older poets are doing. Contributors include Elisavietta Ritchie, Laurie Spier, Anthony Piccione, Donald Levering.* Irreg; $6/3 issues; 1970; 32pp; 8½x5½; 500 circ; lo. Reports 6 wks. Pays copies only. Ads: $50/p; $25/½. Discounts: 20-40% agent, trade. COSMEP.

Blacksuade Boot Press, **Barry McSweeny,** 53 Ramilles Road, Blackfen, Sidcup, Kent, UK. ALP.

BLACKWOOD'S MAGAZINE, William Blackwood & Sons Ltd., **Douglas Blackwood,** 32 Thistle St., Edinburgh EH2 1HA, UK. Articles, poetry. Blackwood's *is Britain's oldest monthly, publishing short stories, poems and articles of a very high standard. Would-be contributors are asked to study the magazine before sending material.* 12/yr; £3/sub; 24p(85 cents)/ea; 1817; 96pp; 7¼x4½"; 11,250 circ; lp. Reports by return. Pays on publication. Ads: £40/page pro rata. Discount: 25% trade.

BLAKE NEWSLETTER, **Morris Eaves, Morton D. Paley,** Dept. of English, Univ. of New Mexico, Albuquerque, NM 87131. Articles, art, photos, criticism, reviews, letters. *Our orientation is scholarly, though we have published some non-scholarly material. Blake was both poet and artist, and we welcome material on either or both aspects of his work:* news items *on exhibitions, publications, etc.;* notes *that run from one to several pages;* discussion *articles for the exchange of opinion;* "minute particulars," *which are mini-notes;* reviews *of books about Blake;* biographical *material. Many of the articles are illustrated.* Q; $5/yr; $2/ea; 1967; 40pp; 8½x11; 500 circ; lo. Reports 4-6 wks. Pays copies only. Ads: $80/p; $55/½. Discounts: agency disc. 10%; individual subs. $4/yrly. Back issues: whole nos.17-18/ $5; whole no.20/$3. Pub'd 4 issues 1973, expects 6 in 1974. COSMEP.

BLEB, **George Ryan,** Box 322, Times Square Sta., New York, NY 10036. Poetry, concrete art. *Open on style and content. Also do translations, reprints, anything unusual.* 2/yr; $1/yr; 75 cents/ea; free sample; 1970; 32pp; 9x6; 500 circ; lo. Reports 3 wks. Pays copies only. Discounts: 50%. CCLM.

BLIMP/REALIT, Reality Studio Arts Workshop (Publications), **Sheril Berkovitch, Mont Goldman, Ray Rich,** Reality Studio Arts Workshop, 23 Hand Court, High Holborn, London WC1, UK. Articles, poetry, fiction, art, cartoons, news items, interviews, criticism, music, letters, longpoems. *Welcome work from anybody. Have found it difficult to find regular contributors recently. Distribution/circulation varies according to number printed. Not always on time but twelve issues are published yearly. As we work on a low finance level sometimes only 5 or 4 sheets are used or less copies are run off. If we have a regular order from several people we can afford to improve the paper without fear of running into debt.* Monthly; 50p/ sub; 5p/ea; S.A.E./sample; 1970; no. pages & size varies; 300-500 circ; mim. Ads: 10p regardless of length; Box Nos. 5p extra. Discounts: students, OAPs, Community groups, free ads. Alternative/Community.

BLUE CLOUD QUARTERLY, Graphic Arts/Blue Cloud Abbey, **Brother Benet Tvedten, O.S.B.,** Blue Cloud Abbey, Marvin, SD 57251. Poetry, fiction, articles, art, photos. *Poetry, short stories, historical and cultural articles . . . all relating to the Indian American. Magazine is limited to sixteen pages.* Q; $1/yr; 25 cents/ea; samples; 1954; 16pp; 6x9; 2,876 circ. Reports within 2 wks. Pays copies only. No ads. Discounts: no bulk discounts for subscriptions. Individual back issues sold 10 cents per copy to schools. Back issues: free to those requesting single copies. Pub'd 4 issues 1973, expects 4 in 1974. American Indian.

Blue Dragon Press (see STARDANCE)

Blue Egg Studio (see NORTH EASTERN ARTISTS DIRECTORY)

Blue Mountain Press (see SKYWRITING)

Blue Wind Press (see also SEARCH FOR TOMORROW), **George Mattingly,** 820 O'Farrell, San Francisco, CA 94109. *Books published:* Skyliner, *Merrill Gilfillan: 1974: prosepoems: 32pp; illus; $2; $15 (lettered & signed);* Something Swims Out, *Darrell Gray: 1972: selected poems: 96pp; illus; $2.50. Forthcoming:* This Too Will Pass, *Sheila Heldenbrand: poems & prose;* Rocky Dies Yellow, *Michael Lally: poems: $2;* Traveling Light, *Steve Toth: poems: $2.* 1970. Discounts: trade 40%; bulk (25+) 45%; wholesale 50%; institution 0%; mag sub agency 20%.

Bluffridge Ltd. (see JEFFREY)

BOGG, Fiasco Publications, **George Cairncross,** 31 Belle Vue St., Filey, Yorkshire, UK. Articles, poetry, fiction, cartoons, satire, news items, criticism. 4/yr; 60p/sub; 15p/ea; 1968; 20pp; qto; 150 circ; mim. Reports vary. No pay. No ads. No discounts. ALP.

BOND, **Greg Laxer,** 58 W 25th St., NYC 10010. Bimonthly; Pays $6/yr. No ads. G.I.

Bond Street Publishers Ltd. (see THE WRITER)

BONES, White Bones Press, **Katherine Greef, Terence Anderson,** RD1, Box 265, Otego, NY 13825. Poetry, fiction, cartoons, parts-of-novels, longpoems, collages, concrete art. *We welcome new & unpublished writers with at least some experience, i.e. don't send your very first poem. We also include those who have published. We are now especially interested in works by women and in visual poetry.* At intervals; $2/2 issues; $1/ea; $1.25/sample; 1967; 80pp; 7x8½; 1M circ; of. Reports 5 min. to 2 yrs. Pays 2 copies. No ads. No discount. Back issues: not available except in complete sets; write for details. None pub'd 1973. COSMEP.

BOOK COLLECTING, **B. Hutchinson,** 42 Trafalgar St., Brighton, UK. *Articles up to 5000 words on book collecting and bibliography.* Monthly; £2/sub; 1968; Pay: £3.15 to £10.50 per 1000 words.

BOOK COLLECTOR, 58 Frith St., London W1V 6BY. 4/yr; 75p/ea; 1952.

BOOK EXCHANGE, **W.K. Fudge,** Sardinia House, Sardinia St., London WC2A 3NW. Book reviews. 12/yr; £2/sub; 1948; 32pp; 8½x5½; lp. Ads: £30/page pro rata; 1p/word.

BOOKLEGGER MAGAZINE, **Celeste West, Valerie Wheat, Sue Critchfield,** 72 Ord St., San Francisco, CA 94114. Articles, art, photos, cartoons, reviews. *We are* *a feminist collective of information freaks.* Bklg. *reviews the independent, alternative press, mainly to increase librarians' awareness of it.* Bklg. *includes resource lists on social change & creative life styles — such as radical therapy, decriminalizing prostitution, self-publishing, energy, worker self-management, etc. We believe Information Is Action, and should be accessible to all people for control over their own lives.* Bi-monthly; $8/yr; $1.50/ea; 1973; 48pp; 7x10; 2M circ; lo. Reports 1 mo. Pays copies only. No ads. Discounts: 10% to agents, and for any bulk (5 + copies) orders; prepaid only. Back issues: $1.50/ea; 10% disc. on 5 + copies ordered. Pub'd 1 issue, 1 book 1973, expects 5 issues, 2 books in 1974. COSMEP, Third World, Women, Food/Ecology, Social change, Resource lists.

BOOKS, National Book League, Clifford Simmons, Jane Austin, assist., National Book League, 7 Albemarle St., London W1X 4BB, UK. Articles, poetry, criticism. *1500 average length of material. Literary figures, home & abroad.* Q; 25p/ea; free sample; 1946; 48pp; demy; 15,000 circ; lp. Reports immediately. Pays £10 per 1500 words. Ads: £30/page.

BOOKS ABROAD, Univ. of Oklahoma Press, Ivar Ivask, 401 W. Brooks St., Room 45-A, Univ. of Oklahoma, Norman, OK 73069. Articles, photos, criticism, reviews. *Average article: 2500 words; average commentary: 1400 words; average review: 250 words. Current belles-lettres discussed in articles & reviewed (600 reviewers in 66 languages). Frequently special topics: a writer (e.g. Ungaretti, Pasternak), a literature, a genre, or literary movement.* $8/yr; $2.50/ea; free sample; 1927; 176pp; 5x8; 3M circ; of; lp. Reports 3 wks. Pays copies only. Ads: $75/p; $40/½.

BOOKS & BOOKMEN, Miss Cis Amaral, Artillery Mansions, 75 Victoria St., London SW1H 0HZ, UK. Articles, interviews, criticism, letters. *No mss. should be sent unless commissioned in writing by the editor.* Monthly; £5.40/sub; 40p/ea; free sample; 1955; 100pp; 11x8½"; lp. Pays: by negotiation. Ads: £100/page. Discounts: 10% publishers; 10% agents.

BOOKSELLER, Philothea Thompson, 13 Bedford Square, London WC1B 3JE, UK. Weekly; £6.20/sub; 1858.

The Bookstore Press, 39 Housatonic St., Lenox, MA 02140. Children's books. *The only unsolicited manuscripts we want are children's books.* Lo. Reports right away. Pay depends. Discounts: trade 40%; library 15%. Pub'd 4 books 1973, expects 4 in 1974. COSMEP.

BOTH SIDES NOW, Free People Press, staff, 1232 Laura St., Jacksonville, FL 32206. *Alternative paper with magazine content in tabloid format. In-depth news, editorials, counter-cultural features, articles, short fiction, satire, poetry, letters, reviews, art, cartoons. We will probably be joining COSMEP, but prefer to do so through COSMEP South, if that materializes, so are waiting on developments there. Were fairly dormant in '73, putting out only one issue and several Penny Press street sheets. Trying to go monthly in '74 with one issue (Feb) out to date. Good authors published include Bill Griffen and Donald Roberts. Bill is a sometimes contributor to* Win, *and Roberts authored our first full-length short story.* Monthly; $2/10 issues; 25 cents/ea; sample; 1969; 20pp; 4-5M circ; lo. Pays copies only. Ads: $100/p; $55/½; $3/col. inch, 3¼ wide col. Discounts: by arrangement. Back issues: 25 cents postpaid. APS.

BOUNDARY 2: A Journal of Postmodern Literature, State Univ. of New York at Binghamton, William V. Spanos, Robert Kroetsch, Dept. of English, SUNY, Binghamton, NY 13901. Poetry, fiction, articles, art, cartoons, reviews, criticism, interviews, plays. *International journal; scholarly and critical work and also creative* *work; restricted to postmodern literature. Recent contributors: Jean Starobinski, Charles Altieri, David Alpaugh, Susan Fromberg Schaeffer, Edward Said, David Antin, Yannis Ritsos, David Ignatow, Samuel Moon, Ihab Hassan, Manolis Anaghnostakis, George Seferis, Odysseus Elytis, Stratis Tsirkas, Jenny Mastoraki, Nathan Scott.* 3/yr; $5/yr; $2/ea; 1972; 260pp; 500 circ; lo. Reports 1 mo. Pay: variable. Ads: $65/p; $35/½. Discounts: 20% trade; 20% agency.

Bowery Press (see MANO—MANO)

BOX 749, Seven Square Press, **David Ferguson,** ed. in chief, **Janden Hogan,** art ed., **M. Elizabeth Clifford, Anderson Craig, Elizabeth Durland, Patricia Eakins, Mary Maud Ferguson, Marc Rangel de Algeciras,** Box 749, Old Chelsea Sta., New York, NY 10011. Poetry, fiction, art, photos, cartoons, satire, music, letters, parts-of-novels, longpoems, collages, plays, belles lettres. Box 749 *is a quarterly magazine of the printable arts – open to all kinds of writing, graphics and music. We have no particular stylistic or ideological bias. We will consider – and would like to serialize – long fiction; we have published one act plays and will consider plays that are full length.* Q; $7/yr; $2/ea; 1972; 64-80pp; 8½x11; 1M circ; lo. Reports 2 to 4 mos. Pays 2 copies. No ads. Discounts: 1 yr. sub. is $6 to libraries; no discounts for single copies. Back issues: $4/ea. except when sold as part of a sub. to a current volume. (Subscriptions are sold by volume only). COSMEP, NESPA.

Bradford-Robinson (see DENVER QUARTERLY)

BRANCHING OUT, **Susan McMaster,** co-ordinating ed., 11443 77 Ave., Edmonton, Alberta, Canada T6G OL9. Poetry, fiction, articles, art, photos, cartoons, interviews, satire, criticism, reviews, letters, parts-of-novels, longpoems. Every 2 mos; $9.50/12 issues; $1/ea; $1/sample; 1973; 44p; 8½x11; 3M circ. Reports 8-10 wks. Pays: copies only. Ads: $165/page (subject to change, 30 days notice); $80/½; no class/wd. No discounts. Back issues: no discount. Pub'd 1 issue in 1973. Women.

BRECHT TIMES, Brecht Times Press, **Peter Langford,** Alexandra Cottage, Kimpton Road, Welwyn, Herts, UK. Poetry. *We have also formed a record label "Brecht Times Records" which is releasing left wing rock music (i.e. rock music with left wing lyrics). So far two albums issued "Red Television" and "Horn on the People's Side"* £*1.25 each, from the above address or any branch of Virgin Records.* 3/yr; 30p/sub; 10p/ea; free sample; 1972; 20pp; A4; 500 circ; mim. Reports: 1 mo. No pay. No ads. Discounts: 33% bookshops. Back issues: none. ALMS.

Brecht Times Records (Record Label), 7 Beadon Road, London W6 7Br, UK. Music. *So far we have released two records:* Horn on the People's Side *(by the Canadian group Horn);* Red Television *(by the English group Red Television). Further information on request.*

Paul Breman Ltd. (see HERITAGE)

BRIDGE, A POETRY QUARTERLY, Bridge Publications, **Nanlee Haston Pitts,** 3726 Hibicus Stree, Coconut Grove, FL 33133. Poetry, longpoems. Bridge Quarterly *seeks traditional, experimental, etc...work from any poet/poetress known or never before in print. Age and/or reputation is of no concern. Competition is tough however. Editor rec. approx. 300 mss. each month, and only prints 15 poets per issue on an average. Seeks small (max. 4x4 inches) pen & ink drawings to be used in illustration (to compliment page). One illustrator per issue. Requests a short biography on poet, illustrator etc. for our files; also require a small selection of work to select from. Is essential contributor see a copy for* *length & width needs – not to mention quality of requirements.* Q; $8/yr; $2.50/each; $1.75/sample; 1971; 30pp; 5½x11; 500 circ; lo. Reports 6 wks max. Pays for poets, playwrites, illustrators: comp. copies of issue in which artist appears; 1 yr sub; $ prizes. No ads. Discounts: contact McGregor, Ellsworth, Faxon, or other agencies for school rates. Back issues: Nos. 1,2,3,4 not for sale (with rare exception to large poetic collections, etc. for $10-$25 a copy). COSMEP, CCLM.

Bridge Publications (see BRIDGE, A POETRY QUARTERLY, TROLL)

Bridgewest Publications (see LAST FLY)

BRIEF, Alasdair Aston (Chairman: Dulwich Poetry Group), 15 Pickwick Road, Dulwich Village, London SE21, UK. *All kinds of poetry from all age-groups and in all styles. Issued free to those attending poetry readings in Dulwich.* Monthly; single copy/free; 1969; 10pp; A4. Reports vary. No pay. No ads. Poetry.

Brimscombe Publications (see BRITANNIA)

Bristol Arts Centre (see POETRY OF THE CIRCLE IN THE SQUARE)

Bristol Women's Liberation Group (see ENOUGH)

BRITANNIA, Brimscombe Publications, M. Brimscombe, 8 St. John's Park, Blackheath, London SW3 7TQ, UK. *A magazine for students of English all over the world. Very lively, well-informed articles dealing with the British and all aspects of life in Great Britain and the British Commonwealth. Length 500-800 words.* 8/yr; £1.25/sub; 1950. Pays on publication.

BRITISH AMATEUR JOURNALIST, *British Amateur Press Association,* BCM/BAPA, London WC1V 6XX, UK.

BRITISH BOOK NEWS, Gillian Dickinson, 59 New Oxford Street, London WC1A 1BP, UK. Criticism. Monthly; £3.60/sub; 30p/ea; 1940; 72pp; 9000+ circ; lp. Ads: £40/page; £24/½; £14/¼.

BRITISH JOURNAL OF AESTHETICS, *Thames & Hudson Ltd.,* **Harold Osborne,** 90a St. John's Wood High St., London NW8, UK. Articles. 4/yr; £3/sub; 75p/ea; 1960; 96pp; 9x6". Reports vary. No pay. Ads: £16/page pro rata. Discounts: 10%.

The British Naturalists Association (see COUNTRY–SIDE)

BRITISH PRINTER, Roy Brewer, 30 Old Burlington St., London W1X 2AE, UK. *Articles on technical and aesthetic aspects of printing processes and graphic reproduction.* Monthly; £5/sub; 1888. Pays: by arrangement.

BROADSIDE SERIES, 12651 Old Mill Pl., Detroit, MI 48238.

BRONTE SOCIETY TRANSACTIONS, *Bronte Society,* Bronte Parsonage Museum, Haworth, Keighley, Yorkshire, UK.

Brontpress Ltd. (see ELIZABETHAN)

Brownstone Publishers, Inc., Andrew O. Shapiro, John M. Striker, 149 E. 81 St., New York, NY 10028. *Brownstone Publishers specializes in helping readers to help themselves. We look for book-length manuscripts devoted to enlightening the layman on how to demand and enjoy his rights, e.g., as a consumer, tenant, unemployed person, married person, hospital patient, or member of a minority group, etc. Law-for-laymen, self-help books.*

Brynmill Publishing Co. (see HUMAN WORLD)

BUCKNELL REVIEW, **Harry R. Garvin,** Bucknell Univ., Lewisburg, PA 17837. *Our journal is scholarly and interdisciplinary and is designed for both the specialist and the generalist. Humanistic, critical, philosophical approaches to the arts and sciences are preferred. Articles of 12-25 typed pages, double-spaced are preferred.* 3/yr; $5.50/yr; $2.50/ea; no sample; 1941; 150pp; 6x9; 800 circ. Reports 3 wks. Pays copies only. Ads: none as yet. Back issues: $2.50/copy. Pub'd 3 issues 1973, expects 3 in 1974. COSMEP.

BUFFALO COLD SPRING (see 23 CLUB SERIES)

BULLETIN FOR FILM AND VIDEO INFORMATION, Anthology Film Archives, **Hollis Melton, Callie Angell,** 80 Wooster St., New York, NY 10012. Articles, interviews, criticism, reviews. *A compilation of information on film- and video-making, distribution, exhibition and programming, film and video study, preservation. Also included is a column of travel information so that film- and video-makers tours can be fully utilized, a selection of articles, reviews, etc. are reprinted in each issue and selected letters are included. Issues run about 4-8 pages.* Bi-monthly; $2/yr; sample; 1974; 4-8pp; 8½x11; 500 circ; lo. Reports: no definite policy. No ads. Discounts: none. Back issues: 25 cents. No issues pub'd 1973, expects 6 in 1974. Film & Video.

BULLETIN OF THE BOARD OF CELTIC STUDIES, University of Wales Press, **D. Ellis Evans, J. Beverley Smith, R.G. Livens,** Univ. of Wales Press, Merthyr House, James St., Cardiff, UK. *Articles on Language and Literature, History and Law, Archeaology and Art.* 2/yr; £3/yr.

BULLETIN OF HISPANIC STUDIES, Liverpool University Press, **Geoffrey Ribans,** School of Hispanic Studies, The University, PO Box 147, Liverpool L69 3BX, UK. *Specialist articles on the language and literatures of Spain, Portugal and Latin America, in English, Spanish, Portuguese and Catalan.* 4/yr; £4/yr; £1.25/ea; 1923. No pay.

BURLINGTON MAGAZINE, **Benedict Nicolson,** 49 Park Lane, London W1, UK. *Deals with the history and criticism of art. Articles of 500-3000 words from authors having special knowledge of their subjects.* Monthly; 65p/ea; 1903. Pays: £3.15 per page.

Burning Deck Press (see DIANA'S BIMONTHLY)

THE BURROUGHS BULLETIN, House of Greystoke, **Vern W. Coriell,** 6657 Locust, Kansas City, MO 64131. Monthly; $15/yr; $2/ea; 1947; 32pp; 8½x11; 2500 circ; lo. Reports 30days. Pays up to 10 copies. Ads: $18/p; $10/½; 6 lines $2/class/wd. Pub'd 4 issues, 2 books 1973, expects 26 issues, 2 bks. in 1974. Lit.

Michael Butterworth Publications (see CORRIDOR)

Byron Press, **John Lucas, Allan Rodway, George Parfitt,** The English Dept., Univ. Park, Nottingham, UK. Poetry. lp. Discounts: 33%.

BYWAYS, **Gerry Loose,** Hedda's Cottage, Arkesden, Saffron Walden, Essex, UK. Poetry. *Concrete in the true sense of the word.* 4-8/yr; 80p/yr; 23p/sample; 1970; 30pp; A4; 300 circ; lp. Reports 1 mo. Pays: by negotiation. ALMS.

The Cadleon Press, PO Box 24, San Francisco, CA 94101.

CAFE SOLO, The Solo Press, **Glenna Luschei,** 1209 Drake Circle, San Luis Obispo, CA 93401. Poetry, articles, art, photos, criticism, reviews, letters, longpoems, *We are doing a series of special numbers now involving guest editors. Our* Issue 7 *is a women' special edited by Lynn Strongin,* Issue 8 *is a Chicano issue edited by Ernesto Padilla. Other future issues include a special Frank Waters'* Indian Summer Harvest *issue and an issue of children's poetry put together by Dick Bakken. I still cling to the Southwest where* Cafe Solo *was founded. And have a strong Chicano bias as the original intent of* Cafe Solo *was to spark a dialogue between Spanish and English.* 2/yr; $2.50/yr; $1.50/ea; 1969; 44pp; 8½x11; 500 circ; offset. Reports within a mo. Pays: $2.50/p. Discounts: any order over 5 books, 40%. Pub'd 2 issues, 1 book 1973, expects 3 issues, 3 bks. 1974. COSMEP, CCLM, Chicano.

Caithness Books, **John Humphries, proprietor,** Janet St., Thurso, Caithness, Scotland, UK. *Publishes books only: Scottish poetry, Scottish lit. crit., Scottish local history.* ALP.

Calder Valley Poets' Society (see PARNASSIAN)

THE *CALIFORNIA QUARTERLY,* **Elliot Gilbert, Karl Shapiro, Diane Johnson,** 100 Sproul Hall, Univ. of Calif., Davis, CA 95616. Poetry, fiction, articles, art, photos, reviews, criticism, interviews, parts-of-novels, longpoems. *Stories should not exceed 5000 words, though we make exceptions. We like "California material" however you care to define that, but don't insist on it. We publish whatever we think is good and recommend that authors glance at past issues. Recent contributors include Charles Simic, Robert Kelly, Karl Shapiro, James Bertolino, Marjorie Green, Jerry Bumpus, Sandra Gilbert, Rosellen Brown, Ann Stanford.* Q; $5/yr; $1.50/ea; 1971; 83pp; 8½x5½; 400 circ; lp. Reports: 4-6 wks. Pays: 2 copies + sub. Ads: $40/p; $25/½. Discounts: we make different arrangements for different circumstances. Back issues: at present, same as single price, $1.50. Pub'd 3 issues 1973, expects 4 in 1974. COSMEP, CCLM.

Barry Callaghan, Publisher (see EXILE)

CAMBRIDGE REVIEW, **Hugh Brogan, Philip Pettit,** 7 Green St., Cambridge, UK. 6/yr; 25p/ea; 1879; 30pp; quarto; 3000 circ. Reports: 2 wks.

CAMELS COMING NEWSLETTER, **Richard Morris,** PO Box 703, San Francisco, CA 94101. Poetry, fiction, articles, art, photos, cartoons, interviews, satire, criticism, reviews, letters, collages, plays, concrete art. *Emphasis on criticism and commentary on the 'underground' lit. scene. Poetry submissions not wanted. Newsletter format.* Irreg; $7/12 issues; free samples; 1972; 4-8pp; 8½x11; 1500 circ; lo. Reports: 1 wk. Pays: copies only. COSMEP, NESPA.

Canada Publishing Company (see ART & LITERARY DIGEST)

THE CANADIAN FICTION MAGAZINE, **R.W. Stedingh,** PO Box 46422, Postal Station G, Vancouver, BC, V6R 4G7, Canada. Fiction, articles, art, photos, interviews, criticism, reviews, parts-of-novels, collages, manifestoes. *Open to both traditional and experimental fiction, no biases. Recent contributors: John Metcalf, Matt Cohen, George Woodcock, Hugh Hood, Robert Harlow, Susan Musgrave, Robin Skelton, Eugene McNamara, Michael Bullock, J. Michael Yates, Leon Rooke, Kent Thompson, David Helwig. The oldest and still the most exciting fiction magazine in Canada. Especially receptive to articles on the aesthetics of fiction.*

Q; $8/yr; $2/ea; $1/sample; 1971; 120pp; 6x9; 1M circ. Reports: 1 mo. Pays: $3/page. Ads:$50/p; $26/½. Discounts: 40% bookstores, jobbers; 50% classroom; 5% agents. Back issues: Nos. 1-3, 5, 6, 9 & 10 are collector's items for libraries only, $25 each. Pub'd 3 issues 1973, expects 4 in 1974. COSMEP. Literary.

CANADIAN LITERATURE, **George Woodcock,** c/o Publications Centre, Univ. of BC, Vancouver 8, BC, Canada.

CANADIAN STEAM MAGAZINE, Richard L. Coulton, **Richard L. Coulton,** Bentley, Alberta, Canada TOC OJO. Articles, reviews, letters. *We are interested in all facets of steam power as used in Canada. 'If it was built or used in Canada, & powered by steam, we are interested.' Articles sent in may be up to 500 words.* Q; $1/yr; 25/ea; 1971; 7pp; 8½x11; mi. Reports vary. Pays on articles only, 1 cent/word. Ads: 10 cents/word.

CANDOUR, **A.K. Chesterton,** Forest House, Liss Forest, Hants, UK. *Politico-economic articles with a national and Commonwealth appeal. 1200-1500 words.* Monthly; 10p/ea. Pays: £5/1000 words.

CANYON CINEMANEWS, **Diane Kitchen,** Industrial Center Bldg., Rm. 220, Sausalito, CA 94965. Poetry, articles, art, photos, interviews, criticism, reviews, letters. *Articles, reviews, & criticisms by and for the independent filmmaker. Interviews with same.* Bi-monthly; $3/yr; 50 cents/ea; free sample; 1967; 16pp; 7½x 9¾"; 2M circ; lo. Ads: $50/p; $25/½; class/wd free. Back issues: 50 cents/ea. Published 4 issues 1973.

Capra Press, **Noel Young,** 631 State St., Santa Barbara, CA 93101. Poetry, fiction articles, art, photos, cartoons, interviews, satire, parts-of-novels, longpoems, plays. *David Meltzer, Henry Miller, Andrei Codrescu, Morton Marcus, James Houston, Anais Nin, Lawrence Durrell, Ross MacDonald, Barry Gifford, Diane diPrima, Richard de Mille, Carlos Reyes.* lp. Reports 1 mo. Discounts: 40% to trade. Pub'd 15 books 1973, expects 12 in 1974. COSMEP.

CARET, **Robert Johnstone, Trevor McMahon, William Peskett,** 31 Marlborough Park Central, Belfast BT9 6HN, UK. Poetry, fiction, art, criticism, letters, longpoems. *Anything of sufficient standard included. Prose preferably not much more than 2000 words. Only work in English and translations. Mostly Irish and British, occasionally American. 3 or 4 line drawings per issue.* 3/yr; 50p ($2.10)/yr; 15p (75 cents)/ea; 1972; 40pp; 800 circ. Reports about 1 mo. Pays copies only. Ads: £7/page; £4/½ page.

THE CARLETON MISCELLANY, **Wayne Carver,** Carleton College, Northfield, MN 55057. Poetry, fiction, interviews, satire, criticism, reviews. *These days, with our budget, we have a strong bias toward short stuff. Fiction up to 7500 words, poetry up to 75 lines, though we will find room for the truly outstanding story or poem if we come across it. I'd like to find some good, informal, impassioned but intelligent criticism, but I don't like rejects from* The Explicator *or A+ term papers on The Grail Theme in the latest masterpoem from an underground press. Recent contributors: Ira Sadoff, James B. Hall, Jack Matthews, and Fred Busch and poets galore – some of them indistinguishable. But good! Good!* 2/yr;
$3/yr; $1.50/ea; $1.50/sample; 1959; 148pp; 8½x6; 1300 circ; lp. Reports 6 wks-2 mos. Pays $8/printed page. No ads. Discounts: agents 60 cents on a $3 sub. Back issues: $1.50/copy. Pub'd 1 issue 1973. CCLM.

CAROLINA QUARTERLY, **Bruce M. Firestone,** Box 1117, Chapel Hill, NC 27514. Poetry, fiction, reviews, part-of-novels, longpoems. *We hold a fiction contest each year which awards prizes to writers under 30 who have not yet published a book-length manuscript. Information on it available on request (send stamped envelope).* 3/yr; $4.50/yr; $1.50/ea; $1.50/sample; 1949; 120pp; 6x9; 1500 circ; lo. Reports 4-6 wks. Pays $5 per printed page + 2 copies. Ads: $100/page, $60/½. Back issues: $2. Pub'd 3 issues 1973. COSMEP, CCLM.

Carpenter Press, **Robert Fox,** Rt. 4, Pomeroy, OH 45769. Poetry, fiction, art, photos. *Plan to concentrate on fiction but will do poetry, too. Hope to do 2 full-length books a year but have to sell* Nobody's Perfect *first. Can't read unsolicited mss. yet.* 1973; lo. Pays by contract. Discounts: Trade, Classroom. Expects 1-2 books in 1974. COSMEP.

Casa de las Americas, G y Tercers, Vedado, Havana, Cuba.

CASA BOLETIN, Casa Editorial, Maria Tello, mag. ed., Leland Mellott, press ed., 362 Capp Street, San Francisco, CA 94110. Casa Boletin can use short poems in Spanish or English or both. Can accept very short articles on current Raza events (esp. in Bay Area). Monthly; $5/yr; 50 cents/ea; 1970; 12pp; 8½x7"; 550 circ; mi; graphics. Pays: copies only. No ads. No discounts. Pub'd 12 issues, 2 books 1973, expects 12 issues, 2 books in 1974. COSMEP, Third World.

Casa Editorial   (see CASA BOLETIN)

CASTRUM PEREGRINI, **M.R. Goldschmidt,** PO Box 645, Amsterdam, The Netherlands. Poetry, articles, art, criticism, reviews, music, letters, longpoems, collages, plays, concrete art. 5/yr; $17 + p&p/yr; $4/ea; 1951; lp. Ads: DM/Hfl. 440/page; DM/Hfl. 220/½. Pub'd 5 issues 1973.

CATACOMB POETS, Catacomb Press, **Rev. Alistair Osborne,** 1 Fulbar St., Renfrew PA4 8PH, Scotland, UK. Poetry. *The series started in the Faculty of Divinity in Edinburgh University. It tries to publish the private poems of the non-poets. These people include professors, housewives, students, ministers, OAPs, businessmen, workers, school pupils, etc. They all write for their own pleasure first of all. The purpose of publishing is partly religious, a kind of celebration of life, but the content of poetry is comprehensive. The series is non profit making on principle, and financial hardship makes it necessary to restrict content to short poems. "For most must walk, though some by natural flying learn from the bitter winds a kind of praise." We try to present a "kind of praise."* 2/yr; 15p/ea; 1972; 24pp; 8x5"; 200 circ; mim. Reports 1 wk. No pay. No ads. Discounts: negotiable. Back issues: 10p sample or order.

Catalyst (see also GAY BOOK NEWS), **Ian Young,** 315 Blantyre Avenue, Scarborough, Ont., Canada MIN 2S6. Poetry, fiction. Catalyst *publishes 2 or 3 chapbooks a year – poetry and stories by gay and non-gay authors. Titles published in 1972; Graham Jackson:* The Apothecary Jar (stories); *Wayne McNeil:* Shells (poetry, illustrated), *Ian Young:* Some Green Moths (poetry). *Authors published in 1974 include: Wayne McNeill, E.A. Lacey.* All books $2. of. Reports very fast. Discounts: 40% (less than 10 copies, 30%). Gay.

CATONSVILLE ROADRUNNER, Moss-Side Press, 28 Brundetts Road, Chorlton

Manchester 21, UK. Articles, cartoons, photos, satire, news items, letters, collages. *Articles not usually more than 2 pages. About 750 words to a page.* Monthly; £1.25/yr; 8p px/ea; free sample; 1969; 20pp; 12x8½"; 5000 circ; off. Ads: no fixed rates. Discounts: usually 25%. Back issues: 5p/ea px. Women, Ecology, 3rd World, Black, Gay, Alternative Press Syndicate.

Cat's Pajamas Press (see also *MOJO NAVIGATOR(E))*, **John Jacob,** 423 S. Humphrey, Oak Park, IL 60302. Poetry, fiction, parts-of-novels. *We're operating on a shoestring and have commitments. Please hold manuscripts until Nov. 1974 at the earliest. Short books will receive serious consideration. Short fiction and short excerpts from novels are welcome, but we also want to encourage the writing and publication of short, self-contained units of fiction. We will be publishing Eric Felderman's 34 page novel* The Book of Lies. *Beat down some of the constricting barriers.* Irreg; price ea/varies; 1969; 8-40pp; page size varies; 250 circ; lo; lp. Reports 1 mo-6 wks. Pays copies only. Discounts: 40% to anyone ordering four or more copies of publications. Back issues: query. Pub'd 1 book 1973, expects 2 in 1974, COSMEP, CCLM.

CAVE: International Magazine of Arts and Ideas, Outrigger Publishers Ltd., **Norman Simms, Tim Pickford, Sefulu Ioane,** 1 Von Tempsky St., Hamilton, New Zealand. Poetry, fiction, articles, interviews, criticism, reviews, parts-of-novels, long-poems. *Translations, especially Pacific Islands, Latin America, and Eastern Europe. Articles sought on, for, about literature as meaningful part of a small nation's life-kulture; interaction of poetry and politics. No word-games, please! We are interested in oral traditions, aesthetic theory, etc.* (NZ): $3/3 issues, $5/6 issues, $1/ea; 72pp; 8x10"; lp. Reports 3 mos. Pays copies only. Ads: (NZ): $30/p; $15/½. Discounts: 33 1/3 to trade; libraries and institutions $5/3, $9/6. Third World.

Caveman Publications Ltd., **Trevor Reeves, Graeme Reeves,** PO Box 1458, Dunedin, New Zealand. Cave *now edited & published by Dr. Norman Simms, 1 Von Tempsky St., Hamilton, NZ. We now remain essentially publishers of collections of poetry, novels, and short stories in book form.* 10 books 1973, expects 11 in 1974.

CELLAR PRESS POEMS, Cellar Press, St. Bridgets, Radcliffe Rd., Hitchin, Herts, **Peter Scupham, John Mole, Roger Burford Mason,** 2 Taylors Hill, Hitchin, Herts, SG4 9AD, UK. Poetry. *We print 6 Cellar Press Poems each year. Each poem is printed in letterpress on laid paper and accompanied by a linocut, woodblock, or line-block illustration. Coloured card covers. Hand-sewn. Series one (1-6) at 50p set pf. Poets are Michael Johnson, Alan Golightly, David Day, John Hadwen, John Fuller and Peter Goodden. Series two (7-12) 60p pf. Poets are Anthony Thwaite, Simon Curtis, Duncan Forbes, Eddie Wainwright, Robert Cassidy, and Paul Matthews. Cheques etc. should be payable to Peter Scupham.* 6/yr; 60p/yr; 1972; 8pp; 200 circ; lp. Reports 2 wks. Pays 10 copies. Discounts: 33% (5 sets or more). ALP.

CENTAUR, **K. Antoinette Graham,** 2257 W. 35th St., Chicago, IL 60609. Fiction, plays. Centaur *wants only short fiction and drama that is imaginative and to the point. Keep it short – 1000 word limit, and payment only to 500 words. Absolutely no poetry.* 2/yr; $3/yr; $1.50/ea; free sample; trade; 1973; 48pp; 5½x8½; lo. Reports 1 mo. Pays 2 cents/wd. Ads: $25/½p. Expects 2 issues in 1974. Experimental.

CENTER, **Carol Berge,** Box 698, Woodstock, NY 12498. *Experimental prose only (including book reviews).* 2/yr; no sub; $1.50/ea + SASE; no sample; 1971; 80pp; 8½x11; 800 circ; lo. Reports pretty quick. Pays: $5/p + copies & sub. to all future issues. Back issues: 1st 3 issues/$50. Pub'd 2 issues 1973.

Center for Contemporary Poetry, **John Judson,** Center for Contemporary Poetry, Murphy Library, Univ. of Wisconsin-La Crosse, La Crosse, WI 54601. Poetry, articles, interviews. *We publish an annual volume under the title* Voyages to the Inland Sea; *emphasis is on midwestern poetry. Each volume includes three poets, with representative poems and an essay by each. Volumes usually run just under a hundred pages. Prices are $6 regular ed., $10 signed. Poets represented: (I) Etter, Knoepfle, Mueller; (II) Pollak, Woods, Hearst; (III) Dana, McGrath, Sebenthall. Vol. IV, available spring '74, with poets Alvin Greenberg, George Chambers, and Raymond Roseliep. Paperback eds. available for Vols. II,III, & IV, at $3.50.* 1/yr; $6/yr; $6/ea; 1971; 88pp; 8½x5½; 500 circ; lp. Mss. not solicited. Discounts: 20% to dealers, jobbers.

Center for Writers, USM (see MISSISSIPPI REVIEW)

CENTERING: A Magazine of Poetry, Years Press, **Richard Thomas,** ATL/EBH/MSU, E. Lansing, MI 48823. Poetry. *Unlike many little magazines,* Centering *contains at least 10 pages of each poet's work. Unfortunately, I am unable to accept unsolicited material until I get more time and money.* Annual; $1/yr; $1/ea; $1/sample; 1973; 48pp; 7½x8; lo. Reports: no unsolicited mss. Pays copies only. No ads. No discounts. Pub'd 1 issue 1973, expects 1 in 1974. COSMEP.

CENTRE 17, **Frank Davies,** 57 Newbiggin Road, Thaxted, Essex, UK. Poetry, fiction, reviews, criticism, interviews. *Nothing frivolous or cliche-politico poems entertained.* Q; 50p/yr; 12½p/ea; 1971; 16pp; quarto; 200 circ; mim. Reports 1-3 wks. Back issues 1 to 3.

CENTRE SPAN, **Martyn Offord,** c/o Mundella Grammer School, Meadows, Nottingham, UK. Articles, photos, news items, interviews, letters. Centre Span *is run from Mundella School using pupils in its reporting and photography. Other local schools also contribute along with community organisations: Tenants Association, Churches, Care Group, Social Service, Youth Clubs, Probation Service, Scouts, Racial Groups, etc. The Corporation Departments of Nottingham also use us as an information and advertising medium. With such a variety of news sources it can be seen that we are a meeting point for all sorts of views and therefore retain a fairly objective standpoint, though we do exert pressure on certain local issues when the needs of the Meadows Community are at stake.* 10/yr; 60p/yr; 3p/ea; 1970; 6-8pp; 15x10"; 1000 circ; off. Ads: £3/col. inch. Community Newspaper.

Century City Educational Arts Project (see INTERMEDIA)

Cepheid Variable Press (see STANLEY)

CEREMONY NEWSLETTER, Ceremony Press, **Clem Gorman,** 15 Arundel Gardens, London W11, UK. Articles, art, cartoons, news items, interviews, criticism, letters, collages. *Information on ceremony. Newsletter is core of non-local community of people interested or involved in ceremony and celebration. Interest in community, the arts (especially music) and community arts. Not radical political.* Monthly; donation/sub; free sample; 1973; 6pp; qto; 500 circ; off. Reports 1 mo. Pays: by negotiation. Ads: negotiable.

CHANGE, The Synergetic Society, **N.A. Coulter, Jr., Lorraine Cullen,** 1825 North Lake Shore Dr., Chapel Hill, NC 27514. Articles, criticism, reviews, letters. Synergetics *is the art and science of evoking synergy in the human mind, in small groups, and in other complex systems.* 6/yr; $3/yr; 50 cents/ea; sample; 1954; 28pp; 8½x11; 150 circ; mi. Reports 30 days. Pays copies only. No ads. Back issues: 50 cents if available. Pub'd 6 issues 1973. COSMEP.

Chaotic Press (see also *MERE ANARCHY)*, **Alexander Chaos,** 51 Mann TCE, North Adelaide, South Australia 5006. Poetry, quotes, graphics. *Publish (& distribute free, around Australia – mailed copies are dependent on postage being sent): 1) Broadsheets 20x14": eg:* Surrealism & Anarchy *(1973);* Pablo Neruda's Poetry *(1974);* Poetry & The Imagination *(1974), 2)* Mere Anarchy *(1973), 3) Books of poetry: eg: Peter Hicks,* Six Pieces on the Events in Chile Sept-Oct 1973 *(1974); John Healey,* Desert *(1972), & similar.*

CHAPMAN, **Walter Perrie,** Drum Park, Trinity Gask, Auchterarder, Perth, UK. Articles, poetry, fiction, art, satire, criticism, music, longpoems.

CHASM, **Garry D. Mitchell,** PO Box 735, Huntsville, AL 35801. Poetry, fiction. *Less than 20 lines; one fiction short story per issue.* Annual; $5/yr; $1.25/ea; no sample; 1973; 18pp; 8x8; 100 circ; lo. Reports flexible. Pays one copy only. Ads. $100/p; $37.50/½; no class/wd No discounts. Back issues: $1.25. Pub'd 1 issue 1973, expects 1 in 1974; no booktitles.

CHEAP AND FAST, The Friends of the Written Word, 2357 N. Buffum, Milwaukee, WI 53212. Cheap and Fast *is a vehicle for the literary and graphic arts, published quarterly, concentrating on short and short short stories and graphics with some poetry. Fiction should be two pages or less, single-space typewritten. Graphics include photos, drawings and illustrations. Poetry should be short, generally, although we have published long poems.* Sample copies 50 cents each. Pays 2 copies. *Make checks payable to the* Friends of the Written Word.

CHELSEA, **Sonia Raiziss, Rose Graubart, assoc. ed.,** PO Box 5880, Grand Central Sta., New York, NY 10017. Yearly; $2.25/ea; 1956; 200pp; 5½x8½; 1M circ; lo. Reports 3 mos. Pays 2 copies. Back issues: on inquiry. Pub'd 1 issue 1973, expects 1 in 1974. CCLM.

CHERNOZEM, Big Deal Press, **Susan L. Deal, Steven L. Deal,** PO Box 404, Gothenburg, NB 69138. Poetry. 3-4/yr; $2.50/4 issues; $1/ea; two 10 cent stamps/sample; 1972; 15pp; 8½x11; 100 circ; mi. Reports 2-4 wks. Pays copies only. Back issues: $1/ea. Pub'd 3 isssues 1973, expects 3 in 1974. COSMEP.

CHESIL, Word and Action, **David Boadella, Elsa Corbluth, Chris Fassnidge, R.G. Gregory,** 1 Back St., Abbotsbury, Weymouth, Dorset, UK. Poetry. Chesil *does not set out to be a general poetry magazine, but a collection of the poems read by* Chesil Poets *at their public readings.* 3-4/yr; 1973; 50pp; mim; off.

The Chestnut Leaf Private Press, **Colin Smith,** 68 Harewood Ave., Hornchurch, Essex, UK. *This is a private press. One of my main works to be printed will be a book on Essex views and poems drawn and composed by myself.* 1968; lp. BPS, BAPA.

CHICAGO JOURNALISM REVIEW, Assn. of Working Press, **Mike Miner, Michael Sneed, Paul O'Connor, Leonard Aronson,** 192 N. Clark, No.607, Chicago, IL 60601. Poetry, articles, art, photos, cartoons, interviews, satire, criticism, reviews, letters. *Specializes in media review, criticism, suggestions.* Monthly; $7/yr; 75 cents/ea; free sample; 1968; 24pp; 8¼x10½; 4M circ. Reports variable. Pays copies only. No ads. Discounts: classroom; negotiable. Back issues: $1. Pub'd 11 issues 1973, expects 12 in 1974. COSMEP.

THE CHICAGO REVIEW, **Thomas Joyce,** Univ. of Chicago, Chicago, IL 60637. Poetry, fiction, articles, art, photos, cartoons, interviews, satire, criticism, reviews, music, letters, parts-of-novels, longpoems, collages, plays, concrete art. *We embrace experimental, little-known, established, and traditional writers, and more* *and more we're also encouraging graphic artists to submit their work. Stylistic inventiveness often reaches extremes, as a glance at the last year's offerings shows. We publish excerpts from works-in-progress and selections often run to considerable length. We do not want Xerox copies or carbon copies, or submissions unaccompanied by SASE. Recent contributors include: Ronald Sukenick, W.S. Merwin, Gilbert Sorrentino, Jerome Klinkowitz, Kenji Miyazawa, George Grosz, Maxwell Geismar, Blaise Cendrars, Eugene Wildman, Yoichi Midorikawa.* Q; $6.95/yr; $1.95/ea; $1.95/sample; 1946; 200pp; 2500 circ; lo. Reports 1-2 mos. Pay varies; 3 copies + yr's sub. Ads: $100/p; $60/½; no class/wd. Discounts: agency and university press: 15% on ads; 10% on subs and back issues. Back issues: send for quotes; in general 50 cents higher per back year. Pub'd 4 issues 1973, expects 4 in 1974. COSMEP, CCLM.

CHILDREN'S BOOK REVIEW, Five Owls Press, **Valerie Anderson,** 67 High Rd., Wormley, Broxbourne EN10 6JJ, UK. 6/yr; £1.25/yr; 25p/ea. Pays: £1.05/ 1000 words.

CHINA QUARTERLY, **David C. Wilson,** Contemporary China Institute, 24 Fitzroy Square, London W1P 5HJ, UK. *Articles of about 8000 words on contemporary China.* 4/yr; £3/yr; 75p/ea. Pays: £50/article.

THE CHOWDER REVIEW, **Ron M. Slate,** 118 Dimmock St., Quincy, MA 02169. Poetry, articles, interviews, criticism, reviews, letters. *Kuzma, Doug Blazek, Linda Pastan, Wm. Stafford, Leonard Nathan, Robert Hass, John N. Morris, Jim McMichael. We respect poems that call into themselves the motions of the world. Types: poems that stand on solid images; traditional forms and free verse; light verse.* 3/yr; $3.50/yr; $1.25/ea; 1973; 40pp; 8½x5½; 600 circ; lo. Reports 2-3 wks. Pays copies only. Ads: $35/p; $20/½. Back issues: $1.25. Pub'd 500 issues 1973, expects 1500 in 1974. COSMEP, NESPA.

Christopher's Books, **Melissa Albers,** 1819 Sycamore Canyon, Santa Barbara, CA 93108. *Recent authors include Robert Peters, Nathaniel Tarn, John Brandi, Robert Durand, Hum es Den Boer, et al. Poetry series (hip-pocket series) requires mss of 50 to 100 pages (not typescript pages, finished book pages). We do not like even to read totally experimental work, incoherent work, concrete or otherwise only-visual work.* Lp. Reports 6 wks. Pay: varies %. Discounts: 2-4 copies/30%; 5 plus/40%. Pub'd 6 books 1973, expects 10 in 1974. COSMEP.

The Cider Press (see HARD CIDER)

CINEASTE MAGAZINE, **Gary Crowdus,** 244 W. 27th St., New York, NY 10001. Articles, photos, interviews, satire, criticism, reviews. *A radical political perspective on the cinema: from ideological implications of Hollywood consumer cinema to revolutionary cinema from the U.S., Europe and the Third World.* Q; $4/yr; $1/ ea; 50 cents/sample; 1967; 56pp; 8½x11; 4M circ; lo. Reports 2-3 mos. Pays copies only. Ads: $100/p; $60/½; no class/wd. Back issues: $1/ea. Pub'd 3 issues 1973, expects 3-4 in 1974. COSMEP, Film.

CINEFANTASTIQUE, **Frederick S. Clarke,** PO Box 270, Oak Park, IL 60303. Articles, art, photos, cartoons, interviews, criticism, reviews, music, letters. *The world's only review of horror, fantasy and science fiction films. Recent issues have interviewed screenwriter Richard Matheson, film director George A. Romero and Don Siegel and actors including Charlton Heston, Roddy McDowall, Vincent Price, etc. In addition to reviews on new films and books, the magazine prominently features interviews with new filmmakers as well established artists, as well as articles on genre history and aesthetics. Each issue is 48 pages, including full color front and* back covers and many full color photographs on the interior, printed on glossy coated enamel. Now in third year of publication. Newstand distribution by De-Boer. Q; $8/yr; $3/ea; $3/sample; 1970; 48pp; 8½x11; 8M circ; lp. Reports approx. 3 wks. Pays min. of 3 copies. Ads: $400/p; $275/½; $1/106 pt. line class/wd. Discounts: 30% available via DeBoer Distributors, 188 High St., Nutley, NJ 07110 in U.S. and Canada. For terms of foreign sale, please contact the publisher. Back issues: 10 in print, contact publisher for details. Pub'd 3 issues 1973. COSMEP.

CIRCLE: a periodical of reversible poetry, Circle Forum, **Mrs. J.M. Gates,** PO Box 176, Portland, OR 97205. Circle *is exclusively dedicated to poetry readable, line by line, either forwards or backwards. Minimum length eight lines. First-time publication of reversible poetry on heritage themes, environmental themes, general themes, protest themes in standard English. Recent contributors include Marcella Caine, Doreen Gandy, Christine Fox, Myrle Dobson.* Q; $3.50/yr; $1/ea; $1/sample; 1973; 16pp; 5½x8½; 200 circ; lo. Reports 2 mos. Pays copies only. No ads. No discounts. Back issues: $1.50 when available. Pub'd 3 issues 1973, expects ten page catalog Summer 1974 only. COSMEP, Research & Experimentation

City Lights Books, **Lawrence Ferlinghetti, Nancy Phillips,** 1562 Grant Ave., San Francisco, CA 94133. Poetry, fiction, interviews, longpoems.

CIVIL LIBERTY, National Council for Civil Liberties (N.C.C.L.), 186 Kings Cross Road, London WC1 9DE, UK. Articles, news items. *News and comments on civil liberties in Britain and Northern Ireland. Subscription includes the Annual Report, information on publications and the paper, "Speak Out."* 12/yr; £1.50/yr; 3p/ea; 1935; 4pp; A3; off. No ads.

CIVIL SERVICE POETRY, Emma, **Ernest Meadowcroft, Mabs Allen,** South Corner, Burses Way, Brentwood, Essex, UK. Poetry. *Mainly restricted to European civil servants but some "guest" poets included. Grammatically high standard, sharply focusing emotion, uncovering hidden truth, with subtle distinction between subject and theme, not normally exceeding 24 lines.* Annual; 20p/ea; 1968; 36-48pp; 7½x4½"; lp. Reports: variable. Pays: one free copy.

CLARITY, **Jennifer Sprague,** 3 Greenway, Berkhamsted, Herts HP4 3JD, UK. Articles, poetry, criticism, letters. *Length of material approx. 750-2500 words. Aimed at intelligent non-specialist who is interested in Christianity; interdenominational, covering a broad spectrum of views & attitudes.* Clarity *is the house magazine of the MENSA Christian Group, a sub-group within MENSA, of members who are interested in Christianity. Contributors are mainly group members, but outside contributors & subscribers are welcome.* 6/yr; 50p/yr; 1968; 20-34pp; ½ fcp; 100+ circ; off. Religious.

CLASSIC FILM COLLECTOR, **Samuel K. Rubin,** 734 Philadelphia St., Indiana, PA 15701. Articles, art, photos, cartoons, interviews, reviews, letters. Q; $5/yr; $1.50/ea; $1/sample; 1962; 64pp; 12x15; 2M circ; lo. Reports indefinite. Pays copies only. Pub'd 4 issues 1973. COSMEP.

Clingstone Press (see AMPERS& MAGAZINE)

CLOUD NINE/"Vancouver Island Poems," Soft Press, **Robert Sward,** 1050 Saint David St., Victoria, BC, Canada V8S 4Y8. Poetry, art, photos, parts-of-novels, longpoems, collages. *Soft Press was founded in 1970. We have published eleven titles since that time dealing largely though not exclusively with Candian authors and themes. Recent contributors include William Stafford (a book titled* In The Clock of Reason), *Susan Musgrave, Sean Virgo, Gary Geddes, Dorothy Livesay,*

Earle Birney and others. Presently committed exclusively to Canadian (West Coast) material. Suggest inquiries in advance of submissions. SASE required. Annual; $3.50 per yr; $3.50/ea; 1970; 60pp; 6x9; 1M circ; lo; lp. Reports 3 mos max. Pay varies; copies. Discounts: 30% to trade; 40% over 5 copies. Back issues: $3.50. Pub'd 2 issues, 2 books 1973, expects 1 issue, 1 book 1974. COSMEP.

CLOVEN HOOF, **Rosemary Polzin,** Box 925, Saginaw, MI 48606. Poetry, fiction, art, photos, parts-of-novels, longpoems. *Prefer intensive brilliance in variegated forms.* Irreg; $2/4 copies; 50 cents/ea; 50 cents/sample; 1969; 50pp; 6x9; 500 circ; lo. Reports 1 mo. Pays copies only. Back issues: 50 cents/ea. None pub'd 1973, expects 6 issues in 1974. COSMEP.

Club Leabhar, Highland Book Club, **Frang Macthomais,** 31 Braeside Park, Balloch, Inverness IV1 2HJ, UK. Poetry, fiction. *Publishers of Gaelic and English fiction, non-fiction and Gaelic-based products. Exists to encourage writers in the Gaelic language. English-language publications sales subsidise Gaelic titles.* Gaelic.

Coach House Press, 401 Huron St. (rear), Toronto, Ont., Canada M5S 2G5.

Coarse Crash Press, **Lawrence Upton,** c/o 18 Clairview Rd., Streatham, London SW16, UK. Poetry. *CCP is an anti-vanity press producing booklets at cost for poets who have still to find their way in the poetry field . . . this being my own egocentric opinion. The main aim of CCP is to take away as much business as possible from those whose only interest in poetry is to use it as a means to take away the would-be poet's money.* Irreg; SAE/IRC for price list; 1973; page size varies; 100-300 circ; mim. Reports 2 wks. Pays: special arrangements.

COASTLINE COLLECTIVE, **Robert M. Benn, John Tsitrian,** 3718 Clarington No. 15, Los Angeles, CA 90034. *Coastline Collective is a new monthly with, as yet, humble format and simple esthetic layout. CC is an energetic attempt to gather together the foremost unacclaimed West Coast writers (and artists) into a zolting but unpresumptuous 10,000 plus package each month. CC is not a traditional small press or literary magazine; but a powerful draft combining Coast writing talents into a residual nexus for what will be a slick and successful national monthly combining the formats of* Esquire/ *the new* Harper's/Coast *with a yet more distinctive format proving that California is where the future is!* Monthly; sub. free; 1973; 10 pp; 8½x11; 200 circ; lo. Reports 2-3 wks. Pays copies only. Pub'd 1 issue 1973, expects 12 in 1974.

Cobra Press, **G.W. Sherman,** 15381 Chelsea Dr., San Jose, CA 95124. *The Cobra Press has printed 3 titles:* The Chemists & Other Poems, *54pp, (1964), $2.25;* The Waiting Tree: Sonnets, *48pp, (1966), $2.15;* The Poet & The Flea, *a prosody book, 64pp, (1969), $2.75. Postpaid.*

CODEX SHAMBHALA, Shambhala Booksellers, **Robert Harrison, Michael Fagan,** 2482 Telegraph Ave., Berkeley, CA 94704. Reviews of books only. *Reviews of new and classic books in the fields of alchemy, astrology, Buddhism, Hinduism, Yoga, Oriental Philosophy, Western mysticism, Sufism, Gurdjieffiana, occult subjects, American Indians, humanistic and analytical psychology. Reviewers must include s.a.e. for reply.* 4/yr; $1/6 issues; 25 cents/sample; 1971; 16-24pp; 8½x11; 4M circ; lo. Reports 3 wks. Pays: $5. Ads: $200/p; $100/½. No discounts. Back issues unavailable. Pub'd 4 issues 1973, expects 4 in 1974. COSMEP, Book reviews.

COE REVIEW, **David H. Kameras,** G.M.U. Box 328, 1220 First Ave. N.E., Cedar Rapids, IA 52402. Poetry, fiction, articles, criticism, reviews, parts-of-novels, longpoems. 3/yr; $1.50/yr; 50 cents/ea; 50 cents/sample; 1972; 70pp; 8½x5½; 300 circ;

lo. Reports up to 3 mos. Pays copies only. Back issues: 50 cents/copy. Pub'd 2 issues 1973, expects 2 books in 1974. Literary.

Cokaygne Press (see RADICAL-TRADITIONALIST PAPERS)

Cold Mountain Press, **Ryan Petty,** 4406 Duval, Austin, TX 78751. Poetry, art, photos, interviews. *Generally poems under 25 lines. Recent contributors: William Stafford, John Haines, Robert Bly, Denise Levertov, Gregory Orr.* 1973; lo; lp. Reports 2 wks. Pays copies only. No ads. Discounts: 40% trade; 20% library. Pub'd 12 postcards & broadsheets 1973, expects 14 in 1974. COSMEP.

COLLEGE ENGLISH, National Council of Teachers of English, **Richard Ohmann, ed., Susan McAllester, poetry ed.,** Wesleyan University, Middletown, CT 06457. Poetry, articles, cartoons, satire, collages. *Poetry, articles, criticism. Reviews are assigned by editor.* 8/yr; $15/yr; $2/ea; 1939; 140pp; 7½x9½; 15M circ; lp. Reports up to 2 mos. Pays copies only. Ads: $290/p; $195/½; 75 cents class/wd. Pub'd 8 issues 1973, expects 8 in 1974. No books.

College Press Service, **Collective of six people,** 1452 Pennsylvania St., Denver, CO 80203. News articles, cartoons, interviews. College Press Service *publishes twice-weekly releases of alternative news and features of interest to the college audience. We have subscriber papers in 47 states. CPS is especially looking for hard news (no editorializing) dealing with militarism, government corruption, the women's movement, consumer protection, and higher education legislation. We also need filler graphics and editorial cartoons and sketches for our graphics pages (4 per week). We also provide active censorship counseling for college journalists (call 303-831-7240).* Twice-weekly; daily papers: $180/yr; 2-3 weeklies: $160/yr; weeklies: $140/yr; less than weeklies: $90/yr; alternatives: make offer. 1962; 8pp; 8½x14; 400 circ; lo. Reports 3 to 4 wks. Pays: $5-$25 per story. No ads. Discounts: libraries $100/yr. Pub'd 60 issues 1973, expects 60 in 1974. UPS, College/alternative news.

THE COLORADO QUARTERLY, **Paul Carter,** Hellems 134, University of Colorado, Boulder, CO 80302. Fiction, articles. *4000-6000 words. Articles written by specialists in all fields in non-technical language for general reader. Stories with plots and understandable characters.* Q; $4/yr; $1/ea; free sample; 1952; 144pp; 6 1/8x9¼; 800 circ; lp. Reports 2-3 wks. Pays 1 copy. No ads. No discounts. Back issues: $1.25 per copy.

THE COLUMBIA FORUM, **Erik Wensberg,** 612 W. 114 St., New York, NY 10025. Poetry, articles, satire, criticism, reviews. *1,000-7,000 words.* Q; $7.50/yr; $1.95/ea; $1.95/sample; $13.50/2 yrs; $18/3 yrs; 1957; 48pp; 8½x11; 10M circ; lo. Reports 2-6 mos. Pays: $250/articles; $75/poems. No ads. Discounts: students, $5. Back issues: $3/ea. Pub'd 4 issues 1973, expects 4 in 1974. COSMEP, General Non-fiction, Poetry.

COME TOGETHER, 5 Caledonian Rd., London N1, UK. Articles, poetry, art, photos. *Of interest to all women and men fighting male domination and all forms of exploitation. All women and queens are welcome to send in articles etc either to London or to Manchester G.L.F., c/o Flat 3, 102 Hathersage Rd., Manchester 13.* 5/yr; 65p/yr; 13p/ea. Women, Gay.

Committee for Prisoner Humanity & Justice (see CPHJ NEWSLETTER)

COMMUNES, Journal of the Commune Movement, Moss Side Press, **No editors, Journal material is chosen by Commune Movement members on arranged Journal**

production weekends, Publications Secretary, Commune Movement, Lochhill Cottages, Ringford, Castle Douglas, Kircudbrightshire, Scotland, UK. Articles, art, letters. Communes *is the official journal of the Commune Movement and we will be pleased to publish any articles on communal living and related subjects (i.e. cooperative ventures). Articles of any length can be used and any practical information will be greatly appreciated.* Q; £1/yr; 24p/ea; 24p/sample; 1968; 24pp; A4; 1500 circ; lo. Reports vary. Pays: no pay, all material is given free. Ads: no adv. rates, will advertise other u/g papers if the same is done for us. Back issues: 24p (include postage). Alternative Society.

The Communication Company, **Daniel L. Dorman,** PO Box 6723, Columbus, OH 43209. Fiction, articles, art, photos, cartoons, interviews, criticism, reviews, music, letters, technical materials, directories & guides. *Published science fiction in 1967-68. Did street mimeo in the Haight (SF) prior. Since then have published several community directories, political pamphlets (Marcuse et.al.), and some articles and poetry and technical work on community organizing and lifestyle. We now have two publishing subdivisions,* The Cider Press *(q.v.) and* Orange Blotter Reality Trust. *We consult on printing & publishing for National Lawyers Guild Columbus Chapter and other groups, and offer technical assistance to all as time and energy permit. Two books in 1973:* Bustbook *(Summer '73) and reprint of* Session Games People Play *by Lisa Bieberman (orig. publ. by Psychedelic Information Center, Cambridge, MA, 1967). Lots more in '74-75, including quarterly newsletter.* Irreg; no sub; write for sample; 1965; page no. & size varies; mi; lo; lp; xerox. Reports 4 wks. Pay varies. Ads: none/varies; no classifieds. Discounts: trade, bulk, classroom (min. order 20 except other editors on letterhead) 25%; institution, agent (min. 10) 15%. Pub'd 2 books 1973, expects 4 issues, 3 books in 1974. COSMEP, UPS.

COMMUNICATIONS CO., Box 41614, Sta. C, San Francisco, CA 94110.

COMMUNITIES, Community Publications Cooperative, **Communitarian Village,** Rt.1, Box 191, Oroville, CA 95965. Articles, art, photos, interviews, reviews, letters. *Material relevant to communes, intentional communities, cooperatives, alternative institutions.* Bi-monthly; $6/yr; $1/ea; free sample; 1972; 64pp; 8½x11; 7500 circ; lo. Ads. $100/p; $50/½. Pub'd 6 issues 1973, expects 6 in 1974. COSMEP.

COMMUNITY COMMENTS, **Staff of Community Service, Inc.,** Box 243, Yellow Springs, OH 45387. *This is pretty much our own writing or that of friends. Four issues are mimeo newsletter style and 2 issues are in depth studies on specific topics.* 6/yr; $3.50/yr; sample; 4-30pp; 8½x11; 500 circ; mi. Special back issue prices. Pub'd 6 issues 1973. COSMEP, Community.

COMMUNITY OF FRIENDS, **Moses Yanes, Rose Anne Yanes,** 13850 Big Basin Way, Boulder Creek, CA 95006. *We publish first time poets and established poets. We encourage submissions from anyone who is attempting to express the reality of his life experience. Our December issue is devoted to children's poetry. We are looking for poetry by children and poetry by adults for children. Some recent contributors include John Yamrus, David Kherdian, Stephen Canada, Alan Burgis, Bruce Mello, Maria Berl Lee, and many other fine poets.* Q; $4/yr; $1.25/ea; free sample; $1.25/specials; 1972; 40pp; 5½x8½; 350 circ. Reports 2-4 wks. Pays 2 copies. Ads: no display; free class/wd. Discounts: 25% library & 40% trade discount. No special back issue prices. Pub'd 4 issues, 5 books 1973, expects 10 issues 1974.

Community Publications Cooperative (see COMMUNITIES)

CONCEPTS—A Magazine of Positive Poetry, Randall, **Robert Rolf Randall,** exec. ed., **Dan Klein & Edmund Miller,** co-eds., Box 4976 Grand Central Sta., New York,

NY 10017. Poetry. *Short (35 line max.) "postivie poetry"* — *(as opposed to negative, self-indulgent, maudlin poetry)* — *stressing the dignity of Man and his ability to overcome obstacles. Address all correspondence to Randall at the above address.* Semi-annual; $1/ea; 1972; 30pp; 6x4; lo. Reports 1 wk. Pays 2 copies. Advertising not accepted. Discounts: only to Randall reps. No back issues available. Pub'd 7 issues 1973, expects 2 in 1974.

CONCERNING POETRY, **L.L. Lee, ed., Robert Huff, poetry ed.,** English Dept., Western Washington State College, Bellingham, WA 98225. Poetry, articles, criticism, reviews. $3/yr; $1.50/ea; 1968; 85pp; 9x6; 300 circ; of. Pays copies only. Ads: $35/p. COSMEP, CCLM.

THE CONCH, Conch Magazine Ltd., **Sunday O. Anozie,** State Univ. of New York, New Paltz, NY 12561. Articles. The Conch *is dedicated to the pursuit of truth and excellence in African literary and cultural criticism. Multidisciplinary and comparative in scope, it explores problems related to sociology, literature, modern structuralism, sociolinguistics, cognitive psychology and the use of mathematics in literary formulation. Since every issue of* The Conch *is literally a special issue, all articles are commissioned. Style is austere and unique to* The Conch. 2/yr; $7/yr person; $9/yr library; $5/ea; sample/library only; 1969; 150pp; 5½x8½; 2500+ circ; lo. Reports 3 mos. Pays 10 offprints. Ads: $200/p; $150/½. Discount and back issue prices: available upon special request. Pub'd 1 double issue, 1 book 1973, expects 1 issue, 1 book in 1974. COSMEP, Third World.

THE CONCH REVIEW OF BOOKS, Conch Magazine Ltd., **Sunday O. Anozie,** State Univ. of New York, New Paltz, NY 12561. Reviews. The Conch Review of Books — *a Literary Supplement to* Conch — *is devoted entirely and exclusively to in-depth and timely reviews of books, films, and records on all subjects related to Africa, in particular, and the entire Black world in general.* 4/yr; $10/yr person; $15/yr library; $3/ea; sample/library only; 1973; 48-60pp; 6x9; 3M circ; lo. Reports 30 days. Pays 10 offprints. Ads: $200 & $150/p; $150 & $100/½; class/wd: 20 cents/20 words min. Discount schedule available upon special request. Back issues: all subscriptions are on a volume-per-year basis. Pub'd 4 issues/per volume 1973, expects 4 in 1974. COSMEP, Third World, Black.

CONFRONTATION, **Martin Tucker,** English Dept., Long Island Univ., Brooklyn, NY 11201. Poetry, fiction, articles, art, photos, interviews, satire, criticism, letters, parts-of-novels, longpoems, plays. *I.B. Singer, Eugene McCarthy, Frances Steloff, David Bisonette, Cynthia Ozick, Sol Yurick, Denise Levertov, besmilr brigham.* Semi-annual; $2/yr; $1/ea; 1968; 102pp; 6x9; 2-3M circ; lp. Reports 6 wks. Pays: $10-$100; copies. No ads as yet. Back issues: $1.50/ea. Pub'd 2 issues 1973. COSMEP.

CONNECTICUT FIRESIDE MAGAZINE, Fireside Press, **Albert E. Callan,** 51 Ingram St., Hamden, CT 06517, or Box 5293, Hamden, CT 06518. Poetry, fiction, articles, cartoons, satire, reviews, letters. *I had hoped to make it a monthly; now hope for 6 issues a year.* 6/yr; $4/yr; 75 cents/sample; 1972; 64pp; 9½x7; 1M circ; lo. Reports 1 mo. Pays: $10 for best short story; copies only for other stuff. No discounts. Back issues: 50 cents for each of first 3 issues. Pub'd 2 issues 1973, expects 5 in 1974.

CONTAC, Contac Publications, **John Freeman,** 6 Main View, Thorne Rd., Stainforth, near Doncaster, Yorks. DN7 5BU, UK. Articles, poetry, art, criticism, music. *All magazines received are reviewed (or at least mentioned if short on space). Any type of poetry or prose is considered. Recent contributors: Andrew Darlington, Tom Land, Steve Sneyd, N.S. Jackson, Hugh Probyn, William Oxley, John Elsberg,*

Richard Austin. 4/yr; 80p/yr; 17p/ea; 10p/sample; 1969; 28-32pp; A4; 200 circ; mim. Reports vary. Pay: negotiable. Ads: negotiable. Discounts: 10% (over 20). Back issues: 10p. ALP.

CONTEMPORA, PO Box 673, Atlanta, GA 30301.

CONTEMPORARY AUTHORS & POETS JOURNAL, **Eileen Reed,** Box 444-L, Brentwood, NY 11717. Poetry. *Sensitive poetry that a person may enjoy and relate to. Send 1-2 poems, 3-16 lines, and return env. We'd rather study one or two of your poems than skim over a bunch. If they're good, you'll be remembered as a good poet here. But a bunch that we think are not good would compound the odds against you. Think about that. Familiarize yourself with good poetry in whatever style you like, perhaps study our sample, before sending.* Q; $24/yr; $5.95/ea paper; $8.95/ea cloth; $4/sample; 1973; 50pp; 8½x5½; 3M circ. Reports within 3 wks. Pays: 50 to 75 cents/poem. Discounts: on request. None pub'd 1973, expects 3 issues in 1974.

CONTEMPORARY REVIEW (incorp. the *Fortnightly),* **Rosalind Wade,** 37 Union St., London SE1, UK. Articles, poetry, fiction, interviews, criticism, music, long-poems. *Ideal max. length 2500-3000 words. Recent contributors include: Peter Archer, Sir Frederic Bennett, John Biggs-Davidson, Gen. Lord Bourne, Donald Bruce, Sir Herbert Butterfield, Dame Margaret Cole, Andrew Faulds, David Fingleton, Lady Gardiner, Val Gielgud, James Hanley, Sir Edward Howard, James Avery Joyce, Kenneth Lindsay, The Earl of Longford, David Loshak, Michael McNair-Wilson, Sir James Pitman, Paul Rose, Baroness Seear, A.L. Rowse, William Kean Seymour, David Steel, Michael Stewart, John Trewin, Terry Tucker, David Vessey, Patrick Wall, Phillip Whitehead, Richard Whittington-Egan.* 12/yr; £4.08/yr; 30p/ea; sample/apply; 1866; 56pp. Reports 1 mo. Pays: £2.50/1000 words. Ads: £25/page pro rata. Discounts: apply.

CONTRABAND MAGAZINE, **Bruce Holsapple, Peter Kilgore, David Empfield,** PO Box 4073, Sta. A, Portland, ME 04101. Poetry, fiction, articles, art, photos, cartoons, interviews, satire, criticism, reviews, music, letters, parts-of-novels, long-poems, collages, plays, concrete art Q; $2/yr; 50 cents/ea; free sample; 1971; 80 pages; 7x8½; 500 circ; lo. Reports 3 mos. Pays 2 copies. Back issues: 35 cents first 6; 50 cents otherwise. Pub'd 2 issues, 2 books 1973, expects 4 issues, 4 books in 1974. COSMEP, CCLM.

CONTRACULTURA, **Miguel Grinberg,** C.C. Central 1332, Buenos Aires, Argentina. Articles, interviews. *Wilhelm Reich, Joe Berke, Allen Ginsberg, Antonin Artaud, Juan Peron, Noel McInnis, Luiz Carlos Maciel.* Monthly; $5/yr; 50 cents/ea; free sample; 1970; 32pp; 2M circ; lp. Reports immediately. Pays copies only. Ads: on request; no class/wd. Back issues: $1/ea. None pub'd 1973, expects 12 issues, 1 book in 1974. UPS.

CONTRIBUTORS BULLETIN, Freelance Press Services, **Arthur Waite,** Freelance Press Services, 67 Bridge St., Manchester M3 3BQ, UK. *A monthly Bulletin of what editors want to buy from Freelance writers.* Monthly; £3.85/yr; 30p/ea; 1962; 10pp; 13x8"; 800 circ; off. Reports 1 wk. Pays: 5p/line. Ads: 4p/word.

COPEMAN, Cope Press, **Copeman Collective,** c/o 146 Great Western Rd., London W11, UK. Articles, poetry, satire, news items. *Anti-psychiatry magazine offshoot of Cope – a group operating in a 'PNP' sort of way, trying to set up communities for freaked out people.* 4/yr; 60p/yr; 15p px/ea; 1974; 32+pp; foolscap; 500+ circ; mim. Ads: £10/page. Discounts: free to any alternative psychiatry mag. organisation etc. Alternative.

Copper Canyon Press (see also *COPPERHEAD*), **Sam Hamill, Jim Gautney,** 19 S. Utica St., Denver, CO 80219. *We are primarily a book publisher; our books are handset then run photo/offset & perfect bound. Limited editions library bound or bound in boards (short discount). We are distributed by Book People, Berkeley. Forthcoming poets include: W.M. Ransom, James M. Mitsui, Robert Hedin, Jack Hirschman, & Deena Metzger. Bias: we* do not *want to receive mss. from poets who have not at* least *read the classics of modernism (i.e. Pound, Rexroth, Olson) to say nothing of the Ta Hsio. We are particularly interested in publishing first books by promising poets.*

COPPERFIELD, Copperfield Canada Press, **Douglas Brown, Dermot McCarthy, Hugh Stewart,** Box 421, Temagami, Ont., Canada. Poetry, fiction, articles, art, photos, interviews, criticism, reviews, longpoems, plays. *No change — still a magazine of the land & North. Each issue now has, however, a thematic outline e.g. No. 5 "The Journal," No.6 "The Ancestor," No.7 "The River," examining issues in Canadian writing.* Irreg; $2/ea; no sample; 1969; 160pp; 500 circ; of. Reports vary. Pays copies only. Ads: $25/p; $15/½. Discounts: one third. IPPA.

COPPERHEAD, Copper Canyon Press, Sam Hamill, Jim Gautney, 19 S. Utica St., Denver, CO 80219. Poetry, articles, interviews, criticism, reviews, longpoems. *Copperhead is especially interested in criticism & translations, reviews, & commentaries. Bias: we are interested in work subsequent/consequent to a study of the Ta Hsio.* Ocassional; sub. price varies; 1974; no. pages varies; 6x9; lo; lp. Reports 2 wks. Pays copies only. No ads. Discounts: 40% on bulk orders. No back issues. Pub'd 4 books 1973, expects 2 issues, 6 books in 1974. COSMEP.

CORDUROY, **Richard Immersi,** 406 Highland Ave., Newark, NJ 07104. Poetry, fiction, art, photos, reviews. *Prose pieces should not exceed 6 double spaced typewritten pages. Black & white art work and photos only.* 2/yr; $2.50/3 issues; $1/ea; 50 cents/sample (for writers); 1968; 50pp; 5½x8½; 300 circ; mi; lo. Reports 2 wks. Pays copies only. Ads: $20/p; $10/½; 10 cents/wd classified. Discounts: 60/40–40% discount. CCLM.

CORMORAN Y DELFIN, (F.F. de Amador), 1805 (1 ° 5), Olivos (FCNBM) Pvcia de, Buenos Aires, Argentina.

CORNHILL MAGAZINE, 50 Albermarle St., London W1X 4BD, UK. Articles, poetry, fiction, photos, criticism. *High literary standard. No contribution previously published in this country is accepted.* 4/yr; 30p/ea; 1860. Pays: by arrangement.

CORRIDOR: New Writings Quarterly, Michael Butterworth Publications, **Michael Butterworth,** 61 Seymour St., Radcliffe, Manchester, UK. Articles, fiction, art, photos, interviews, criticism, letters. *Fiction magazine that voices new kinds of writing styles and ideas. Exciting to read and informative "behind-scenes" talks with authors, their books reviewed, news of events and publications. SF element. Recent issues have contained: J.G. Ballard, Michael Moorcock, Hilary Bailey, Peter Finch, Richard Konstalanetz, and many others. Material up to 5000 words or 5-6 A4 size pages. Artwork any size.* 4/yr; 80p/yr; 25p/ea; 1971; 32pp; 1000 circ; off. Reports 2-4 wks. No payment yet. Ads: £10/inside page; £12.50/back cover; 1p per word. Discounts: 33% over 5. Back issues: 20p/copy 2-4.

COSMEP NEWSLETTER, PO Box 703, San Francisco, CA 94101.

COSMIC PAPER, (formerly *FOX),* **The Cosmic Paper Folks,** Prins Hendrikkade 142, Amsterdam, Netherlands. Poetry, articles, art, photos, interviews, reviews, letters, comics. *New age magazine. Recent contributors: Ram Dass, Pir Vilayat*

Khan, Yogi Bhajan, Stephen Gaskin. *(Latest issue included).* 4/yr; $1/ea; $1/sample; 1972; 32pp; 2500 circ; lo. Pays free copies. Ads: $50/½p; $25/¼p. Discounts: more than 10 copies: 40% plus shipping. Back issues: single copy: no discount; bulk: 50% plus shipping. Pub'd 3 issues 1973, expects 4 in 1974. UPS.

COSMOPOLITAN CONTACT, Pantheon Press, **Romulus Rexner,** PO Box 26531, Los Angeles, CA 90026. Articles, cartoons, interviews, criticism, reviews, letters. Cosmopolitan Contact — a polyglot magazine — *promotes intercultural understanding & intellectual growth as means toward the reduction of intergroup and international tension and conflict.* Irreg; $2/yr; 50 cents/ea; 1961; 32pp; 6x9; 2M circ; lo; lp. Pays copies only. Ads: 10 cents/wd. Back issues: 25 cents. Planetary Legion for Peace (PLP).

COTTONWOOD REVIEW, **Michael Smetzer et. al.,** Box J, Kansas Union, Univ. of Kansas, Lawrence, KS 66045. Poetry, fiction, art, photos, interviews. *We are open to a wide variety of styles if the work is well done. We are particularly interested in contemporary translations. Chapbooks are generally by invitation.* Some recent contributors include: Jack Anderson, Colette Inez, Danny Rendleman, Lyn Lifshin, Reg Saner, David Ohle, John Judson, and Victor Contoski. 2/yr; $3/yr (includes chapbooks); $2/ea; $1/sample; 1965; 70pp; 8½x11; 800 circ; lo. Reports 2 mos. Pays copies only. No ads. Discounts: trade 40%; bulk negotiable. Back issues: Spring 73 & Winter 73-74=$1.25; Winter 69-70 to Fall 72=$1; special set Winter 69-70 to Winter 73-74=$5.50 (6 issues). Pub'd 2 issues 1973, expects 2 issues, 1 book in 1974. COSMEP, CCLM.

Richard L. Coulton *(see CANADIAN STEAM MAGAZINE, RLC'S MUSEUM GAZETTE)*

COUNTERPLAY, Gordon & Breach, **Ken Handel, Barbara Graustark,** Gordon & Breach, One Park Ave., New York, NY 10016. Poetry, fiction, articles, art, photos, interviews, satire, criticism, reviews, letters, parts-of-novels, longpoems, collages, plays, concrete art. Counterplay *is an anthology/digest of the counterculture press. Material relates in some way to the counterculture, though each issue has a separate issue theme.* Q, $9.50/yr; $3/ea; no sample; 1974; 64pp; 8½x11; lo. Ads: $300/p; $175/½. Discounts: 50% distributors (min. order 50); 40% bookstore (min. order 5); 10% sub. agencies.

COUNTER-SPY, **Organizing Committee for a Fifth Estate,** PO Box 647, Washington DC 20044. Articles. *We are totally oriented towards intelligence copy.* Q; $6/yr; $1.50/ea; $1.50/sample; 1973; 32pp; 8x10; 3M circ; lo. Ads: $400/p; $200/½; $1 class/wd. Discounts: 50 cents each if ordered 2 mos. in advance. No back issues. Pub'd 4 issues 1973, expects 4 in 1974. Independent.

THE COUNTRYMAN, **Crispin Gill,** Sheep St., Burford, Oxford OX8 4LH, UK. Articles, poetry, cartoons, photos, criticism. *Concern with life in the countryside of all kinds, but no townie sentimentalising.* 4/yr; $5.50/yr; 35p/ea; 1927; 208pp; 125x182mm; 60,000 circ; off. Reports 1-2 wks. Pays: £12/1000 words. Ads: £135-110/page; £57/½. Discounts: trade 25%. Ecology.

The Countryman Press, **Peter Jennison, Barbara Yeomans,** Taftsville, VT 05073. Book-length, regional nonfiction. 1973; lo. Discounts: trade: 1 copy 25%; 5-99=40%; 100+=45%. Pub'd 2 books 1973, expects 3 in 1974. COSMEP, NESPA.

COUNTRY-SIDE, The British Naturalists Association, **Anthony Wootton,** 13 Bishopstone Rd., Stone, Nr. Aylesbury, Bucks HP17 8QX, UK. Articles, photos, news items, letters. *Serious, authoritative,* original *articles, observations, etc. on mainly*

British Wild Life and the country-side. Length varies. Illus. black and white photos; accurate line-drawings (occasionally). 3/yr; 75p/yr; 30p/ea; 18p pf/sample; 1905; 48-52pp; 5½x8½"; 2500 circ; lp. Reports vary. Pay: nil. Ads: £10/page; £5.50/½; £2.75/¼; 2p/word. Discounts: publishers 10%; agents 15%. Back issues: 18p pf. Ecology, Natural History.

Covent Garden Press Ltd., 80 Long Acre, London WC2E 9NG, UK. ALP.

COYOTE'S JOURNAL, Coyote, **James Koller, Franco Beltrametti,** PO Box 629, Brunswick, ME 04011. Poetry, articles, longpoems. Irreg; no subs; price for ea copy differs; no sample; 1964; 100pp; 5½x8; 1M circ; lo. Reports vary. Pays: copies. No ads. Discounts: usual book wholesale to distributors & stores. Back issues: no special prices. Pub'd no issues 1973, expects 1 in 1974.

CPHJ NEWSLETTER, Committee for Prisoner Humanity & Justice, CPHJ (attn. Ron Silliman), 1029 Fourth St., No.37, San Rafael, CA 94901. Articles, interviews, criticism, reviews, letters. *Recent articles included an analysis of length of sentence per crime by different races; a study on Prolixin; lists of free literature available to prisoners . . . Forthcoming: interview w/Carol Parker of Connections re that groups folding, an analysis of the big prison lockdown in California, parole changes in Ohio, new disciplinary rights in Minnesota; book reviews, interviews . . .* Q; sub. free; single copy free; sample free; 1971; 8pp; 8½x14; 3M circ; mi. Reports 3 mos. Pays copies only. No ads. Some back issues from volumes 1 & 2, but many are out of print. Pub'd 3 issues 1973, expects 4 in 1974. Prison.

CRACKER, **Ed Jones,** 5 Spittal St., Edinburgh 3, UK. Articles, news items, interviews, criticism. Fortnightly; £3/yr; 15p/ea; free sample; 1971; 20pp; 11x9"; 4000 circ; off. Reports vary. Pay: negotiable. Ads: £20/page.

Creative Books, **John & Regina Hicks,** PO Box 5162, Carmel, CA 93921. Photos, photo histories. 64pp; 8½x11; lo. Discounts: trade, bulk & library discounts available. Pub'd 1 issue 1973, expects 1 in 1974. Three books 1973. COSMEP.

THE CRESSET, Valparaiso University Press, **Kenneth F. Korby,** Valparaiso Univ., Valparaiso, IN 46383. Poetry, fiction, articles, art, photos, interviews, criticism, reviews, music. Monthly except July & Aug; $3/yr; 35 cents/ea; free sample; 1936; 28pp; 8½x11; 5200 circ; lo. Reports 90-120 days. Pays: $5 per printed page; 10 copies. No ads. Discounts: agent $2; 2 yrs $3.85; students $1. Pub'd 10 issues in 1973.

CRISIS AND CHANGE, **Alana Cohen,** Social Science Institute, Washington Univ., St. Louis, MO 63130.

The Crossing Press (see NEW: AMERICAN & CANADIAN POETRY)

Crow Mountain Pressworks (see BLACK WOLF)

CSA Press, Inc. (see ORION)

Cuddles Press Ltd., **John Horder,** 18 Hanover Park, London SE15, UK. ALP, Maha Baba.

CURRENT, **Grant S. McClellan,** Plainfield, VT 05667. Articles, interviews, criticism. Current *is a digest of published and unpublished material.* 11/yr; $10/yr; $1/ea; free sample; 1960; 64pp; 7x10; 10M circ; of. Reports 1 mo. Ads: $225/p; $175/½. COSMEP.

CURTAINS, Pressed Curtains, **Paul Buck,** 12 Foster Clough, Hebden Bridge, Yorkshire HX7 5QZ, UK. Articles, poetry, fiction, art, interviews, criticism, longpoems. *The magazine presents new English writing from such as Dug Oliver, Peter Riley, Rosmarie Waldrop ... and French writing in translation from such as Blanchot, Bastaille, Jabes, Noel, Laporte, Pleynet, Royet-Journoud. Directions and tensions in the magazine precludes virtually all unsolicited material received. Last issue, a double issue of 173 pages. Spring 1974 issue to be a triple issue of around 300 pp.* 4/yr; £1 ($4)/yr; 25p ($1)/ea; 1971; 60pp; qto; 400 circ; mim. Reports 1 wk. Pays copies. Literature.

THE CURWOOD COLLECTOR, **Ivan A. Conger,** 1825 Osaukie Rd., Owosso, MI 48867. Poetry, fiction, articles, photos, criticism, reviews, letters, anything pertaining to James Oliver Curwood. *A non-profit fanzine for people interested in the life and works of James Oliver Curwood. Recent contributors: G.M. Farley (Maryland), Raoul Conac (France). Back issues always available.* 3-4/yr; $2/4 issues; 50 cents/ea; 1972; 8-14pp; 8½x11; 200 circ; mi; of. No ads. Discounts: $4 postpaid for each 10 copies of any one issue. Back issues: $2 for a volume (4 issues). Quantity rates as above.

Cycle Press, 18 Warren Pl., Brooklyn, NY 11201.

CYMBELINE, Cymbeline's Cosmic Cataclysms Inck., **Cymbeline Collective,** c/o 15 East Hill, Colchester, Essex, UK. Articles, poetry, fiction, art, cartoons, photos, satire, news items, interviews, criticism, music, letters, longpoems. *First issue due out March 21st. Style will be alternative/underground, with strong community bias. It will be an organ of communication between members of the Cymbeline (People's) Collective, and between the collective and manifestations of alternative activity everywhere; locally based, but intergalactic in implication. All content is dependant upon contributions received.* 12/yr; 50p/yr; 8p/ea; 1974; 16+pp; A4; 500 circ; off. Ads: £24/page; £13/½; £7/¼; £1.20/col. inch; 2p/word. Women, Ecology, Occult, 3rd World, Black, Gay, SF, Alternative/Community.

CYNGOR CELFYDDYDAU CYMRU (see WELSH ARTS COUNCIL)

CYPHER, Cypher Press, **James Goddard,** Plovers Barrow, School Rd., Nomansland, Salisbury, Wilts., UK. Articles, art, cartoons, interviews, criticism, letters. *Any length material considered. Must be literate and written in an interesting style. No bias. Recent contributors: Kingsley Amis, James Blish, Brian W. Aldiss, Harry Harrison, Bob Shaw, J.G. Ballard, Cy Chauvin, Greg Bedford, Jack Gaughan, Judith Anne Lawrence and others. As from issue 11 Cypher will be printed by lithography.* 4/yr; £1/yr; 25p/ea; 1970; 60+pp; A4; 300 circ; mim. Reports almost immediately. No pay. Ads: on request. Discounts: none. SF.

Cypher Press (see also *ARCANUM, CYPHER),* **James Goddard,** Plovers Barrow, School Rd., Nomansland, Salisbury, Wilts, UK. *Publishes:* Cypher, Arcanum *and* J.G. Ballard: A Bibliography (2nd edition in preparation).

D.S.P. (see GROPE)

DACOTAH TERRITORY, Territorial Press, **Mark Vinz,** PO Box 775, Moorhead, MN 56560. Poetry. *Biased against the merely academic, the merely linguistic. Recent contributors: McGrath, Bly, Frumkin, Simpson, Snyder, Rezmerski, Gordon, Cardona-Hine, Merwin, Stafford, Ignatow, Blazek, Greenberg, & Gershgoren. Note: with issue No.4 (Winter 1973), pages, price, & press run have increased. Nos. 5&6 will be specials, guest edited — so we will not be reading unsolicited mss. seriously until Summer 1974.* 3/yr; $2.50/yr; $1/ea; 1971; 64pp; 7x8½; 1M circ; lo. Reports 1 wk to 2 mos. Pays copies only. No ads. Discounts: 20%. Back issues: 4-6 available

51

at $1/ea. Pub'd 3 issues, 3 books 1973, expects 3 issues, 9 books 1974. COSMEP, CCLM.

DAEDALUS, 7 Linden St., Harvard Univ., Cambridge, MA 02138.

H. S. Dakin, Publisher, **H.S. Dakin,** 3456 Jackson St., San Francisco, CA 94118. Technical. *Published:* High-Voltage Photography *by H.S. Dakin, 1974, 65pp, 8½ x11" paperback, $5. High-voltage photography, known also as Kirlian or corona-discharge photography, is an experimental technique for making photographic prints or visual observations of electrically conductive objects with no light source other than the luminous corona discharge which appears around conductive objects in a high-voltage, high-frequency electric field.* Pub'd 1 book 1973, expects 1 issue, 1 book in 1974. COSMEP.

THE DALHOUSIE REVIEW, **Dr. A.R. Bevan,** Killam Memorial Library, 4th Fl., Halifax, Nova Scotia, Canada B3H 4H8. Poetry, articles, criticism, reviews. Q; $6/yr; $2/ea; plus 50 cents hndlg outside Canada. 1921; 200pp; 6x9½; 1100 circ; lo. Reports: between editor & contributor. Pays: $1/page. Ads: $50/p; $30/½. Discounts: agents: 25% disc. on subs., 15% on ads. Back issues: from $6 to $2 plus carrying charges. Pub'd 1 Vol. in 1973, expects a small increase each year in number of books.

DANCE SCOPE, **Seymour Barofsky,** 245 West 42nd St., New York, NY 10019. *A magazine of American dance.* 2/yr.

Dancing Patch Press (see ZERO ONE)

DARK TOWER, Cleveland State University Press, **Mitch Hansen,** University Center, c/o Cleveland State Univ., Cleveland, OH 44115. Poetry, fiction, art, photos, cartoons, criticism, collages, plays (short). Dark Tower *Award: three $5 awards to authors we find particularly interesting because of the experimental nature of their work or the excellence of their performance in their genre.* 40pp; 6x9; 700 circ; lo. Reports min. 2 mos. in advance. Pays copies only. Pub'd 2 issues 1973, expects 2 in 1974.

DARKWATERS, **Colleen McElroy,** PO Box 22246, Seattle, WA 98122. Poetry, fiction, art, photos, interviews, criticism, longpoems. $7.50/yr; $2/ea; 1973; 4x5½; 500 circ; lo. Reports 3 mos. Pay, ads, discounts, back issues: N/A. Pub'd 1 issue 1973, expects 4 in 1974. COSMEP, Third World, Black.

DATR, Smoothie Publications, **John Noyce,** 67 Vere Rd., Brighton BN1 4NQ, UK. Articles, poetry, art, cartoons, concrete. *Short poems, preferably by the lesser published names.* Irreg; 20p/ea; 1971; 30pp; A4; 200 circ; mim. Reports vary.

Daughters of Bilitis (see SISTERS)

Christopher Davies Ltd. (see POETRY WALES)

DAWN, The Wichita Falls Alternative, **Craig Canan,** PO Box 1822, Wichita Falls, TX 76307. Poetry, articles, art, photos, cartoons, interviews, reviews, music, letters. *Published monthly by Craig Canan. "Progressive poetry" is solicited.* Dawn, The Wichita Falls Alternative *is a member of the Underground Press Syndicate and subscribes to the College Press Service, Liberation News Service and Zodiac News Service.* 6/yr; $6/yr; 25 cents/ea; $3/½ yr; 1972; 20pp; tabloid; lo. Ads: $52.80/p; $30/½; free class/wd. Discounts: 40%. Back issues: 25 cents. COSMEP, APS, LNS, ZNS, CPS.

Dawn Press, 42 Homersham Rd., Kingston-on-Thames, KT1 3PN, UK. Lp. BPS.

DAY BY DAY, Loverseed Press, **Ronald Mallone, manag. ed., M. Gibson, reviews ed.,** Woolacombe House, 141 Woolacombe Rd., Blackheath, London SE3, UK. Articles, poetry, fiction, satire, interviews, criticism, letters. *Any poems or stories should be short. Basically we use factual material, which must be carefully authenticated. We do not use satire which is aimed at particular individuals. Articles (unless by arrangement) should not exceed 1000 words. Letters should not exceed 300 words. Unsolicited mss. should be accompanied by SAE or IRCs. Subtitle is "News Commentary, Digest of National and International Affairs & Review of the Arts." We review art, books, films, opera, plays, etc. and report countycricket and Test matches in England.* 13/yr; £1.40/yr; 13p/ea; 1962; 16pp; 13x8"; 11,000 circ; mim. Reports 3-21 days. Pays: by arrangement. Ads: 4p/word; display by arrangement. Discounts: 5% (20 or more copies).

DEATH RATTLE, Kitchen Sink Enterprises, **Denis Kitchen,** PO Box 5699, Milwaukee, WI 53211. Cartoons, comic strips. *Richard Corben, John Pound, Tim Boxell, Peter Poplaski, recent contributors. Please note that we do* not *publish poetry.* Q. Back issues: 65 cents.

DECAL POETRY REVIEW, **Meic Williams,** 52 Dan-y-Coed Road, Cyncoed, Cardiff, UK. Articles, poetry, fiction, criticism. 2/yr; £1/yr; 50p/ea; 1972; 80pp; 8¼x 5¾"; 600 circ; off. Pays copies only. Ads: £10/page; £7/½.

DECEMBER MAGAZINE, **Curt Johnson, Bob Wilson,** Box 274, Western Springs, IL 60558. Poetry, fiction, articles, art, photos, interviews, satire, reviews. Irreg; $8/4 issues; $2.50/ea; $2/sample; 1958; 256pp; 5½x8½; 1500 circ; lo. Reports 4-8 wks. Pays copies only. Ads: $100/p; $60/½. Discounts: 40% trade, 20% classroom. Back issues: available from Xerox Univ. Microfilms. COSMEP, CCLM.

DECIDUOUS, **Christopher Franke,** 4208½ Whitman Ave., Cleveland, OH 44113. Poetry, collages, concrete art. Up Against The Wall, *a broadside, copyright 1971 by Christopher Franke, 20x26", $1.00. Various "poem-collage leaflets" by Christopher Franke, $1.00.* Page One, *a broadside, copyright 1970 by Christopher Franke, 19x25", o/p.* Irreg; $1/yr; 5/10/25 cents/ea; sample; 1pp; page size varies. Reports vary (inquiry brings response). Pays copies only. Ads: negotiable. Discounts: yes. COSMEP.

Michael deHartington, 60 Oxford St., London W1A 4WD, UK. Poetry, fiction. Gay.

DELTA, **Michael Launchbury, Peter Middleton,** 524 Fulwood Rd., Sheffield 10, UK. Poetry, fiction, criticism, letters. 3/yr; 75p/yr; 25p/ea; free sample (30p overseas); 1953; 45pp; 8½x5½"; 1000 circ; lp. No pay. Ads: £20/page; £12/½. No discounts. Back issues: 25p in UK; 30p overseas or 1.25.

Delta Can, **Glen Siebrasse,** 351 Gerald St., Lasalle, Que., Canada H8P 2A4. Poetry, art. *Canadian poetry only.* 1964; lp. Reports 1 mo. Pays 15% royalties. Discounts: 40% bookstores, 20% wholesalers. Pub'd 1 book 1973, expects 5 in 1974.

DENVER QUARTERLY, Bradford-Robinson, **Burton Feldman,** Dept. of English, Univ. of Denver, Denver, CO 80210. Poetry, fiction, articles, criticism, reviews. 4/yr; $6/yr; $1.50/ea; $1/sample; 1966; 120pp; 1M circ. Reports 2-4 wks. Pays: $5/page prose; $10/page poetry. Pub'd 4 issues 1973, expects 4 in 1974.

DESCANT, TCU Press, **Betsy Feagan Colquitt,** Dept. of English, Texas Christian Univ., Fort Worth, TX 76129. $2/yr; 75 cents/ea.

DESCANT, **Karen Mulhallen,** PO Box 314, Sta. P, Toronto, Ont., Canada M5S 2S8. Poetry, fiction, articles, art, photos, cartoons, interviews, satire, criticism, reviews, music, letters, parts-of-novels, longpoems, collages, plays, concrete art. 2/yr; $4/yr; $2/ea; $1.50/sample; 1970; 80pp; 9x6; 600-1M circ; of; lp. Reports 4 mos. Pays copies only. Discounts: 20%. Back issues: varies with issue no. − $2.50 and up. Pub'd 2 issues 1973, expects 2 in 1974. General arts, etc.

Deuce of Clubs Press, Marseille Spetz, PO Box 4682, Sacramento, CA 94825. Poetry, fiction, satire. Pub'd 2 books 1973, expects 1 in 1974. Fantasy.

DHARMA, **Larry Buttrose, Donna Maegraith, Stephen Measday, John Franklin,** PO Box 5, Prospect, South Australia 5082. Q; $1.50/yr; 25 cents/ea; 1971; 32pp; 7x8; 500 circ; lo. Reports coupla mos. Back issues: 20 cents/ea. Pub'd 3 issues 1973, expects 4 issues, 2 books in 1974. COSMEPA.

DIAGONAL CERO, Calle 7, No.546, 2 °E., La Plata, Pvca. de Buenos Aires, Argentina.

THE DIAL-A-POEM POETS LP, Giorno Poetry Systems, **John Giorno,** 222 Bowery, New York, NY 10012. Poetry. *LP records of solid gold poetry readings in dynamite short selections with 40 poets in each 2-record album.* The Dial-A-Poem Poets LP, *GPS 001, 1972.* The Dial-A-Poem Poets DISCONNECTED, *GPS 003, 1974.* $6.98/ea. COSMEP, CCLM, Third World, Women, Black, Gay.

DIANA'S BIMONTHLY, Burning Deck Press, **Tom Ahern,** 71 Elmgrove Ave., Providence, RI 02906. Poetry, fiction. *Need submissions of 10-20 poems (or several stories) in order to select a sampling of 5-6 pieces by an individual. Contributors recently: Rochelle Owens, Terry Stokes, Christopher Middleton, William Bronk, Walter Hall, Charles Hine, Keith & Rosemarie Waldrop, Bruce Andrews, Ron Silliman, Michael Lally, Terence Winch, Lyn Lifshin, Opal Nations, Robert Peters, Eugene McNamara, George Tysh, Alan Kornblum, David Antin, Richard Kostelanetz, many others, usually 10-15/issue. Before submitting, persons should definitely see the magazine. Most work solicited.* 6/yr; $5/yr institutions, $2.50/yr individuals; 50 cents/ea; 50 cents/sample; 1972; 40pp; lo; lp. Reports 1 day to 1 wk. Pays 3-5 copies only. Ads: arranged; no class/wd. Discounts: 40% off to dealers, stores, agents. Back issues: where available (1st issue o.p.) $5/ea. Pub'd 6 issues 1973, expects 6 in 1974.

THE DICKENSIAN, The Dickens Fellowship, 48 Doughty St., London WC1N 2LF, **Dr. Michael Slater,** Birkbeck College, Malet St., London WC1, UK. Articles, criticism. *Specialist journal referring to Dickens, his life & works, with Victorian background information and book reviews, reports on Fellowship (International) activities and strong critical and academic articles.* 3/yr; £2.50/yr(UK); £3/yr overseas; 1905; 68pp; oct; 2000+ circ; lp. Reports: arrange with editor first. Pay: nil. Ads: £25/page(UK); £30/page(overseas) pro rata. No discounts.

EMILY DICKINSON BULLETIN, Higginson Press, **Frederick L. Morey,** 4508 38th St., Brentwood, MD 20722. Articles, criticism, reviews. *4000 word maximum; MLA style sheet; contributors: Jay Leyda, Lawrence Perrine, William White, George Monteiro (all professors). Also academics from Finland, Japan, and India.* Semi-annual; $5/yr; individuals, $10/yr libraries; $3/ea; $3/sample; 1968; 50pp; 5x8; 250 circ; lo. Reports 1 mo. Pays 1 copy only. Ads: $90/p; $50/½; Discount: 10%. Back issues: $10 annually, $50 complete file. Pub'd 2 issues 1973, expects 2 in 1974. COSMEP, MLA: Editors of Learned Journals Modern Language Assn., NYC.

Dildo Press (see THE REGINALD A FESSENDEN MEMORIAL RADIO/TIMES/ ARE)

DIMENSION, **A. Leslie Willson,** PO Box 7939, Austin, TX 78712. *Original contemporary literature from published writers whose language is German, with translations.* 3/yr; $9:$12/yr; $4/ea; 1968; 200pp; 6x9; 600 circ; lo; lp. Reports 3 mos. Pays: modest. No ads. Discounts: 20%. Back issues: $4/ea (Vol.I out of print, available University Microfilms). Pub'd 4 issues (special issue on East German literature) in 1973, expects 3 in 1974. CCLM.

A DIRECTORY OF AMERICAN POETS, Poets & Writers, Inc., 201 West 54 St., New York, NY 10019. A Directory of American Poets *is a unique reference work. It includes names, addresses, teaching interests, publications, and other information for about 2000 contemporary American poets. In addition to information about authors, the Directory provides names and addresses of 450 organizations that sponsor readings and workshops. A service section provides listings of anthologies, films, videotapes, what organizations to contact for information of special interest to writers, and other types of information.* Coda, *the supplemental newsletter published by* Poets & Writers, Inc., *keeps Directory readers up-to-date on changes and new information. Purchasers of the Directory receive* Coda *at no additional charge.* Coda *is published 7 times a year. Cost: $6 (paperback); $12 (hard-bound).* 160pp; 8½x11; 5M circ.

THE DC GAZETTE (The Gazette Supplement), **Sam Smith,** 109 8th St. N.E., Washington, DC 20002. Articles, art, photos, cartoons, interviews, satire, criticism, reviews, music, letters. Monthly; $6/yr; 50 cents/ea; sample; 1966; 28pp; 10x15; 3M circ; lo. Reports vary. Pays copies only. Ads: $135/p; $67.50/½; 10 cents class/wd. Expects 12 issues in 1974. COSMEP, UPS.

Dixie Dung Beetle Press (see APALACHEE QUARTERLY)

Dock Leaves Press (see ANGLO-WELSH REVIEW)

Doggeral Press (see FOUR DOGS MOUNTAIN SONGS)

Dolemen Press, 8 Herbert Place, Dublin 2, Eire, UK. IPA.

DOOR, **Larry Remer,** Box 2022, San Diego, CA 92112. Articles, photos, interviews, reviews, music. Door *has expanded in the last year to cover both LA and San Diego. While the San Diego office is still the main one, our LA address is:* Door, *PO Box 4010, Van Nuys, CA 91412. No sexploitive ads are run.* 2/mo; $6/yr; 25 cents/ea; 25 cents/sample; 1968; 20pp; 10x14; 14M circ; lo. Ads: $285/p; $145/½; 50 cents class/wd. Discounts: inquire. Back issues: $1/ea. Pub'd 24 issues 1973, expects 24 in 1974. UPS.

DORSET: The County Magazine, Dorset Publishing Co., **Rodney Legg, Colin Graham,** Milborne Poert, Sherborne, Dorset DT9 5HJ, UK. *Ecological and environmental news and features.* 12/yr; £4/yr; 25p/ea; 1967; 60pp; 7x9¼"; 10,000 circ; lp. Pays: £5/1000 wds. Ads: £66/page pro rata. Discounts: 25% post paid by us.

DOWNSIDE REVIEW, **Dom Daniel Rees,** Downside Abbey, Stratton-on-the Fosse, Bath, UK. Articles, criticism. 4/yr; £2/yr; 50p/ea. Pays: by arrangement. Theology/Metaphysics/Monastic History.

THE DRAGONFLY, **Duane Ackerson,** 309 W. 22nd St., Eugene, OR 97405. Poetry, fiction, articles, satire, criticism, reviews, longpoems, collages, concrete art. *Try to represent a variety of good writing, both verse and prose poetry/experimental fiction; I have done special anthologies or pamphlets on prose poetry* (A Prose Poem Anthology), *poetry related to ecology* (Recycle This Poem), *and, most recently, a pamphlet of one line poetry (entitled* "But Is It Poetry?": An Anthology of

One Line Poems); planned for the next few months (that is, by June, 1974) are special pamphlets or issues devoted to science fiction influenced poetry and student (elementary, high school, and college) poetry. Recent contributors: Edson, Kuzma, Simic, Stafford, Trudell, Reed, Meyers, Hewitt, etc. Q; $3.50/yr; $1/ea; $1/sample; pamphlets: $1/ea; 1969; 60pp; 5½x8½; lo. Reports 1 day to 6 mos. Pays: copies only: 2 contrib. Ads: $15/p; $10.50/½; no class/wd. Discounts: 10% to subscription agencies and classrooms. Back issues: *A Prose Poem Anthology* ($15); "But Is It Poetry?": An Anthology of One Line Poems (1st ed. $5; 2nd $1). Pub'd 1 issue, 1 book 1973, expects 3 issues, 2 books 1974. CCLM.

Dragon's Teeth Press, **Cornel Lengyel,** El Dorado National Forest, Adam's Acres West, Georgetown, CA 95634. COSMEP.

THE DRAMA REVIEW, **Michael Kirby, Paul R. Ryan,** 32 Washington Pl., Rm. 74, New York, NY 10003. Articles, photos, interviews. *Publishes documentation of historical and contemporary trends in the full range of the performing arts.* Q; $9.50/yr; $3/ea; 1955; 160pp; 7x10; 15M circ; of. Reports 1-2 mos. Pays: 2 cents/wd. Ads: $287/p; $172/½. Discounts: 15% agency; 2% cash. Back issues: $3. Pub'd 4 issues 1973, expects 4 issues, 2 books in 1974. COSMEP, CCLM.

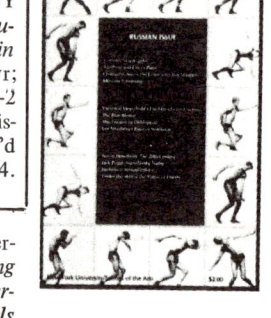

DRAMATIKA, **John Pyros and Daughter,** 390 Riverside Dr., New York, NY 10025. Plays. *Performing pieces solicited: brief critiques related to the performing arts (avant-garde preference). Materials sought: biographers for a series of pamphlets;* especially interested in segments, and/or chapters from unpublished m.a. and Ph.D. thesis. Payment, rights, etc. negotiable. Contributors: Hugh Fox, Fred Lazarus Light, Vito Acconci, Jackson MacLow, Sheila B. Weinstein, Gil Scott-Heron, Stu Horn. Semi-annual; $4/yr; $2/ea; $2/sample; 1968; 50pp; 8x11; circ. varies; lo. Reports 1 mo. Pays copies only. Discounts: negotiable. Pub'd 2 issues 1973, expects 2 in 1974. COSMEP, CCLM.

DRIFTWOOD-EAST Quarterly International, **Marjorie Look Drake,** 95 Carter Ave., Pawtucket, RI 02861. Poetry, articles, "constructive" criticism, reviews. *Poem limitations – 20 lines per. All styles, no pornography; no overly religious or political themes.* Readers from 10 to 98 years. Dr. Robert Ambacher, Dr. Charles Angoff, Dr. Fred Raborg, Jr., Gertrude Maglutz (CA), May Gray (AR), Robert Halsey (Australia), Mabel Sheldon (London), Roberta Goldstein, Dr. Louis J. Cantoni, Dr. E.R. Mignault. Q; $5/yr; $1.50/ea; $1.50/sample; 1973; 76pp; 6x9; 700 circ; lo. Reports 2 wks. Pays copies only. No ads. I do free book reports for subscribers. Discounts: univ., all libraries, 10% discount if paid in 30 days. Back issues: $2. Pub'd 3 issues 1973, expects 4 in 1974. Poetry, no affiliations.

Driftwood Publications, **Brian Wake,** 58 Exeter Rd., Bootle 20, Lancashire, UK. Poetry, longpoems. *Now up to No.9 in* Driftwood Poets *series. Forthcoming: 'Anthology of Driftwood Poets' 80pp of poems – 60p per copy.* Driftwood *has agreed to acknowledge Merseyside Arts Association for aid.* Irreg; £1.50/sub; 1968; 24pp; 500-1000 circ; off; lp. Pays copies. Discounts: 33 1/3% on 1 doz. or more. ALP.

Druid Heights Books, **Elsa Gidlow,** Camino del Canyon, Muir Woods, Mill Valley, CA 94941. *Not accepting mss. at this time.* Pub'd 1 new book in 1973. COSMEP, Women.

DRYAD, **Neil Lehrman,** 2943 Broderick St., San Francisco, CA 94123, **Merrill T.**

Leffler, PO Box 1656, Washington, DC 20013. Poetry, art, photos, criticism, reviews, longpoems. *No limit on length of material. Morton Marcus, John Logan, John Logan Jr., Frank Dwyer, Rod Tellema.* Semi-annual; $4/yr; $2/ea; 1967; 80 pp; 6x9; 750 circ; lo; lp. Reports up to 3 mos. Will pay for work in the future with new grant. Discounts: 20% to subscription agents. Back issues: $2-$6 depending on availability. Pub'd 1 issue 1973, expects 2 in 1974; expects 4 books in 1974. COSMEP, CCLM.

DUBLIN MAGAZINE, **John Ryan, Anthony Cronin, Tom Haran,** Elstow, Knapton Rd., Dun Laoire, Co. Dublin, Eire   . Articles, poetry, fiction. *length up to 5000 words.* 4/yr; 30p/ea. Pays: by arrangement.

Duck Down Press (see SCREE)

Duende Press (see FERVENT VALLEY)

THE DURHAM UNIVERSITY JOURNAL, **M.E. James,** 43 North Bailey, Durham DH1 3EX, UK. Criticism. *Mss. and books for review should be sent to the editor, M.E. James, 43 North Bailey, Durham, England. All correspondence on other matters relating to the Journal should be sent to the Registrar, Univ. Office, Old Shire Hall, Durham. Subscriptions should be made payable to 'University of Durham.'* 3/yr; £1+15p pst/yr; 35p+5p/ea; no sample; 1876; 250-300pp; 7¼x4"; 800 circ; lp. Reports 3 mos. No pay. Ads: 1 issue: £12/page; £8/½; £6/¼; 3 issues: £33/page; £22.50/½; £16.50/¼. Discounts: normal to agents. Back issues: Microfilms of past issues of the Journal from 1876 (Vol.I) to 1967 (Vol.LIX; new series Vol. XXVIII) are now available from University Microfilms Inc., 300 North Zeeb Rd., Ann Arbor, Michigan, USA, to whom enquiries should be addressed.

DUST, Dustbooks, PO Box 1056, Paradise, CA 95969. (see also *Dustbooks, SMALL PRESS REVIEW). Some gab of rejuvenating this currently-suspended title as the result of two publishing events: Len Fulton's novel* The Grassman *by Thorp Springs Press, and Gary Elder's anthology* Back West *by San Marcos Press. There's a plethora of serious western-genre writers with no place to go, and* Dust *is projected as a semi-annual anthology for them beginning perhaps in 1975. The publisher solicits editorial ideas and vision.* Style *will be focussed – not "stance." Don't send manuscripts, but do send names and interests.* COSMEP, ALP, ALMS.

Dustbooks (see also *DUST, SMALL PRESS REVIEW),* **Len Fulton, ed., James Boyer May, Ellen Ferber, assoc. eds.,** PO Box 1056, Paradise, CA 95969. Nonfiction, poetry, fiction, photos, longpoems. Dustbooks *is a small-press imprint that covers three lines of publishing activity: A literary periodical* (Dust, *currently suspended), a series of chapbooks of both prose and poetry, and a series of trade periodicals that detail information about the books, literary magazines, authors and editors from the small and underground presses. Since the early Sixties the publisher has been fully committed both to putting contemporary literature into print, and to researching and defining its sources and vehicles. Annually publish* Directory of Little Magazines and Small Presses, Directory of Small Mag/Press Editors and Publishers, Small Press Record of Books, *and other trade titles. We have published poetry chapbooks, non-fiction, prose, and will bring out* Honey Dwarf, *a novel by Gene Detro in fall, 1974, plus a women's anthology and a Folsom Prison anthology; also the first title in our "Living Poets" Series,* Hugh Fox *on the work of Charles Potts. Esp. open to short, experimental novels by women.* Lo. Founding member of COSMEP. CCLM, ALP, ALMS.

Dustbooks, U.K. (see Headland Publications)

E. G. Publications (see EARTH GARDEN)

E. M. Press (see ALOES BOOKS)

EARTH GARDEN, E.G. Publications, **Irene & Keith Smith, eds. & publ.,** PO Box 111, Balmain, New South Wales, Australia 2041. Articles, photos, interviews. *Practical "how to" stories on self-sufficiency, natural farming and gardening, building, raising animals, the back-to-the-Earth movement, with an Australian bias (also New Zealand writers) and a pioneering flavour. Din Kum Aussie stuff on the world's new (last?) frontier.* Q; $9.50/yr; $2/ea; $2/sample; 1972; 60pp.; 8½x10½ inches; 9500 circ; of. Reports 1 mo. Pay: varies, about $A35 per 1000 words, + several copies. No ads. Discounts: wholesale (seamail) 10 copies @ $1.20 ea; we pay postage; retail sets of *EG 1-10* cost $18, *we mail.* Pub'd 4 issues 1973, expects 4 issues, 1 book in 1974.

EARTH'S DAUGHTERS, 944 Kensington Ave., Buffalo, NY 14215.

East African Publishing House, Koinange St., PO Box 30571, Nairobi, Kenya, Africa.

EAST END INDEPENDENT, Scrub Pine Studios/Tangential Bivalve Corp, **Karl Grossman, ed. in chief, Van Howell, pub., Ray Maichen, mang. ed.,** PO Box 400, Bellport, NY 11713. *Primarily local (eastern Long Island) news analysis. Some politics and "culture," but primarily focusing on local environment in an economic-sociological context.* Fortnightly; $5/yr; 20 cents/ea; 20 cents/sample; 1974; 16pp; 10x14 tabloid; 7500 circ; lo. Reports 2 wks. Ads: $150/p; $90/½; $2/20 wds class/wd. Back issues: 20 cents. None pub'd 1973, expects 24 issues, 2 books in 1974. Third World (somewhat), Black (somewhat), Food/Ecology, Local muckraking and interviews.

East Midlands Arts Association, 1 Frederick St., Loughborogh, UK.

Easter Island Books, 23 Moorhouse Rd., London W2, UK. *Set up in 1971 to publish, very occasionally, extended books & non-books. Publications: David Coxhead: "Zig-Zag; a postcard serial" (silver blocked leatherette hardbacked folder 12.5x20cm containing 20 postcards mailed from Asia, Africa & Europe, together with title and end-cards; limited edition of 26 copies lettered A-Z. Letterpress, litho, rubber stamp, & handwritten, bound, signed...* £15. *Susan Hiller: "The way to divine life" (litho and notebook) 9.5x5cm edition of 100, unsigned, spiral bound)* 50p.

EBORACUM, **P. Brookesmith, Osric Allen, bus. & adv.,** Derwent College, Univ. of York, Heslington, YO1 5DD, UK. Articles, poetry, fiction, interviews, longpoems, plays. *We occasionally publish fiction up to a novel length of c. 72,000 words, serialised or in a single issue, but only very rarely accept material of over 10,000 words, and 3000 to 6000 for fiction/articles/interviews is our preferred length. A strong arts bias.* 3/yr;£1/yr; 1963; 49pp; 10x7½; 2000 circ; lp; off. Reports 3 wks. Pay: varies with quality of material. Ads: £40/page pro rata. Discounts: 10% series of 3.

ECO CONTEMPORANEO, **Miguel Grinberg,** C.C. Central 1933, Buenos Aires, Argentina. Poetry, letters, longpoems. *Nicanor Parra, Ernesto Cardenal, Allen Ginsberg, Antonin Artaud. (Also publishes an independent newsletter on revolutionary Ecology).* Bi-mo; $10/yr; $2/ea; $2/sample; 1961; 64pp; 2M circ; lp. None pub'd 1973, expects 6 issues in 1974. UPS, MNS.

ECOLIT, **Gerald Haslam,** Dept. of English, Sonoma State College, Rohnert Park,

CA 94928. Poetry, fiction, articles, cartoons, interviews, satire, reviews. *This journal aims at introducing environmental awareness in English classes. Publishes all the above for every level from pre-school up, as well as bibliographies & teaching units. Seeks submissions.* 2/yr; $1/yr; 50 cents/ea; free sample; 1972; 50pp.; 9x11; 300 circ; mi. Reports 2 wks. Pays 2 copies. No ads. Back issues: 50 cents/ea. Food/Ecology, COSMEP.

ECOLOGIST, E.R.D. Goldsmith, 73 Kew Green, Richmond, Surrey, UK. *Length 300-3000 words. Magazine should be studied for level and approach.* Monthly; 25p/ea; 1970; Pay: £10/1000 words. Ecology.

EDDA. Scandinavian Journal of Literary Research, Universitetsforlaget, Box 307 Blindern, Oslo 3, Norway, **Ase Hiorth Lervik,** Univ. of Tromso, 9000 Tromso, Norway. Bi-mo; $10/yr; $3/ea; sample; 1914; 60-70pp; 6½x9¾". Ads: $100/p; $60/½. Back issues: $3. Pub'd 6 issues 1973.

EDGE, The Edge Press, **D.S. Long, William L. Fox, J.E. Weir, Robert Stowell,** PO Box 25042 Victoria St., Christchurch, NZ. Poetry, fiction, articles, art, photos, interviews, criticism, reviews, parts-of-novels, longpoems, plays, concrete art. *Primarily poetry, fiction, graphics. A tri-quarterly international literary magazine based in NZ. Basically we are a New Zealand literary magazine with about 50% overseas content. Some theme issues: 5/6, S.F. Directions; 8/Modern Poetry in Translation; 19/Poetry in Translation from Australasia & The South Pacific; 7/ listed all current sources of NZ poetry; 8/MPT 19 lists all existent Australasian & South Pacific literary magazines. See our catalogue for recent contributors.* Tri-Q; $4.50/yr and $1.50/ea (NZ); $6/yr and $2/ea (any other currency); sample; $1.50/ea. 1971; 64pp.; 9x7; 1-3M circ; lp. Reports 1 wk (SAE + postal coupons suff for type of return post. req.) Pays 2 copies + token cash on publication. Ads: $25/p (NZ); $30/p (other currencies). Discounts: 33 1/3% trade disc. in NZ; 40% elsewhere sale or return. Back issues: consult catalogue. Note: all subs. to Whitcoulls Ltd. Mag. Dept., Private Bag, Cristchurch, NZ. COSMEP, COSMEPA, YWEP, Association of Handcraft Printers (NZ), NZ Book Council.

The Edge Press (see also *EDGE*), **D.S. Long, William L. Fox, J.E. Weir, Robert Stowell,** PO Box 25042 Victoria St., Christchurch, New Zealand, also: 1127 Codel Way, Reno, NV 89503, and c/o McBride & Broadley, Wood Cottage, Nash Rd. Great Horwood, Near Bletchley, Bucks, U.K. Edge: *a tri-quarterly international literary magazine based in New Zealand;* Edge Broadsheets: *a series of handset & printed poetry broadsheets;* Edge Newsletters: *poems & information;* Edge Press/CPCL Books: *a series of craft edition hardback collections; Also occasional publications including* Gar(r)otte'. *For further info. consult our catalogue for publication shortly (at press).*

Editorial Associates (see THE IDLER)

ELAN, Poetique Litteraire et Pacifiste, **Louis Lippens,** 31 Rue Foch, 59126 Linselles, France. Trimestriel; 15F/yr; 12-16pp. Discounts: remise 25%.

ELITE MAGAZINE, Somars Enterprises, 269 High Town Rd., Luton, Beds. LU2 OBZ, UK. *An exciting adult contact magazine for single people and married couples with various erotic interests.* 20p/sample.

The Elizabeth Press, **James L. Weil,** ed., Carroll Arnett, Simon Perchick, assoc. ed., 103 Van Etten Blvd., New Rochelle, NY 10804. *Books of poems & essays. Our* list is committed through 1976, and we are considering no further titles at this time.

ELIZABETHAN, Brontpress Ltd., **Lewis Sheringham,** 355 Ashford Rd., Staines, Middlesex, UK. Articles, fiction, cartoons, photos. *Stories up to 2000 words. Articles up to 1000 words. Suitable for boys and girls between ten and eighteen.* Monthly; £2.40 pf/yr; 17½p/ea. Pays: by arrangement.

ELLIPSE, Faculte Des Arts, Univ. de Sherbrooke, Sherbrooke, Que., Canada.

Ember Press (Thames Ditton) (see LAISSEZ–FAIRE, LITTACK, NEW HEADLAND)

Emerald City Press (see YELLOW BRICK ROAD)

EMK (The Edward M. Kennedy) QUARTERLY, **James Spada,** 101 Chester Ave., Staten Island, NY 10312. *EMK has ceased publication, but 8 back issues are available for $1 each. Together, they form a lively, comprehensive history of American politics from 1969 to 1972, especially in regard to Senator Edward M. Kennedy. Write for information and content descriptions.* 1969; 30pp; 8½x11; lo.

Emma (see CIVIL SERVICE POETRY)

EMPTY BELLY, Orphan Press, **Charles Tidler,** Box 14, Ganges, BC, Canada V0S 1E0. Poetry, fiction, articles, interviews, criticism, reviews, letters, longpoems. *The poet and the peasant are one. Cleverness must subside to the craft.* Irreg; Libraries only: U.S., $10/4 issues; Canada, $6/4 issues; $1/sample; 1967; no. of pp & size vary; 200 circ; mi; lo. Reports 2 wks to 2 mos. Pays 6 copies; copies only. Ads: $50/p; $30/½. Discounts: query. Back issues: query. Pub'd 1 issue 1973, expects 3 in 1974.

EMPTY BOAT, **Ben Goldberg,** Box 42, Brandywine Sta., Schenectady, NY 12309. Poetry, fiction, articles, interviews, satire, criticism, reviews, letters, parts-of-novels. *After a sad start we're finally rolling. Expect 2 issues by end of summer. We "recycle." Mark all previously published submissions "reprint," give date of pub., who pub. & address of pub. Affectionate toward "new writers." No academic or tea party odes please. We are a Marxist mag: "Say the magic word and the duck will come down and give you $100." Recent contributors: Number A: E.R. Baxter, John Bennett, David Condit, Joel Deutsch, Al Masarik, Peter Wild; Number B: Harley Elliott, Gene Fowler, Tom Johnson, Ron Koertge, Joe Ribar, Rod Tolloss, F. Keith Wahle.* 2/yr; $2/3 issues; $1/ea; 50 cents /sample; 1972; 45pp; 4½x5¾; 1M circ; mi. Reports 1 wk-1 mo. Pays copies only. Ads: "barter" – send book, mag, idea, thing, etc. If we like it we'll plug it. Discounts: by arrangement. Back issues: none such. No issues pub'd 1973, expects 3 in 1974.

EMPTY ELEVATOR SHAFT, **Bruce Leary,** PO Box 27004, San Francisco, CA 94127. Poetry, fiction, art, photos, cartoons, satire, music, parts- of-novels, longpoems, collages, plays, concrete art. *Since the last directory, i've found i'm not as open as i'd indicated... all styles are read, answered, accepted & rejected – but the technique must be perfected and keen. there must also be some movement – inner, mental, language or flexed muscle – not just several hundred hopeless words piled line upon line. also spending more time producing small chapbooks than the mag.* $4/4 issues; $1.25/ea; $1.25/sample; 1972; 64pp; page size varies; 500-1M circ; lo. Reports: lightning to methuselah. Pays copies only. Ads: make offer/p; pub'd 1 issue, 2 books 1973, expects 2 issues, 4 books in 1974. Independent.

EMU, **Ann Karkalas, James G. MacDonald,** Glasgow Univ., Dept. of Extra-Mural & Adult Education, 57-59 Oakfield Ave., Glasgow G12 8LW Scotland, UK. Articles, poetry, fiction, art, cartoons, photos, satire, criticism, music, concrete. *At the moment contributions are invited only from members of classes run by Glasgow University Dept. of Extra-Mural & Adult Ed.: EMU is in effect an extramural students magazine, & is mainly distributed among the students — although on sale to the public too. Emphasis on creative work by new writers etc.* Annual; 15p/ea; 10p pf/sample; 1971; 30pp; 24x17½cm; 1000 circ; lp. Reports 3 wks. Ads: £25/p; £15/½.

ENCOUNTER, **Melvin J. Lasky, Anthony Thwaite,** 59 St. Martins Lane, London WC2N 4JS, UK. Articles, poetry, art, criticism, letters. Encounter *is an international review of politics, literature and the arts. Estimated readership 120,000 worldwide. In-depth articles up to 15,000 words.* Monthly; $14 ($15.50 by air)/yr; $1.25/ea; 1953; 96pp; 10x7"; lp. Ads: £100/p.

ENCRES VIVES, **Michel Cosem,** Engomer, 09800 Castillon, France. Poetry, longpoems, collages. 50-100 pp.; 4/yr; of. Pub'd 4 issues 1973.

ENCUENTRO, **Alberto Luis Ponzo,** Italia 830, Castelar, Provicia de Buenos Aires, Argentina.

Energy Blacksouth Press (see HOO–DOO)

ENGLAND, Royal Society of St. George, **R.H. Gibbons,** 4 Upper Belgrave St., London SW1, UK. *Articles on all aspects of English life, conservation, history, travel, industry, entertainment, sport, arts and crafts.* 4/yr.

ENGLISH, English Association, **Margaret Willy,** 1 Brockmere, 43 Wray Park Rd., Reigate, Surrey, UK. Articles, poetry, criticism. 3/yr; 52½p/ea. Pay: by arrange.

English Centre of International P.E.N. (see INTERNATIONAL P.E.N. BULLETIN OF SELECTED BOOKS)

ENGLISH DANCE AND SONG , English Folk Dance and Song Society, **Tony Wales.** Cecil Sharp House, 2 Regents Park Rd., London NW1 7AY, UK. Articles, cartoons, photos, criticism, music, letters. 4/yr; £ 1/yr; 20p/ea; 1936: 40pp; 9¾x7¼, 12,000 circ; lp. Ads: £ 35/p; £20/½; 3p/word. Discounts: agency 10%.

Enitharmon Press, **Alan Clodd,** 22 Huntingdon Rd., East Finchley, London N2 9DU, UK. Poetry. lp. Reports 2 mos. Pays: royalty.

ENOUGH, Bristol Women's Liberation Group, Women's Centre, 11 Waverley Rd., Bristol 6, UK. Articles, poetry, fiction, cartoons, interviews. *All material comes from Bristol Women's Liberation Group members.* About 1/yr; price/ea varies; 12p/sample; 1969; 40pp; page size varies; 800-1000 circ. No pay. No ads. Discounts: 33%. Back issues: 10p. Women.

ENVOI, **J.C. Meredith Scott,** Lagan nam Bann, Ballachuiish, Argyll, Scotland, UK. Envoi *indicates — poetry, brief, traditional not barred. Non-political and noticeably erotic.* 3/yr;, £ 1/yr; 33p/ea; 1956; 22pp; 6x8"; lp (may become off. before next issue). Pay: by arrangement. Discounts: often 33%. Back issues: of 48 issues only 46-47 available.

EPOCH, **William Gummer,** 2a Lebanon Rd., Croydon, Surrey CR0 6UR, UK. Articles, poetry, cartoons, photos, interviews, criticism, letters. Ecology.

EPOCH, 251 Goldwin Smith Hall, Cornell Univ., Ithaca, NY 14850

EPOS, Rollins College, **Evelyn Thorne, Jean West Mackenzie,** Crescent City, FL 32012. 3/yr; $3/yr; $1/ea; $1/sample; 1949; 36pp; 6x9; 500+ circ; lp. Reports 1 wk. Pays copies only. No ads. No discounts. Pub'd 4 issues 1973, expects 3 in 1974. Poetry.

EQUAL TIME, **Hugh Seidman, Frances Whyatt,** 463 West St., Apt. D1016, New York, NY 10014. Poetry. *Equal Time was conceived as an anthology and contains the work of some 65 poets from all around the country. On this basis we do not plan to have another issue at present, tho that may change in the future.* One issue; 1972; 100pp; 9x12; 1M circ; ty. NESPA.

EQUALITY, **Richard Fichter,** coordinator, 28 E. Vine, Oxford, OH 45056, and 6 Frankfurt-Main, Postfach 2803, Germany. Poetry, articles, art, reviews, photos, cartoons, letters, collages. *The Do-it-yourself contact paper prepared entirely by the readers that guarantees you a free and equal voice and invites your participation.* Irreg; donation; 30 cent stamp/ea; 1965; 16pp; 6x8½; 500 circ; lo. No pay. No ads. Back issues: 30 cents. Everybody.

Erdesdun Pomes (see OSTRICH)

Erratica Press, **Don Dorrance,** 626 Milwaukee, So., Milwaukee, WI 53172. Poetry, fiction, satire, longpoems, plays. *Interested in literature with quality of professionalism the only criteria. No politics, no special interest, but a moderate degree of good taste.* Irreg; $2/yr; 50 cents/ea; 1971; 40pp; 4x5½; 200 circ; lo. Reports 2-4 wks. Pays copies only. Discounts: 35%. Pub'd 1 issue 1973, expects two double issues for 1974 at $1/ea. COSMEP.

ESPONTANEO, Hellric Publications, **Ottone M. Riccio,** Hellric House, 39 Eliot St., Jamaica Plain, MA 02130. Fiction, parts-of-novels. *Fiction only, including parts-of-novels. A bit overstocked & behind schedule, but still reading mss.* Irreg; $2.50/4 issues; 75 cents/ea; 75 cents/sample; 1972; 26pp; 8½x11; 500 circ; lo. Reports days to wks. Pays 5 copies + sub. No outside ads. Discounts: only on 20 or more copies or subscriptions. 50%. Back issues: 75 cents/ea. Expects 4 issues in 1974. Independent.

ESSAYS IN CRITICISM, **Stephen Wall, Christopher Ricks, F.W. Bateson,** advisory ed., Editorial: Stephen Wall, Keble College, Oxford; Business: F.W. Bateson, Brill Aylesbury, Bucks, UK. *Primarily an English Journal with Oxford bias, articles from abroad also welcome, especially if they continue some articles already raised in these pages.* 4/yr; £3 ($9)/yr; £1/$3/ea; 1951. Back issues: Nos. I-XXI (1951-1971) have been re-issued by Messrs Swets & Zeitlinger (Kiezersgracht 471 & 487, Amsterdam, Holland).

Estuary Press (see TANGENT POETRY QUARTERLY)

ETC: A Review of General Semantics, **Thomas M. Weiss,** College of Education, Univ. of Wyoming, Laramie, WY 82070, **Elizabeth Bartlett, Poetry ed.,** Aptdo 19, Comala, Colima, Mexico. Poetry, articles. *Poetry mss. are to be accompanied by international coupon & self-addressed envelope. All other mss. must be sent in duplicate with s.a.s.e. Recent poetry contributors: William Stafford, David Ignatow,* **Larry Rubin,** *Donald Finkel, Lewis Turco, Miriam Maloy, Helene Mullins,*

Joan Colby, Frances Hall, Evelyn Eaton, Constance Urdang. Recent article contributors: J. Samuel Bois, Weller Embler, Alfred Fleischman, Eugene Gingerich, Elwood Murray, Harold F. Vollmer.4/yr; $6/yr; $1.50/ea; 1943; 100pp; 6x9; 5M circ. Reports 3 mos. articles, prompt on poetry. Pays copies only. Pub'd 4 issues 1973, expects 4 in 1974. COSMEP.

THE EUGENE AUGUR, Augur Publishing Co., **Wayne Gordon, Sue Jacobs, Brian Livingston, Sally Ooms**, 454 Willamette, Eugene, OR 97401. *We are interested in printing original material on Oregon or the West. Should be written in a concise style because of space limitations: 500-1000 words if possible.* 2/mo; $5/yr; 20 cents/ea; 25 cents/sample; 1969; 16-24pp; 11x17; 3M circ; lo. Reports 3 wks. Pays copies only. Ads: $196/pg ($4 per column inch); $98/½; class. inch rate. Discounts: 15% to ad agencies. Back issues: 25 cents if available. Pub'd 14 issues 1973, expects 20 in 1974. UPS.

EULOGY, **Phil Spencer, Sherry Manebridge**, 65 Southdown Rd., Portslade, Brighton BN4 2HL, UK. Articles, poetry, fiction, art, cartoons, criticism. mi.

EUREKA, **Allan Burgis**, Tellusborgsvagen 45 BIII, 126 33 Hagersten, Stockholm, Sweden. Poetry, fiction, articles, art, cartoons, longpoems, collages, concrete art. *Eureka has readers/subscribers/contributors in Scandinavia, U.K., U.S.A. & elsewhere in western Europe. All non-English material is translated & printed in both the original version & in a translated version. I am particularly interested in getting prose & graphics from the U.S.A. (there is no shortage of poetry so far). In six issues, EUREKA has featured over 20 Americans including James Tate, Stephen Canada, Moses Yanes, Ray di Palma, David Gitin, Maria Gitin, Emilie Glen, Arthur W. Knight, Glee Knight, John Yamrus, Donald Moyer etc. Other contributors include Gunnar Harding, Opal Nations, Paul Brown, Jim Burns, Sona Akesson, Tina Morris, Dave Cunliffe, Pierre Joris, Alexis Lykiard, Allan Burgis, Antonio Claudio Carvalho, Barry Edgar Pilcher, Peter Finch, Chris Torrance etc.* 4/yr; $4/yr; $1/ea; 75 cents/ sample; 1972; 65pp; A4; 350+ circ; mi. Reports 2 wks-1 mo. Pays: one copy per contributor. Back issues: 75 cents when available. Pub'd 3 issues 1973, expects 3-4 in 1974.

EUROPEAN JUDAISM, **Anthony Rudolf**, Kent House, Rutland Gardens, London SW7, UK. Articles, poetry, fiction, interviews, criticism, letters. *Recent contributors include George Oppen, Edmond Jabes, Elaine Feinstein, Jakov Lind, A. Alvarez, M. Hamburger. The name of the magazine describes its orientation.* 2/yr; £ 1.30 ($3.30/yr) 65p ; ($1.90)/ea; 1966; 56pp; 9½x7";lp. Reports 1 mo. Ads: £20/p.

EVERYMAN, *Cuyahoga Community College*, **Christopher Franke**, 2900 Comm. College Ave., Cleveland, OH 44115. Poetry, fiction, articles, art, photos, cartoons, interviews, criticism, collages, concrete art. *Charles Bukowski, Cyril A. Dostal, Gerald Locklin, Harold Witt, Russell Atkins, & others.* 2/yr; $2.50/yr; $1.25/ea; sample; 1964; 100pp; 7x10; 1M circ; lo. Reports vary. Pay varies; 2 copies. Discounts: 60-40; 20; 10; 40-60, etc. Back issues: o/p. Pub'd 1 issue 1973. COSMEP, literary.

Excello and Bollard *(see also SANDWICHES)*, 66b Whitstable Rd., Canterbury, Kent CT2 8EB, UK. Poetry, fiction, satire, longpoems, plays. *Free Booklets. Press is also agency for artwork of Paul Lamprill.* A4; mim. ALP.

Exeter College, Exeter (see SUZANNE)

EXILE, **Barry Callaghan, pub.**, Box 546, Downsview, Ont., Canada. Poetry, fiction, art, photos, music, parts-of-novels, longpoems, plays. No length demands: have published complete plays and novels. Q; $7/yr; $2/ea; 1972; 140pp; of. Reports 3-4 wks. Pay varies. No ads.

EXPANDED MEDIA EDITIONS (see also SOFT NEED), **Udo Breger**, D-34 Gottinger Gronerland 21, West Germany. *Initially E.M.E. started with a multi media box giving an idea of German art of the late sixties. Conceptual art & concrete poetry by internationally known authors. A couple of free jazz records followed. Then Jack Kerouac hit me again & E.M.E. now does mostly prose by "beat authors" & those who followed after. And sometimes we really get nasty with it. Last year a new series of books & compact cassettes was begun. Among others these authors are contributing: Mary Beach, William Burroughs, B. Demattio, Jorg Fauser, Ian H. Finlay, Allen Ginsberg, H. Guthrie, Brion Gysin, G. Malanga, Claude Pileiu, J. Ploog, Allan Praskin, C. Weissner. All this started in 1970.*

THE EXPATRIATE REVIEW, **Roger W. Gaess, Wyatt James, Edouard Roditi, Euro. adv. ed., Martin Steingesser, assoc. ed.**, PO Box D, Staten Island, NY 10301. Poetry, fiction, articles, interviews, parts-of-novels, longpoems, plays. *Recent contributors: Douglas Blazek, Walter Lowenfels, William Burroughs, Daniela Gioseffi, Tommy Livingston, Rochelle Ratner, Patricia Goedicke.* 2/yr; $2.50/yr; $1.25/ea; 1970; 48pp; 5½x8½; 750 circ; lo. Reports 1 wk-1 mo. Pays copies only. COSMEP.

EXPRESSION ONE, **Les Surridge**, 117 Forest Rise, Waltham Forest, London E17 3PW, UK. Articles, poetry. 4/yr; $1.50/yr; 15p/ea; 24pp; 8x6½", lp.

EXPRESSIVE ARTS REVIEW, **Robert Alexander**, Box 202, 140 4th St., Brentwood, NY 11717. Poetry. *Sensitive poetry that a person may enjoy and relate to. Send 1-2 poems, 3-16 lines, and return env. We'd rather study one or two of your poems than skim over a bunch. If they're good, you'll be remembered as a good poet here. But a bunch that we think are not good would compound the odds against you. Think about that. Familiarize yourself with good poetry in whatever style you like, perhaps study our sample, before sending.* Q; $24/yr; $5.95/ea paper; $8.95/ea cloth; $4/sample; 1973; 50pp; 8½x5½; 3M circ. Reports within 3 wks. Pays: 50 to 75 cents/poem. Discounts: on request. None pub'd 1973, expects 3 issues in 1974.

Eye Publications, **Terri Hooley**, 21 Deramore Dr., Belfast BT9 5JR, UK. *For three years ID magazine fought off printers bills, bombs and apathy to survive in Belfast. "The Rise & Fall of ID" is a collection of goodies from past issues. All the money we raise will go into producing more magazines. Send 15p minimum payable to Terri Hooley.*

Fabian Society (see THIRD WORLD)

THE FALCON, **W.A. Blais, poetry ed., T.E. Porter, fic. ed.**, Mansfield State College, Mansfield, PA 16933. *No limit on length. Some recent contributors: Albert Goldbarth, Mike Finley, Siv Cedering Fox, Russell Edson.* Bi-annual; $2/yr; $1/ea; free sample; 1970; 100pp; 6x9; 1500 circ; lo. Reports 6 wks. Pays $5 to $25. Ads: exchange ads only. Discounts: 40% to trade or agent. Back issues: available only on microfilm. Pub'd 2 issues 1973. COSMEP, CCLM.

FANTASIAE, The Fantasy Association, **Ian M. Slater**, PO Box 24560, Los Angeles, CA 90024. *Features listings and criticism of past and current fantasy (in books, magazines, arts, and media) for adults and children, including tra-*

ditional, weird, and heroic stories, etc., but generally excluding science fiction. Feature articles by professional authors (recently including Katherine Kurtz, Marion Zimmer Bradley, David Gerrold, Mary McDermot Shideler, L. Sprague de Camp) and illustrators, notes on critical and historical works, conference and convention listings, bibliographies, and letters are especially featured. Most articles 500-1000 words, some longer, preferably factual. Letters (from members) may be on any fantasy-related topic, and there is an attempt to present a *variety of opinions whenever possible.* Monthly; $4/yr; 35 cents/ea; 1 sample; 1973;14p; 8½x11; 400-500 circ; lo. Ads: $10/pg; $5/½. No discounts. Back issues: 35 cents ea; Pub'd 9 issues 1973, expects 12 in 1974.

FANTASY ADVERTISER INTERNATIONAL, Derek G. Skinn,**Derek G. Skinn,** 116 Western Rd., Goole, Yorkshire DN14 6RD, UK. Articles, fiction, art, cartoons, interviews, letters. *Recent contributions: Interview with Frank Bellamy SGA, FSIA, FRSA. Most editorial material concerns science fiction and fantasy. in comics, books, magazines and films. Was referred to by Penthouse as "The Exchange & Mart for fantasy collectors." 60% of editorial & advertising content comics orientated. Though limited run, has readers in 19 countries.* 8/yr; £1/yr; 15p/ea; 1965; 52pp; A4; 1000 circ; off. Pay: varies with quality of contribution. Ads: £4/page (private); £12/page(trade). No disc. Comics, SF.

THE FANTASY ASSOCIATION (see FANTASIAE)

FAPTO, 441 Northdown Rd., Margate, Kent, UK. Articles, poetry, art, cartoons, photos, interviews, criticism, music, letters. 36/yr; £3.50/yr; 15p/ea; 1971; 32pp; 16x10; 12,000 circ; mim; off. Pays: by arrangement. Ads:£120/page;£70/½; 5p/word. UAPS.

THE FAR POINT, University of Manitoba Press, **George Amabile,** 605 Fletcher Argue Bldg., Univ. at Manitoba, Winnipeg, Canada. Poetry, reviews, letters. *Our bias is toward the poem which is imaginative and realistic at once, and which is fresh, taut, and free of cliche & mannerism.* 2/yr; $3.50/2yrs; $1/ea; free sample; 1967; 72pp; 6x9; 1M circ; of. Reports 2-6 wks. Pays copies only. Ads: $75/p; $50/½. Discounts: 20% sub. agencies & bookstores. Back issues: **$2**/1 - 3.

FATE, Athol Publications, **Kay Worgan,** Athol St., Douglas, Isle of Man, UK. *Serious articles on the unknown, the mysterious, supernatural — anything that seems inexplicable. Length 500-2000 words.* Monthly; 15p/ea; 1954. Pays:£3/1000 wds. or on merit. Occult.

THE FAULT, **Terrence Ames, Lit., Tom Rowe, art,** 41186 Alice Ave., Fremont, CA 94538. Poetry, Fiction, articles, art, photos, cartoons, interviews, satire, criticism, reviews, music, letters, parts-of-novels, longpoems, collages, plays, concrete art. *We've given up trying to shape the magazine into a preconceived image. As an issue gathers momentum, its genes determine the style and format.* 2/yr; $2/yr; $1 or trade; 1972; 100p; 6x9; 500 circ; lo; lp. Reports 1 wk. Pays grants & copies. No ads. Discounts: 40%. Back issues: $1. Pub'd 2 issues 1973, expects 2 in 1974; 1 book 1973, expects 4 in l974. COSMEP. CCLM.

The GRASSMAN

FELLOWSHIP. Fellowship Books, **James Forest, Diane Leonetti,** Box 271, Nyack NY 10960, Poetry, articles, art, photos, interviews, reviews, letters. *Very little poetry. Peace-related articles. Most articles in 1000 to 2000 word length.* Monthly; $6/yr; 60 cents/ea; free sample; 1915; 16-24p; 8½x11; 13M circ; lo. Reports 1 mo. Pays copies only, 10-20. Ads: no full pg; ½pg, write for rates. Discounts: 25%. Back issues: varies, 60 cents to free. Pub'd 11 issues 1973, expects 11 in 1974; 1 book 1973. COSMEP, Pacifist.

FELLOWSHIP IN PRAYER, Fellowship in Prayer, Inc., **Paul Griffith,** 200 E. 36 St., New York, NY 10016. Bi-mo; $3/yr; 50 cents/ea; 1949; 36pp; 2M circ; lo. Reports: not long. Pays copies only. No ads. Discounts: can be arranged. Back issues: 35 cents/ea. Pub'd 6 issues, 6 books 1973, expects 6 issues, 1 book 1974.

FEMALE ARTISTS PAST & PRESENT, (see Women's History Research Center)

THE FEMINIST PRESS (also WOMEN'S STUDIES NEWSLETTER), Box 334, Old Westbury, NY 11568. The Feminist Press is a non-profit, tax-exempt educational and publishing organization founded to challenge sexual stereotypes in books and schools and libraries. We publish three series of high-quality, low-cost paperbacks: feminist biographies, reprints of women's work from the past, and nonsexist children's books. Also educational materials in women's studies plus the Women's Studies Newsletter, a quarterly report of news in nonsexist teaching, at all levels of schooling. We also conduct inservice education workshops on sex-role stereotypes, for teachers, and have organized community workshops on children's books. $25/for a selection of books; price each varies; 1970; 120 pp; 5x7"; lo. Reports several months. Pays: no advances, earnings split 50/50. Discounts: 40% to booksellers; 25% to libraries. About 12 publications, 10 books 1973, expects 16 publications, 12 books in 1974. COSMEP, Women.

FEMINIST STUDIES Feminist Studies, Inc., **Ann Calderwood,** 417 Riverside Dr., New York, NY 10025. Poetry, fiction, articles, interviews, criticism, reviews, (only lengthy, substantive reviews), longpoems. *The journal was "founded for the purpose of encouraging analytic responses to feminist issues and analyses that open new areas of feminist research and criticism."* 3/yr; $6/yr person; $9/yr library, institutions, etc; $2/ea; no sample; 1972; 128pp; 6x9; 1200 circ; lo. Reports 4-6 wks. Pays copies only. Ads: $150/p; no ½ page or class/wd. Back issues: N/A. Pub'd Vol.I, No.1-4 in 1972-73. Women, Scholarly, Interdisciplinary.

FERRY PRESS , 177 Green Lane, London SE9, UK. Poetry. *Publishers of new writing in English & American — for all the usual reasons we rarely publish unsolicited mss.* ALP.

FERVENT VALLEY, Duende Press, **Larry Goodell,** Box 571, Placitas, NM 87043. Poetry, art. *Joby, Pearlman, Bravoli, Dawson, Raworth, Wilson, Bukowski, Karassic, Goodell, Meadow.* $1.50/ea; 1964; lo. Reports: submissions only after inquiry. Discounts: trade. COSMEP.

Fiasco Publications (see BOGG)

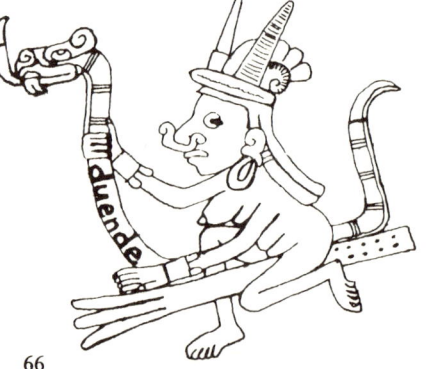

Fiction Collective, English Dept., Brooklyn College, Brooklyn, NY 11210. Fiction Collective *is an expanding writers' cooperative founded by a group of established novelists dedicated to publishing serious, literary fiction. We see ourselves not as The* Fiction Collective *but as a group of novelists who hope to indicate by example that collaborative publishing is a workable alternative. We edit each other's books, do our own designing and promotion – that is, come to our readers without the intercession of a publisher. We intend to do seven or eight books a year. Our first publications are:* Reruns *by Jonathan Baumbach,* Museum *by B.H. Friedman, and* Twiddledum Twaddledum *by Peter Spielberg; to be followed by* Statements, *an anthology of new fiction from writers associated with the Collective. Forthcoming novels include work by Jerome Charyn, Leslie Epstein, Raymond Federman, Jack Gelber, Steve Katz, Jascha Kessler, Barton Midwood, Mark Mirsky, and Ronald Sukenick. Subscription rate for all 3 novels (paperback) is $10.*

FICTION INTERNATIONAL, **Joe David Bellamy,** Dept. of English, St. Lawrence Univ., Canton, NY 13617. Fiction, interviews, criticism, reviews, parts-of-novels. *Because of our editorial commitment to publishing fiction, we are no longer able to read unsolicited poetry submissions. No hard-and-fast length limitations on fiction, though we rarely use short-shorts or mss. over 30pp. No taboos. Especially receptive to innovative forms and idiosyncratic styles. Contributors: Joyce Carol Oates, Albert Drake, Raymond Federman, Gary Gildner, Ihab Hassan, Jerome Klinkowitz, Robert Scholes, William Stafford, Ronald Sukenick, Gordon Weaver.* 2/yr; $4/yr; $8/yr institution; $2/ea; 1973; 150pp; 5½x8½; 5M circ; lp. Reports 2-6 wks. Pays $5-$150. Ads: $80/p; $45/½. Discounts: 25%.

THE FIDDLEHEAD, **Kent Thompson,** The Observatory, Univ. of New Brunswick, Fredericton, NB, Canada. Poetry, fiction, art, reviews. *Literary magazine of strong Canadian emphasis. (We are swamped with would-be contributors; it is becoming a very difficult magazine to break into, particularly for non-Canadians.) Our 29th year.* 4/yr; $6/yr Can., commencing with issue No.102; $7/yr U.S.; $1.50/ea; no sample; 1945; 120pp; 5½x8½; 700-900 circ; lo. Reports approx. 6 wks. Pays: $5/printed page. Ads: $50/p; $26/½. Discounts: bookstores 33 1/3%; agents 50 cents/subscription. Back issues: $2. Pub'd 4 issues 1973, expects 4 in 1974.

Figtree Press, Star Route, Box 91, Claverack, NY 12513.

FILM, **Peter Cargin,** 81 Dean St., London W1, UK. Articles, photos, news items, interviews, criticism. *Film news, criticisms etc.* Monthly; £3.50 ($9.15)/yr; 25p/ea; free sample; 1954; 24pp; A4; 3000 circ; off. Reports 2 wks. Pays: by arrangement. Ads: £50/page; £28/½; £15/¼; £8/1/8; Advertising managers: Adpress, 29 Cavendish Road, Redhill, Surrey. Movies.

FILM COMMENT, **Richard Corliss, Melinda Ward,** 1865 Broadway, New York, NY 10023. Articles, photos, interviews, criticism, reviews, letters. *The content of the magazine is all related to the cinema whether it be interviews with directors, actors and actresses, articles on every aspect of the cinema (past and present), or reviews of film books. Recent contributors: Andrew Sarris, Molly Haskell, Robin Wood, Raymond Durgnat, Roger Greenspun, Stuart Byron, Jonathan Rosenbaum, Steven Farber, Paul Schrader, Stanley Kauffmann.* Bi-mo; $9/yr; $1.50/ea; 1962; 68pp; 8½x11; 8M circ. Reports 2 wks. Pays 2 cents/wd. Ads: $250/p; $140/½. Back issues: $2. Pub'd 6 issues, 1 book 1973, expects 6 issues in 1974.

FILM HERITAGE, Wright State Univ. Press, F. Anthony Macklin, Film Heritage/College of Liberal Arts, Wright State Univ., Dayton, OH 45431. Articles, photos, interviews, criticism, reviews. Film Heritage is a quarterly journal devoted to analyses of films and rediscoveries of un-

derrated films. Length of material: approx. ten pages double spaced, typed. Style: Univ. of Chicago: A Manual of Style. Recent contributors: Dwight Macdonald, John Simon, Stanley Kauffmann, Andrew Sarris, Foster Hirsch, Birgitta Steene. 4/yr; $3/yr; 75 cents/ea; free sample; 1965; 40pp; 5½x8½"; 2M circ; lo. Reports 6 to 8 wks. Pays copies only. Ads: $80/p; $40/½. Discounts: agency rates available. Back issues: V.1=$3/ea; V.2 & 3=$2/ea; all others=$1/ea. Pub'd 4 issues 1973, expects 4 in 1974. COSMEP.

FILMS BY AND ABOUT WOMEN (see Women's History Research Center)

Firebird Publications, **David Allan Stringer,** c/o The Bookshop, 153 Woodhouse Lane, Leeds 2, Yorks., UK. Poetry, longpoems, plays. *Usually entire collections of one persons writings. Preference — emotional/narrative/lyrical verse rather than concrete/experimental avantegarde styles. Some publications:* Poems *by P. Newbold, 5p (3½p post).* Ebenezer Elliot: Poet of the Poor, the field, the furnace 1781-1847, *12p (3½p post).* England/Drumflowers/Sun Songs *by David Stringer, 5p (3½p post).* In the land of the Gorsedd Dard - Cornish Poems, *David Stringer, 20p (4½p post). Also Tom Maguire (Poet 1865-95)/Peter Robinson/Info sheet on request.* 4-5/yr; price/ea varies; sample/postage; 1967; 30pp; A4; 500+ circ; off; mim. Reports 2-3 wks. Pays: any profits after print cost covered. No ads. Discounts: 25-33%. ALP.

FIRELANDS ARTS REVIEW, The Rudinger Foundation, Inc., **Joel D. Rudinger, mang. ed., Julius T. Kosan, art ed.,** Firelands Campus, Huron, OH 44839. Poetry, fiction, art, photos. *Poetry — no limits or restrictions. Fiction — 3000 words max. no porno or erotica.* Annual; $1.50/yr; $1.50/ea; $1/sample; 1972; 72pp; 8½x5½; 1M circ; lo. Reports 4 wks max. Pays: depends on $ available. Ads: $100/p; $75/½; no class/wd. Discounts: 20% off on orders of 10 or more; 20% off for classroom use. Back issues: $1. Pub'd 1 issue 1973. COSMEP.

Fireside Press (see CONNECTICUT FIRESIDE MAGAZINE)

1st Casualty Press, c/o N.C. Pouchet, PO Box 501, Port of Spain, Trinidad, West Indies.

First Media Press (see THE SILENT PICTURE)

FITS Printing & Publishing Collective, **A Collective of 4 women and 4 men,** 2680 21 St., San Francisco, CA 94110. Poetry, fiction, articles, art, photos, cartoons, interviews, satire. *We do labor-donated printing for the liberation struggles of Third World people, women, workers, gay people and prisoners. We also print for community-based medical clinics, legal projects and cultural groups. We collectively own and control our machines, and share all skills. As the contradicitons of this imperialist society become clearer, revolutionary culture emerges. As publishers, we aid in the development of this culture, providing an opportunity for writers and printers to have mutual control over production. Our publishing will reflect the transformations of people stuggling to be free. We welcome your responses to our books.* Lo. Discounts: 40%. Pub'd 1 book 1973, expects 3 in 1974. COSMEP, Revolutionary literature.

5 Associates, **Anne Helms,** 1021 Edgewood Rd., Redwood City, CA 94062. *5 Associates publishing company has in the past been a vehicle for photographic works by Ansel Adams. Now looking for new material & subjects. Only limit is good taste and money! Not limited to photographic works; in fact, we would like to see some new non-fiction type work.* 1953; lo. Reports 3 wks. Pay: negotiable. Discounts: standard. COSMEP, Women, Food/Ecology, American Indian.

Five Owls Press (see CHILDREN'S BOOK REVIEW)

FLASH ART, Flash Art Edizioni SRL, **Giancarlo Politi,** Via Donatello 36, 20131 Milano, Italy. Articles, art, photos, interviews, criticism, reviews. Every 2 mos; $20/yr; $2/ea; 1967; 80-100pp; 310x225; 25M circ; lo. Reports 1 mo. Pays: check. Ads: $550/p; $300/½. Discounts: agency 15%; payment to order 3%; 8 issue contract 10%. Pub'd 6 issues 1973, expects 6 in 1974; 4 books 1973. Art.

Floating Hair Press (see MANTRAS)

The Florida Press (see POCKET POETRY MONTHLY)

FLOWER PATCH, **Anne & David Lazell,** 127 Tower Rd. South, Warmley, Bristol BS15 5BT, UK. Articles, art, satire, music, letters. *We reproduce old-time drawings, prints etc. linked to material on natural history, old-time journalism, work of Flora Kliekmann (pioneer ecologist) satire on modern "technology," co-operative ideas.* 6/yr; £1/yr; 1971; 24pp; A4 folded; several hundred circ; off. Reports: a.s.a.p. Pays: by arrangement. Ads not usually accepted. Back issues: 12p/copy. ALMS, Women, Ecology, Humour, Memories.

FOCUS ON FILM, The Tantivy Press, **Allen Eyles,** 108 New Bond St., London W1Y OQX, UK. Articles, interviews, criticism. *A magazine that documents the history of the cinema in exact detail and specialises in subjects and areas generally neglected elsewhere. Contributors need to be exceptionally well informed on their subjects.* Q; £1.60/yr; 35p/ea; 1970; 68pp; 9½x6½; lp. Reports 1-2 wks. Pays: maximum £25. Ads: on application. Discounts: for series. Back issues: sold at current issue price. Cinema.

FOCUS/MIDWEST, Focus/Midwest Publ. Co., Inc., **Charles L. Klotzer,** PO Box 3086, St. Louis, MO 63130. Poetry, articles, interviews, criticism, letters. *The only independent magazine of facts, interpretation and analysis, presenting political, social, cultural and literary issues on the local, regional and also national scene of direct interest to the reader in or observer of the middle west. Without taboos, it enjoys exploring controversial and suppressed subjects. Also excellent poems, art works, and state/national voting records.* Bi-mo; $5/yr; 85 cents/ea; samples; 1962; 40pp; 8½x11; 5M circ; lo. Reports 4-6 wks. Pays upon publication. Discounts: 20%. Back issues: $1.50. Pub'd 6 issues 1973, expects 6 in 1974.

Focus/Midwest Publ. Co., Inc. (see FOCUS/MIDWEST, ST. LOUIS JOURNALISM REVIEW)

Folk/Frog Press (see also *THIS IS NOT THE TITANIC),* **C.S. Crowther,** PO Box 15407, Salt Lake City, UT 84115. *Poetry/individual book length manuscripts/under 80pp approx. "I place no editorial bounds upon work submitted. I find that when I decide to publish/or not to publish a certain peom, it usually boils down to a matter of personal taste."* 4 bks/yr; $7.50/yr; $2.25/ea; $2/sample; 1973; 65-80pp; 5½x8; 1M circ; of. Reports 2 mos. Pays 10% after overhead is met + any work that Folk/Frog Press publishes during a year. No ads. Discounts: 40% to booksellers. Back issues: $2.

FOLK MASS AND MODERN LITURGY, Resource Publications, **William Burns,** 6244 Rainbow Dr., San Jose, CA 95129. Poetry, articles, art, photos, cartoons, interviews, satire, criticism, reviews, music, letters, collages, plays. *1000-2500 words.* 8/yr; $8/yr; $1.50/ea; free sample; 1973; 32pp; 8¼x10 7/8; 3500 circ; lo. Reports 4-6 wks. Pays 2 copies. Ads: rates by arrangement; no class/wd yet. Discounts: 10%. Back issues: $1.50/ea. Pub'd 1 issue 1973, expects 8 in 1974. Religious.

FORESIGHT, **John W.B. Barklam, Mrs. J. Barklam,** 29 Beaufort Ave., Hodge Hill, Birmingham B34 6AD, UK. Articles, poetry, news items, letters. *Articles of any length up to 1000 words approx. on subjects of philosophy, mysticism, occultism, UFOs and allied subjects. Small poems related to the above subjects are also accepted.* Bi-mo; 90p pf/yr; 15p pf/ea; 1970; 24pp; 5¾x8¼"; 1500 circ; mim. Reports 1 wk. No pay. Ads: £7/page; £4/½; £2/¼; 2p/word. Discounts: negotiable. Back issues: 11p pf. Occult, Philosophy, Mysticism.

FOUR DOGS MOUNTAIN SONGS, Doggeral Press, **Alice Karle and Thor,** Rt. 1, Box 193 See Canyon, San Luis Obispo, CA 93401. Poetry, art, letters, longpoems. *For now we are taking poetry and artwork (especially linoleum blocks and block prints, also woodblocks) that can be reproduced using hand-set type on a letterpress. Will take articles, letters, etc. if they are exceptional. Also will take artwork that must be reproduced offset occasionally. The definite emphasis is on poetry and block prints though.* Kenneth Rexroth, Ling Chong, Doren Robbins, Barbara Szerlip, Robyn Bell, John Wilson. 1/yr; $4/yr; $6/ea; 1973; 20-60pp; 17x13 folded to 8½x13; 240 circ; lp. Reports 2 wks. Pays 1 copy or more by request. No ads. Discounts: $4 no bulk because so few copies this issue. Any discount is $4 price. Back issues: $2. Poetry.

FOUR QUARTERS, **John J. Keenan,** La Salle College, Philadelphia, PA 19141. Poetry, fiction, articles, art, interviews, criticism. Q; $3/yr; 75 cents/ea; 1951; 48 pp; 6x9; 700 circ; lp. Reports 6 wks. Pays: $5/poem; story, article/up to $25 + 3 copies. No ads. No discounts. Back issues: $1. COSMEP, CCLM.

THE FOUR ZOAS, a journal of poetry and letters, **M. Gordon,** RFD Campbell Rd., Ware, MA 01082. 3-4/yr; $7.50/yr; $2.50/ea; 1972; 40pp; 7x9; 500 circ; lp. Reports 1 wk to 2 mos. Pays copies only for the present. Discounts: usual trade. Back issues: Issue 1&2 is priced at $4.50. Pub'd 1 book 1973, expects 3 issues and 1 book in 1974. COSMEP, CCLM, NESPA, Third World.

FOXFIRE, The Foxfire Fund, Inc., **Eliot Wigginton,** Rabun Gap, GA 30568. *Due to a tremendous backlog of folklore material, we will only occasionally be printing the poetry section that was once a feature of each issue. Our real emphasis now is on articles (factual) about the people of the Southern Appalachians and their customs. Photographs are welcomed if they are part of the article.* Q; $5/yr; $1.25/ea; 1967; 80pp; 7½x10; 10M circ; lo. Reports 3 wks. Pays copies. No ads. Back issues: price list furnished on request. COSMEP, CCLM.

FPS—the Youth Liberation News Service, Youth Liberation Press, **a staff collective,** 2007 Washtenaw Ave., Ann Arbor, MI 48104. Articles, cartoons, reviews, politics. *FPS prints articles about the oppression and liberation of young people in society. The schools, the family, juvenile justice and the workplace are common areas of discussion.* Monthly (during school yr); $5/yr kids; $8/yr adults; $12/yr instit; $1/ea; 25 cents/sample; 1970; 26pp; 8½x11; 750 circ; lo. Reports 1 mo. Pays: only on special arrangement. Ads: $100/p; $60/½; 25 cents class/wd; consult ad dept. for changes. Discounts: inquire. Back issues: $15 for all available (33 out of 35). Pub'd 8 issues, 2 books 1973, expects 8 issues, 2 books in 1974. COSMEP, UPS, Youth.

FRAGMENT, **F.G. Bissenden,** 41 Fabian Rd., Fulham, London SW6 7TY, UK. Articles, poetry, fiction. 2-3/yr; free single copy; 8pp; 5x4"; 250-300 circ; hand lever. No pay. No ads.

Fragment Press (see also *PLOUGHMAN),* **Gary Oliver,** PO Box R.217, Royal Exchange, Sydney, NSW, Australia 2000. Poetry. Circ. no more than 25 copies; lo; Albion lp. No ads. No back issues.

FRAGMENTS, A Literary Review, **Kenneth MacLean, poetry, Edwin Weihe, prose,** 212 Marion Hall, Seattle Univ., Seattle, WA 98122. Poetry, fiction, art. *We are a professionalized university undergraduate literary magazine printing the best we can find outside and inside our campus writing community. Costs necessitate short poetry and fiction in all but a few outstanding instances. Open to material other than poetry, fiction and art, but these take a definitely primary position so that criticism, photography, etc is not invited.* 1/yr; $1.50/yr; $1.50/ea; 1971 in present form (1959 previous); 65-70pp; 700 circ. Reports 6-8 wks. Pays copies only (2).

FREE LANCE MAGAZINE, **Casper L. Jordan, J. Stefanski, Russell Atkins,** 6005 Grand Ave., Cleveland, OH 44104. *Recent contributors: David Jaffin, Charles Angoff, Ben Tibbs, Dave Axelrod, Aaron Kramer, L. Eric Greinke, Lorenzo Thomas, etc.* Semi-annual; $2/yr; $1/ea; no sample; 1950; 80-110pp; half 8½x11; 500 circ; lo. Reports irreg. Pays copies only. No ads. Back issues: left up to reprints. Pub'd 1 "double issue" 1973, no books. COSMEP, CCLM.

Free Life Editions, Inc., **Chuck Hamilton, Mark Powelson, Sharon Presley,** 41 Union Square West, New York, NY 10003. Art, non-fiction. *We publish books dealing with issues related to personal, social, and political freedom. Our books emphasize non-authoritarian, non-coercive approaches to social problems. Our titles include reprints of libertarian and anarchist classics as well as significant new contributions to the contemporary libertarian and non-authoritarian perspective. Recent tiles include* Our Enemy The State *by Albert Jay Nock,* As We Go Marching *by John T. Flynn,* The Anarchist Collectives *ed. by Sam Dolgoff with an intro by Murray Bookchin,* The State *by Franz Oppenheimer, and* The Unknown Revolution *by Voline.* 140-720pp; 5½x8½; of. Reports: depends. Pay: depends. Discounts: regular bookstore rate is 40%. Pub'd 2 books 1973, expects 5 in 1974. COSMEP, Libertarian, Anarchist.

Free People Press (see BOTH SIDES NOW)

Freelance Press Services (see CONTRIBUTOR'S BULLETIN, FREELANCE WRITING & Photography)

FREELANCE WRITING & Photography, Freelance Press Services, **Arthur Waite,** Freelance Press Services, 67 Bridge St., Manchester M3 3BQ, UK. Q; £1.20/yr; 1954; 36pp; 9x6; 3,000 circ; off. Reports 1 wk. Pays: £4 per 1000. Ads: £15/page and pro rata.

Friends of Malatesta, Inc., **Robert & Anne Dickens,** Box 72, Bidwell Sta., Buffalo, NY 14222. *Anarchist/libertarian.* Third World, Women, Black Food/Ecology, American Indian, Prison, Chicano, Anarchism, Gay, COSMEP.

The Friends of the Written Word (see CHEAP AND FAST)

Fringe Press (see LUNATIC FRINGE)

Frog in The Well Press, **Wendy Batson, Robert Cooney, Will Kirkland,** 667 Lytton St., Palo Alto, CA 94301. Poetry, fiction, articles, art, photos, cartoons, interviews, satire, criticism, reviews, parts-of-novels, longpoems. *We're a pamphlet experiment at bringing social change issues to middle class folks who often have little that is 'revolutionary' to identify with. Inexpensive & attractive reprints, poetry sheets, critical reviews, essays, fiction, etc. Few books; distributors & printers.* Often; price/ea varies; 1972; 8pp; 8½x11; lo. Discounts: 20% on orders over $5. Many issues expected in 1974.

From Here Press (see also *HAIKU MAGAZINE)*, **William J. Higginson,** Box 2702, Paterson, NJ 07509. Poetry, art, photos. *Please: no mss. without query first! Expect to begin series of 'Small Poem Pamphlets' summer 1974, with work by Larry Wiggin, Michael McClintock, myself & Yosa Buson (tr.) featured in first three numbers.* From Here Press publishes Haiku Magazine, *and the pamphlet series grows out of the interaction between haiku and other varieties of poem, particularly concrete and realistic, found poems, etc. The 'SPP' will be a subscription series, and pricing etc. not yet finalized at this time. Inquiries invited.* 1974; lo; lp. Reports: immediate. Pays: 50% net profit + 10 copies. No ads. Discounts: trade, 5 or more copies, 40%. Expects 2-3 books in 1974.

Fuller D'Arch Smith, **Martin Booth, Jean Overton Fuller,** 60 Oxford St., London W1, UK.

Funch Press (see also *THE HORBLY GNOME, THE PAN AMERICAN REVIEW)*, **Seth Wade,** 1100 West Samano, Edinburg, TX 78539. *Concrete & related work, mostly. One book in 1973,* These Fragments I Have Gathered For Ezra, *Andrew Suknaski; at least one in 1974,* Electronic Salad, *Richard Latta. Beyond present commitment, might consider small works if they struck me as great.* Mi; lo; lp. Discounts: 40% (on some items 50%) trade.

FWBO MAGAZINE, Friends of The Western Buddhist Order, **Upasaka Ananda,** Aryatara Buddhist Community, 3 Plough Lane, Purley, Surrey, England, UK. *Articles on all aspects of Buddhism by practicing Buddhists. Emphasis on Western application and relation with contemporary thought in philosophy and Arts. Poetry and review section.* Articles, poetry, art, photos, interviews, criticism, letters. Biannual; £1/yr; 50p/ea; 50p/sample; 1968; 40pp; qto; 200 circ (sub), 300 circ (direct); off; Pay: nil. Ads: by arrangement. Discounts: nil. Back issues: 50p. Philosophy/Arts.

GAIRM, Gairm Publications, **Derick S. Thomson,** 29 Waterloo St., Glasgow G2, Scotland, UK. Articles, poetry, fiction, cartoons, photos, satire, interviews, criticism, music. *All material printed in Gaelic.* 4/yr; £1.20/yr; 25p/ea; 1952; 100pp; 21x13.5cm; 2000 circ; lp. Pay: nominal. Ads: £30/page; £17/½. Back issues: yes.

GALAXIA 71, Grupo Escritores de Venezuela, **Mr. Modesto Vargas Lopez,** Apdo 4023, Carmelitas 101, Caracas, Venezuela. Poetry, articles, art, photos, interviews, criticism, reviews, parts-of-novels. Bi-mo; $5/yr; $1/ea; free sample; $1/other; 1971; 20pp; 5M circ; lo. Ads: $30/p; $15/½; $1/10 words class/wd. Discounts: 10%. Back issues: 8 numbers special price $5. Expects 6 issues, 1 book in 1974.

The Gallery Press: Gallery Books, **Peter Fallon,** 19 Oakdown Rd., Dublin 14, Eire, UK. Poetry, longpoems. 3-4/yr; price/ea varies; 1970; 32-100pp; 8½x5½"; 1-2000 circ; lp. Reports 3 wks. Pay: negotiable. Discounts: 33%. ALP, Irish Publishers Association.

GALLIMAUFRY, Grossman Publishers, **Mary MacArthur, Richard Grossman,** 359 Frederick, San Francisco, CA 94117. Poetry, fiction, art, photos, satire, criticism, reviews, letters, parts-of-novels, longpoems, collages, plays, concrete art. *Biased only in favor of quality. Will consider all schools traditional or experimental. Would like to encourage fiction, longer poetry. Walter Lowenfels, Clarence Majors, Harold Carrington, Paul Vangelisti, Steve Shutzman, Olga Cabral, Nanos Valaoritis, Tom Sobel, Susan Schaeffer, Keith Abbott.* 3/yr; $2/yr; 65 cents/ea; 65 cents/sample; 1973; 48pp;

8½x11; 5M circ; lo. Reports 3 mos. max. Pays copies only (10). No ads. Discounts: available on request. Back issues: $1. Pub'd 2 issues 1973, expects 3 in 1974.

GAMBIT, Calder & Boyars Ltd., **Irving Wardle**, 18 Brewer St., London W1R 4AS, UK. Articles, criticism, plays. *Full and short-length plays by contemporary writers, neglected authors, translations of foreign works.* 4/yr; 75p ($2.50)/ea; 1963. Pay: by arrangement.

THE GAR, **Hal Wylie, Carolyn Wylie**, Box 4793, Austin, TX 78765. Poetry, fiction, articles, plays, concrete art. The Gar *tries to put art to the service of the cultural revolution of our times, especially as it relates to central Texas. We mix journalism and poetry, and believe that the old conceptions of genres are no longer functional. We welcome submissions.* 6/yr; $3/yr; 25 cents/ea; free sample; 1971; 32pp; 8½x11; 1500 circ; lo. Reports 1 mo. Pays copies only. Ads: $35/p; $20/½; 5 cents class/wd. Discounts: contact us. Back issues: 50 cents/ea. Pub'd 6 issues 1973, expects 6 in 1974; 1 book 1973. UPS.

GAY BOOK NEWS, Catalyst, **Ian Young**, 315 Blantyre Ave., Scarborough, Ont., Canada MIN 2S6. *A bulletin of notices and reviews about new books & periodicals relevant to the subject of homosexuality.* Approx. 2/yr; $2/yr institutions; 50 cents/ea individuals. Gay.

GAY NEWS, **Denis Lemon, Peter Mundy, David Seligman, Mike Mason**, 62a Chiswick High Rd., London W4 1SY, UK. Articles, poetry, fiction, cartoons, photos, news items, interviews, criticism, letters. Fortnightly; £4/yr; 15p/ea; 20p/sample; 1972; 20pp; A3; 18000 circ; off. Pay: N.U.J. min. Ads: £75/page; £40/½; £26/¼; £15/1/8. Discounts: agency 12½%; publishers 5%. Gay.

GAY SUNSHINE, **Radical Gay Men's Collective**, Box 40397, San Francisco, CA 94140. *A newspaper of gay liberation.* $6/12 issues; $8/12 issues overseas and Canada; $10/12 issues 1st class; 50 cents/sample.

GAY WORLD, Insight, **Deric R. James**, 118 Windham Rd., Bournemouth, Hants, UK. Articles, photos, satire, news items, interviews. *Interviews with well-known personalities, Theatre and Film reports, Book review, dates of various meetings, short stories and Pin-Ups of the dishiest guys to hit the camera.* 4/yr; £2.50 ($7)/yr; 75p/ea; free sample; 1965; 40pp; 9x6"; off. Reports 2 wks. Pays: by negotiation. Ads: £10/page pro rata; 1p/word (Box no. 15p). Back issues: 50p. Gay.

THE GAZETTE SUPPLEMENT (see THE DC GAZETTE)

GEGENSCHEIN, **Eric B. Lindsay**, 6 Hillcrest Ave., Faulcon Bridge, NSW, Australia 2776. Articles, art, cartoons, interviews, satire, criticism, reviews, letters. Geg *is a personal journal, nominally about science fiction and any related subject, but there are no restrictions on subject or length of contributions.* 5/yr or more often; $1/3 issues; 40 cents/ea; sample/if you send an interesting letter; trade with other magazine; 1971; 20pp; 8x10; 240 circ; mi; lo. Reports 2 wks + mail time. Pays: 1 copy + reprints if requested before printing. Ads: display not available; class/wd free if room available. Discounts: none. Back issues: none. Pub'd 4 issues 1973, expects 6 in 1974. COSMEP, COSMEPA.

Gemini (see MADRONA)

The Generalist Assn., Inc. (see THE SMITH)

GENESIS III, Philadelphia Task Force on Women in Religion, **Nancy E. Krody, mang. ed.**, PO Box 24003, Philadelphia, PA 19139. Articles, reviews. *We cover* news in the field of women in religion, nationally (to some extent internationally) and ecumenically. This includes info on conferences, resources, and women's groups; book reviews and abstracts of articles; suggestions for action; news of individual women and denominational action (such as task forces on women in church & society). 6/yr presently; $2/yr; sold only by vol; free sample; 1971; 10 pp; 8½x11; 425 circ; lo. Pays 1 copy. No ads. Discounts: can be arranged for college-class use (approx. half price for 12 to same address). Back issues: $2/vol. Published 6 issues 1973. COSMEP, Women in religion.

THE GEORGIA REVIEW, John T. Irwin, Lustrat House, Univ. of Georgia, Athens, GA 30602. Recent contributors: Marion Montgomery, Robert Beum, Van K. Brock. Q; $3/yr; $1/ea; no sample; 1947; 157pp; 6¾x10; 1,800 circ; lp. Reports 1-2 mos. Pays: 1 cent/word prose; 50 cents/line poetry. Ads: $60/p; $35/½; no class/wd. Back issues: $1/ea. Pub'd 4 issues 1973.

Germainbooks, J.W. Backus, 91 St. Germain Ave., San Francisco, CA 94114. To be published late 1974: Una Stannard, Mrs. Man. COSMEP.

Gerry de la Ree, Gerry de la Ree, 7 Cedarwood Lane, Saddle River, NJ 07458. *I use fantasy-type material – articles, memoirs, considerable artwork and usually publish 400 to 650 paperbound copies and 50 to 65 hard-bound copies of each book.* Discounts: dealer: 5-9 copies, 30%; 10 or more, 40%. Pub'd 5 books 1973, expects 4 in 1974.

GHOST DANCE, Hugh Fox, N.W. Werner, assoc., P. Ferlazzo, ad., Leslie Tracy, asst., ATL/EBH/MSU, E. Lansing, MI 48823. Poetry, concrete art. *Looking both for new form and content. Poetry isn't antiquarian for us, nor is it "non-functional," but a tool for thought-/idea-exploration, so that whatever's on the foreward-wave in science or art should be reflected in our pages. Suspect the 1970's will be a decade of "head"-exploration ("consciousness-expansion explored systematically"), so especially on the lookout for experimental psych-related work. Same goes for pre-historical anthropology. We could be a forum for exploring ways of translating the untranslated (Linear Script A, for example).* Q; $2.50/yr; 75 cents/ea; 75 cents/sample; 1968; 32pp; 8½x5½; 300 circ; lo. Reports 1 day. Pays 1 copy; copies only. No ads. No discounts. Back issues: 75 cents. Pub'd 4 issues 1973, expects 4 in 1974; 1 book 1973, expects 2 in 1974. COSMEP, CCLM, Ambiguous.

GINGER, Ruth Cohen and others, 9 Poland St., London W1V 3DG, UK. Articles, photos, news items, interviews, letters. *700-1000 words. Basically aimed at one parent families and others concerned with their welfare. Gives information of social policy developments which have implications for one parent families in the U.K. Also information on action for change which one parent families have taken or can take. Contributors besides one parent families themselves have included experts on social benefits, adult education etc.* Monthly; £1.50/yr; 13p/ea; 1973; 16 pp; A5; circ going up; off. Pay: none to contributors. Ads: none at present. Back issues: 13p + postage. Women, Social Work.

Giorno Poetry Systems *(see THE DIAL-A-POEM POETS LP)*

THE GISSING NEWSLETTER, Pierre Coustillas, 10, Rue Gay-Lussac, 59110 La Madeleine, France. Articles, criticism, reviews. *Any contribution about George Gissing and his circle.* Q; £1/yr individual; £1.50/yr institution; 1965; 20pp; 250 circ; lp. Reports fortnightly. No pay.

Glebe Press *(see OLD FRIENDS)*

Glide Publications, 330 Ellis St., San Francisco, CA 94102.

GLOBAL TAPESTRY JOURNAL, B.B. Books, **Dave Cunliffe**, 1 Spring Bank, Salesbury, Blackburn, Lancs BB1 9EU, UK. Articles, poetry, fiction, art, cartoons, photos, satire, interviews, criticism, letters, longpoems, plays, collages. *Contemporary poetics. Copy concerned with alternatives, counter-culture, anarchism, nonviolent revolution, vegetarianism, ecology, living cheaply, yogic breathing, psychoexperimentation, psychedelic drugs. Recent contributors have included Michael Horovitz, Mark Hyatt, Tina Morris.* 4/yr $6/yr; $1.50/ea; $1/sample; 32pp; A4; 1000 circ; off. Reports as soon as possible. Pay 1 copy. Ads: $25/page; $13/½; 30 cents/word. Discounts: 33% trade. ALP, Expanding creativity Cosmic Liberation.

GNOSTICA NEWS, Llewellyn Publications, **Ronald Wright**, PO Box 30159, St. Paul, MN 55165. *Poetry, fiction, articles, art, photos, cartoons, interviews, satire, criticism, reviews, music, letters, parts-of-novels, longpoems, collages, plays, concrete art. 5,000 word maximum.* Monthly; $5/yr; 50 cents/ea; free sample; 32pp; 11x17; 30M circ. Reports 2 wks. Pays: 1 cent/wd. Ads: $340/p; $180/½; 25 cents class/wd. Discounts: 50%. Back issues: $1. Pub'd 10 issues: 1973, expects 12 in 1974. Occult.

THE GODDARD JOURNAL, 304 Publications, Rolling Board, Box 595, Goddard College, Plainfield, VT 05667. Poetry, fiction, art, photos, interviews, parts-of-novels, longpoems, collages, plays, concrete art. *Gluck, Ungerer, Bosch, Kuzma, Lifshin, Oybek, Halpern. Open to most forms of writing & graphics.* 2/yr; $1.50/yr; $1/ea; sample usually on request; 1968; 66pp; 9x6; 1M circ; lo. Reports vary greatly. Pays 5 copies. Discounts: usual 40% bookstore disc. Pub'd 2 issues 1973, expects 2 in 1974; 8 books 1973. COSMEP

GOD'S LIGHT, Guru Bawa Fellowship, **Mitch Gilbert**, Carriage House, 5820 Overbrook Ave., Philadelphia, PA 19131. *We accept pieces in whatever form as long as their subject matter is of a spiritual nature. They are printed in either of the following two sections of the magazine: 1) On the Path, 2) Lord Knows We Try.* Every 1½ mo; $3.50/10 issues; 35 cents/ea; 1974; 20pp; 6 5/8x9½; 300 circ; lo. Ads: display not set; no class/wd. Discounts: retail 30%. Pub'd 2 books 1973, expects 3 in 1974. COSMEP, Spiritual.

Golden Atom Publications, **Larry & Duverne Farsace**, c/o Golden Atom, PO Box 1101, Rochester, NY 14603. Poetry, fiction, articles, art, photos, reviews, letters. *We publish many one-shots, some with a huge number of pages, such as the current World Poetry, Part 1.* 1939; 12-100pp; 500+ circ; mi. Reports 2 wks. Pays: $4-12/fiction; 25 cents/line poetry. 1st Fandom, Intern'l Who's Who in Poetry.

GOLDEN ROSE SERIES, Headland Publications, 56 Blakes Lane, New Malden KT3 6NX, UK. Poetry. *A series of fine poems finely presented in limited editions of 150 numbered copies and 26 lettered, signed copies. Only the best of work by known poets considered for this series.* 20pp ($1)/ea unsigned; 75p ($3)/ea signed; 1973; 4pp; 9x6"; 176 circ; lp. Pay: royalties. Discounts: 33% trade.

THE GOLIARDS, 3515-18th St., Chuckanut Village, Bellingham, WA 98225.

Golgonooza Press, **Brian Keeble**, 76 Suffolk Rd., Ipswich, Suffolk 1P4 2Ez, UK. Articles, poetry, longpoems. *The Press derives its name from William Blakes divine City of Arts and Crafts. Publishes works of prose & poetry which by their spirit encourage a dialogue between spiritual values and the problems of the practising contemporary artist.* 3/yr; 1973; 15pp; off. Reports: no unsolicited mss. Discounts: trade.

GONE SOFT, **Ron Bogan, John Currier,** c/o Salem State College, Salem, MA 01970. Poetry, fiction, art, photos, cartoons, interviews, plays. *We dislike obscure poems. Poetry must carry some meaning for the reader. We will look at anything;* biographical info must be sent with material. *May 1974 issue features Ginsberg, Corso, and Orlovsky.* 2/yr; $2/yr; $1/ea; $1/sample; 1972; 64pp; 5½x9; 2500 lo. Reports up to 4 mos. Pays: copies only. Back issues: $5/first issue; $2/others. COSMEP.

Good Elf Publications, **Lawrence Upton,** c/o 18 Clairview Rd., Streatham, London SW16, UK. *No limit to the range of material used. I do not limit myself that way. If I like what is sent in it will be used.* 12/yr; 1969; 500 circ; mim; off; lp. Reports 1-10 days. Pays: ad hoc arrangements. Discounts: 33%.

GOOD ELF/VISST, **Lawrence Upton,** c/o 18 Clairview Rd., Streatham, London SW16, UK. Articles, poetry, cartoons, satire, criticism, letters, longpoems. "Visst" *is the reviews section of G.E. and is not available seperately. I try to avoid bias. Length of material and style — no rules. Depends how I feel. 1974 — goes over to 2-4 pages in Swedish.* "Good Elf" 2/yr; "Visst" 4/yr; 20p /ea; 1970; 25pp; 10x8; 1000 circ; mim; off; lp. Reports 1-10 days; Pays: 1 copy of mag. Ads: £2.50/page; £1.60/½. Discounts: 33%. Back issues: on application. ALMS, ALP.

GOOD NEWS, Arete Ink, **Steve Kraus,** 239 East 2nd St., New York, NY 10009. Poetry, articles, art, photos, cartoons, satire, criticism, reviews. *Covers the good things happening.* Irreg; 25 cents/ea; 50 cents/sample; 1966; 20pp; tabloid; 10M circ; of. Reports 1 wk. Pays copies only. Ads: $60/p; $35/½.

THE GOODFELLOW CATALOG OF WONDERFUL THINGS, Temporary Gymnasium Press, **Christopher Weills,** PO Box 4520, Berkeley, CA 94704. Photos. *The Goodfellow Catalog is a mail order catalog meant to aid craftspeople in marketing their wares. Its purpose is also to introduce quality crafts to the general public and further stimulate the renaissance of good craftsmanship.* 1/yr; $2.50/ea; 1974; 112pp; 8½x11; 5M circ; lo. Discounts: available upon request. Expects 1 issue in 1974. COSMEP.

THE GOODFELLOW NEWSLETTER, Temporary Gymnasium Press, **Christopher Weills,** PO Box 4520, Berkeley, CA 94704. Articles (about crafts), art (line drawings), book reviews (about crafts). *The Goodfellow Newsletter is a monthly crafts review published to serve the many divergent craftspeople and their trade. The Newsletter contains articles, book reviews, lists of upcoming crafts fairs, information on craft suppliers and generally serves as a helpful and handy guide for craftspeople everywhere.* 1/mo; $1.50/yr; 25 cents/ea; sample/upon request; 1973; 8pp; 10x8"; 1500 circ; lp Reports 2 wks. Pay: not set. Ads: $35/p; $20/½; free class/ word. Discounts: upon request. Back issues: 25 cents. Pub'd 4 issues 1973.

Gordon & Breach (see COUNTERPLAY, NATURAL LIFE STYLES, RADICAL SOFTWARE)

GPU NEWS, **Eldon Murray, Alyn Hess, Robert Stocki, art ed.,** PO Box 90530, Milwaukee, WI 53202. Poetry, articles, art, photos, cartoons, interviews, satire, criticism, reviews, music, letters. Monthly; $5/yr; 50 cents/ea; 1971; 24-32pp; 8¼x 10½; 1500 circ; lo. Pay: negotiated with known authors only. Ads: $45/p; $30/½ the 1st time, $22.50 repeat; class/wd. $2/col. inch, $1.50 repeat. Min $10 design fee for ads if not camera ready submission. Back issues: 50 cents/ea. Pub'd 10 issues 1973 (two were double month issues), expects 10 in 1974. COSMEP, Gay Liberation.

GR/EW Books (see also GROSSETESTE REVIEW), **Tim Longville, John Riley, buss. manag.,** 10 Consort Crescent Commonside, Pensnett Staffordshire, UK. Bus/ address: 4 Gledhow Wood Close, Leeds 8, UK. *31 books published; 8 in 1973. Complete catalogue, combined with Index to vols. 1-8 of* Grosseteste Review *available on request. Among books published:* The White Stones, *by J.H. Prynne, poems;* The Welsh Poems, *by John James, versions of medieval Welsh poems from the Hendregadredd mss.;* Cells, *by Jim Burns, prose pieces;* What Reason Was, *by John Riley, poems.* 1966; lp to '70, off. now. Discounts: 33 1/3%.

GRANDE RONDE REVIEW, **Ben L. Hiatt,** 907 River Way, Folsom, CA 95630. Poetry, fiction, articles, art, photos, cartoons, interviews, satire, criticism, reviews, letters, parts-of-novels, longpoems, collages, concrete art. *We're going through changes. Look for some crazy mimeo work in coming year. The format and frequency very much depend on the editor's sobriety and whim. Overstocked as of spring '74 with everything but that will change as summer comes to Lower Folsom. Send me the stuff that is just too fucking hairy for anyone else.* Varies; $6/yr; $1/ea; $1/sample; 1964; no. & page size vary; 500 circ; mi; lo. Reports 1 min. to 1 yr. Pays 3 copies. No ads. Discounts: 50% to anyone on 3 or more copies; no consignment. Back issues: query. Pub'd 1 issue, 2 books 1973. CCLM.

GRANITE, **George M. Young, Jr., prose ed., Anselm Parlatore, poetry ed., Dorothy Beck, mang. ed.,** Box 774, Hanover, NH 03755. Poetry, fiction, interviews, criticism, letters, translations. 2-3/yr; $5/3 issues; $2/ea; 1971; 150pp; 9x6; 1M circ; lo; lp. Reports 2 wks. Pays copies only. Discounts: 40% to trade. Back issues: $3. COSMEP, CCLM.

Granny Soot Publications, **Colin Browne,** PO Box 171, Sannichton, BC, Canada. Poetry, fiction, parts-of-novels, longpoems, plays. *We only publish books so far – no magazine yet.* 1970; lo. No books pub'd 1973, expects 2-3 in 1974.

Graphic Arts/Blue Cloud Abbey (see BLUE CLOUD QUARTERLY)

GRAPHIKTRAKT, published & designed by Ted Smith Graphics, St. Louis, **Eugene Warren,** 107 South Rolla, Rolla, MO 65401. Poetry, fiction, imaginative prose. *We plan a series of short items, each by a single author, and each individually designed. We are primarily interested in material which articulates a basic Christian perspective, though it need not be explicit, and should not be merely didactic or sentimentally devotional.* GraphikTrakt One: Rumors of Light, *eleven poems by Eugene Warren plus graphics in broadside/poster; 75 cents.* 4/yr; $3.50/ 6 issues; varies/single; 1974; 500 circ; lo. Reports 6 mos. Pays copies. Discounts: 30% trade.

GRASS ROOTS, **David & Meg Miller,** Box 900, Shepparton 3630, Australia. Articles, interviews, lifestyles. *We're into natural sensible living. The editors live on a farm etc. Factual/lifestyle material needed.* Q; $A4.50/yr; $A1.25/ea; 1973; 64pp; Qto; 5M circ; of. No ads. Pub'd 2 issues 1973, expects 4 in 1974. COSMEP, UPS, COSMEPA.

GRAVIDA, **E. Romaine Murphy,** 157 E. Hartsdale, Hartsdale, NY 10530. Poetry. *Gravida is edited by the Women's Poetry Collective: we also conduct workshops. Recent contributors have been Lyn Lifshin, B. Holland and an interview with Terry Stokes.* 4/yr; $3/yr; $1/ea; 1973. Reports 6 wks. Pays copies only. Expects 4 issues 1974. COSMEP.

GREAT NEWSPAPERS REPRINTED, Peter Way Ltd., **Peter Way, David Sharp, Brian Lake,** 28 James St., Covent Garden, London WC2E 8PA, UK. 12/yr; £1.80/ yr; 15p/ea; 1970; 16pp; 20x15"; 80,000 circ; Ads; on application. History.

Great Society Press, **Angelo De Luca,** 101 Morris St., Phillipsburg, NJ 08865. Poetry. 35 cents/ea; 1960; 16pp; 5x7; 300 circ. of. No payment.

THE GREAT SPECKLED BIRD, Atlanta Cooperative News Project, PO Box 7847, Atlanta, GA 30309. Poetry, articles, art, photos, cartoons, interviews, satire, criticism, reviews, music, letters. Weekly; $7/yr; 25 cents/ea; free sample; 1968; 24pp; 10¼x15; 10M circ; lo. Reports 3 wks. Pay: negligible. Back issues: 50 cents per copy. Pub'd 50 issues 1973, expects 51 in 1974. UPS.

GREEN EGG, PO Box 2953, St. Louis, MO 63130. Occult.

Green Horse Publications (see also PLATFORM), **Andrew Cozens,** 'Avalon', London Rd., Stockbridge, Hants SO20 6EJ (all orders to this address please), **Duncan Tweedale,** 13 Windsor House, Lawn St., Winchester, Hants SO23 8DT, UK. Poetry, longpoems. *Current series produced in co-operation with* Platform *magazine (Andrew Cozens). Other publications produced previous to this series, including the defunct magazine "Black Eggs" are available from 13 Windsor House, Lawn St., Winchester. Recent issues include a booklet of Greek surrealist translations, translation of Mirko Lauer's "Common Grave" by David Tipton, poems by Tony Curtis.* About 4/yr; 50p/sub; 10p/ea; 1969; 20pp; A5; 150 circ; lp. Reports: commisioned work only. ALP.

Green Knight Press, PO Box 512, Amherst, MA 01002.

Green Note Music Publications, **Straw Dog, Ceel,** PO Box 4187, Berkeley, CA 94704. Music. Guitar instruction manuals; music information texts. 1970; 84pp; 8½x11; lo. COSMEP.

THE GREENFIELD REVIEW, **Joseph Bruchac iii, Carol Bruchac,** Greenfield Center, NY 12833. *We are interested primarily in contemporary poetry. Once a year we devote an issue to African poetry and we have a deep interest in the writing of Third World people, though we are open to good work from anyone. Recent contributors include Kofi Awoonor, Duane Niatum, Bruce St. John, Frank Chin, Lawson Inada, Ross Talarico, Emily Borenstein, Leslie Silko, Simon Ortiz, Dennis Brutus, Anne Pitrone, Rod Tulloss, William Hathaway, Ingrid Wendt, Michael Harper, Amerigo Casiano, Mei Berssenbrugge, John Gill, Collette Inez, James Grabill, William Witherup.* Q; $4/yr; $1/ea; 84pp; 1M circ; of. Reports 2days to 2 mos. Pay varies, usually $5 + copies. Discounts: usual trade disc. Back issues: Vol.1, No.1/$20, No.2/$5, No.3/$5. Pub'd 3 issues 1973, expects 4 in 1974; 7 books 1973, expects 6-8 in 1974. COSMEP, CCLM, NESPA, Third World.

Greenfield Review Press, **Joseph Bruchac,** Greenfield Center, NY 12833. *We publish about 6 titles a year. Thus far we've done books by mostly Third World Writers: Ron Welburn, Kalu Uka, Wendy Rose, Kofi Awoonor, Tanure Ojaide, Duane Niatum (Black American, Nigerian, Indian, Ghanaian) for example, and we are very favorably inclined toward manuscripts from such writers. We do not automatically reject manuscripts from any other writers, however, although we do feel that most of them have other outlets. We offer a straight split of profits — 50% — on sales to anyone whose book we publish, but we usually only publish about 500 copies and try to keep the prices reasonable — say about $1 for a 40 page book.*

GREEN'S MAGAZINE, **David Green,** Box 313, Detroit, MI 48231. Poetry, fiction. *Arthur Hailey, Marjorie Holmes, James Goldwasser, John Ditsky, Anne Long, Lawrence Taylor Carter. Stories 1-3000 preferred; poems to 40 lines preferred. Strong characterization essential.* Q; $3/yr; $1/ea; 48pp; 5½x7½; 2M circ; lo. Reports 6 wks. Pays up to $25. Ads: $100/p; $60/½. Discounts: 40%. Pub'd 4 issues 1973, expects 4 in 1974. COSMEP, CCLM.

GROPE, D.S.P., **Mike Smith, Nick Dowson,** 2 Cumberland House, Orton, Penrith, Cumberland, UK. Poetry, art. *Tries to include a wide range of poems, taken on their own merits rather than to fit in with preconceived ideas. Frequency of publication at this stage depends on sales. Perhaps there is a slight Lake District Bias – in poets if not in content!* Bi-annual; 20p/ea; 1971; 24pp; 500+ circ; off. Reports 1-2 wks. Pay: nil. Ads: £4/½p. Back issues: "Grope Again" No.2 15p. Poetry.

GROSSETESTE REVIEW, Grosseteste Review Books (GR/EW Books), **Tim Longville,** 10 Consort Crescent, Commonside, Pensnett, Staffordshire, UK. Articles, poetry, fiction, interviews, criticism, letters, longpoems, plays. *No limit to length of contributions. Recent contributors: George Oppen, Gilbert Sorrentino, Donald Davie, Carl Rakosi, John Riley, J.H. Prynne, Douglas Oliver, Hugh Kenner, Charles Tomlinson, Peter Riley, Kris Hemensley, William Bronk, Cid Corman, Franco Beltrametti, Peyton Houston, James Kaller, Michael Chamberlain, Michael Palmer, etc.* Q;£1 ($4)/yr; 30p($1)/ea; 1968; 64pp; 5½x8½; 400 circ; off. Reports 2 wk. Pays copies. Ads:£10/page; £6/½; £4/¼. Discounts: 33 1/3%. Back issues: back set: 6 yrs 22 issues/ £8; single copies pre '73/50p.

Grossman Publishers (see GALLIMAUFRY)

THE GROVE, Naturist Foundation, **Editorial Committee,** Brockenhurst, Sheepcote Lane, Orpington, Kent BR5 4ET, UK. Articles, photos, news items, criticism, music, letters. *House journal of Naturist Foundation and associated Sun Societies. Contributions, with or without illustrations, welcomed from other naturist interest; no payment offered!* 3/yr; £1/yr; 50p/ea; 1950; 16pp; 9½x7½; 750 circ; lp. Pay: nil. Ads: £ 12/page; £6.50/½; £4/¼. Discounts: 10% 3 insertions. Back issues: 3 for £1. Naturist.

Grupo Escritores de Venezuela (see GALAXIA 71)

THE GUARDIAN, **Irwin Silber, Jack A. Smith,** 33 W. 17 St., NYC 10011. Articles, photos, reviews, letters. Weekly; $12.50/yr; 35 cents/ea; free sample; 1948; 20pp; 11½x16; 22M circ; lo. Pays: $15. Ads: $300/p; $175/½; 75 cents class/line. Discounts: 20 cents/copy. Back issues: 50 cents. Pub'd 50 issues, 2 books 1973, expects 50 issues, 2 books in 1974. Political.

Guild of Undergraduates, Liverpool University (see PLUM)

Guildford Poets Press (see WEYFARERS)

Guru Bawa Fellowship (see GOD'S LIGHT)

Gyst Publications (see THE RUFUS)

EN HAA, Apartado 19211, Correos de Quinta Crespo, Caracas 101, Venezuela.

Russ Haas Press (see NAUSEA ONE)

HAIKU MAGAZINE, From Here Press, William J. Higginson, Box 2702, Paterson, NJ 07509. Poetry, articles, art, photos, criticism, reviews, letters. *We're here to abolish the haiku fad. (Almost got swamped in 1973, but two issues out already in 74, two to come).* Q; $6/yr (1975); $2/ea; $1/sample; 1967; 40pp; 5½x8½; 330 circ; lo. Reports 2 wks to 1 mo. Pays copies only. Ads: query. Discounts: trade, 40%; sub. services, 10%; 5 or more copies. Pub'd none 1973, expects 4 in 1974

HALLAMSHIRE & OSGOLDCROSS POETRY EXPRESS, Headland Publications, **Gerald England,** 745 Abbeydale Rd., Sheffield S7 2BG, UK. Articles, poetry, news items, interviews, criticism, letters. *Covers those aspects of poetry not usually covered by other little mags. Articles generally solicited but ideas welcome. Submissions of poetry are not required. Topics covered include Vanity Presses, Arts Councils, French Poetry, Poetry & Communication, Alternative Presses of 19th cent. Contributors include Michelle Loi, Stewart Brown, Norman Hidden, Howard Sergeant, Ben Dyson. All magazines/books received are mentioned if not reviewed.* Irreg; £2 ($8)/life sub; sample/postage; 1972; 6pp; 13x8;2000 circ; mi. Reports vary. Pay: free copies (unlimited number). Ads: 2p/word (min.50p) Box numbers 15p. Back issues: 2p/page xerox copies from Cyril Smith, Langwith House, Well, Bedale, Yorkshire DL8 2PD.

HAMPSHIRE, **Dennis Stevens,** 39 Above Bar, Southampton SO1 ODX, UK. *Factual articles of 500-1000 wds. on all aspects of Hampshire & Hampshire life, past and present.* 12/yr; 15p/ea. Pay: £5.25/1000 words.

HAMPSHIRE POETS, **Mrs. Katharine Sparks,** 7 Leep Lane, Alverstoke, Gosport, Hants PO12 2BE, UK. Poetry, news items, criticism. *Length of poems pref. 20-35 lines/free verse and contemporary techniques where craftsmanship is employed/ bias towards socialist and protest ideas if contained in good construction/traditional-lyrical if irresistible: recent contributors: Robert Morgan, Robert Shaw, A.L. Hendriks.* 2/yr;65p/yr; 28p/ea; free sample; 1969; 36pp; 8½x6;under 500 circ; off. Reports 3 days. No pay. No ads. No discounts. Back issues: 10p.

The Handcraft Press (see ARENA: A LITERARY MAGAZINE)

HANGING LOOSE, **Robert Hershon, Emmett Jarrett, Dick Lourie, Ron Schreiber, Denise Levertov,** cont ed.., 231 Wyckoff St., Brooklyn, NY 11217. *Recent contributors: Harley Elliott, Kathleen Wiegner, Michael Lally, Robert Peters, Jim Gustafson, C.W. Truesdale, Donna Brook, Halvard Johnson, Katy Akin, Daniela Gioseffi.* Q; $3.50/yr; $1/ea; 1966; 72pp; 5½x8½; 1200 circ; of. Reports 8 wks. Pays occasionally if we've got some money, otherwise 3 copies. No ads. Discounts: to bkstores and agents. Back issues: on request, some full sets available. Pub'd 2 issues 1973, expects 4 in 1974; expects 2 books 1974. COSMEP, CCLM.

Hanuman Publications, **Hanuman Collective,** Box 1069, Ojai, CA 93023. Poetry. *Hanuman believes that earthly events proceed from spiritual causes (you might call that a bias) and would expect a similar understanding from any contributors.* Pub'd 3 books 1973. Spiritual.

HAPPINESS HOLDING TANK, Stone Press, **Albert & Barbara Drake,** PO Box 227, Okemos, MI 48864. Poetry, articles, art, photos, criticism, reviews, letters. *We've been emphasizing poetry, information, printing processes, people, and are still moving in those directions. To keep it fun rather than a chore we've been doing posters, pamphlets, etc., and there's more ahead. Philip Whalen, Earle Birney, Wm. Matthews, Ed Ochester, Wm. Stafford, etc. No mss. during summer please.* 3/yr; $3/yr; $1/ea; $1/sample; $4/poetry pack; 1970; 50pp. 8½x11; 300 circ; mi; of. Reports 1 wk. Pays copies only. Ads: $15/p;(open to exch.). Discounts: 40%. Back issues: a few sets available (No.1-No.12) for libraries. Pub'd 3 issues 1973, expects 3 in 1974; 3 books 1973, expects 3 in 1974. COSMEP, CCLM.

Harbour Publishing (see RAINCOAST CHRONICLES)

HARD CHEESE - A Journal of Education, Liverpool Free Press Group, **Ted Bowden,** 95a Shooters Hill Rd., Blackheath, London SE23 8RL, UK. Articles, satire, interviews, criticism, letters. *Any length, any form, left biases.* 15p/ea; 1973; 60-80pp; A5; 2-3000 circ. No pay. Ads: nogotiable. Sociology/Education.

HARD CIDER, The Cider Press, **Daniel L. Dorman, Karen Wachsman, Pat Ryan, Debbie Klein, Sue Engle,** PO Box 10113, Columbus, OH 43201. Poetry, fiction, articles, art, photos, cartoons, interviews, satire, criticism, reviews, music, letters, parts-of-novels, longpoems, collages, plays (maybe in special edition or book). *Three issues only in 1974; quarterly thereafter. We're in the market for shop equipment, too; anybody got a broken-down 16x20 process camera? We do as much in our own shop as we can to keep production costs down; we're part of a not-for-profit corporation and feel the pinch all the time. Always in the market for manuscripts, especially short stories. Also need photos and art. First issue included Judy Shepps Battle, A.D. Winans, Arthur & Glee Knight, Gil Williams, Irving Stettner, Danette Hoffman, Diane Powell, John King, e. Romaine murphy, et.al.* Q; $4/yr; $1/ea; $1/sample; 1973; 48-64pp; 8x11; 2500 circ; lo; intaglio. Reports 4 wks. Ads: $60/p; $35/½; no class/wd. Discounts: min. order 20 copies, 25% off; orders of 50 copies or more, 40% off; instit.; prisons, libraries, min. order 5 at 25% off. Pub'd none in 1973, expects 3 issues, 1 book in 1974. COSMEP, UPS.

Headland Publications (see also Dustbooks, U.K., GOLDEN ROSE SERIES, HALLAMSHIRE & OSGOLDCROSS POETRY, PROMONTORY), **Gerald England, Vivienne Finch, Directors.** 56 Blakes Lane, New Malden, Surrey KT3 6NX, and 745 Abbeydale Rd., Sheffield S7 2BG, UK. Poetry, art, criticism, longpoems, concrete. *Original poetry in pamphlet form. New and established authors including James Kirkup, Anna Adams, Colin Simms, Penelope Shuttle. U.K. agents for Dustbooks Directories. Write or phone ol-942 0979 for a copy of our latest catalogue.* 15p /sample; 1970; 1p mainly. Reports up to 3 mos. Pay: royalties. Discount 33% trade. ALP.

HEADLOCK, **Susan Grathwohl, Kenneth Koprowski,** 43 Payne St., Hamilton, NY, 13346. Poetry, articles, art, photos, cartoons, interviews, criticism, reviews, longpoems. *Headlock is a socialist/feminist magazine of poetry, extended reviews, essays and reporting. We are still putting together issue one and wish to solicit contributions.* Sporadic; price ea/not fixed. Reports 1 mo. or less. Pays copies only. Discounts: 40% standard. COSMEP, Women, Political.

HEALTH & EFFICIENCY, **Leslie L. Bainbridge,** 38 North Audley St., London W1, UK. Articles, photos, letters. *Includes the official Monthly Bulletin of the Central Council for British Naturism.* 26/yr; 30p /ea; 1900; 90pp; 7¼x5¼"; 1p .Ads: 5p/word (min.£1.50). Naturist.

*HEALTH RIGHTS NEWS,***Judith Gardiner, chairperson of ed. board,**831 S. Loomis St., Chicago, IL 60607. Articles, art, photos, cartoons, interviews, reviews, letters. *HEALTH RIGHTS NEWS is the newspaper of Medical Committee for Human Rights. We are interested in all health movement activities. We seek analyses of the American health care system; relevant book reviews, art & graphics; reports of projects & activities relevant to health workers, health science students, patients rights, health institutions, mental health, women's health movement, occupational health, etc.* 6/yr or less; $5/yr; free sample; 1967; 12-16pp; 16½x11½; 12M circ; 1p. Reports 1 mo. Pays copies only. Ads: $200/½pg; $100/¼; $50/1/8; class/wd 19 or less/$20. Discounts: Bulk, 25cents/copy to 25 copies; 15 cents/copy for larger numbers. Medical Movement.

HEALTH TEAM,National Association of Health Students, **Mike Sinason,** 15a Alexandra Mansions, West End Lane, London NW6, UK. Articles, poetry, cartoons, photos, satire, news items, interviews, criticism, letters. 4/yr; 40p/yr; 5p/ea; 1973; 24pp; 11¾x8¾"; 10,000 circ; off. Reports 7 days. Pays: by arrangement. Ads: £70/page; £40/½; £30/third page.

HEART, Young Virgin Weasel Enterprises, **John-Peter Horsam, Pip Giles, Chris Coxhill, Robert Burgess, Wendy Harvey,** 47 Williamson Rd., Para Hills, South Australia 5096. Poetry, art. *Contributors: Locals: [Horsam, Giles, Coxhill, Harvey, Buttrose, Hope (not A.D.)] and Rae Desmono Jones, S. Flavell, G. Langford, E.M. Bennett, D.S. Long, etc.* 4/yr; $2/6 issues; 25 cents/ea; 20 cents/sample; 1973; 30pp; ½ foolscap; 500 circ; lo. Reports 2-3 wks. Pays 1 free copy per poem. Ads: negotiable, not usually used. Discounts: 25% for order of 10 or more. Back issues: 2nd issue=15 cents/ea; 3rd issue=25 cents/ea; plus postage. Pub'd 2 issues 1973, expects 4 in 1974. COSMEPA.

HEIRS MAGAZINE, **Alfred Garcia, Ernest J. Oswald, Bruce Spenberg,** 657 Mission St., Rm 205, San Francisco, CA 94105. Conceptual art, poetry, fiction, articles, art, photos, interviews, satire, criticism, reviews, music, parts-of-novels, long-poems, collages, plays, concrete art. *We are interested in contemporary works of art, poetry and prose in any language from any country. Very interested in theatre and film, – plays, scene plays, and articles both in the U.S. and in other countries.* $4.50/yr; $1.25/ea; $1/sample; 1968; 68+pp; 8½x11; 2M circ; lo. Reports 6 to 12 wks. Pays: token $ and copies. Ads: $115/p; $80/½; $40/¼. Back issues: query by letter for rates please. Pub'd 1 issue 1973, expects 3 issues, 2 books 1974. COSMEP, CCLM.

The Heliopolis Press (see NEW WORLD HAIKU)

Heller & Son, Publishers, **Richard Heller,** 90 Daisy Farms Dr., New Rochelle, NY 10804. Non-fiction. *We are book publishers, at this point, primarily of trade (quality) paperbacks. Our first book was The New Earth Catalog, published in 1973 and our next book is the People's Yellow Pages of America, to be published in May, 1974.* 1972; of. Reports 6 wks. Discounts: trade discount. Pub'd 1 book 1973, expects 2 in 1974. COSMEP.

HELLRIC CHAPBOOK SERIES, Hellric Publications, **Ottone M. Riccio,** Hellric House, 39 Eliot St., Jamaica Plain, MA 02130. Poetry, fiction, plays. *Overstocked in all depts. Will not read new mss. during 1974.* Irreg. $ea/varies; no%/sample; 1968; no. pp varies; 5½x8½; 500 circ; of. Pay: arranged, + copies. Discounts: only on 20 or more copies, 50%. Pub'd none in 1973, expects 2 books in 1974. Independent.

Hellric Publications (see AB INTRA, ESPONTANEO, HELLRIC CHAPBOOK SERIES, PYRAMID)

HERE NOW, **Tom Kelly,** 22 Torquay Parade, Hebburn-on-Tyne, Co. Durham, NE31 2AD, UK.

HERITAGE,Paul Breman Ltd., **Paul Breman,** 1 Rosslyn Hill, London NW3 5UL. UK. Poetry. *Recent contributors: Arna Bontemps, Sebastian Clarke, Waring Cuney, Eseoghene (Lindsay Barrett), Robert Hayden, Dudley Randall, Conrad Kent Rivers.* 4/yr; $2.50/ea; 1962; 24pp; 8½x5½"; 500 circ;lp. Reports longish. Pays: 5-10% royalties. Discounts:40% trade. Black.

*HERITAGE, HERITAGE PRESENTS
. . . , Heritage,* **Richard Garrison,** PO Box 721, Forest Park, GA 30050. *We are a comic and graphic continuum publisher – utilizing classic comic characters and current renderings of the character by the world's finest comic artists. In conjunction, we publish prints, smaller books, color posters. Utilize enamel paper, square binding, full-process color, etc.* Intermittent; $5/ea; 1971; 72pp; 8½x11; 3M circ; lo. Reports: we do not solicit actively. Pay: varies. No ads. Discounts: we offer one-copy price only, no disc. at this time. Special back issue prices: none. Pub'd 1 issue (also one set of posters, one 12 page book) 1973, expects 2 books 1974,COSMEP.

The Heron Press, **Bruce Chandler,** Box 225, Deerfield, MA 01342. Poetry, art, letters, parts-of-novels, longpoems, plays. *Heron is a ltd. edition press, completely hand produced, with the occasional use of a high-powered press. Usually type is handset and attention to the finer hand made papers is observed. We print small books & broadsides usually poems– but entertain ms. of all forms.* Whenever possible; price/ea varies with each title; 1967; 16pp; pg size varies; 1p. No ads. Discounts: 40% to bkstores only. Pub'd 1 issue 1973, expects 3 in '74.

HEY LADY,Morgan Press, **Edwin H. Burton II,**1819 N. Oakland Ave., Milwaukee, WI 53202. Poetry, art, photos. *No biases. Recent contributors: Gibbons, Blythe Ayne, Lifshin, Ann Menebroker, D. Margoshes, J. Evans, A. Dewey, Dacey, C. Petroski, Finley, O.H. Winn, Hillebrand.* 6/yr; free sub. 1969; 32pp; 5x11 & up; 500 circ; lo; lp. Reports 2-3 wks. Pays copies only (10-200). No ads. Discounts: free, as are all our bks. Back issues: free when available. Pu'd 4 issues, 1 book 1973, expects 6 or more issues, 3-4 books in 1974. COSMEP, CCLM.

HIBERNIA, **John Mulcahy,** 179 Pearse St., Dublin 2, Eire. *Of interest to Irish people at home and abroad, including books, writers, theatre, the arts, etc.* Fortnightly; 12p/ea; 1936. Pays: by arrangement.

Hierophant Press, **Thomas Kerrigan,** 15141 Sutton St., Sherman Oaks, CA 91403. Poetry. *Hierophant Magazine folded in 1972 after 7 issues. In the future, Hierophant Press will publish one book of poetry a year. It will accept no unsolicited manuscripts of poetry.* 1/yr; $2/ea; 1970; 50 pp; 5x8;2M circ; lp. Reports 3 wks Pays 2 copies. No ads. No discounts. No back issues.

HIGGINSON JOURNAL OF POETRY, Higginson Press, **Frederick L. Morey,** 4508 38th St., Brentwood, MD 20722. Poetry, articles. art, photos, cartoons, criticism, reviews. *50% poetry and criticism of Emily Dickinson; also reforms of Col. T.W. Higginson, her mentor: black, women's lib., world govt.etc.* Semi-annual; $10/yr libraries, $5/yr individual; $3/sample; 1968; 50pp; 8½x11; 200 circ; lo. Reports 1 mo. Pays 1 copy. Ads: $90/p; $50/½; either class/wd. Discounts: 10% Backissues: $20 for all in print. No partial fulfilment. Pub'd 2 issues 1973, expects 2 in 1974; expects 1 book in 1974. COSMEP, Third World, Women, Black, Modern Lang. Assn. editors sec.

Higginson Press (see EMILY DICKINSON BULLETIN, HIGGINSON JOURNAL OF POETRY)

High Orchard (see SHAVIAN)

Highland Book Club (see CLUB LEABHAR)

THE HILLINGDON WRITER, **John C. Keeble**, 16 Hoppner Rd., Hayes, Middx. UB4 8PY, UK. Articles, art, photos, letters. *Local Borough magazine but articles and letters on Leisure time activities, nature and the potential of ordinary folk are accepted from other sources. Max. 2000 words* Bi-annual; £1/continuous sub; 15p/ea; 1967; 60pp;A5; 1000 circ; off. Reports usually return. Pays: usually none. Leisure magazine.

Hilltop Press (see LUDD'S MILL)

Hippopotamus Press, **Roland John**, 26 Cedar Rd., Sutton, Surrey, UK. Poetry, criticism, longpoems. *Plans are to produce twelve pamphlets this year, possibly some criticism, essays on a particular poet, maybe an anthology of Hippopotamus Press poets in* ɔ 75. *Biases against nonsense, lazy syntax, typographical oddities unless they serve the poem. For: sense both in content and technique. Experimental poetry must be poetry; not glimpses into the workshop. Length immaterial, provided the work is good.* 45p (£1)/ea; 1973; 28pp; lp. Reports 2 wks. Pays: royalty or by arrangement. Discounts: 25% under £5; 33% over £5. ALP. Poetry.

HIRAM POETRY REVIEW, **David Fartus, ed.in-chief, Hale Charfield, ed.**, PO Box 162, Hiram, OH 44234. Poetry, reviews, letters, longpoems, concrete art. *All poetry is from unsolicited submissions. Reviews by invitation only. High quality, serious poetry only. No carbons or other duplication copies are read. It is a waste of time to send manuscripts as a "last resort" — after they are dog-eared and dirty from handling by editors of the "paying"slicks. Recent contributors include: Wm. Aiken, Franklin Brainard, Wm. Virgil Davis, Felix Pollak, Harley Elliott,J. Garmhausen, S. R. Lavin, Lyn Lifshin, David Schloss, Peter Wild, Charles Edward Eaton, et.al.* 2/yr; $2/yr; $1/ea; free sample; 1966; 34pp; 6x9; 500+circ; lo. Reports 1 mo. Pays 2 copies + one-yr. sub. No ads. Discounts: Bkstores 40%; subs. agency 50% Back issues: No2/$50; No.3/$20; No.4/$5; No.5-10/$2; all others $1. COSMEP, CCLM.

HISTORY OF CHILDHOOD QUARTERLY: *The Journal of Psychohistory,* **Lloyd deMause**, 2315 Broadway, New York, NY 10024. Articles, reviews. *Childhood in past; psychohistory.* 4/yr; $14/yr; $3.50/ea; 1973; 160pp; 6x9; 6M circ; lo. Reports 1 wk. Pays 50 copies. Ads: $200/p; $100/½. Discounts:10%. Back issues: $3.50/ea. Pub'd 4 issues 1973. COSMEP, History.

THE HOLLINS CRITIC , **John Rees Moore**, Box 9538, Hollins College, VA 24020. Poetry. *Each issue is based on a review essay of a contemporary author's work to date, of about 4500 words, no footnotes. No unsolicited essay manuscripts. Short poems are published in almost every issue. The other features are a front picture of the author under discussion, a checklist of his writing and brief sketch of his career. Available in Microform from Zerox Univ. Microfilms, 300 North Zeeb Rd., Ann Arbor, MI 48106.* 5/yr; $3/yr ($4/yr Canada and elsewhere); 65 cents/ea; 1964; 15p; 7x10; 1M circ. Reports 2-3 mos. Pays: $100 essay; $20 poems. No ads. No discount. Back issues: from Zerox Univ. Microfilms. Pub'd 6 issues 1973, expects 5 in 1974, COSMEP, CCLM.

Holmgangers Press, **Gary Elder**, 22 Ardith Ln., Alamo, CA 94507. Poetry, fiction, art, photos, satire, music, longpoems, collages, plays, concrete art, regional history. *Books, chapbooks only — 20-150 pages; style just right; bias against anything everyone else might do; first book Wally Depew's Nine Essays On Concrete Poetry, next a book of Dean Phelps'Montana Stories.* 1974; lo. Reports wk to mo. Pay: negotiable. Discounts: 40%. Expects 3-5 books 1974. COSMEP, Anomalous.

HOLY BEGGAR'S GAZETTE, House of Love and Prayer Publications, **Steven L. Maimes, Elana Rappaport,** 1456 9th Ave. San Francisco, CA 94122. Poetry, articles, art, photos, reviews. *Teachings from Rabbi Shlomo Carleback, stories from Hasidic Rebbes and Jewish mysticism.* 4/yr; $5/yr; $1.25/ea; $1/sample; 1971; 24pp; 8½x5½; 1500 circ; lo. Reports 2 wks. Pays copies only. Ads: $40/p; $20/½; no class. Discounts: Trade: 40% for under 10 copies; 50% for 10 or more copies. Back issues: $1/ea. Pub'd 4 issues 1973, expects 4 in 1974. COSMEP.

Homestead Press, **Remi and Sharon Barron,** Star Rt., Pine Ridge, Auberry, CA 93602. Reviews. *We are a new, small press. We publish books on owner-building, homesteading, organic gardening etc. We are also starting a mail order book service for the "back to the land" movement. Our catalog will cost $1.00–refundable with first book purchase.* Lo.

Honeysuckle Publishing Company (see AUNT HARRIET'S FLAIR FOR WRITING REVIEW)

HOO–DOO, Energy Blacksouth Press, **Ahmos Zu-Bolton II,** 103 Ollie St., DeRidder, LA 70634. *In HOO-DOO I: Antar Sudan Katara Mberi, Ron Welburn, Carolyn Chew, Brenda Torres, Kalamu Ya Salaam, Russell Chew, Jerry Ward, Eusi Matata, Dudley Randall, May Miller, Pinkie Gordon Lane, Lorenzo Thomas.* Varies; $1.50/sample, 1973; 40pp; pg size varies; lo. Reports vary. Pays copies only. Discounts: contact editor. Pub'd 1 issue 1973, expects 3 in 1974. Black.

HOPKINS RESEARCH BULLETIN, Hopkins Society, 162 Turkey St., Enfield EN1 4NW. *Also have published Kathleen Raine's 1972 lecture "Hopkins, Nature and Human Nature." Autographed edition limited to 125 copies.* £5; Annual; £2 ($6)/yr; libraries; £4 ($12)/yr; 1969.

THE HORBLY GNOME, Funch Press, **Seth Wade,** 1100 West Samano, Edinburg, TX 78539 *Concrete, phenomena related thereto, prose poems, sometimes verse: all experimental work. Not really a mag anymore but an annual anthology. Following the lead of Assembling & how of Ovum in Uruguay, I am asking contributors to have their own reproduction done– or do it themselves, any method– & send me 300 8½x11 copies of up to 4 pages. But let me see the work first, sending xeroxes or whatever. New series will go like* the horbly gnome 1975 *etc. A name change too is possible. Some THG contributors: Richard Latta, Michael Gibbs, Michael Joseph Phillips, Glyn Pursglove, Clemente Padin.* Annual; $2.50/yr; 1970; 8½x11; 300 circ; Production: all & any. Reports 1 wk to 1 mo. Pays several copies. Discounts: 50% trade. Pub'd 1 issue 1973, expects 1 in 1974. COSMEP.

Horsehead Nebula Press, **F.A. Nettelbeck,** 12655 Flat St., Boulder Creek, CA 95006. Poetry. *Still here in shadows hoping to emerge with books of poetry/ thanx for waiting.* COSMEP.

House of Greystoke (see THE BURROUGHS BULLETIN)

House of Love and Prayer Publications (see HOLY BEGGAR'S GAZETTE, TZADDIKIM)

HOUSEMAN SOCIETY JOURNAL, **Graham Speake,** 74 Duns Tew., Oxford, UK.

Hub Publications Ltd. (see ORBIS)

THE HUDSON REVIEW, 65 East 55 St., New York, NY 10022.

HUERFANO: A LITERARY ORPHANAGE, **Dowling Campbell, J.M. Ferguson, Jr.,** Box 15700, N.A.U., Flagstaff, AZ 86001. Poetry, Fiction, satire, parts-of-novels, longpoems. *+ personal, informal essay, rich in tone and atmosphere and a sense of place. + character sketch.* 2/yr; $2/yr; $1/ea; $1/sample; 1973; 32pp; 5½x8½; 50 circ; lo. Reports 1 mo. Pays 3 copies only. Ads: inquire. Pub'd 2 issues '73, expects 2 in 1974. Literary.

LA HUERTA, **Gerald McCarthy,** Box 27 B, Lakeville, NY 14480. *Dave Kelly, George Chambers, Terry Stokes, Lyn Lifshin, Sister Zubena, Diane Kruchkow, W. S. Merwin, James Mechem, Jack Hirschman, Mike Waters, Douglas Musella, William Matthews, Russ Banks, etc.* 3/yr; $2.50/yr; $1/ea; 1970; 80pp; 6½x9; 700 circ; lo. Reports 1 mo. Pays 2 copies. Ads: $50/p; $25/½. No discounts. Back issues: $1 plus postage (25 cents). Pub'd 1 issue 1973, expects 3 in 1974. COSMEP.

HUMAN WORLD, Brynmill Publishing Co., 130 Bryn Rd., Brynmill, Swansea SA2OAT, UK.

THE HUMANIST MAGAZINE, Prometheus Books, **Paul Kurtz,** 923 Kensington Ave, Buffalo, NY 14215. Bi-monthly; 8/yr; $1.50/ea; 1941; 48pp; 8½x11; 28,500 circ; lo. Reports 4-6 wks. Ads: $390/p; $215/½; 30 cents/wd. Discounts: 40%. Back issues: $2. Pub'd 6 issues 1973. COSMEP.

Hummingbird Press, (see HYACINTHS AND BISCUITS)

HUMOROUS HOTCHPOTCH, Belvedere Publications, **Valery Fraser,** Adelphi Chambers, Hoghton St., Southport, UK. Articles, poetry, fiction, cartoons, photos, satire, interviews, criticism, letters. *Material should not exceed 1,000 words. We require good clean* humor. Bi-monthly; 25p /ea; 1973; 44pp; 10x7½"; 10,000 circ; off. Reports 2 wks. Pay: good. Ads: £40/page pro rata. Discounts: none. Back issues: 15p.

HURON REVIEW, Walden Press, **Frank Hamilton,** 423 South Franklin Ave., Flint, MI 48503. Poetry, fiction. 2/yr (spring, fall); $2.50/yr; $1.25/ea; $1/sample; 1974; 36pp; 300 circ; lo. Reports 2 wks. Pays copies only. No ads. COSMEP.

HYACINTHS AND BISCUITS, Hummingbird Press, **Jane R. Card,** Box 392, Brea, CA 92621. Poetry, articles, art, satire, reviews. *Also use short biographical sketches of poets – short sketches of local scenes. Some recent contributors are: Paul Rider, Edna Fuchs, E.G. Eidenier, J. William Myers, William Dauenhaur, Pauline Barrese, Jesse Paul Reichman, Richard Latta.* 6/yr; $5/yr; $1/ea; $1/sample; 1969; 48pp; 5½x8½; 1M circ; lo. Reports 1 wk to 1 mo. Pays: $1–$10; 6 free copies with sub. Ads: class./wd. $4/inch. Discounts: 50%. Back issues: 50 cents. Pub'd 6 issues 1973, expects 6 in 1974; expects 1 book in 1974. COSMEP, Chicano, Black, Am. Indian, Prison.

HYPERION, Thorp Springs Press, **Paul Foreman, Judy Hogan, Foster Robertson,** 2311–C Woolsey, Berkeley, CA 94705. Poetry. 3-4/yr; $4/yr; $1/ea; $1/sample; sample free to impoverished poets who send postage; 1969; 60pp; 8½x5½; 2M circ; lo. Reports 2-6 mos. Pays: copies only; may be paying $2-5/p given upturn in fortunes. No ads; some announcements of poetry we think important. Discounts: 40% usual trade disc; inquire for classroom use. Back issues: inquire. Pub'd 3 issues 1973, expects 3 in 1974; 9 books 1973, expects 12 in 1974. COSMEP.

I. S. Publishing Company, (see Workers' Power)

THE IDLER, Editorial Associates, **James Parkhill-Rathbone,** The Old Crown, Crown Rd., Wheatley, Oxford, England.   Articles, poetry, art, photos, music, letters. *2000 words max. length; essay style, or letters. Recent contributors: Marina Vaizey, William Gerhardie, Peter Hutchison, Josephine Saxton, Margaret Haley, June South. Mood and style important-languid but observant. Material includes old engravings, woodcuts, ornamental initials, pendrawings. Each issue is carefully built around a possible quietist idea in which nothing is too humble to be a subject. Some material comes from medieval writing, eighteenth century writing, which is placed alongside contemporary work, not to compete but to supplement, the general effect being one of gentleness without sentiment. Though the* Idler *has a social conscience, it takes very little notice of ephemeral social preoccupations, is not political, is non-academic...but not escapist since what it deals in has been part of reality for several thousand years. Samuel Palmer did this in paint.* Irreg; 50p/sub; 12½p/ea; free sample; 1968; 8pp; 15x12½"; 1000 circ; Tabloid. Reports 4 wks. Pays: £3/1000 words; illustrations as agreed. Ads: by arrangement. Discounts: 10%.

Illuminations Press, **Norman Moser,** 1510 San Antonio No.1, Austin, TX 78701. Poetry, fiction articles, art, photos, cartoons, reviews, letters, longpoems, collages, plays. *Books scheduled only for '74-5.* No sample; 1965; lo. Reports 3-6 mos. Pays copies only. No discounts. Back issues: $75/Patron's Sub. − No. 2 Folio & all subsequent; No.3 mag=$25; No.4 mag=$15; $5 for 5 or more assorted tabloids, books, mags etc. Pub'd 1 issue, 1 book *(Jumpsongs)* 1973, expects 1-2 books in 1974. COSMEP, ALP, CCLM.

IMAGO, Beaver Kosmos, **George Bowering,** 2499 West 37th Ave., Vancouver, BC, Canada V6M 1P4. Poetry. *Imago 20, now at press, is a super issue, the final one. Beaver Kosmos Folios will continue to appear.* 2/yr; $1/ea; $1/sample; 1964; 48pp; 5x7; 400 circ; lo. Reports 2 wks. Pays copies only. No discounts. Back issues: $1. Pub'd 2 issues, 3 books 1973, expects 1 issue, 3 books in 1974.

IMK Publications (see MAYBE, Worlds of Fandom)

Impulse Publications Ltd., **Paul Harris,** 28 Guild St., Aberdeen AB9 2AE, UK. *Scottish non-fiction.*

IN-OUT PRODUCTIONS, **Ulises Carrion,** Reguliersgracht 103, Amsterdam, Netherlands. Language, poetry, art. *We are solely interested in language-oriented poetry as opposed to word-oriented poetry.* Mi. Pub'd 7 books 1973, expects 10 in 1974.

Inca Press (see also SUNTEMPLES), **Phil Silva,** PO box 769, La Jolla, CA 92037. *Inca Press is interested in publishing poetry, art & photography in its quarterly journal Suntemples and is always looking for new talent to publish in small paperback form. We are especially interested in publishing work that would have a general appeal, such as how-to pamphlets oriented to an audience seeking alternatives to a dehumanizing, unecological society. Looking for contributors and members for S.T.E.G.O. Newsletter and organization. STEGO is an acronym for the Save The Earth Guerilla Organization, and is an organization dedicated to propagating and promoting the ideas of Paolo Soleri, the founder of Arcology. We are willing to consider all manuscripts that are typed and accompanied by a stamped self-addressed envelope.*

INDEX ON CENSORSHIP, Writers and Scholars International Ltd., **Michael Scammell,** 35 Bow St., London WC2R 7AU, UK. Articles, poetry, fiction, news items, interviews, criticism, letters, longpoems. *The magazine offers an international and thorough approach to all types of censorship (censorship for political reasons mainly) from the Soviet crackdown on writers to the repression in Brazil and including England & Ireland. Each issue features 5 or 6 articles by writers, lawyers, teachers, poets, journalists; among contributors have been Solzhenitsyn,*

Nadine Gordimer, Don Tyerman, Anthony Smith, George Mangakis, Ludvik Vaculik, Josef Brodsky, Wolf Bierman and many others. *Also features* Index-Index, *a country by country chronicle of instances of repression. No political affiliation. Publishes poems, interviews and fiction by censored writers and academics.* 4/yr; £3/yr; 75p/ea;1972;120pp; 24x17 cm;1500 circ; lp. Reports 2 mos. Pays: £10/1000 words. Ads: £30/page pro rata. Discounts: none. Back issues: 60p until Jan. 1, '74, then 85p; pf. Censorship.

The Indian Historian Press, Inc., 1451 Masonic Ave., San Francisco, CA 94117. *Founded by the American Indian Historical Society, and its official publishing agency. We publish books and other informational materials by and about Native Americans.*

THE INDIAN PUBLISHER & BOOKSELLER, *Popular Book Depot Printing Division*, **Mrs. Nirmala Bhatkal, Mr. Sadanand Bhatkal**, c/o Popular Book Depot, Dr. Bhadkamkar Marg, Bombay 400 007, India. Articles, Photos, interviews, letters. Monthly; Rs20.00/yr; Rs2.00/ea;1950; 32pp; 25x18.50 cms; 3200 circ; lp. Ads. Rsl35/p; Rs70/½. Back issues: Rs45 complete set. Pub'd 12 issues 1973, expects 12 in 1974.

INDIGO—*The Voice of American Poets, Randall*, **Robert Rolf Randall; periodic guest editors**, Box 4976, Grand Central Sta., New York NY 10017. Poetry. *Poems with general interest themes around 35 lines by American poets. Address all correspondence to Randall at the above address.* Monthly; $1/ea; 1974; 30pp; 6x4; lp. Reports 1 wk. Pays copies only (2). Adv. not accepted. No discounts except to Randall reps. No back issues available. Expects 11 issues in 1974.

INDOCHINA FOCAL POINT, **Carol Kurtz, Paul Ryder, Susan Wind, Jack Nicholl**, 181 Pier Ave., Santa Monica, CA 90405. Poetry, articles, photos, cartoons, interviews, reviews. 2/mo; $4/yr; 10 cents/ea; free sample; 1973; 6pp; broadsheet; 6M circ; lo. Pay case by case. Pub'd 9 issues 1973. Anti-war.

INLET, **Bruce Guernsey**, Virginia Wesleyan College, Dept. of Eng., Norfolk, VA 23502. Poetry, fiction. *Short poems and fiction of all kinds, though we tend toward the traditional. Recent contributors include William Meredith, Dabney Stuart, Diane Wakoski, William Matthews. Handsomely printed on fine paper.* Mss. read from Sept-March, only. 1/yr; free; 1971; 36pp; 8½x8½;lp. Reports 1 mo. Pays 3 copies. No ads. Independent.

THE INQUIRER, *Inquirer Publishing Co. Ltd.*, **Fred M. Ryde**, 1-6 Essex St., London WC2, UK. Articles, poetry, photos, interviews, criticism, music, letters. *Articles not more than 1000 words on religious, ethical or social issues from a liberal and rational viewpoint.* Fortnightly; £2.40/yr; 4p/ea; free sample; 1842; 4pp; 17x12"; 3500 circ; off. Reports 1 wk. Pays: £5. Ads: 10p/line; £1/col. inch, £6/¼p.

INSIDE OUT MAGAZINE, *Aberdeen Peoples Press*, **Chrissy McKean, Tony Stark, Geoffrey Andrews, Drew Clegg**, 49 Meadowside, Dundee, Scotland, UK. Tel. 22940 or 643367. Articles, poetry, fiction, art, cartoons, photos, satire, news items, interviews, criticism, music, letters, longpoems. *Aberdeen Peoples Press print the magazine but we have smaller offset-litho facilities and run our own print-shop. We can print up to 12x8" (approx.) - business cards/letterheads/small books, etc.* Monthly; £1.70/yr; 10p/ea; 1973; 24pp; 12x8½"; 1500 circ; off. Ads: £20/page pro rata; 5p/word, Box no. 10p. Discounts: 25% shops/streetseller. Back issues: 5p. Women, Ecology, Occult, Black, Gay, SF, A.P.S.

INSIGHT MAGAZINE, *Insight*, **Deric R. James**, 118 Windham Rd., Bournemouth, Hants., UK. Articles, photos, satire, news items. *A magazine exploring the Occult* *in depth from the Intuitive angle. Contents include: Psychic research, Spiritualism, Comparative Religion, Witchcraft, Occult Fraternities, The Tarot, Ancient British Mysteries.* 4/yr; £1 ($4)/yr; 25pp ($1)/ea; free sample; 1965; 40pp; 9x6"; 5000 circ; off. Reports 2 wks. Pays: by negotiation. Ads: £5/page pro rata. Back issues: 17p. Occult.

INSIGHT PUBLICATIONS, **Jon M. Harvey,** 18 Cefn Rd., Mynachdy, Cardiff CF4 3HS, **Robert J. Curran,** 7 Lever Rd., Portstewart, Co. Derry, N. Ireland, UK. Poetry, fiction, art, cartoons, satire, longpoems. *We publish collections (both one-author and anthologies) of prose and/or poetry on any subject of suitable quality, as well as comics. Literary material length: anything short of novel length (30,000 word max.). Proposed publications for 1974.* Caedman Never had it as Good *by Gerald England;* Old Drunk Eyes Haiku and other Poems *by Briton Connors;* Please Preserve this Mo (nu) ment *by Rosamund Stanhope;* Lisbon Revisited *Pesoa tr., J.C.R. Green;* Where the Yahoos Are *by Gregory FitzGerald; and* Witch World 1 *(comic). Also in 1974/75 a Lovecraft Anthology* Spawn of the Unknown *edited by Paul Bergland featuring the work of American contributors.* 1974; off. Reports 1 mo. Pays copy only. No ads. Discounts: 25% on 10 or more.

INTAK, Yorkshire Poets' Association, **Hon. Sec. Lyn Cooper,** 24 Laverdene Dr., Totley Rise, Sheffield S17 4HH, UK. Annual: £1/membership; 25p px/ea; 1971; 28pp; 9x5"; 200 circ. Back issues: *Intak,* '71 and '72 @ 20p each.

Interim Books (see MAGAZINE (Six))

INTERMEDIA, Century City Educational Arts Project, **Harley W. Lond,** 10508 W. Pico Blvd., Los Angeles, CA 90064. Poetry, fiction, articles, art, photos, cartoons, interviews, satire, criticism, reviews, music, letters, parts-of-novels, longpoems, collages, plays, concrete art. *Hope to be out by Fall of this year. Start out as monthly cultural-art-resource-news-mag for Los Angeles specializing in listings/ reviews/criticisms of all art forms, including* Small Press Publishing, *performing arts, important resources for survival (government, welfare, cheap things, craftsmen, etc.). Hopefully a "whole-earth-yellow-page-resource-guide" of the arts and survival communications. Want fiction, graphics, etc. to round out each issue.* Monthly; 1974; lo. Reports as soon as possible. Pub'd none in 1973, expects 4 issues, 1974. COSMEP, News-mag.

INTERNATIONAL P.E.N. BULLETIN OF SELECTED BOOKS, English Centre of International P.E.N., **David Carver, Kathleen Nott, acting ed.,** 62-63 Glebe Place, London SW3, UK. *A bilingual (English-French) guide, backed by U.N.E.S.-C.O., to notable books belonging to literatures of lesser currency. Most numbers contain articles and reviews from several countries, but there have also been eleven special numbers devoted to one country, the most recent being on Bulgarian literature. A new series devoted to particular themes have been projected; the first two to Criticism and International Children's Books.* 4/yr; 68p($2.60)/yr; 17p/ea; 1950.

INTERNATIONAL TIMES, 286 Portobello Rd., London W11, UK. Articles, poetry, fiction, art, cartoons, photos, satire, news items, interviews, criticism, music, letters, collages, concrete. 26/yr; £4.80/yr; 15p/ea; free sample; 1966; 24pp; 15½ xll; 25,000 circ; off. Reports vary. Pay varies. Ads: £80/page pro rata; 5p/word. UAPS.

INTERPLANETARY NEWS, **Mike Parry, Alfred Edwards,** 15 Nealden St., Stockwell, London SW9 9QX, UK. Articles, fiction, art, cartoons, photos, interviews, criticism, letters. 12/yr; £2.16/yr; 18p/ea; 1957; 24pp; 8x6½; 300 circ; off. Reports 1 mo. Pay: negotiable. Ads: £1/page pro rata; 2p/word. Discounts: 33%. SF.

INTERSTATE, **Carl D. Clark, Loris Essary,** 4319 Airport Blvd., Austin, TX 78722. Poetry, fiction, articles, art, photos, satire, criticism, reviews, music, letters, parts-of novels, longpoems, collages, plays, concrete art. *All forms of creative acts are considered for publication, regardless of form or genre. We are not interested in critical or non-creative secondary work. Beginning with* Interstate Two, *a Supplement of Opinion will be included in the magazine in the form of insert to provide space for reviews, correspondence and information flow of all sorts. Contributors to* Interstate *include J. Michael Yates, Richard Kostelanetz, Larry Eigner and John Unterecker.* 4/yr; $4/yr; $1.50/ea; 1974. 56pp; 5½x8½; 300 circ. Reports 1-4 wks. Pays copies only. Ads: negotiable. Discounts: to merchandisers/none to libraries. COSMEP.

INTREPID, **Allen DeLoach,** PO Box 1423, Buffalo, NY 14214. Poetry, fiction, art, photos, interviews, criticism, letters, parts-of-novels, longpoems, collages, plays. *Please read the magazine before submitting mss.* Q; $5.50/4 issues; $/ea varies; free sample; 1964; 80pp; 8½x11; 1M circ; lo. Reports 3 mos. Pays copies only. No ads. Back issues: on request. Pub'd 4 issues 1973, expects 4 in 1974. COSMEP.

Intrepid Press (see 23 CLUB SERIES)

Intrepid Trips Information Service (see SPIT IN THE OCEAN)

INVISIBLE CITY, Red Hill Press (Los Angeles & Fairfax), **John McBride, Paul Vangelisti,** 6 San Gabriel Dr., Fairfax, CA 94930. Poetry. *Is a tabloid collection (on durable stock) of poetry, translations, reviews and statements, published whenever enough good material is available. Recently featuring Franco Fortini, Corrado Costa, Adriano Spatola, Franco Beltrametti, Rene Depestre and Mohammed Dib. Also original work and translations by: Mike Finley, Jack Hirschman, J.L. Mezzetta, Sam Hamill, Carolyn Stoloff, Robert Peters, Venantius Fortunatus, and others.* 3-4/yr; $2/3 issues; 1971; 16pp; 17x11; 1100 circ; lo. Reports 1 mo. Ads: none for sale. Back issues; full sets No.1-16=$20; some issues available singly or in bulk. Pub'd 3 issues 1973, expects 3 in 1974. COSMEP, CCLM.

THE IOWA REVIEW, 453 E.P.B., Univ. of Iowa, Iowa City, IA 52240.

IREGO, **Jack Libert,** PO Box 679 Lenox Hill Sta., NYC 10021. Fiction, satire, drama. 1965; of. Discounts: 40%; Wholesalers: 50%

IRISH BOOKLORE, Blackstaff Press Ltd. **Aiken McClelland, Jim Gracey, Diane Gracey,** 15 Donegall Square South, Belfast BT1 5JE, UK. Articles, criticism, letters. *Substantial articles (up to 25,000 words) on subjects of Irish literary and bibliographical interest. (Shorter items also). Reviews of Irish & bibliographical books. Notes and queries. Letters.* 2/yr; £2/yr; £1.40/ea; 1971; 150-200pp; 6x9½; 750 circ; lp. Reports varies about 2 mo. Pay: nil. Ads: £25/page; £14/½; £8/¼; 10% reduction/series. Discounts: trade subs. £1.80 + carriage. Back issues: all out of print. Irish Bibliography.

IRON, Iron Press, Tyneside, **Peter J.G. Mortimer,** 31 Beverly Terrace, Cullercoats, Northumberland, England, UK. Poetry, fiction, art, cartoons, photos, satire, plays, concrete. *Iron is primarily a literary magazine which attempts an even balance between prose and poetry. Short stories considered up to 5000 words. Poetry from one line upwards. Also keen to see graphic work (line drawings mainly). Centre pages often devoted to this. Visual side of* Iron *v. important, great use made of photos, art work etc; No political bias, but political literature always considered. No regional bias (first three editions contained work from Europe, Africa and America plus N.E. writers).* 4/yr; 60p/yr; 15p/ea; 1973; 36pp; A4; 700 circ; off.

Reports 1 wk. Pay: none—hope to pay from summer '74. No ads.

Iron Horse Publishing Co., **Michael Juliar,** PO Box 1182, Northland Center Sta., Southfield, MI 48075. *We are only publishing our own style of comic book, which we call* A Montage Book. *Our only author-artist is Sanho Kim. Each book is about 128 pages and is $1.50. We are not creating politically or satirically-oriented literature; we are trying to create a commercial product to entertain our readers. But it is very different in style, fromat, story telling, art technique than any other commercial comics or head comix. In fact, it is similar to many Oriental comic books.* 1973; lo. Discounts: trade, 40% (5 or more); bulk, agent: write to publisher. Pub'd 1 book 1973, expects 1 in 1974. Comic book oriented.

IRONWHORSEBOOKS, **PN, Wally & Linda Depew,** 819-17 St., Sacramento, CA 95814. *Each issue is a 8½x11 printed sheet cut into 16 relatively equal pieces – there are variations on this but it gives the general idea. We have done the printing for the first few but will prefer to consider printed (200 copies) material. We will then cut, collate & cover. Single copies 25 cents + postage. Or send a buck for a few.*

ISLANDS: A New Zealand Quarterly of Arts & Letters, **Robin Dudding,** 4 Sealy Road, Torbay, Auckland 10, New Zealand. *Prices listed are all for outside NZ and quoted in NZ dollars – payment preferably by bank draft because of exchange fluctuations.* Q; $7.50/yr; $2/ea; $2/sample; 1972; 112pp; 8½x6"; 2M circ; lo; 1p. Reports vary. Pay varies. Ads: $30/p; $18/½. Discounts: 33 1/3% trade for 2 or more; 20% of retail for agencies. Back issues: all at $2. Pub'd 4 issues 1973, expects 4 in 1974.

ISTHMUS, **J. Rutherford Willems,** 1429 Leavenworth No.303. San Francisco, CA 94109. Poetry, fiction, articles, art, photos, interviews, criticism, reviews, parts-of-novels, longpoems, plays. *Biases are for a marriage of phenomenology, kabbalah, surrealism, cubism, totemism, and biology.* 2/yr; $6/yr; $3/ea; $3/sample; 1971; 150pp; 7x10; 800 circ; lo. Reports 1-2 mos. Pays 2 copies. No ads. No discounts. Pub'd no issues, 2 books 1973, expects 3 issues in 1974.

Ithaca House, **Baxter Hathaway, Lynn Shoemaker, Jim Bertolino, David McAleavey, Bill Larson, Merry Forresta, Allen Forresta, Bob Minkoff,** 108 N. Plain St., Ithaca, NY 14850. Poetry, fiction. lo; 1p. Reports 3 mos. Pays copies only. Distributed by Serendipity Books (June 1, 1974). Pub'd 6 titles 1973, expects 12 in 1974. COSMEP.

J & C Transcripts (see JEAN'S JOURNAL)

J. Mark Press (see ALL-TIME FAVORITE POETRY, AMERICAN SCENES, BEST IN POETRY, POETRY OF OUR TIME, POETRY OF THE YEAR, POEMS OF SIGNIFICANCE)

JAM TO-DAY, **Poetry: Judith & Don Stanford, Floyd Stuart; Prose/reviews: Fred Cook,** PO Box 249, Northfield, VT 05663. Poetry, reviews. Prefer shorter poems, any style from traditional to avant garde. *We've published Harley Elliott, Hugh Fox, Milton Kessler, David Kherdian, Lyn Lifshin, David Smith, Dabney Stuart.* 2/yr; $2.50/yr; $1.50/ea; 1973; 48pp; 5½x8½; 300 circ; lo. Reports 3-6 wks. Pays 2 copies to each poet printed. Pub'd 1 issue 1973, expects 2 in 1974. COSMEP, NESPA.

JANUS–SCTH, Sangre de Cristo, **Rhoda de Long Jewell,** 1325 Cabrillo Ave., No. 12, Venice, CA 90291. Poetry, reviews. Q; $2.75/yr; 75 cents/ea; 75 cents/sample; 1964; 44pp; 5½x8; 750 circ; 1p. Reports 1 wk. Pub'd 4 issues 1973.

JEAN'S JOURNAL, J & C Transcripts, **Jean Calkins,** Box 15, Kanona, NY 14856. Poetry, articles, reviews, letters. *Only restriction is within the limitations of good taste.* Q; $5/yr; $1.25/ea; 50 cents/sample; 1963; 70pp; 5½x8½; 450 circ; mi. Reports 2 wks. Pays: awards only. Ads: $14/p; $7/½; 5 cents class./wd. Back issues: $1/ea. Pub'd 4 issues 1973, expects 4 in 1974; 23 books 1973. UPS.

THE JEFFERSONIAN REVIEW, **Frank Conneen III,** PO Box 3864, Charlottesville, VA 22903. Poetry, fiction, articles, art, photos, cartoons, reviews, parts-of-novels, longpoems, plays. *Like to see things from "unknown struggling writers," though we don't discriminate against the established. Have no limitations on length, style, etc. No concrete biases, material accepted depends on changing moods of the editors.* 6/yr; $5/yr; $1/ea; $1/sample; 1973; 96pp; 6x9; 1M circ; lo. Reports 2-4 wks. Pays copies only. Ads: $40/p; $20/½; $10/¼. Discounts: 25%. Pub'd 3 issues, 1 book 1973; expects 6 issues, 1 book 1974. COSMEP.

JEFFREY, Bluffridge Ltd., **Michael Anderson, Alex McKenna,** PO Box 804, London W4, UK. Articles, cartoons, photos, letters. *Gay fiction and information. Gay personal ads, and photos.* Monthly; £3/yr; 75p/ea; 60p/sample; 1972; 48pp; 3000 circ; off. Pay: variable. Ads: 5p per wd. Gay.

JEWEL OF AFRICA, International House 5-13, Univ. of Zambia, Box 2379, Lusaka, Rep. of Zambia, Africa.

JOHNSONIAN NEWS LETTER, **James L. Clifford, John H. Middendorf,** 610 Philosophy Hall, Columbia Univ., New York, NY 10027. *We use news items and short articles up to 300 words – all dealing with the 18th century.* 4/yr; $3/yr; US; $3.50/yr foreign; $1/ea; 1940; 12pp; 1100 circ; lo. Reports mo. or so. No pay. No ads. No discounts. Back issues. $1/issue. Pub'd 4 issues 1973.

John Jones Cardiff Ltd., **John Idris Jones,** 41 Lochaber St., Cardiff CF2 3LS, UK. *Mostly a) sport and b) books written in Welsh background. Factual sports handbooks, illustrated about 15,000 words.* off. Reports 2 wks. Pays: royalties + 20 free copies. Discounts: 33% trade; 20% singles. ALP.

JOURNAL OF COMMONWEALTH LITERATURE, Oxford University Press for the University of Leeds, **Arthur Ravenscroft,** School of English, Univ. of Leeds, Leeds LS2 9JT, UK. Articles, interviews, criticism. *Subscriptions to Oxford Univ. Press, Subscription Dept., Press Rd., Neasden, London NW10 ODD.* 3/yr; £3.50/yr; 95p/sample; 1965; 100pp; 5½x8½"; 1000 circ. Reports 2 mos. Pays: articles £4/1000 words; reviews £3/1000 wds. Back issues: £1.30 (1973); 90p (1970-1972) px. Third World.

JOURNAL OF MODERN LITERATURE, **Maurice Beebe,** Temple Univ., Philadelphia, PA 19122. Articles, interviews, criticism, reviews. 5/yr; $8/yr; $2/ea; sample; 1970; 160pp; 7x10; 2200 circ; lo. Reports 6 wks. Pays: $100/articles. No ads. Pub'd 3 issues 1973, expects 5 in 1974. COSMEP.

JOURNAL OF NARRATIVE TECHNIQUE, **George Perkins, Paul Bruss, David Geherin, Jay Jernigan, Paul McGlynn, Ronald Trowbridge,** English Dept. Eastern Michigan Univ., Ypsilanti, MI 48197. Criticism. *JNT is a scholarly magazine with a small international circulation. Essays run generally from 15 to 25 typed pages. Contributors should follow MLA style.* 3/yr; $3/yr; $1/ea; 1970; 65pp; 6x9. Reports 1-4 mos. Pays copies only. No ads.

JOURNAL 31, Smoking Mirror Press, **David Plumb, Robert Spence,** Box 2109, San Francisco, CA 94126. *We have recently decided to publish* Journal 31 *as an annual with more pages & more prose. We are doing this in order to devote time to* *other projects i.e. chapbooks, broadsheets etc. We are looking for experiment prose but will read everything that comes our way. Prefer not more than 350 words. We will continue to publish poetry & all ms. will receive personal attention in the way of personal reply.* Recent contributors: Ron McClure, Faye Kicknosway, Nancy Kline, Robert Peters, Wayne Miller, Bob Kaufman, Sergei Yessenin, Paul Mariah, Dan Propper, Doug Blazek. Annual; $4.50/yr; $1.25/ea; $1/sample; 1972; 120p; pg size varies; 500-600 circ; lo. Reports 1-30 days. Pays: token or copies. Ads: $50/pg; $25/½pg. Discounts: 30% classroom. Back Issues: No.1 $5; No.2 $3. Pub'd 1 issue 1973, expects 1 in 1974; 1 book 1973, expects 3 in 1974. CCLM.

JOURNAL OF WORLD EDUCATION, **Mrs. Leah R. Karpen,** 3 Harbor Hill Dr., Huntington, NY 11743. Poetry, articles, art, photos, cartoons, interviews, reviews, letters. *Articles run between 250 and 1000 words. Authors should request a back issue for style. Seeking especially cross-cultural experiences by students.* Recent contributors: Ronald Gross, Nobuo Shimahara, many others. Q; $5/yr students, $10/yr libraries, $15/yr (membership) individuals; $1/sample; 1970; 16p; 8½x11; 4M circ; of. Reports 1 mo. No pay. Ads: on request; class/wd $5/line. Back issues: $1/ea if available; also on microfilm. Pub'd 4 issues 1973, expects none in 1974. Education.

Journeyman Press, **Emil Antonucci,** PO Box 4434, Grand Central Sta., New York, NY 10017. Poetry, art. *My press has been exclusively devoted to works of Robert Lax. Hope to do some other poets some day, but Lax work so fine, and I am in such deep rapport with it usually, that it is perfect verbal expression of all I want to do in book design. I am an artist rather than editor & press is really not a literary activity in usual sense. Therefore, I don't solicit any mss.* 1959. Expects 3 issues in 1974.

Juniper Press (see Northeast/Juniper Books)

Kanchenjunga Press, **Miki Sheffield (Ms.),** 22 Rio Vista Lane, Red Bluff, CA 96080. Poetry. *Publications to date: Robert Bringhurst,* The Shipwright's Log *(1972); Kerry Shawn Keys,* Swallowtails Gather These Stones *(1973); Robert Bringhurst,* Cadastre *(1973). U.S. Distributor for the Sono Nis Press of Vancouver, BC, Canada. Titles in production for release in 1974: Kerry Shawn Keys,* JadeWater. 1972; lo. Discount: 40% to bkstores and distributors. Pub'd 2 books 1973, expects 3 in 1974. COSMEP.

Kansas State Printer (see THE MIDWEST QUARTERLY)

The Kanthaka Press, **Alex Jack,** 246 Tappan St., Brookline, MA 02146. *First book 1974 is* 221A Baker Street: The Adamantine Sherlock Holmes, *by Hapi, from the Coptic* The Victorian Book of the Dead. *A study of racialism in Watson's account and new adventures of Holmes in Tibet & a Mahayanist masterspy in London. 144 pages illus., offset, paperback, $2.95 postpaid, 40% trade discount.* 1973. COSMEP.

KARAMU, **Allen Neff, Carol Elder, Gordon Jackson,** Eng. Dept., Eastern Illinois Univ., Charleston, IL 61920. Poetry, fiction, art, criticism, parts-of-novels, longpoems. 1-2/yr; $1/ea; $1/sample; 1966; 75-80pp; 5x7"; 300 circ; lo. Reports up to several mos. Pays copies only. No ads. Back issues: samples on request. Pub'd 1 issue 1973.

Norman Kark Publications (see LONDON MYSTERY MAGAZINE)

KAYAK, Kayak Books, **George Hitchcock,** Bonny Doon Rd., Santa Cruz, CA 95060. Poetry, short prose, critical articles, Q; $4/yr; $1/ea; 1964; 72p; 5½x8½; 1400 circ; of. Reports 2 wks. Pays copies only. Ads: $40/p; $20/½. Discounts: standard. Back issues: $2/ea. Pub'd 4 issues, 2 books 1973; expects 4 issues, 3 books in 1974. CCLM.

KEEPSAKE POEMS, Keepsake Press, **Shirley Toulson, Roy Lewis,** 26 Sydney Rd., Richmond, Surrey, UK. Poetry. 8/yr; £1.75/yr; 25p/ea; 1972; 4pp; 8½x6¾; 180 circ; off; lp. Reports 2-3 wks. Pays: by agreement. No ads. Discounts: 33% 2 or more copies. ALP.

Kenfig Press, **Arthur Smith,** 41 Heol Fach, Cornelly, Pyle, Glamorgan CF33 4LN, UK. Articles, poetry, fiction, art, cartoons. 4pp; 8x6½; 150 circ; mim. Pays copies only. BAPA.

KENT: Journal of The Men of Kent and Kentish Men, **Alan Rye,** Cornwallis House, Pudding Lane, Maidstone, Kent., UK. 4/yr.

KENTUCKY FOLKLORE RECORD, Kentucky Folklore Society, **Charles S. Guthrie,** Box 169, Western Kentucky Univ., Bowling Green, KY 42101. Articles, photos, reviews, music. *Articles: 500-3000 words; expository style; related to some phase of folklore, preferably that of Kentucky. Use MLA Style Sheet for documentation. Reviews: Reviews of books having some bearing on some phase of folklore, preferably that of Kentucky. Music and songs: Original collections from oral tradition, preferably annotated according to Child, Bronson, Laws, or some other standard collection.* Q; $3/yr; 75 cents/ea; free sample; 1955; 24p; 5¾ x 8¾; 400 circ; of. Reports 4 wks+. Pays copies only. Discounts: 25% to agents & trade only, none to others. Back issues: vols. 6-18 complete $28.

KIL-KAAS-GIT, **Tamara Smid, advisor,** Box 166, Craig, AK 99921. Poetry, articles, art, photos, interviews. *Magazine records Tlinget & Haida culture, crafts, legends, etc. Material is collected by students through interviews & observation.* 4/yr; $6/yr; $2/ea; 1973; 48pp; 8½x11; 500 circ. Reports: not available. No pay. No ads. No discounts. Back issues: $2. Pub'd 2 issues 1973, expects 3 in 1974. American Indian.

KINESIS, **Virginia Kidd,** Box 278, Milford, PA 18337. Poetry. *Behind and overstocked — no submissions accepted in 1974 (until I deal with backlog).* Irreg; 50 cents/ea; 24pp; 8½x11; 100 circ; mi. Reports same day — usually, not always but I try. Pays copies only. No ads. Back issues: all out of print. COSMEP.

THE KIPLING JOURNAL, **Roger Lancelyn Green, B. Litt: M.A. (Oxon),** The Kipling Society, 18 Northumberland Ave., London WC2N 5BJ, UK. Articles. *Published for members of The Kipling Society and concerned entirely with his life and works. Articles up to 2,500 words.* Q;£1.75/yr; 1927; 24pp; 5½x8½; 1000 circ.

Kirkwall Press (see ORCADIAN)

Kitchen Sink Enterprises (see DEATH RATTLE, SNARF, WEIRD TRIPS MAGAZINE)

KNOW NEWS SERVICE, Know Inc., PO Box 86031, Pittsburgh, PA 15221.

KONGLOMERATI, **Richard Mathews,** 5719 29th Ave. South, Gulfport, FL 33707. Poetry, fiction, art, cartoons, music, parts-of-novels, longpoems, plays, concrete art. *Recent contributors: Gerard Malanga, Richard Kostelanetz, Peter Meinke, Anne Waldman, Lyn Lifshin, F.A. Nettelbeck, and the konglomerati.* 2/yr; $2.50/yr; $1.50/ea; 1971; 60pp; 300 circ; lo;lp. Reports 2 wks, but varies. Pays copies only. Discounts: 40% over 10 copies. COSMEP.

Konocti Books (see SIPAPU)

KONTEXTS, Kontexts Publications, **Michael Gibbs,** 31 Pinhoe Rd., Exeter, Devon, UK. Concrete. *Kontexts is devoted primarily to concrete/experimental poetry from all over the world. Recent contributors: Jiri Valoch, Ian Breakwell, Jochen Gerz, Robert Lax, John Giorno.* Irreg; £1($4)/yr; 30p($1)/ea; 1969; 40pp; mostly A5; 250 circ; mim; off. Ads: on application. Discounts: 33% on 6 or more. Back issues: issue 2: 20p(50 cents); issues 1 & 3 out of print. ALP.

KRAX, **G.A. Rhodes, A. Robson, D. Pruckner,** Flat 3, 60 York Place, Harrogate, Yorkshire, UK. Articles, poetry, fiction, satire, longpoems, plays, concrete. £1/sub; 18p/ea; 1972; 16pp; 8¼x6"; 300 circ; off. Reports approx. 1 mo. No pay. Ads: £2/page pro rata. Discounts: 15p wholesale. Poetry.

KROKLOK, Writers Forum, **Dom Silvester Houedard,** 262 Randolph Ave., London W9, UK. Articles, sound poetry, concrete. *This is intended to be an anthology of concrete/sound poetry to be completed in 21 issues. 3 issues to date.* Irreg; £1/yr; 25p/ea; 1971; 32pp; A4; 500+ circ; mim. Discounts: trade 33%. ALMS.

Kropotkin's Lighthouse Publications, **Jas. Huggon,** c/o Houseman's Bookshop, 5 Caledonian Rd., London N1, UK. Poetry, anarchy, pacifism. *Pamphlets, posters and postcards have been produced, and a Calendar. 2 pamphlets in 1973, hopefully 3 in 1974.* 1968; mim; off; lp. Discounts: 33% px; libraries 10% px. ALP, Anarchy, Pacifism, Poetry.

KUKSU Press (see KYOI/KUKSU: A Journal of Backcountry Writing)

Kulchur Foundation, **Lita Hornick,** 888 Park Ave., New York, NY 10021. Poetry, fiction, art, photos, cartoons, parts-of-novels, longpoems, concrete art. 128pp; 7½ x10; lp. Pays: $500. Discounts: 40% bookstores; 20% libraries. Pub'd 2 books 1973, expects 2 in 1974. COSMEP, Women.

KYOI/KUKSU: A Journal of Backcountry Writing, KUKSU Press, **Dale Pendell,** Alleghany Star Route, Nevada City, CA 95959. Poetry, fiction, articles, art, photos, interviews, reviews, music. *Some criticism, letters and plays. Mostly unknown west coast poets & writers. Emphasis on back-country, rural material – but consider any material of quality, especially if connected thematically, spiritually, or politically (?), with what.(ever) we, the rivers, & the pinetrees are up to out here. Recent contributors: Gary Snyder, Vinson Brown, Steve Sanfield, James Ekedal, Steve Levine ...* 2/yr; $5/yr; $1/ea; 1972; 64pp; 6x8½; 1M circ; lo. Reports 1 wk-1 mo. Pays copies only. Ads: $30/p; $20/½. Discounts: trade, bulk, agent: 40%; prisons, asylums, etc: upon request, tho appreciate stamps. Back issues: *KYOI No.2*/50 cents. Pub'd 1 issue 1973, expects 2 in 1974. COSMEP, Ecology, American Indian, Backcountry.

L MAGAZINE, **Curtis Faville,** 2021 Francisco No.301, Berkeley, CA 94709. Poetry, articles, photos, criticism, reviews. *As yet, only poetry has been printed. Plans to do other things – in the wings.* 2/yr; price/yr varies; price/ea varies; 1971; 45-50pp; 7x7; 300 circ; lo. Reports 1 wk. Pays 2 copies per contribution. Discounts: 40% trade. Pub'd 1 issue 1973.

THE LADDER, **Ms. Gene Damon,** PO Box 5025, Washington Sta., Reno, NV 89503. Poetry, fiction, articles, art, photos, cartoons, interviews, satire, criticism, reviews, music, letters, parts-of-novels, longpoems, plays. *Material must pertain to women, with primary emphasis on lesbians. Recent work by poets: Lynn Strongin, Rita Mae Brown, Martha Shelley, Rochelle Holt. Recent fiction by: Jane Rule, F. Ellen Isaacs, Rochelle Holt. Art column by: Sarah Whitworth. Art by: Georgia O'Keeffe, Romaine Brooks, Audrey Flack, etc.* 6/yr; $7.50/yr; $1.25/ea; 1956; 56pp; 5¼x8¼; 1750+ circ; photo of. Reports 15 days. Pays copies only. Ads: $80 /p; $45/½.

LAISSEZ FAIRE, Ember Press (Epping), **William Oxley, John David Beugger,** 27 Brook Rd., Epping, Essex, England, UK. Criticism. Irreg; 10p/ea.

Lake Grove Printing (see SAILING THE ROAD CLEAR)

THE LAKE SUPERIOR REVIEW, **Cynthia Willoughby,** Box 724, Ironwood, MI 49938. 3/yr; $2.75/yr; $1/ea; $1/sample; 1969; 48pp; 600 circ. Reports 6-8 wks. Pays 2 copies. Ads: $100/p; $50/½. Discounts: 10% off on 20 or more books. Back issues: $2/ea. Pub'd 3 issues 1973, expects 3 in 1974. COSMEP, CCLM.

Lame Johnny Press (see SUNDAY CLOTHES)

THE LAMP IN THE SPINE, **Patricia Hampl, James Moore,** PO Box 3372, St. Paul, MN 55165. Poetry, fiction, articles, art, photos, interviews, satire, criticism, reviews, longpoems. *Committed to publishing essays on poetry, politics, feminism and psychology – and how all these relate to each other. A continuing feature, "American Poetry in and out of the Cave" by co-ed James Moore has discussed the work of Kinnell, Merwin, Wright, Levertov and Ignatow. Other essays (by co-editor Patricia Hampl) on women writers and (by Eqbal Ahmad) on the Vietnam War and (by Dr. W.D. Roll) on parapsychology. Many long poems. Contributors include Robert Bly, Kathleen Fraser, Thomas McGrath, Wendell Berry, Gregory Orr, Marge Piercy, Sonya Dorman, Wm. Matthews but especially many young poets, not well known. We used an authors payment grant from CCLM to commission 2 essays and to run an essay contest in order to show our interest in this form.* 3/yr; $3/yr; $1/ea; 1971; 108pp; 5½x8½; 900 circ; of. Reports: we try for 2 wks. Pays 5 copies. Ads: inquire; we have had no ads so far. Back issues: $1/ea as long as they last (No.3 and No.5 are out of print). COSMEP, CCLM.

LASER, **Brian Meek, Philip Hemelryk, Philip Vince,** 58b Fellows Rd., Hampstead, London NW3 3LJ, UK. *Articles on effect of technology on society. Recent contributors: Magnus Pyke, Prof. Arnold Bender and Cesare Marchetti of Euratom.* 4/yr; £1/yr; 25p/ea; 40pp; qto; 200 circ; off. No pay. Ads: £25/page. Ecology.

LAST FLY, Bridgewest Publications, **Derek Telling, John Clements,** 2 Silveys Cottages, Catbrain Lane, Bristol BS10 7TJ, UK. Poetry, fiction, art, longpoems. *Last Fly is a new magazine concerned with the image as a new reality, i.e. used to disturb often impossible fantasies evoking possible truths within the images' framework. First issue includes Penelope Shuttle, Denis Goacher, Peter Redgrove, Henry Graham, Nicki Jackowska, Paul Matthews, Martin Booth, Derek Brake. Also published "Peace Poster" designed by Terry Wiltshire in red and gold, 15p. "Honourable Discharge" a booklet by John Clement, 25p.* 1/yr; 40p($1.75)/ea; 1973; 56pp; 8x6"; off. Discounts: 33% (3 or more). ALP.

Latimer New Dimensions Ltd., **John L. Smith,** 104 Earl's Court Rd., London W8 6EG, UK. Art, cartoons, photos, music. *Also: theatre, mazes, occult, architecture, crafts, alternative living. In 1973 five books were published. We anticipate 12-15 in 1974.* 1970. ALP.

The Laurel Press (see OPENSPACES)

LAVA: An International Journal of Modern Poetry, **G.P. Vimal,** 26/53 W.E.A., New Delhi-110005, India. *We are an international magazine and will be publishing poetry of all the countries in English translation. We are looking forward for poetry, subscription, donations and ideas for* Lava. $10/yr. Pays copies only; plan to give prizes for good poetry. *Every contribution must include International (Postal) reply coupons.*

Lavender Press, PO Box 60206, 1723 W. Devon, Chicago, IL 60660. *Has published 2 anthologies of lesbian poetry and graphics.* Thunder From The Earth *is still available at $1.50/copy. Plans to publish a lesbian novel by an established writer and 2 collections of poetry by individual women poets during 1974. Other possibilities are a songbook and a book of graphics.*

LAVENDER WOMAN, **we are a collective,** PO Box 60206, 1723 W. Devon, Chicago, IL 60660. Poetry, articles, art, photos, interviews, reviews, letters, longpoems. *We solicit material only from women and it must deal with issues which are relevant to lesbians.* Every 6 wks; $8/yr instit; $4/yr individual; 50 cents/ea; 65 cents/ea outside Chicago; 1971; 16pp; 10x15; 1500 circ; lo. Reports 6 wks-2 mos. Pays copies only. Ads: $5 up to 50 words class/wd. Discounts: bulk orders keep 15 cents for every copy sold. Back issues: institutions: Vol.I=$2/issue; Vols.II&III =$1/issue.; individuals: Vol.I=$1/issue; Vols.II&III=50 cents/issue. Pub'd 7 issues 1973, expects 8 in 1974. Women, Gay.

League of Socialist Artists, **Maureen Scott,** 18 Camberwell Church St., London SE5, UK. Articles, poetry, art, cartoons, criticism, longpoems, plays. *Marxist-Leninist, Socialist, progressive arts, artists, theoretical, agitational. Socialist poets, Socialist Artists, Socialist film.* Odd times; free sample; 1972; 20pp; A4; 500 circ; off. Reports 1 wk. Discounts: 33% bookshops/agents. Arts.

LEAVES OF TWIN OAKS, Twin Oaks Publications, **Pammy Wammy,** Twin Oaks Community, Louisa, VA 23093. Poetry, articles, art, photos, letters. *Most of the material is written by the members of Twin Oaks, an experimental community of 50 people living on a farm in Louisa, VA. It describes what life on a rural commune is like, and we see it as an important contribution to the community movement.* Bi-monthly; $3/yr; 50 cents/ea; 1967; 16pp; 8½x11; 900 circ; of. Reports: n/a. No pay. No ads. Pub'd 5 issues 1973, expects 6 in 1974. COSMEP.

LEEDS STUDENT, Regent Press, **Ian Coxon,** 155 Woodhouse Lane, Leeds, UK. Cartoons, photos, news items, interviews, criticism, letters. *Student orientated. Financed by advertising and grants from Leeds Polytechnic and Leeds University Students Unions. Aimed at all students in higher education in Leeds.* Weekly in term; £2/yr; 3p/ea; 1970; 12pp; 10x14"; 4000 circ; lp. No pay. Ads: £90/page; £1.15/col. inch. Discounts: 20% series of 10.

Leicester University Students Union (see RIPPLE)

L'ESPRIT CREATEUR, Artes Graficas Soler, S.A. (Valencia), **John D. Erickson,** Box 222, Lawrence, KS 66044. Articles, interviews, criticism, reviews. *We are interested in the critical interpretation of French Literature. Each issue presents analyses of the literary production of a single author or works falling within a literary movement or mode. We are interested in the investigation of non-literary phenomena and in the history of literature only secondarily. We look with interest on the new trends in methods of critical analysis in France and invite works using those methods as well as more traditional methods that hold the text as primary. Length of articles: 4000 max; reviews of critical works on French lit: 700* *words*. Q; $4/yr; $1.25/ea; 1961; 90pp; 26x42 picas; 1100 circ; lp. Reports 3-6 mos. Pays 5 copies to author. Ads: $60/p (1 time); $40/½; no class/wd. Discount: 10% to sub. agents. Back issues: all $1.25, except summer 1971 ($3.50).

LEWIS CARROLL CIRCULAR, **Trevor Winkfield**, 14 Wesley Rd., Leeds 12, UK. *An occasional publication of hitherto scarce, unpublished or "lost" Carrolliana.* Occasional; £1($3)/ea; 1973; 60 circ.

THE LEY HUNTER, **Paul Screeton,** 5 Egton Drive, Seaton Carew, Hartlepool, Co. Durham TS25 2AT, UK. Articles. *A magazine of ancient skills and wisdom, dealing with leys, megaliths, folklore, cosmology and UFOs. The forum for "live" archaeology.* Monthly; £1.50/yr; 13p/ea; 1969; 12pp; A4; 270 circ; mim. Reports 1 mo. Pay: nil. Ads discouraged. Discounts: 33%. Occult.

LIBERAL NEWS, Liberal Party Organisation, **Philip Young,** 7 Exchange Court, Strand, London WC2R OPR, UK. Articles, cartoons, photos, news items, interviews, criticism, letters. 26/yr; £1.95/yr; 6p/ea; free sample; 1946; 8pp; 17x11½; 8,500 circ; off. Reports 7 days. Pay: varies. Ads: £65/page; £35/½; 3p/word (box nos. 10p). Discounts: wholesale newsagents 40%; library agents 10%. Back issues: 10p.

LSM (Liberation Support Movement) Press, PO Box 94338, Richmond, BC, Canada V6Y 2A8. LSM *publishes books and pamphlets on the liberation struggles in Africa and on imperialism. We also reprint the offical movement bulletins:* Mozambique Revolution, Angola In Arms, PAIGC Actualities, Zimbabwe Review *and* Namibia News *for North American distribution. Details for* Mozambique Revolution *are below, but information applies generally for other periodicals.* Q; $3/yr; 75 cents/ea; no sample; 1968; 36pp; 8½x11; 1M circ. No ads. Discounts: bookstores & organizations: 50% disc. with standing orders of 10 copies per bulletin or more. Back issues: $1/ea (published Q since 1971). Pub'd 5 issues (12 total), 8 books 1973; expects 4 issues (20 total), 11 books in 1974. Third World.

LIBERTARIAN STRUGGLE, **rotating editorship amongst local ORA groups,** Production Collective, 63 Middleton St., Hull., UK. Cartoons, photos, news items, interviews, letters. *Monthly paper of the Organisation of Revolutionary Anarchists: to make libertarianism relevant in the class struggle.* Monthly; £1/yr; 5p px/ea; 1973; 8pp; A2; 2000 circ; off. Reports 3 wks. Ads: free to libertarians.

LIBRARIANS FOR SOCIAL CHANGE, **John Noyce,** 67 Vere Rd., Brighton, Sussex, England, UK. Articles, poetry, art, cartoons, news items. *Shortest articles. We try to relate librarianship to what is going on in the world. A group of radical librarians having the same name has been formed.* 3/yr; 60p/yr individuals; 80p/yr libraries; £1.50/yr overseas; 20p/ea; 1972; 30pp; A4; 400+ circ; mim; off. Reports 2-3 wks. Ads: on application. Discounts: library agents 25%; bookshops 33% 5 or more. ALP, Librarianship.

LIBRARY HISTORY, **Miss A.M. Pryde,** Middle Temple Library, London EC4Y 9BT, UK. Articles, bibliographies, criticism. 2/yr; £1.50($5)/yr.

LIBRARY REVIEW, **W.R. Aitken,** W & R Holmes (Books), 98-100 Holm St., Glasgow, UK. 4/yr; £1.80/yr. Pays: £4.50/1500 words.

LIGHT: A Poetry Review, **Roberta C. Gould,** Box 1105, Stuyvesant Sta., New York, NY 10009. Poetry. *The poem makes it — prefer shorter poems — concise writing.* 3/yr; $3/yr; $1.15/ea; $1/sample; 1973; 64pp; 5x6; 1M circ; lo. Reports: 3 mos. Pays copies only. No ads. Discounts: bookstore, 65 cents (35% off), over 5 copies. COSMEP, 3rd World, Women, Chicano, Black, Food/Ecology, American Indian, Gay.

Light, Powder and Construction Works (see POWDER MAGAZINE)

Limestone Press, **Charles Hine**, 71 Elmgrove Ave., Providence, RI 02906. Intermittent; $10/ea; no sample; 1971. Pays some copies. No ads. Discounts: 40%. Expects 6 books 1974. Third World, Food/Ecology, American Indian, Nomadic.

LINES REVIEW, **Robin Fulton**, M. MacDonald, Edgefield Rd., Loanhead, Midlothian, Scotland, UK. Poetry, criticism, longpoems. *Catchment area basically Scottish: occasional features in translation from Europe.* 4/yr; $3/yr; $1/ea; 1952; 50-60pp; 8½x5½; 700 circ; lp. Reports: by return. Pays: by arrangement. Ads: by arrangement. Discounts: 30% trade.

Lionhead Publishing (see ROAR)

LITERARY SKETCHES, 707 Monumental St., Williamsburg, VA 23185.

THE LITERARY SUPPLEMENT, Nothing doing (formally in London), **Anthony Barnett**, Editorial: Johan Grundt Tanum, Karl Johans gate 43, Oslo 1, Norway; Subs: Publisher, 25 Woodhall Dr., London SE21 7HJ, UK. Literary texts. *Gratis to persons px. Libraries – prepaid subscription: rate for nos. 1-99* £30 or $95 by air. 12 issues published in 1973. Literary texts in any language and in translation. Previously unpub. work only. Contributors in '73: Auster, Blanchot, Borges, du Bouchet, Casares, Chaloner, des Forets, Gjerstad, Grossinger, Haslam, Jabes, Laporte, MacSweeney, Oliver, Philpott, Riley, Ruberg, Waldrop. Irreg; 1972; 4pp; A4; 150 circ; mim or off. Reports immediate. Pays: copies. Literature.

THE LITERARY SUPPLEMENT–WRITINGS, Nothing doing (formally in London), **A. Barnett**, consultants: **J.H. Prynne, C. Royet-Journoud, R. Waldrop,** 25 Woodhall Dr., London SE21 7HJ, UK. Literary texts. *No.1 contains: Jabes,* Answer to a Letter *(trans. Waldrop); J.H. Prynne,* Es lebe der Konig *(in English); Paul Celan,* Conversation in the Mountains *(trans. Waldrop). No.1 has 20pp. Price: £1.95 or $4.95. Series not on sub. Individual orders only on pub. of each.* 1/yr; 1973; 9x6¼; 200 (print) circ; lp. Reports: no unsolicited mss. Literature.

LITERATURE & IDEOLOGY, Progressive Books & Periodicals, Ltd., The National Publ. Ctr., PO Box 727, Adelaide Sta., Toronto 210, Canada.

LITMUS, **Charles Potts**, 574 3rd Ave., Salt Lake City, UT 84103. Irreg; $5/yr; 64pp; 500+ circ. Reports immediately. Pays copies only. No ads. Back issues: inquire. Pub'd 1 book 1973, expects 3 in 1974. COSMEP.

LITTACK, Ember Press (Epping), **William Oxley**, 27 Brook Rd., Epping, Essex, England, UK. Articles, poetry, fiction, art, satire, interviews, criticism, letters, longpoems. *No bias on length; quality only criteria. Contributors: Robert Graves, Kathleen Raine, Ian Hamilton Finlay, Hugh MacDiarmid, Lawrence Durrell, Walter Perries, Richard Burns, Anthony Johnson, Ronald Duncan, Anthony Rudolf, Hugo Manning, Duncan Glen, Tom Scott, David Jaffin, Cal Clothier, Kathleen Abbott. Objective: to establish a climate of new poetics for U.K.* 2/yr; £1($4)/yr; 40p($2)/ea; 1972; 100pp; 8½x6"; 400 circ; off. Reports: US 1 mo. UK 1 wk. Pay: negotiable. Ads: £25/page pro rata. Discounts: 33½% trade. Back issues: set of 1-5/£10.

THE LITTLE REVIEW, **John McKernan**, PO Box 2321, Huntington, WV 25724. 2/yr; $2.50/yr; $1.25/ea; 1969; 32pp; 8½x11; 800 circ. Reports wk-mo. Pays copies. No discounts. COSMEP. Poetry.

LITTLE WORD MACHINE, **Nick Toczek,** 103 Moorhead Lane, Shipley, Yorkshire, UK. Articles, poetry, fiction, art, photos, interviews, criticism, concrete. 4/yr; £1/yr; 28p/ea; 1972; 50-60pp; 5½x8; 1000 circ; off. Reports 2 mos. Pays: 1-2 copies. Ads: £12/page pro rata.

Liverpool Free Press Group (see HARD CHEESE)

LIVING BLUES, Living Blues Publications, **Jim & Amy O'Neal,** PO Box 11303, Chicago, IL 60611. Articles, art, photos, cartoons, interviews, satire, criticism, reviews, music, letters. *Features & interviews on the black American blues tradition: 1000 words & up. Reviews: 200-500 words. Recent contributors: Pete Welding, Paul Oliver, Dave Alexander, Eric Kriss.* Q; $2.40/yr; 75 cents/ea by mail, 60 cents/ea newsstand; 1970; 40pp; 8¼x10½; 3500 circ; lo. Reports 2-8 wks. Pays: $10-$25; copies only for reviews. Ads: $75/p; $45/½; 10 cents class/wd. Discounts: write for ad rate card. Disc. for 3 or more ads. Back issues: 75 cents/ea. Pub'd 4 issues 1973, expects 4 in 1974.

Llewellyn Publications (see GNOSTICA NEWS)

LOCUS, Locus Publications, **Charles & Dena Brown,** Box 3938, San Francisco, CA 94119. Reviews. *Magazine subtitle:* The Newspaper of the Science Fiction Field. Bi-weekly; $6/18 issues individual; $10/yr library; 40 cents/ea; 40 cents/sample; 1968; 4-10pp; 8½x11; 2M circ; lo. No unsolicited material. Ads: $60/p; $40/½. Discounts: 40% off, plus postage, on 10 or more copies. Back issues: 25 cents, but not current year. Pub'd 24 issues 1973, expects 24 in 1974. COSMEP, Newspaper, Science-fiction.

LOL, Welsh magazine, printed (offset) and printed (1st August) by Y Lolfa, Talybont, Ceredigion (Cardiganshire) SY24 5ER, Wales, UK. Satire, cartoons, nudes, *Twll Tin Pob Sais.* Annual; 20p/ea; 25p/ea by post; 1965; 44pp; 10x7½". **Elwyn Ioan, Robat Gruffudd.** ALP.

THE LONDON COLLECTOR, Wolf House Books, **Richard Weiderman, Frank Girard, James E. Sisson,** 1420 Pontiac Rd., S.E., Grand Rapids, MI 49506. Poetry, articles, art, photos, cartoons, interviews, criticism, reviews, letters. *The London Collector publishes articles of interest to fans and students of Jack London. One topic is discussed each issue. Wolf House Books reprints rare ephemera & other scarce London material. Future plans call for further reprinting of desirable material as well as a series of monographs by contemporary London scholars.* Irreg; $1/yr; 50 cents/ea; no sample; 1970; 20pp; 5½x8½; 130 circ; lo. Reports immediate. Pays 12 copies. Discounts: 40% five or more.

LONDON MAGAZINE, **Alan Ross,** 30 Thurloe Place, London SW7, UK. Articles, poetry, fiction, photos, criticism. 6/yr; £5/yr; 90p/ea; 1954; 160pp; 6x8"; lp. Reports 2 wks-1 mo. Pays: by arrangement. Ads: £50/page pro rata. Discounts: 10%. Back issues: none.

LONDON MYSTERY MAGAZINE, Norman Kark Publications, **Norman Kark,** 268-270 Vauxhall Bridge Rd., London SW1 1BB, UK. Fiction. *Macabre, ghosts and whodunits up to 4000 words. Must be strong and novel in plot.* 4/yr; 25p/ea; 1949. Pays: by arrangement.

LONDON REVIEW, 7 The Priory, Priory Park, Blackheath, London SE3, UK.

LONDON WELSHMAN, London Welsh Association, **Tudor David,** 157-163 Grays Inn Road, London WC1, UK. Articles, poetry, news items, letters. 4/yr; 15p/ea; Pays: £1.05/1000 words minimum.

LONG ISLAND REVIEW, **Stephen Sossaman, Edward Faranda,** Box 10, Cambria Hts., NY 11411. Poetry, fiction, articles, interviews, criticism, reviews, parts-of-novels, longpoems. *Submissions should be intelligent, well-crafted, purposeful. New writers welcome, but all should see an issue before submitting. Especially interested in material for issues on poetry as social criticism, the dramatic monolog, the Latin American novel, and the sociology of literary forms. Poetry by Vietnam veterans always welcome. We're for writers and readers, not literary critics, so query any especially esoteric articles. No length limits within reason. Paging James Dickey, Anne Hussey.* 3/yr; $3/yr; $1/ea; $1/sample; 1973; 40pp; 5½x8; 300 circ; lo. Reports 3-4 wks. Pays 2 copies. Ads: $10/p; $6/½. Discounts: 40%. Pub'd 2 issues 1973, expects 3 in 1974. COSMEP.

Lookout Free Press. Press as such is defunct. Imprint may be used in future on specific publications still in works but will be printed by other presses. We no longer have a mailing address & all mail will be returned by P.O. if old address(es) are used. Mi. Pays copies only. Expects 1 book in 1974.

LOON, **D.L. Emblen, Richard Speakes, Richard Welin,** PO Box 11633, Santa Rosa, CA 95406. Poetry, translations. *We want to publish first-rate poetry. We have no restrictions as to subject matter, style, form, or length.* Loon No.2 *will include poems by Donald Hall, John Haines, Werner Aspenstrom.* Loon No.1 *included poems by Peter Wild, John Vernon, Bill Wertheim.* 2/yr; $2/yr; $1/ea; $1/sample; 1973; 60pp; 5½x8½; 150 circ; lo. Reports 2-4 wks. Pays 2 copies. No ads. Pub'd 1 issue 1973, expects 2 in 1974.

LORE AND LANGUAGE, **J.D.A. Widdowson,** Survey of Language and Folklore/ Archives of Cultural Tradition, Dept. of Eng. Language, The University, Sheffield S10 2TN, UK. Articles, poetry, fiction, news items, interviews, criticism, letters. *Articles & items for those who share an interest in local language, customs & traditions.* 2/yr; 30p px/yr; 15p px/ea; 1969; 20pp; quarto; 1000 circ; off. Reports 3 wks. Back issues: 5p to 15p px.

Los Angeles Free Press, 6013 Hollywood Blvd., Los Angeles, CA 90036.

Lotus Press, **Morris Howard,** PO Box 601, College Park Sta., Detroit, MI 48221. Poetry. *We are interested in poetry of literary merit, regardless of style or subject matter. Our primary interest is black poets who have been caught in the middle by editors who either don't think they're black enough or don't think they're universal enough, but we are interested in non-black poets as well. We are a fledgling company whose only offerings to date are two books by Naomi Long Madgett, but with the purchase of our own equipment, we are planning to expand.* 1972; 64pp; 5½x8½; Gestetner method. Reports 4-6 wks. Pay: negotiable. Discounts: 20-40% disc. for libraries, bkstores, schools. Pub'd 2 books 1972, none in 1973; expects 4 books in 1974. Black.

Love Street Books, **Jim Wortham,** PO Box 58163, Louisville, KY 40258. Poetry. *I publish poetry books only. Since I do not have much money I am just publishing my own poetry and books for other poets who will pay for printing costs. The three books which I have published are all easy reading love poems – free verse and stream of consciousness. Books published so far, 1974:* Touching You Touching Me *by Jim Wortham ($1.95) 64pp;* Fragile Moments *by Barbara Whitener ($1) 24pp;* Looking Down From Heaven *by Bob Ward ($1) 24pp.* COSMEP.

Loverseed Press (see DAY BY DAY)

LUDD'S MILL, Ludd's Mill Poetry Publishing Cooperative, **S. Sneyd, coordinator, A. Darlington, art coordinator,** 4 Nowell Place, Almondbury, Huddersfield HD5

8PB, Yorks, England, UK. Poetry, fiction, articles, art, photos, cartoons, interviews, satire, criticism, reviews, music, letters, longpoems, collages. *The magazine is owned by a co-operative. Shares cost £1 & shareholders receive free subscription, their work & influence on direction of magazine encouraged. Biases are probably unconscious. Anti-authoritarian, anti-classidemic, anti-excessive seriousness, anti-elitist.* Approx. 6 monthly; $1.60/4 issues; 40p pf/4 issues (UK); 40 cents/ea (US, incl. post.); 10p + 3p post/ea (UK); sample/same as price ea; 1971; 24pp; A4; 600 circ; lo. Reports as soon as possible. Ads: £5 or $11.50/p; £2.25 or $5.75/½; class/wd: by arrangement (also for reprint inserts). Discounts: 3p per copy booksellers, streetsellers, for 10 or more copies. Back issues: £1($2.50) post free, sets: issues 3-8 (6 copies). Pub'd 2 issues 1973, expects 2 in 1974.

LUNA MONTHLY, Luna Publications, **Ann F. Dietz,** 655 Orchard St., Oradell, NJ 07649. *Recent contributors: Frederik Pohl, Mark Purcell, J.B. Post. Science fiction and fantasy literature oriented. News, reviews,* **no** *fiction or poetry.* Monthly; $4.25/yr; 50 cents/ea; 50 cents/sample; 1969; 32pp; 5½x8½; 1M circ; lo. Pays copies only. Ads: $8/p; $4.50/½; 2 cents class/wd. Back issues: Nos.1-19=75 cents ea; No.20 to current=50 cents/ea. Pub'd 6 issues 1973, expects 10 in 1974. Science Fiction Publishers Association.

LUNATIC FRINGE, **John H. Coutermash, Helene Baak,** Box 237, South Salem, NY 10590. Poetry, cartoons, satire. Q; $3/yr; $1/ea; $1/sample; 1970; 36pp; 6½x 9; 600 circ; mi; lp. Reports 1 wk. Pays: none; copies only: just folks in jail. Ads: open. Discounts: penal & mental institutions are free. Back issues: none.

LUNCH, 59 Bridge Lane, London NW11, UK. Articles, poetry, fiction, art, cartoons, photos, satire, interviews, criticism, letters. *Articles not exceeding 2000 words. Intelligent informative commentary on homosexuals in society. For men and women. No contact ads.* 12/yr; £2.80/yr; 25p/ea; 1971; 32pp; 9x6¾; 3000 circ; off. Ads: £15/page pro rata; 2p/word. Gay.

LUNE, **Denise Taler, Jim Drayton, Alan Ball, publ.,** Box 91, Bellmore, NY 11710. Poetry, fiction, articles, art, photos, cartoons, interviews, satire, criticism, reviews, music, letters, parts-of-novels, longpoems, collages, plays, concrete art. *A magazine of time and space including poetry, fiction, art, science and politics to educate/ entertain with a working class/revolutionary foundation. Some poets: Barbara Holland, Lyn Lifshin, Susan Fromberg Schaeffer, Jared Smith.* Goal is to become monthly; $1.50/3 copies; 60 cents/ea postpaid; 60 cents/sample; 1973; no. pages & size varies; 2M circ (projected); lo. Reports 1 mo. Pay: negotiable; usually copies only. Ads: $40/p; $20/½; 10 cents class/wd. Discounts: 40% to booksellers; 40% on orders of 5 or more to same address. Back issues: 60 cents. Pub'd 1 issue, 2 pamphlets 1973, expects 3 issues in 1974.

LYRICAL IOWA, **Ruth DeLong Peterson,** 202 Sunset Dr., New London, IA 52645. *Only poetry by Iowa residents. Annual poetry contests (top prizes $15 for general classification poems and a number of special classifications varying from year to year). Submit material Jan. 1 to Feb. 15 of each year. Top poems submitted win prizes and/or publication. Non-profit organization, Iowa Poetry Association. Membership $2.50/yr. Membership not necessary for competition or publication.* 1/yr; $2/yr; 1946; 128pp; 6x9; 700 circ; lp. Reports in April. Pays: only prizes. No ads. Back issues: all years since 1965 available at $2/ea.

THE LYTTON RECORD, Orchard Press, **Howard Cooper-Brown (general),** Eric F.J. Ford (executive), 125 Markyate Rd., Dagenham, Essex, RM8 2LB, UK. *Dissemination of work/life/times and influences on & from Edward Bulwer-Lytton (1803-1873). Author, dramatist, poet & statesman.* Annual; £2/yr; 60p/ea; 1973; 40pp; A5; 100 circ; off. Reports 3 mos. Pays copies. Ads: £10/page. Discounts: 20% agents.

MADRONA, Gemini, **Charles Webb, J.K. Osborne, John Levy, Vassilis Zambaras,** 4332 4th N.E., No.3, Seattle, WA 98105. Poetry, fiction, articles, art, photos, cartoons, interviews, satire, criticism, reviews, parts-of-novels, longpoems, plays. *We favor intelligent imaginative, lively writers with the discipline & technical skill to capture their intelligence, imagination & liveliness on the page. We encourage the use of humor, & are, we hope, open to anything. No formulated biases. Recents contributors: Hugo, Levertov, Zimmer, Finkel, Bly, Edson, Stafford, Wagonner, Ignatow, Bukowski.* 3/yr; $5/yr; $1.50/ea; $1.50/sample; 1971; 75pp; 7x8; 500 circ; lo. Reports 2 wks to 1 mo. Pays 1 yr sub. Ads: $40/p; $20/½; no class/wd. Discounts: 40% to dealers. Pub'd 3 issues, 2 books 1973; expects 3 issues, 2 books in 1974. COSMEP, CCLM.

Mag Press, **John Kay,** 3802 La Jara, Long Beach, CA 90805. Poetry, fiction. *Now publishing books exclusively.* Lo. Pays copies only. Discounts: 40%.

MAGAZINE (Six), Interim Books, **Kirby Congdon,** Box 35, New York, NY 10014. Poetry, articles, interviews, criticism, reviews, letters. 2/yr; $10/ea; 1964; 5½x8½; 500 circ; lo. Reports 2 wks. Pays copies only. Back issues: Magazine Four: $2; Magazine Three: $2. COSMEP, CCLM.

Magic Circle Press, **Valerie Harms, Adele Aldridge,** 31 Chapel Lane, Riverside, CT 06878. Fiction, art, photos, criticism. *Our books are based on original art & written material. All books are done in quality paper and have a visual statement to make. We do not publish poetry. We are limited in time and committed in budget now so we can't consider unsolicited manuscripts, but will respond to queries.* 2 bks/yr; 1972; lo. Pay depends, 15% authors royalty. Discounts:trade 40%. COSMEP NESPA, Women.

MAGIC INK, Underground/Alternative Press Service/Europe, **Ian King,** B.C.M. Box 9620, London WC1V 6XX, UK. *Magic Ink is sent free to over 400 papers, news agencies and groups throughout the world. It is primarily an internal newsletter made up of various reports from papers plus news items.* UAPS/Europe.

MAINE EDITION, **Stephen Cook,** 22 Bridge St., Topsham, ME 04086. Poetry, articles, art, photos, interviews, criticism, reviews, music, letters, longpoems, collages, plays, concrete art. *Recent contributors: Robert Bly, James Humphrey, Kathleen Spivak, Arthur Greger, Lyn Lifshin.* Monthly; $5/yr; 60 cents/ea; 1972; 20pp; 8½x11; 2M circ. Reports 4 mos. Pays 2 copies. Ads: $100/p; $50/½; no class/wd. No discounts. Back issues: 30 cents. Free of organizations.

THE MAINSTREETER, Scopcraeft Press, **Antony Oldknow,** 1118 Cherry St., Grand Forks, ND 58201. Poetry, articles, interviews, criticism,reviews. Irreg; $1/ea; 75 cents/sample; 1971; 28pp; size varies; 350 circ; lo. Reports irreg. Pays copies only (2). Back issues: 50 cents/ea where available – applies to nos. 1-5. Pub'd 1 issue, 1 book 1973; expects 2 issues, 4 books in 1974.

THE MALAHAT REVIEW, The Univ. of Victoria, **Robin Skelton,** The Univ. of Victoria, PO Box 1700, Victoria, BC, Canada V8W 2Y2. Poetry, fiction, articles, criticism, reviews, letters, longpoems, plays.

MALENKA, **Brian Moses, Jeffrey Bleakley,** Eastbourne College of Education, Darley Rd., Eastbourne, Sussex, UK. Poetry, art. *Malenka is a separate sheet mag, the whole being contained in an envelope and stamped* Malenka. *Includes poetry and graphics. Object to give each poet included a full 2 sides for either a selection of work or a longer piece. Contributors include: Alexis Lykiard, Ian Robinson, John Rice, R. Gregory, Dick Russel, Paul Lampril, etc.* 3/yr; 10p/ea; 5p/sample; 1972; 12pp; qto; 200 circ; mim. Reports 1-2 wks.

Malpelo Press, **Lee Mallory,** 1429 Hialeah Ct., Fayetteville, NC 28301. Poetry.

MANKIND QUARTERLY, **Dr. R. Gayre of Gayre,** 1 Darnaway St., Edinburgh EH3 6DW, UK. Articles, photos. *Articles on ethnology, human heredity, ethnopsychology, anthropop-geography.* 4/yr; £1.50/yr; 40p/ea. Pays: £1.05/page.

MANO-MANO, Bowery Press, **Larry Lake,** 5539 Wheeling St., Denver, CO 80239. Poetry, fiction, articles, art, photos, cartoons, interviews, satire, criticism, reviews, music, letters, parts-of-novels, longpoems, collages, plays. Mano-Mano/2 – *Bukowski, Neal Cassady, Joan Clifford, de Prima, Russell Edson, Eigner, James Holmstrand, Kerouac, Ken Kesey, Wm. J. Margolis, James Ryan Morris, Stuart Z. Perkoff, Tony Scibella, Frank T. Rios, Patchen, Ben Talbert.* $4/yr; $1.50/ea; 1968; 75pp; 5x8; 1500 circ; lo. Reports 2 wks. Pays: $5/poem + 3 copies. Ads: $100/p; $55/½; 10 cents class/wd. Discounts: 20%. Back issues: *MM/2,* $3; *MM/1,* $4. Pub'd no issues, 4 books 1973, expects 2 issues, 3 books in 1974.

MANROOT, **Paul Mariah, Richard Tagett,** Box 982, South San Francisco, CA 94080. Poetry, fiction, articles, art, interviews, criticism, reviews, music, letters, parts-of-novels, longpoems, collages, plays, concrete art. *We still want the word to grow flesh. We have some of the finest contributors in the world writing today. What we do need is readers. If you don't know the work of Jack Spicer then don't waste our time by submitting. Not interested in "good poems." Contributors: Eigner, Lonidier, Valaoritis, Strongin, Turks, Borsa & Genet, Prevert, Char, Codrescu, Eluard, Luster & Grossinger ... Please do not submit material after September 1975. We are stopping publication with* ManRoot No.12 *& will be unable to use any new material after that time.* 2/yr; $5/4 issues; $1.50/ea; 1969; 120pp; 1M circ; lo. Reports 5-60 days. Pays: $2+/page if grant, copies normally. Ads: $35/½. Discounts: 33% bulk. Back issues: some copies available; please inquire. Pub'd 2 issues 1973, expects none or 2 in 1974. CCLM.

MANTRAS, Floating Hair Press, **Alan Britt, Joyce Britt,** 4408 Carlyle Rd., Tampa, FL 33615. Poetry, art. Mantras: An Anthology Of Immanentist Poetry *is the only full length book done by* Floating Hair Press *so far and It sells for $3/copy. Anyone wanting to review the anthology will be sent a copy. Short pamphlets sent free upon request.* Once; $3/ea; sample/review; 1972; 100pp; 5½x8½; 650 circ; mi; lo. Reports: am *not* seeking mss. at present. Pays copies only. Discounts: 40% bookstores; 20% classroom. Back issues: $3. Pub'd 1 book 1973, expects none in 1974.

MANUSCRIPTS, **Paul V. Lutz,** 1023 Amherst Dr., Tyler, TX 75701. Articles. *Deals with various aspects of manuscripts, their collective use, preservations.* Q; $10/yr; $3/ea; 1948; 76pp; 5½x8; lp. Reports 1 mo. Pays copies only. Ads: $100/p; $65/½; 10 cents/wd.

MANY SMOKES, Sun Bear & Wabun (Bear Tribe), PO Box 5895, Reno, NV 89503. Poetry, fiction, articles, art, photos, cartoons, interviews, satire, criticism, reviews, music, letters. Best to be Indian related. Q; $2/yr; 50 cents/ea; 50 cents/sample; 20pp; 8x10; lo. Reports: as soon as possible. Pays copies only. Ads: $300/p; $150/½; 15 cents class/wd. Discounts: 35 cents/copy wholesale; 50 cents/copy retail. Pub'd 4 issues 1973, expects 4 in 1974. American Indian.

MARGINS: A review of little mags & small press books, **Tom Montag, Karl Young,** assoc. ed.; Contrib. eds: Geoffrey Cook, John Jacob, Angela J. Peckenpaugh, Martin J. Rosenblum; Canadian contrib. ed: John Shannon; News notes ed: Diane Kruchkow, 2912 N. Hackett, Milwaukee, WI 53211. Articles, photos (with articles), interviews, criticism, reviews, letters (relevant). *We survey the alternative/*

small publishing scene in America and elsewhere; features cover significant books and mags, looks at presses and publishing ventures, concerns relevant to small publishing; also shorter reviews of recent small books and mags in "In the Margins." We have published a focus on Women's Writing, on American Indian Writing, on the Role and Responsibility of the Review Journal and Reviewer; on Small Press Distribution World-wide, will have focus on Prison Writing and Grants in upcoming issues. Also starting our contemporary writing symposia series soon; these will be guest edited symposia on writers of significance with pieces by a variety of critics. Margins intent is to report on, evaluate, criticize, create alternatives in contemporary writing, publishing, and reading. A recent issue, Feb.-March 1974, contains features on Lamp In The Spine, Burning Deck Press, Some of Us Press, Four Women's Journals, and Michael Ondaatje's Rat Jelly; also The Living Z: a guide to the literature of the counter-culture, the alternative press and little magazines by Noel Peattie, and Prospects: the possibility of rejuvenation and what is to be done by Richard Kostelanetz from his End Of Intelligent Writing; as well as other reviews and comment. 6/yr; $3.50/yr; 75 cents or $1/ea; 60 cents/sample; 1972; 64pp; 8½x11; 1,250 circ; lo. Reports 2 wks to mos. Pays: copies only except by arrangement. Ads: $20/p; $12/½; no class/wd; smaller ads available. Discounts: 40% disc. to bookstores and bulk; additional 15% to distributors; 50% on orders of 100 or more in bulk. Back issues: No.2, 40 cents; Nos. 6-9, 60 cents/ea; No. 10, 75 cents. Pub'd 6 issues 1973, expects 6 in 1974.

THE MARKHAM REVIEW, **Joseph W. Slade,** Horrmann Library, Wagner College, Staten Island, NY 10301. Articles, photos, criticism, reviews. *Deal only with criticism of literary, political, and social figures of the period 1865-1940 in America. Maximum length of articles is 6000 words. MLA stylesheet. Contributors usually though not always university professors.* 3/yr; free; 1968; 20pp; 8½x11; 2M circ. lo. Reports 4 wks. Pays copies. No ads. No discounts (free). Back issues: available from University Microfilms.

THE MASSACHUSETTS REVIEW, **John Hicks, Lee R. Edwards,** The Massachsetts Review, Memorial Hall, Amherst, MA 01002. Poetry, fiction, articles, art, photos, interviews, criticism, reviews, music, letters, parts-of-novels, longpoems, plays. 4/yr; $9/yr; $2.50/ea; 1959; 250pp; 2100 circ; lp. Reports 1-2 mos. Pays: money and copies. No class/wd. Pub'd 4 issues 1973, expects 4 in 1974. CCLM.

MATE, **Alistair Paterson,** Box 5670, Wellesley St., Auckland, New Zealand. Poetry, fiction. *Subsidized by the New Zealand State Literary Fund. Material required: New Zealand poetry and short stories, short extracts from novels in progress. Some contributors: Kendrick Smithyman, Bruce Beaver, Louis Johnson, Ian Wedde, Hone Tuwhare, Kevin Ireland.* Bi-annual; $2/yr; $1/ea; 1957; 60pp; 5x8; 800 circ; lo. Reports 3 wks at most. Pays: yes; 2 copies. Ads: $20/p; $12/½. Discounts: 33 1/3% trade only. Back issues: 50 cents/ea. Pub'd 2 issues 1973, expects 2 in 1974. Independent.

MATRIX, **Charm & Idell,** Box 4218, No. Hollywood, CA 91607. Poetry, fiction, articles, art, photos, cartoons, interviews, satire, reviews, longpoems, collages, plays. *Must be new age thought or at least excellent works for women. Contributors include Alta, Elsa Gidlow, H. Luster, Ann Deagon, J. Hirschman, J. Herms, D. Meltzer, Anais Nin, D. Rhodyar, Diane Di Prima, Lyn Lifshin, Daisy Alden, Cameron etc, etc. Translations by K. Rexroth etc. Vol.III published 1973 was/is last issue. All 3 vols. still available. Theme of No.3: "The initiated female soul."* $5/yr; 1970; 50pp; 600 circ; of. Pays copies only. No ads. Discounts: 40% to dealers. COSMEP, Women.

MAYBE, Worlds of Fandom, IMK Publications, **Irvin M. Koch, Bryan Jones,** c/o 835 Chatt. Bk. Bldg., Chattanooga, TN 37402. Articles, art, cartoons, interviews, criticism, reviews, letters (rarely). *Prefer 600-1800 words. Any style. Prefer informative, interesting, or constructive.* Bi-monthly or more often; $2.50/6 issues; 50 cents/ea; sample on whim; 1969; 20pp; 8½x11; 250$^{\pm}$100 circ; lo. Reports immediately if SASE. Pays copies only. Ads: $8/p; $4/½; no class/wd. Discounts: 10 copies for resale $3.75 + postage. Pub'd 12 issues 1973, expects over 7 in 1974. Science Fiction/Fantasy.

Maynard Press, **Cedric Cullingford,** 8 Rangers Square, London SG10, UK. Poetry. ALP.

MEANJIN QUARTERLY, **C.B. Christesen, OBE,** Univ. of Melbourne, Parkville, Victoria 3052, Australia. Poetry, fiction, articles, criticism, parts-of-novels. Q; $A12/yr; 1940; 160pp; 9½x6½; 3600 circ; lp. Reports 3 mos. Pays: upon publication. Ads: $200/p. Discounts: 25% trade disc. Pub'd 4 issues 1973, expects 4 in 1974.

MEDICAL HISTORY, **Wellcome Institute for the History of Medicine, Edwin Clarke, M.D., F.R.C.P.,** 183 Euston Rd., London NW1 2BP, UK. Articles, photos, news items. 4/yr; £4/yr; £1.10/ea; 1957; 106pp; 5x8"; 1200 circ; lp. Reports 2 wks. Pay: nil. Ads: £15/page; £8.50/½. Back issues: £1.50/issue if available.

Menard Press, **Anthony & Brenda Rudolf,** 1 Primrose Gardens, London NW3 4UJ, UK. *Poetics and translated poetry. 2 books/1973. 3 books/1974. Have a programme, so no submissions for the time being.* Lp; off. ALP.

MERE ANARCHY, Chaotic Press, **Alexander Chaos,** 51 Mann TCE, North Adelaide, South Australia 5006. Poetry, art. *Original poetry, quotes, graphics, short short stories. Criteria are: simple in the words, contemporary in the concerns, self-aware in the attitudes.* Intermittent; free + postage/yr; 1973; 24pp; 10x8"; 500 circ; lo. No pay. Ads: free if accepted. Pub'd 1 issue 1973. Poetry.

MERIDIAN, Rondo Publications Ltd., **Trevor Kneale,** 155/157 The Albany, Old Hall St., Liverpool L3 9EG, UK. Poetry. *"Broad mainstream"* — *monitors best of the established, encourages rising talents. Basically, a poetry anthology of new work; not a review medium. Recent contributors: Alan Brownjohn, Jim Burns, Miles Burrows, Peter Dale, David Jaffin, Lotte Kramer, John Mole, Peter Redgrove, Harriet Rose, John Stathatos, Jon Stallworthy, Edward Storey, Gordon Symes, Tony Connor, Anthony Edkins, David Grubb, Phoebe Hesketh, Elizabeth Saxon, Penelope Shuttle, Eddie Wainwright, George Barker, Thomas Blackburn, Jack Clemo, Donald Davie, Peter Dent, Douglas Dunn, Elizabeth Jennings, George MacBeth, Brian Patten, R.S. Thomas, David Wevill, etc.* Q; £1.20/yr; 35p/ea inc. post; 1973; 34pp; (3 col-card cover); A5; circ rising rapidly UK & abroad; off; lo. Reports 2 wks. Pay varies. Ads: £18/page; £9.50/½; £5/¼. Back issues: 35p (few available). Mainstream.

MERIP REPORTS, **Middle East Research and Information Project,** Box 48, Cambridge, MA 02138. Articles, reviews. *We publish material dealing with the middle east, particularly U.S. involvement there and liberation struggles of M.E. people. Direct reports included. Political orientation is anti-imperialist and marxist.* Monthly; $6/yr; $12/yr non-pro. institutions; 50 cents/ea; sample; 1971; 28pp; 8½x11; 2500 circ; lo. Reports 6 wks. Pays copies only. No ads. Discounts: 40% for orders of 5 or more copies of each issue. Back issues: 50 cents/ea. Pub'd 11 issues (bimonthly, July-Aug) in 1973. Third World.

MERLIN'S MAGIC, **Merlin F. Teed,** 419–91 St., Brooklyn, NY 11209. Poetry, fiction, articles, reviews. 6/yr; 30 cents/ea; 1959; 4pp; 8½x11; 350 circ; mi. Reports 2 wks to 1 mo. No pay.

Merseyside Arts Association (see ARTS ALIVE MERSEYSIDE)

METANOIA, An Independent Journal of Radical Lutheranism, **Douglas C. Stange,** 2126 University Ave., Dubque, IA 52001. Articles, art, photos, interviews, reviews, letters. *Material — articles that run about 5-6 double-space type-written pages. Style — interpretative rather than descriptive, forceful rather than milk-toast. Biases — leftist, in the old Christian Socialist tradition. Non-violent unless . . . Contributors include Joseph Fletcher, Harvey Cox, Martin Niemoeller, John C. Cooper, Connie Parvey, et.al.* Q; $3/yr; $1/ea; free sample; $8/3 yrs; 1969; 12-16pp; under 1M circ. Reports 2-3 wks. Pays copies only. No paid ads, sometimes carry free ads for selected "causes." Discounts: bulk rates available; They vary according to the size and format of issue; Prices per issue quoted upon request. Religion.

MICHIGAN QUARTERLY REVIEW, University of Michigan, **Radcliffe Squires,** 3032 Rackham Bldg., Ann Arbor, MI 48104. Poetry, fiction, articles, criticism, reviews, parts-of-novels, longpoems. Q; $6/yr; $1.50/ea; 1962; 100pp; 7x10; 3M circ; lo. Reports 2-3 wks. Pays 50 cents/line poetry; $10/p prose; $7/p reviews; + 3 copies. Ads: $125/p. Discounts: 15% agent — advertising; 10% agents — sales. Back issues: $2/ea. CCLM.

Midnag Publications, Mid Northumberland Arts Group, Ashirgton, Northumberland, UK.

THE MIDWEST QUARTERLY, **Rebecca Patterson,** Kansas State College, Pittsburg, KS 66762. Q; $2.50/yr; $1/ea; free sample; 1959; 110pp; 6x9; 1M circ; lp. Reports 2-3 mos. Pays copies only. COSMEP.

MIH Publications (see also *MUGWUMPS' INSTRUMENT HERALD),* 12704 Barbara Rd., Silver Spring, MD 20906. *We publish reprints of old musical instrument catalogs, primarily from the turn of the century through the end of the 1920s. We also publish* The Mugwumps' Reader, *which contains all the articles that appeared in the first two volumes of* Mugwumps' Instrument Herald, *the magazine of folk instruments. Commencing with Summer, 1974, we will publish books which pertain to various other aspects of folk musical instruments. The first will be a text about American folk instruments; it is intended for use in Folklore programs and for general interest reading. Then we will do 2 or 3 instruction books on how to play certain intstruments; these may be book and record combinations.*

THE MINNESOTA REVIEW, **Roger Mitchell; Assoc. eds: Lyman Andrews, James Atlas, Victor Contoski, M.L. Raina,** Box 5416, Milwaukee, WI 53211. Poetry, fiction, articles, art, photos, interviews, satire, criticism, reviews, parts-of-novels, longpoems, plays. *No style restrictions. Interested in all good work, "creative" and "critical." Special interest in Marxist ("engaged," "committed") writing. Recent contributors: Jon Silkin, Fredric Jameson, Tom Wayman, Graham Good, Greg Kuzma, Darko Suvin, Doug Blazek, The Living Newspaper, David Posner, more.* 2/yr; $3.50/yr; $2/ea; $2/sample; 1960; 150pp; 8½x5½; 1M circ; of. Reports 1-3 mos. Pays: $5-$10 when available. Ads: $40/p; $20/½, (both photo-ready copy); no class/wd. No discounts. Back issues: most available, prices on request. Pub'd 2 issues 1973, expects 2 in 1974.

MINORITY RIGHTS GROUPS AND REPORTS, MRG (Press), **B. Whitaker,** MRG, 36 Craven St., London WC2, UK. *Specially commissioned reports only. Reports already published include those on the Basques, The Africans predicament in Rhodesia, What future for the Amerindians Of South America, The two Irelands etc.* 5/yr; £2.50/yr; 45p/ea; 1970; 30pp; 1000 circ. Third World.

Mirrora Press Limited, M.J. Sharon, PO Box 3979, West 10th Ave., Vancouver, BC, Canada V6B 3Y6. Poetry, fiction, articles, art, photos, cartoons, interviews, satire, criticism, reviews, music, letters, parts-of-novels, longpoems, collages, plays, concrete art. Mirrora Press Limited is interested in any and all materialist works of art and/or criticisms thereof. Any serious work will be given serious consideration all others will be trashed. We are also interested in science and are in fact scientists, so empirical and philosophical works will be considered as well. Lp. Pays: contract. Discounts: a quarterly journal is to be forth coming sometime around September '74. Write for further information. Anarchist.

MISSISSIPPI REVIEW, Center for Writers, USM, **Gordon Weaver, Jesse McCartney, Walter Everett, D.C. Berry,** Southern Sta., Box 37, Hattiesburg, MS 39401. Poetry, fiction, reviews, parts-of-novels, longpoems. *Academic, but, hopefully, not pedantic; open to all modes, forms, values, types – Guy Owen, Elizabeth Spencer, David Madden, Daniel Curley, James Whitehead – not regional!* 3/yr; $3/yr; $1.50/ea; free sample; 1972; 100pp; 9x12; 500 circ; lo. Reports 1 wk to 3 mos. Pays: $3/p prose; $5 per poem. Ads: exchange. No discounts. Back issues: $1.50. Pub'd 2 issues 1973, expects 3 in 1974. COSMEP, CCLM.

MR. COGITO, **Robert A. Davies, John M. Gogol,** Box 627, Pacific Univ. Forest Grove, OR 97116. Poetry, art, translations. *Poetry and poetry translations, as well as line drawings. First two issues included Herbert, Ridland, Curtis, Masarik, Stafford, LaGuin, and Russell. Open to poets of any school. Prefer strong imagery, heightened language, emotional impact.* 3/yr; $3/yr; $1/ea; $1/sample; 1973; 24pp; 4x11; 500 circ; lo. Reports 1-2 mos. Pays 3 copies. Pub'd 1 issue 1973, expects 2 in 1974. COSMEP.

Mitre Press, 52 Lincolns Inn Fields, London WC2A 3NW, UK.

Mockingbird Press, **Tuli Kupferberg,** 381 East 10th St., New York, NY 10009.

MODERN FICTION STUDIES, **Wm. T. Stafford, Margaret Church,** Dept. of Eng., Purdue Univ., W. Lafayette, IN 47907. Criticism, reviews. Q; $6/yr individuals; $7/yr institutions; $2/ea; sample; 1955; 140pp; 6x9; 4500 circ; lp. Reports 2-4 mos. Pays copies only. No ads. No discounts. Back issues: $2. Pub'd 4 issues 1973.

THE MODERN LANGUAGE JOURNAL, George Banta Co., Menasha, WI, **Charles L. King,** University of Colorado, Boulder, CO 80302. Articles, reviews. *Length of articles: 6-40 double-spaced typewritten pages; reviews: 500 words MLA style sheet, revised edition. Some recent contributors: Peter Boyd-Bowman, Theodore Anderson, Dwight Bolinger, Stephen A. Freeman Twaddell.* 6/yr; $6/yr; $1.50/ea: 1916; 80pp; 9x10; 9,500 circ; of. Reports 3-6 mos. Ads: $150/p; $90/½.

MODERN LANGUAGE REVIEW, **Prof. C.P. Brand,** David Hume Tower, George Square, Edinburgh EH8 9JX, UK. *Articles and reviews of a scholarly or specialist character, on English, Romance, Germanic, and Slavonic languages and literatures.* 4/yr; £8.50/yr. Pays: offprints.

MODERN POETRY IN TRANSLATION, Modern Poetry in Translation Ltd., **Daniel Weissbort,** 10 Compayne Gardens, London NW6 3DH, UK. Poetry, interviews, criticism, longpoems. *Only translations, very few 'imitations.' Recent contributors: Vasko Popa, Octavio Paz, Yves Bonnefoy, Edmond Jabes, Nichita Stanescu, Harry Martinson, Rolf Jacobsen . . .* 4/yr; £2.40/yr; 60p/ea; 1964; 32pp; 8½x10½; 1500 circ; lp. Reports 3 mos or more. Pay varies. Ads: £30/page pro rata. Back issues: list available on request.

MOJO NAVIGATOR(E), Cat's Pajamas Press, **John Jacob,** 423 S. Humphrey, Oak Park, IL 60302. Poetry, fiction, art, photos, criticism, reviews. *Recent contributors have included Bill Ransom, A.G. Sobin, Ben Hiatt, Michael Lally, Ann Menebroker and many others. Staid material will be returned. If you can know the magazine before submitting, fine. Sending a cover letter is a nice gesture. We're biased toward experiments with integrity. If you're lyric, be off-the-wall. We always get behind what we publish.* Irreg; $3.50/4 issues; $1/ea; $1/sample; 1969; 48pp; 5½x8½; 350 circ; lo. Reports 3-4 wks. Pay: varies. Discounts: 40% disc. on multiple orders of 4 or more. Pub'd 1 issue, 1 book 1973; expects 2 issues, 2 books 1974. COSMEP, CCLM.

MOLE EXPRESS, 100 Oxford Rd., Manchester 13, UK. Tel.061-273 2180 or 061-226 3458. Articles, fiction, cartoons, photos, satire, news items, interviews, criticism, music, letters. *Nothing longer than say 2500 words unless* really *sensational. Could say we were politically biased left-wing.* Monthly; 80p/yr; 6p/ea; sample/ free maybe; 1970; 20pp; 13x8"; 2000 circ; off. Reports vary. Pay: negotiable; not usually. Ads: £20/page pro rata. Discounts: 10%. Back issues: cheap! Community.

MOMENTUM, **William Mohr, Harley Lond, asst. fic. ed.,** Momentum, c/o Century City Educational Arts Project, 10508 W. Pico Blvd., Los Angeles, CA 90064. Poetry, fiction, articles, art, longpoems, plays. *The fourth issue of* Momentum *will contain Leland Hickman's* Tiresias 9:A & 9:B. *Another issue will be the* Collected Poems *of Sophia Castro-Leon, a Los Angeles poet who died in 1972. Some other contributors include Dennis Ellman, Ann Christie, Harry Northup, James Krusoe, Wanda Coleman, John Harris, William Iwamoto, Richard Martin, and other excellent L.A. poets.* 4/yr; $6/yr; $1.50/ea; 1973; 60-80pp; 300 circ; lo. Reports 2 days-3 mos. Pays copies only. Expects 4 issues 1974. COSMEP.

Monad Press, **George Weissman,** 410 West St., New York, NY 10014. Monad Press *is the publishing imprint of the Anchor Foundation, Inc.* Monad *publishes books on social history and philosophy.* Discounts: distributed by Pathfinder Press, Inc.

MONDAY MORNING WASH, Monday Morning Press, **Tom Montag,** 2912 North Hackett, Milwaukee, WI 53211. Poetry, fiction, articles, interviews, criticism, reviews, letters, parts-of-novels, longpoems. *Suspended after first issue. No.1 available for $1.*

THE MONSTER TIMES, The Monster Times Publishing Co., **Joe Kane,** 11 W. 17th St., NYC 10011. Articles, cartoons, interviews, criticism, reviews, letters. *The Monster Times uses articles on horror films, comics and fantasy-related subjects.* Monthly; $6/yr; 60 cents/ea; 60 cents/sample; 1972; 32pp; 10x15; 80M circ; lo. Reports 2 wks-1 mo. Pays: $15-$50. Ads: $500/p; $300/½. Discounts: 6 pages in 6 issues under prior contract 6% disc; 12 pages in 12 issues 9% disc. Back issues: $1-$2. Pub'd 11 issues 1973, expects 12 in 1974.

MONUMENT IN CANTOS AND ESSAYS, Monument Press, **Victor Myers,** Rt.10, Columbia, MO 65201. Poetry, fiction, art, photos, parts-of-novels, longpoems. *I seek work of excellence, contemporary relevance, evocative imagery and a concern for the survival and sacramental appreciation of the earth as an organic whole. All submissions are returned with comments, but discourage all but works of serious craftsmanship.* Annual; $1/yr; $1/ea; sample/cost of current bk rate post; 1968; 50pp; 5½x8½; 300 circ; of. Reports 3 mos. Pays one $25 prize annually; 2 copies. Ads: $35/p; $25/½. No discounts. Back issues: $1.50. COSMEP.

MOON SHINE, **Tina Fulker,** 6 Oxford Close, Edmonton, London N9, UK. Poetry, fiction, art, criticism. *This magazine is not to be confused with any glossy cover* *effort, nor is its aim to be part of any intellectual scene. It's merely an outlet and anyone who writes poetry is welcome to contribute work.* Q; 60p/yr; 15p/ea; 1972; 18pp; qto; 150 circ; off. Reports 1 month.

Moonbird Publications, Robert Richardson, 52 Holtspur Ave., Wooburn Green, High Wycombe, Bucks, UK. Poetry, art, cartoons, photos, longpoems, collages, concrete. *In Feb. 1974 publishing* Tole Lege, *poems by Geoffrey Cook, approx. 36pp, 60p($1.90) px. Also still avail.* The Song of Aino *(Finnish Folk Poem) trans. Keith Bosley & illus. Richard Kennedy, 28pp; 35p($1.50) pf, 50 copies signed by trans. & illus. at £1($3). Would like to make contact with small press poetry and general publishers in other countries – with a view to possible joint publications. Still intend to start a mag, biased towards poetry but including general items. Would like mag to develop as an art-form of its own. Interested to hear from anyone willing to contribute/help circulate.* 1971; A5; 500 circ; off. Reports up to 2 mos. Pay: arranged. Discounts: 33% retailers. ALP, Poetry.

Morgan Press (see HEY LADY)

Morning Star Press (see THE PHOENIX)

E.J. Morten (Publishers) (see PETERLOO POETS SERIES)

MOSAIC, David K. Gast, 1555 Murray Ave., El Cajon, CA 92020. Poetry. *Currently featuring Southwestern poets, but open to quality poetry regardless of source. Contributors include; Burwell, Edson, Kuzma, McCord, Piercy, Strongin, Stafford.* Q; $3/yr; $1/ea; 50 cents/sample; 1973; 24pp; 6½x8½; 1-200 circ; lo. Reports 2 wks. Pays copies only. No ads.

Moss-Side Press (see CATONSVILLE ROADRUNNER, COMMUNES)

MOUNTAIN GAZETTE, Mike Moore, 1801 York St., Denver, CO 80206. Poetry, fiction, articles, photos, interveiws, satire, criticism, reviews, letters. Monthly; $5/yr; 50 cents/ea; free sample; 1966; 32pp; 10x15; 10M circ; lo. Reports 30 days. Ads: $400/p; $200/½; no class/wd. Back issues: 50 cents when available. Pub'd 12 issues 1973, expects 12 in 1974; expects 6 books in 1974. Ecology.

MOUNTAIN LIFE & WORK, staff of: Council of the Southern Mountains, Drawer N, Clintwood, VA 24228. Poetry, articles, photos, cartoons, interviews, criticism, letters. *We solicit our material & rarely use material sent by miscellaneous contributors. The only regional publication in Appalachia covering a broad range of activities and issues concerning mountain people. Monthly, covers regional news, analysis, and reports by community groups and labor groups in Appalachia. Frequent coverage of such issues as strip mining, underground mining, Forest Service land condemnation, Corps of Engineers projects, industrial safety and health in non-coal industries in Appalachia, textile mills in the region, community organizing. Published by the Council of the Southern Mountains.* $5 per year subscription only; $10 membership in the Council included. Monthly; $5/yr; 50 cents/ea; 1925; 24pp; 8x11; 5M circ; lo. No pay. Discounts: 30% for 10 or more. Back issues: $1 per issue, less 30% for 10 or more – on issues prior to current year; 50 cents per issue, less 30% for 10 or more – on issues in current year. Pub'd 11 issues, 1 book 1973; expects 11 issues, no books in 1974. Appalachian.

MOUTH OF THE DRAGON, Andrew Bifrost, 18 Cornelia St., New York, NY 10014. Poetry, longpoems. Mouth of the Dragon *is a poetry journal into male love. With its contributors and readers it will explore the varieties of experience which enable a man to love another man. The first issue will be out May 1st and will in-*

clude work by Edward Field and Jonathan Williams among others. Poems may be of any length or style. Q; no subs; $2/ea; 1974; 50pp; 5½x8½; lp. Reports 2 mos. Pays copies only. No ads. Discounts: $1.20 per issue on orders of 10 or more. Back issues: none yet. Pub'd no issues in 1973. COSMEP, Gay.

MOVING OUT, **Gloria Dyc, Margaret Kaminski, Dee Durkee, Sharon Shaw, Gail Steslick, Julie Jensen,** 169 Mackenzie Hall, Wayne State Univ., Detroit, MI 48202. Poetry, fiction, articles, art, photos, interviews, criticism, reviews, music, letters, parts-of-novels, longpoems, collages, plays. *Feminist literary and arts journal. We welcome quality material from women. We are not interested in articles which are quickly dated since we only come out twice a year. Recent contributors: Marge Piercy, Susan Fromberg Shaeffer, E.M. Broner, Anais Nin. SASE.* 2/yr; $1.50/yr; 75 cents/ea; sample/for institutions; 1970; 75pp; 8½x11; 2M circ; lo. Reports 3 to 6 mos. Pays copies only. No ads. Discounts: special rates for bulk orders; write. Back issues: available: V.2, No.1; V.2, No.2; V.3, No.1; V.3, No.2. Pub'd 2 issues 1973, expects 2 in 1974. COSMEP, Women.

MRG *(see MONORITY RIGHTS GROUPS AND REPORTS)*

MUGWUMPS' INSTRUMENT HERALD, MIH Publications, **Michael I. Holmes,** 12704 Barbara Rd., Silver Spring, MD 20906. Articles, art, photos, cartoons, interviews, criticism, reviews, music, letters. *We are a magazine specializing in material related to folk musical instruments. We publish stories and articles about construction and repair of instruments, histories of the old companies, profiles of contemporary instrument makers, and photographs of important or interesting instruments. We also provide a classified marketplace for listings of instruments for sale, trade or wanted to purchase.* Bi-mo; $6/yr; $1/ea; $1/sample; 1972; 32pp; 5½x8½; 2M circ; lo. Reports usually immediate. Pays: free sub + free ads; 6 copies. Ads: $40/p; $25/½; $1 for 3 lines class/wd. Discounts: 50% for those selling retail; 12½% to sub service; all others, retail. Back issues: $1 when available; most are out of print. Pub'd 6 issues, 3 books 1973; expects 6 issues 1974.

John Muir Publications, PO Box 613, Santa Fe, NM 87501. *Books we have published to date:* How to Keep Your VW Alive *and* The Velvet Monkey Wrench *by John Muir;* People's Guide to Mexico *by Carl Franz;* La Vida De Dos Novios *by Martin Vinaver (Love story and color illustrations by 9 year old);* Boomkitchwatt *a novel by Don Hendrie, Jr.;* Windows, *watercolors, drawings, poems by David Miller. Coming soon:* The Art of Self Defense for Gentle People *by Rolf Cahn.* Pub'd 7 books 1973, expects 2 in 1974.

THE MUNDANE EGG QUARTERLY, **J.F. Knight, L.M.C. Knight,** 81A Johnston St., Annandale, NSW, Australia 2038. Poetry. *A magazine for poetry about religious experience. Drawings are commissioned to accompany individual poems.* Q; $2/yr; 60 cents/ea; 60 cents/sample; 1973; 30pp; ½ foolscap; 100 circ; lo. Reports vary. Pay varies. No ads. No discounts. Back issues: 60 cents/ea. Pub'd 4 issues 1973, expects 4 in 1974.

MUNDUS ARTIUM: A Journal of International Literature & the Arts, **Rainer Schulte,** Ellis Hall, Ohio Univ., Athens, OH 45701. Poetry, fiction, articles, art, photos, music. *Foreign poetry presented bilingually. Interdisciplinary focus on the arts. Does not publish representational works. Translations of recent poetry and fiction. Recent contribs: Morton Feldman, W.S. Merwin, Jean Ipousteguy, Michael S. Harper; sections on recent Swedish, Venezuelan and French-speaking poets.* 2/yr; $6/yr; $3.50/ea; 1967; 180pp; 6x9; 1M circ; lo. Reports 1 mo. Pay varies. Ads: $70/p; $40/½; no class/wd. Discounts: bkstores 33%; agent 10%. Pub'd 2 issues 1973, expects 2 in 1974. CCLM.

MUSE, Birmingham Poetry Centre, **Geoff Charlton, John Dalton,** c/o B.M.I., Margaret St., Birmingham B3 3BS, UK. Poetry, fiction, art, criticism, letters. *Mainly Midlands contributors – plus special features of writers and poets known on the small magazine scene. Submissions invited. Articles and prose up to 1250 words.* Min/Ann; 20p/sub; 15p pf/sample; 1971; 60pp; 500 circ; off. Reports 2 mos. Pays copy. Ads: negotiable. Discounts: 25%.

Museum of New Mexico Press (see EL PALACIO)

MUSHROOM, Yardbird Press, **Peter Fiore,** 3310 Bainbridge Ave., Bronx, NY 10468. Poetry, fiction, articles, cartoons, interviews, music, letters, parts-of-novels, longpoems, concrete art. *Poetry in all its forms. Right now I have a preference for short mind-snapping prose. Experimental prose, in all genres. Recent contributors: Stuart Dybek, Dennis Dooley, Jesus Papoleto Melendez, Warren Herendeen, Chris Bell, Len Galiulo, Al Drake, A. Poulin, Art Beck, Lorraine Harr. I like to hear many strong voices.* 3/yr; $3.50/4 issues; $1/ea; $1/sample; 1974; 30-40pp; 8½x 5½; 2-400 circ. Reports 1 mo. Pays 2 copies. No ads. Expects 3 issues 1974.

MUSIC AND LETTERS, Oxford University Press, **Sir Jack Westrup,** Maycroft Hurland Lane, Headley, Bordon, Hants GU35 8NQ, UK. Articles, criticism, music. *Not specialized in scope, being open to the discussion of anything from primitive music to the latest experiments in the laboratory. But preference is given to contributors who can write, who have a respect for the English language and are willing to take the trouble to use it effectively.* Q; £2($6)/yr; 60p/ea; free sample; 1920; 130pp; 6x9¾; 3500 circ. Ads: £20/page & pro rata.

MUSICAL OPINION, **Laurence Swinyard,** 87 Wellington St., Luton, UK. Articles. *500-2000 words of general musical interest, organ and church matters. No verse.* Monthly; 15p/ea; 1877. Pays: on publication. Music.

MUSTANG REVIEW, **Karl Edd, Marjorie Appell,** 212 S. Broadway, Denver, CO 80209. Poetry, art, reviews. *12-14 lines poetry, metaphoric, suggest you have written for about a 5 yr. min. before you try us & that you be familiar with ancient Chinese poetry or the modern Imagists, we are not for amateurs nor for academicians.* 2/yr; $2/yr; $1/ea; 50 cents/sample; 1967; 24-30pp; 5½x8½; 400 circ. Reports 1-3 wks. Pays copies only. Ads: $40/p; $25/½. Discounts: agent 20%. Back issues: only a few left. Standard prices (½ off to students). Pub'd 2 issues 1973, expects 2 in 1974; expects 1 book in 1974.

MYTHPRINT, **Laurence J. Krieg, mang. ed.,** 1616 Brooklyn Ave., Ann Arbor, MI 48104. Art, interviews, criticism, reviews, letters. Mythprint *is the monthly bulletin of the Mythopoeic Society, which is people interested in Tolkien (hobbits), C.S. Lewis (Narnia,* Perelandra . . .*), and Charles Williams* (Descent into Hell, Region of the Summer Stars). *We love books, and we love to talk about them: a bit of fantasy, a bit of science fiction, a bit of mysticism.* Mythprint *runs news of upcoming events, plus letters, reviews, and discussions. Lengthy articles and reviews are published in* Mythlore, *the society's journal.* Monthly; $3/yr Assoc. Mem.; $6/ yr Actv. Mem.; 35 cents/ea; 2 free samples; 1968; 16-20pp; 5½x8½; 600 circ; lo. Reports 2-4 mos. Pays copies only. Ads: $20/p; $11/½ (camera ready). Back issues: 1968,'69,' 70 @ 15 cents; 1971 @ 25 cents; 1972, '73, '74 @ 35 cents. Pub'd 12 issues 1973. Hobbit.

NAMIBIA NEWS, 10 Dryden Chambers, 199 Oxford St., London W1R 1PA, UK. Third World.

NANIH WAIYA, **Bradley Alex,** Rt.7, Box R-42, Philadelphia, MS 39350. Poetry, articles, art, photos, interviews, letters, longpoems. Q; $8/yr; $2/ea; 1973; 60pp; 1M circ; lo. No ads. Discounts: 10%. Expects 4 issues in 1974. Am. Indian.

National Anti-Vivisection Society (see ANIMALS' DEFENDER & ANTI-VIVI-SECTION NEWS)

National Association of Health Students (see HEALTH TEAM)

National Book League (see BOOKS)

National Council for Civil Liberties (N.C.C.L.) (see CIVIL LIBERTY)

National Council of Teachers of English (see COLLEGE ENGLISH)

NATURAL LIFE STYLES, Gordon & Breach, **Sally Freeman,** Gordon & Breach, One Park Ave., NYC 10016. Articles, art, photos, interviews. Q; $9/yr; $3/ea; no sample; 80pp; 8½x11; 10M+ circ; lo. Ads: $300/p; $175/½. Discounts: 50% distributors (min. order 50); 40% bkstore (min. order 5); 10 % sub. agency.

Naturist Foundation (see GROVE)

NAUSEA ONE, Russ Haas Press, **Leo Mailman, David Scott, art direc.,** PO Box 4261, Long Beach, CA 90804. Poetry, fiction, art, photos, cartoons, reviews, longpoems, concrete art. *Gerald Locklin, John Bennett, Judson Crews, Linda King, Robert Peters, Lyn Lifshin, Ronald Koertge.* 3/yr; $3.50/yr individual; $5.50/yr libraries; $1/ea; 1972; 48pp; 5½x8½; 400 circ; lo. Reports 1 mo. Pays 2 copies. Ads: $30/p; $15/½; class/wd. 20 cents per word. Discounts: 40% bkstores. Pub'd 4 issues 1973, expects 3 in 1974. COSMEP.

Navyug, Delhi, India (see ROOPVATI (The Nymph))

NEGRO AMERICAN LITERATURE FORUM, School of Education, Indiana State Univ., **Hannah L. Hedrick,** Dept. of English & Journalism, ISU, Terre Haute, IN 47809. Articles, art, photos, interviews, criticism, reviews, concrete art. *Review articles covering most of the books appearing in Black Am. Lit. Want photographs of original art work by Black Americans. Publish interviews.* Q; $4/yr; $1/ea; 1967; 36-40pp; 8½x11; 900 circ; lo. Reports 4-6 wks. Pays: complimentary copies only. Discounts: agents, $3/yr. Back issues: $1/issue. Pub'd 4 issues 1973, expects 4 in 1974. Black.

NEPTUNE'S KINGDOM, **Martin Gleeson,** 5 Victoria Terrace, Kilkee, Co. Clare, Ireland.   Poetry. Occasionally; 10p/ea; sample pf; 1972; 36pp; 8½x5½; 3-500 circ; off.

NEVERSELL MONTHLY, **Jethro Somes, Robert Lloyd Griffiths III, Roger Ordway,** 3006 Porter St., N.W., Washington, DC 20008. Poetry, fiction, articles, art, photos, cartoons, interviews, satire, criticism, reviews, music, letters, parts-of-novels, longpoems, collages, plays, concrete art. *Any and all. We pay well upon publication. No biases.* 12/yr; $10/yr; $1/ea; no sample; 1973; 156pp; 8x10½; 12M circ. Reports no longer than 1 mo. Pays $30 per page. No ads. No discounts. Back issues: no back issues so far. COSMEP, UPS, ALP, CCLM, COSMEPA.

NEW: American & Canadian Poetry, The Crossing Press, **John & Elaine Gill,** Trumansburg, NY 14886. Poetry, articles, criticism, reviews, letters. *A poetry & views* magazine with equal *emphasis on poetry & poetry* views. *Recent contributors: Robert Peters, Marge Piercy, Alta, Wm. Witherup, Al Purdy.* 2/yr; $2.75/yr; $1.50 /ea; $3.25/yr institu; lo. Reports 4-6 wks. Pays copies only. Back issues: $3/issue. Pub'd 3 issues, 6 books 1973; expects 8 issues 1974. COSMEP. CCLM.

NEW BLACKFRIARS, **Rev. Herbert McCabe, O.P.,** The English Dominicans, Blackfriars, Oxford.,UK. *Length 2-3000 words. A critical review, surveying the field of theology, philosophy, sociology and the arts, from the standpoint of Christian principles and their application to the problems of the modern world.* Monthly; 25p/ea. Pays: by arrangement.

NEW CHASE CHAT, S.A.T.R.A. and Churches of St. Ann's, **Rev. Peter Jordan,** 21 Courtenay Gardens, St. Ann's Nottingham, NG3 4QG, UK. Articles, poetry, cartoons, photos, news items, interviews, letters. *New Chase Chat attempts to be a community newspaper to serve the St. Ann's area of Nottingham. The Editorial Board consists of representatives of the St. Ann's Tenants' and Residents' Association (S.A.T.R.A.) and of four churches in St. Ann's (Anglican, Methodist, Baptist and Independant Methodist). S.A.T.R.A. and the churches each have their own page to express their views; the remaining pages being, in principle, devoted to community news, views etc.* Monthly; 3p/ea; 1973; 8pp; 15x10"; 1100 circ; off. Reports 2 wks. Ads: 60p/col. inch.

NEW CROSS & BROCKLEY TELEGRAPH, 170 New Cross Rd., London SE14, UK. Articles, art, photos, news items, criticism, letters. *It is a community paper which is put together by a group of people in the area, and aims to inform people of what is going on in the area as well as campaigning on issues which need to be taken up.* Monthly; 40p/yr; 4p/ea; 1970; 8pp; 11x16"; 2,200 circ; off. Ads: £1/ column inch. Back issues: 2p/ea.

NEW DEPARTURES, **Michael Horovitz,** Piedmont, Bisley, Stroud, Glos GL6 7BU,   UK. Articles, poetry, fiction, art, cartoons, photos, satire, interviews, criticism, music, letters, plays, collages, concrete. *"In 1959 Michael Horovitz brought out an exotic magazine called* New Departures. *It was hot to handle in the zero weather of that time. It tended towards characters like Raymond Queneau, John Cage, Jack Kerouac, Gregory Corso, Robert Creeley, Anselm Hollo ... It came out of the bohemian colonies of Europe and America" – Adrian Mitchell.* Irreg; £1.50($4.50)/yr; 36p($1.25)/ea; no sample; 1959; 100pp; 9x6½"; 5000 circ; off. Reports: immense; no mss. wanted for present. Pays: by arrangement. Ads: £50($125)/page pro rata. Discounts: by arrangement. ALP, Arts.

NEW GERMAN STUDIES, **Rex Last, Alan Best,** German Dept., Univ. of Hull, Hull HU6 7RX, UK. Articles, poetry, fiction, art, criticism, plays, concrete. *Keith Dickson, David Heald, R.C. Andrews, Keith Bullivant, Frank Fowler, Michael Butler.* 3/yr; £2/yr individuals; £2.50/yr institutions; 1973.

NEW HEADLAND, Ember Press (Epping), **William Oxley,** 27 Brook Rd., Epping, Essex,   UK. Poetry, longpoems. *Roy Fuller, William Plomer, James Kirkup, David Jaffin, Cal Clothier, Richard Burns, Anthony Johnson, Lotte Kramer, Patricia Martland, Stanley J. Thomas, Colin Nixon, Leon Spiro, William Poskett, Vivienne Finch, Gerald England, Nina Steane, etc.* 4/yr; £1/yr; 25p/ea; 1969; 30pp; 10x8"; 200 circ; xerox. Reports: 1 mo (US); 1 wk (UK). Pays: copies. Ads: £10/page. Discounts: 33% trade. Back issues: £10 set.

NEW HUMANIST, Rationalist Press Association, **Christopher Macy, Roger Manvell,** assoc. ed., 88 Islington High St., London N1 8EL, UK. Articles, poetry, cartoons, photos, criticism. Monthly; £2.25/yr; 15p/ea; free sample; 1972; 32pp;

210x250mm; 8000 circ. Reports 1 mo. Pays: £10/1000. Ads: £60/page; £32/½; £18/¼. Discounts: publishers 10%.

NEW INTERNATIONALIST, Battley Bros., **Peter Adamson**, 74a High St., Wallingford, Berks., UK. Articles, poetry, cartoons, photos, news items. Monthly; £3/yr; 25p/ea; free sample; 1973; 28pp; A4; 20,000 circ; off. Reports 2 wks. Pays: £12.50/1000 words. Ads: £100/page pro rata. Discounts: 15% agency. Back issues: 30p a copy. Third World.

NEW LETTERS, **David Ray**, Univ. of Missouri, Kansas City, MO 64110. Poetry, fiction, articles, art, photos, interviews, criticism, reviews, letters, parts-of-novels, longpoems. *Occasional Special Issues, e.g. on Richard Wright, on Jack Conroy, on African and Caribbean literature. The best in contemporary poetry, fiction, personal essay and photography. Small payment on publication.* 4/yr; $8/yr; 128pp; 9x6; lo. Ads: $100/p (25% discount on contract of 4 ads); $60/½. Back issues: $5 single copy (most issues of *University Review* and *U. of Kansas City Review,* predecessors of *New Letters* available back to 1934). Pub'd 4 issues 1973, expects 4 in 1974. COSMEP, CCLM.

NEW ORLEANS REVIEW, **Marcus Smith**, Loyola Univ., New Orleans, LA 70118. Poetry, fiction, articles, art, photos, interviews, criticism, reviews, music, plays. *Highest quality work. Recent contributors include Ernest Gaines, Al Young, Norman Mailer, Robert Joe Stout, Lester Granger, Natalie Petesch, Thomas Johnson, Rosemary Daniell.* Q; $6/yr; $1.50/ea; $1.50/sample; 1968; 96pp; 8½x11; 1M circ; photo set. Reports 2 wks-2 mos. Pays: $50/prose; $75/cover art & portfolio; $10/poetry & photos; copies only to reviewers. Discounts: agency rate $5 per year. Back issues: V.2; V.3, No.1, $1.25/ea; V.1 microfiche at 50 cents/issue. Pub'd 3 issues 1973, expects 4 in 1974. COSMEP, CCLM.

NEW POLITICS, New Politics Publishing Co., **Julius Jacobson**, New Politics, 507 Fifth Ave., New York, NY 10017. Political: American Politics, Latin American, European, Third World, Eastern European, Middle East, Labor Movement, Socialist. Recent contributors: David McReynolds, James Petras, Noam Chomsky, Julius Lester. Q; $5/yr; $1.25/ea; 1961; 100pp; 6x9; 5M circ; lp. Ads: $200/p; $125/½. Discounts: 20%. Pub'd 4 issues 1973, expects 4 in 1974.

THE NEW RENAISSANCE, **Louise T. Reynolds, Olivera Sajkovic, June Beale, Louise E. Reynolds**, 9 Heath Road, Arlington, MA 02174. Poetry, fiction, articles, art, photos, interviews, satire, criticism, reviews, parts-of-novels, plays. *Overstocked in fiction and poetry; query, enclosing sase, for non fiction, outlining article or essay. Recent contributors: Tom Lyons, Bill DelVisco, Sheila Thompson, Gordon Weaver, Lorca (in D.M. Pettinella translation) Fred White, R.D. Lakin, Barbara Holland, Madeleine Costigan.* 1-2/yr; $5.50/4 issues; $1.70/ea; $1.70/sample; 1968; 72pp; 6x9; 1M circ; lp. Reports 9-14 wks. Pays: $12.50 & up for fiction; $5 for poems. Discounts: agents, etc. 25%; newsstand, etc 30%; over 20 copies, 20%; over 35 copies, 25%; 50 or more copies, 30%, single issues. Back issues: *tnr No.1,* $3.20; all others, Nos.2-7, $1.70. Pub'd 1 issue 1973, expects 2 in 1974. CCLM.

NEW REVIEW (formerly THE REVIEW), **Ian Hamilton**, 11 Greek St., London W1, UK. Articles, poetry, fiction, interviews, criticism. *The first new literary monthly to be founded in Britain for more than a decade. There will be an extensive and topical reviews section, regular literary bulletins from abroad, lively and* *informed coverage of news and controversy and regular articles on painting, music, theatre and cinema. Contributors include A. Alvarez, Roy Fuller, Douglas Dunn, Robert Lowell, Brian Aldiss, Peter Porter, Malvyn Bragg.* Monthly; £12 ($30)/sub; 1962 (as *The Review)*; 1974 (as the *New Review)*.

THE NEW SALT CREEK READER, Windflower Press, **Ted Kooser,** 1720½ C. St., Lincoln, NB 68502. Poetry, interviews, criticism, reviews, letters, longpoems. *During the past year we have published four issues, including the poetry of Leonard Nathan, Denise Levertov, William Dickey, Robert Wallace, Colette Inez, Richard Shelton, Peter Wild, Stephen Dunn, Steven Osterlund, Greg Kuzma, and many others. Our Fall '73 number was a book of poems by William Kloefkorn, and we hope to do one regional collection like his each year. At the present we are not reading book manuscripts, only poetry for the magazine. We will print all of the good poems we get. If forced to admit to any preferences, we would have to say that we like the brief, image-centered poem of consequence. Nothing clever.* 3-4/yr; $3.50/yr; $1/ea; $1/sample; 1967; 50pp; 5½x8½; 400 circ; lo. Reports 2 wks. Pay varies; $2 per poem at present while grant lasts. No ads. Discounts: available on request. Pub'd 3 issues, 1 book 1973; expects 3 issues, 1 book in 1974. COSMEP, CCLM.

THE NEW SCHOLAR, **V.H. Kjonegaard, M.T. Arguello, bk. rv. ed.,** College of Arts & Letters, San Diego State, San Diego, CA 92115. Articles, criticism, reviews. *In the last year we have begun publishing review essays on Movies! Have also gotten more into the essay & translations – will be publishing translations (with commentary) of some of Pablo Neruda's 1930's material.* 2/yr; $4/yr; $2.25/ea; samples available; 1969; 140pp; 6x9; 800 circ; of. Reports 60 days. Pays copies only. Ads: $100/p; $60/½. COSMEP.

NEW SCHOOLS EXCHANGE NEWSLETTER, **Bill Harwood, Grace Dailey,** Pettigrew, AR 72752. Poetry, articles, art, photos, cartoons, interviews, criticism, reviews, letters, longpoems, collages. *We are a national clearinghouse for alternative education. The newsletter is oriented to alternative education – non age specific.* 2/mo (one as expanded magazine, and one as newsletter); $10/yr; $12/yr instit; 50 cents/ea; free sample; 1968-9; one 40pp, other 8pp; 8½x7; 3M circ; lp. No pay. Ads: no charge (2nd class status) as a service at our discretion. Discounts: will work out individual terms; annual *Directory of Alternative Schools:* 10 or more $1.80/ea (retails for $3). Back issues: 25 cents/ea; many available (presently on issue No.113). Pub'd 20 issues 1973, expects 20 in 1974. Education–Alternatives:

NEW SHETLANDER, 23 Knab Rd., Lerwick, Shetland, UK.

NEW UNITY, Box 891, Springfield, MA 01101. Poetry, articles, art, photos, cartoons, interviews, satire, criticism, letters. *Pro-labor, pro-worker, for a democratic economy.* 12/yr; $2.50/yr donation; 10 cents/ea donation; 8 cent stamp/sample; 1971; 8pp; tabloid; 5M circ; lo. Reports vary. No pay. No ads. Discounts: (5 or more) bulk orders for sale: 5 cents/ea, sell for 10 cents + postage; bulk orders for free: 4 cents/ea + postage. Back issues: 8 cent stamp. UPS, Workers.

NEW WORLD HAIKU, The Heliopolis Press, **Joseph Earner,** Box 256, San Fernando, CA 91340. Poetry, articles, longpoems, collages. *Haiku and senryu poetry; some "regular" poems occasionally. We tend toward the new and experimental in haiku, i.e., we are attempting to lift it from the giant birdbath of "women's verse." Standards therefore very high. Recent contributors of note: Michael McClintoch, Cid Corman.* Q; $4/yr; $1/ea; $1/sample; 1973; 24pp; 8½x5½; 500 circ; lo. Reports 2 wks. Pays contrib. copies; copies only. Pub'd 2 issues 1973, expects 2 in 1974. COSMEP, Poetry.

NEW WRITING FROM ZAMBIA, **David Simpson**, PO Box 1889, Lusaka, Zambia. Poetry, fiction. *Accepts only Zambian-relevant material or from citizens, residents or ex-residents.* Q; $2.50/yr and 37 cents/ea (post free); group membership available $4/yr includes free Q. mag and free monthly bulletin of news, comments & hints; 1964; 28pp; 9¼x7, print area 8x5½; 800 circ; lo. Ads: K20 or $33.35/p; K10 or $16.70/½; 2n or 3½ cents class/wd. Discounts: sales agent 33 1/3%; sub. agent 20%. Back issues: to members only 12 cents/ea. Pub'd 4 issues 1973, expects 4 in 1974.

THE NEW YORK CULTURAL REVIEW, **Daniel M.J. Stokes**, 1807 60th St., Brooklyn, NY 11204. Poetry, articles, plays. *Articles on anything, cultural news, you name it, we need it.* Q; $5/yr; 1974; 8½x11.

NEWLETTERS, Beyond Baroque Foundation Publications, **George Drury Smith, James Krusoe, Alexandra Garrett**, 1639 W. Washington Blvd., Venice, CA 90291. Poetry, fiction, articles, interviews, criticism, reviews, letters, parts-of-novels, concrete art. *News of the western literary community, poetry and prose primarily by western writers, commentary and letters from all over, news of interest to writers, including grants, publishers needing manuscripts, close scrutiny of the current publishing crisis. Free to anyone requesting it. $5 contribution brings* Newletters *by first class mail, plus all other Foundation Publications, including* Beyond Baroque *(q.v.) and chapbooks.* 6-8/yr; free; 1972; 24pp; 8½x11; 4M circ; lo. Reports 4-6 wks. Ads: $100/p; $60/½; class/wd $5 per col. inch (col. width 2 inches); 20% disc. to ad agencies or for camera/ready. Discounts: sub agency disc. for Foundation publications 20%. Back issues: generally not available. Pub'd 6 issues 1973, expects 8 in 1974. COSMEP, CCLM.

Newport Press (see *VILLAGE REVIEW*)

NEXUS, **Bruce Pilgrim** *(new ed. will be appointed in May, '74)*, Wright State Univ., Dayton, OH 45431. Poetry, fiction, art, photos, cartoons, satire, longpoems. *We print the best material we can find but refuse to limit ourselves to specific styles, genres or categories. Love to see any and all things, especially from previously unpublished writers and artists. Recent contributors are people you never heard of – but whom you may well hear of in the future.* 4/yr; $2/yr; 50 cents/ea; 50 cents/sample; 1965; 48pp; 8½x11; 1M circ; lo. Reports 2 mos. Pays 2 copies. No ads. Discounts: 20% disc. to trade, classroom, institution, agents. Back issues: 50 cents. Pub'd 2 issues 1973, expects 4 in 1974.

NIGHTWINGS (Silver, Tarzan & the Apes, Armpit), **Tim Rubald**, PO Box 244, Moorpark, CA 93021. Poetry, fiction, articles, art, photos, cartoons, interviews, satire, criticism, reviews, music, letters, parts-of-novels, longpoems, collages, plays, concrete art. *Open mail right away & if not interesting it comes back fast, sometimes not even making it out the P.O. door. Please consider the wait a compliment tho not necessarily an acceptance. This is being written on April 3, 1974. Style/biases: runs from the elegant to the gross; forget the thick, stodgy, academic. Like the neverending sinuousity of sweetness & stench & the creator in his seething majesty or his mother or the seven dwarfs going apeshit.* Pat Nolan, Loren Paul Caplin, Douglas Blazek, Keith Abbott, Philip Lopate, Bruce Andrews, Lyn Lifshin, Michael-Sean Lazarchuk, Joel Deutsch, Norman Mallory, David Gitin, Ken Weston, Anne Waldman, Frederick Lazarus Light, Ron Silliman, Charles Tidler, Charles Bukowski, Clark Coolidge... Irreg; $2/ea; $2/sample; 1969; 8½x11; 200 circ; mi; lo. Reports: if I don't like em you get em back quick; if i do it takes... Pays copies. Ads: $90/p; $60/½; 20 cents class/wd. Discounts: standard. Back issues: *Armpit* No.2, $2; *Silver*, $2; *Tarzan & the Apes*, $7. Expects 2 issues 1974. COSMEP.

NONE, Treacle Press, **Bruce McPherson,** 102 Benefit St., Providence, RI 02903. *First publication: March 15, 1974,* Shamp of the City-Solo, *a novel by Jaimy Gordon, offset, letterpress, & silkscreen, 6x9 inches, 150 pages, eleven drawings by James Aitchison. $2.95 paperbound: ISBN 0-914232-00-2. Press run: 1000.* Lo; lp; silkscreen. Discounts: trade: 40% thru RPM Distributors; text: 20%. Expects 4 books in 1974. COSMEP, NESPA.

NORTH, **Norman Smithson,** 55 Woodsley Rd., Leeds LS6 1SB, UK. £1/3 issues; price/ea varies; off. Back issues: 35p pf.

NORTH AMERICAN MENTOR MAGAZINE, **John Westburg Associates, Publishers, John Westburg,** 1730 Lincoln Ave., Fennimore, WI 53809. *Contributors: Merrill G. Christophersen, Theodore Halaki, James Richard Hurst, Janis Pallister, Lauren Lowenkron, David Crosby, Rod Steier, Jan Stuart, Barbara K. Shepherd, Harold O. Wang, Charles H. Howe, Emilie Glen.* Q; $9/yr; $3/ea; $1/sample; 1964; 75-90pp; 8½x11; 1300 circ. Reports 6 mos or less. Pays 1 contrib. copy; no payment for poetry. Ads: make query. Back issues: make query as to availability; $5 per back number except for Vols.I,II. Pub'd 4 issues 1973, expects 4 issues, 2 books 1974. COSMEP, CCLM, Literary and Political.

THE NORTH AMERICAN REVIEW, **Robley Wilson, Jr., Peter Cooley, poetry ed.,** Univ. of Northern Iowa, Cedar Falls, IA 50613. Q; $6/yr; $1.50/ea; $1/sample; 1815; 80pp; 8½x11; 3M circ; lo. Poetry, fiction, articles, photos, criticism. Reports 8 wks. Pay: $10/pub. page. Ads: $60/p; $35/½; 10 cents/wd. Discounts: 20% to agents. Newsstand distributor: Eastern News. CCLM.

NORTH EASTERN ARTISTS DIRECTORY, Blue Egg Studio, **David Stringer, Terry Heally,** 84 Woodhouse Lane, Leeds 2, UK. *This will be a directory of all kinds of artists and craftsmen/women in the area North of the Trent, East Derbyshire, including Derwent Valley, Yorkshire, Durham & Northumberland.* 20p px/ea; 1974.

NORTH 7, Highlands & Islands Development Board, Bridge House, Bank St., Inverness IV1 1QR, UK. Articles, photos, news items, interviews. North 7 *is published roughly quarterly to give up-to-date information about all aspects of development in the Highlands and Islands of Scotland. Each issue concentrates on a particular aspect of development (i.e. transport, North Sea oil) with support material in the form of news items, photo reports and book reviews. The articles are written by professional journalists.* 4/yr; 20p/yr; 5p/ea; free sample; 1967; 24pp; A4; 7000 circ; off. Pays: £2/100 words. No ads. Back issues: free as available.

THE NORTH STONE REVIEW, Tendon Press, **James Naiden; contrib. eds: Michael Tjepkes, Sigrid Bergie,** University Sta., Box 14098, Minneapolis, MN 55414. *Contributors: David Ignatow, Sigrid Bergie, Robert Bly, Ralph J. Mills, Jr., Herbert Morris.* $1.50/ea; $1/sample; 1971; 130pp; 8½x4½; 1250 circ; lo. Reports 2 wks. Pays 2 copies; copies only. Ads: $55/p; $35/½. Discounts: 40% to stores, etc. Pub'd 1-2 issues 1973, expects 1 in 1974. COSMEP, CCLM, Open to all.

North-Western Arts Association, 52 King St., Manchester M2 4YL, UK.

NORTH YORK POETRY (formerly York Poetry), **Colin Simms,** 37 Ouse Lea, Clifton, York YO3 6SA, UK. Poetry, longpoems. *Mature original work only, and* *more interested in regional* concern *than origin. Dialect, tourists' and new writers especially welcome. Recent contributors include Cal Clothier, Gerald England, Eleanor Makepeace and Jane Wilson. Every fourth issue takes the form of an anthology; those in between are each devoted to the work of a single author.* Varies; £1/5 issues; 25p/ea; 1971; 12-40pp; 9x5"; 500 circ; lp. Reports soon as possible. Pay: still hoping! No ads. Discounts: please apply. Back issues: please apply, list available. Ecology.

Northern Writers, 34 Cedar Lane, New Hey, Rochdale L16 4LQ, UK. Fiction. *An independent imprint whose aim is to publish original fiction by new writers.*

NORTHEAST/JUNIPER BOOKS, Juniper Press, **John Judson,** 1310 Shorewood Dr., La Crosse, WI 54601. Poetry, criticism, reviews, longpoems. *We solicit any work of quality that has a human being behind it, and whose words help shape his awareness of being human. This always comes before fashion, reputation, or ambition in our eyes.* Northeast Special Issue *spring 1974. Experimental Fiction issue guest edited by George (Bonnyclabber) Chambers. Recent Juniper Books: No.8* Astronomers, Madonnas, and Prophesies *by Victor Contoski; No.9* Chambersburg *by George Chambers; No.10* News From a Backward State *by Robert Flanagan; No.11* Bone Flicker *by John Woods; No.12* The Resident Stranger *by Harley Elliott.* 2/yr (with a Juniper Book); $6/yr; $1/ea (Northeast); $2/ea (Juniper Book); 75 cents/sample; 1963; 44-48pp; 8½x7; 500 circ; mi; lo. Reports 3-6 wks. Pays copies only. No ads. Back issues: write for bibliography & price list. CCLM.

NORTHERN JOURNEY, **Craig Campbell, David McDonald, Valerie Kent,** PO Box 4073, Sta. E, Ottawa, Ont., Canada. Poetry, fiction, articles, art, photos, criticism, reviews, letters, parts-of-novels, longpoems, collages, plays, concrete art. 2/yr; $3.50/yr; $2/ea; 1971; 100pp; 6x8¾; 1M circ; lo. Reports 1 mo. Pay: variable; 2 one yr. subs. Discounts: trade: 5-10 copies 35%; over 10, 40%; agency: 10%. Back issues: No. 1 & 2 available for $3.50. Pub'd 1 issue 1973, expects 2 in 1974. Canadian Periodical Publ. Assoc.

NORTHERN LIGHT (The Far Point), **George Amabile,** Univ. of Manitoba, Winnipeg, Manitoba, Canada R3T 2NZ. Poetry, interviews, reviews. *We want fresh, imaginative poetry, about real-life experience. We like the surreal, the mystical, the lyrical, as it comes out of experience. We do not like chatty, or excessively "personal" poems, nor do we admire academic poetry.* 2/yr; $1/ea; $1/sample; 1968; 72-98pp; 6x9; 1M circ. Reports 1-4 mos. Pays 5 copies. Ads: $100/p; $65/½. Discounts: 40%. Back issues: No.1, $5; Nos.2,3&4, $3.50; Nos.5,6&7, $2. We didn't publish in 1973; expect 2 issues 1974.

NORTHWEST REVIEW, University of Oregon Press, **Michael Strelow, mang. ed., Paul Scotton, fic. ed., Jim Heynen, poetry ed.,** Univ. of Oregon, Eugene, OR 97403. Poetry, fiction, art, photos, reviews, parts-of-novels, longpoems. *Quality fiction, poetry, book reviews – (poetry, fiction – Northwest emphasis).* Q; $4/yr; $1.50/ea; $1/sample; 1956; 128pp; 6x9; 1500 circ; lo. Reports 1-2 mos. Pays 3 copies; copies only. Ads: exchange only. Discounts: wholesale (90 cents/copy) 40%; consignment ($1.20/copy) 20% agents. Back issues: $1 examination copy. Pub'd 3 issues 1973. CCLM.

NORTHWOODS NEWSLETTER, Northwoods Press, **Robert W. Olmsted,** Box 24, Bigfork, MN 56628. Poetry, fiction, articles, art, photos, interviews, satire, criticism, reviews, longpoems, plays. *No restrictions, but we are poor. Larry Minkin soon.* 8/yr; $2/yr; 40 cents/ea; SASE for sample; 1972; 20-24pp; 5½x8½; 600+ circ; lo. Reports 1 mo. Pay: token in 1974; copies. Ads: $30/p; $17/½; 10 cents class/wd. Discounts: 20% for 1-10 copies; 40% for 10 + copies. Back issues: 25 cents/ea. Pub'd 5 issues, 12 books 1973; expects 8 issues, 23 books 1974. COSMEP.

Northwoods Press (see THE APOLLO, NORTHWOODS NEWSLETTER)

Nosferatu Press (see STONEY LONESOME)

NOTABLE AMERICAN POETS, Winston-Paramount Books Subsidiary, **Linda Nash,** 110-Cooper St., Drawer 338, Babylon, NY 11702. *Send one or two poems, 3-16 lines, and stamped return env. Our aim is to keep a running index of all the poets we publish and what editions they appeared in, to enable readers to follow particular poets. We want poetry that will give pleasure to others – not the poet wrapped up in himself. We're open to all styles and subjects, provided the work has artistic merit. Wise to study a copy.* Q; $5.95/paper; $8.95/cloth; $3.95/sample; 1973; 50pp; 8½x5½; 3M circ. Reports within 3 wks. Pays: 50 to 75 cents/poem. Pub'd 1 issue 1973, expects 4 in 1974.

NOTES & QUERIES: for Readers & Writers, Collectors & Librarians, **J.C. Maxwell, E.G. Stanley,** English Faculty Library, Manor Rd., Oxford OX1 3UQ, UK. *Typescripts on any matter of English Language or on medieval literature should be sent to E.G. Stanley, Queen Mary College, Univ. of London, 327 Mile End Rd., London E1 4NS. All other notes and queries to J.C. Maxwell, English Faculty Library, Manor Rd., Oxford OX1 3UQ.* 12/yr; £5($13)/yr; 50p($1.30)/ea; 1849.

NOTES ON MISSISSIPPI WRITERS, PO Box 433, Southern Sta., Hattiesburg, MS 39401.

Nothing doing (formally in London) formally Nothing doing in London (see also *LITERARY SUPPLEMENT),* 25 Woodhall Dr., London SE21 7HJ, UK. The Literary Supplement. The Literary Supplement, Writings. Nothing doing in London (ceased). *Books: consult latest (1974) catalogues of* Little Presses of Great Britain. 1966. ALP.

NOTTINGHAM FRENCH STUDIES, University of Nottingham, **Professor Lewis Thorpe,** The University, Nottingham NG7 2RD, UK. Criticism. *Articles 6000 words. French literature – 1600 to now. English & French articles.* 2/yr; £1/yr; £1/ea; 1962; 50pp; 7x9½"; 500 circ; lp. Reports 1 mo. Discounts: trade 50p. Back issues: 50p.

NOTTINGHAM MEDIAEVAL STUDIES, Nottingham University Press, **Professor Lewis Thorpe,** Nottingham Mediaeval Studies, The Univ., Nottingham NG7 2RD, UK. Articles. *This is a learned journal, dealing with mediaeval European literature, language, history, art, music, etc.* Annual; £1.25/ea; 1957; 90-100pp; 7½x9"; 500 circ. Reports 1 mo or so. Pays: none. No ads. Discounts: trade price £1.

Noumenon Press, **Carl D. Clark, Loris Essary, Eric Vogel,** PO Box 7068, University Sta., Austin, TX 78705. Noumenon Press *will begin issuing books in the summer of 1974. We are receptive to material of all types. Payment is by royalties.*

NOVEL: A Forum on Fiction, **Mark Spilka,** Box 1984, Brown University, Providence, RI 02912.

NUCLEUS, PV Publications, **Malc Payne,** 4 Wealden Close, Crowborough, Sussex, UK. Poetry, art, concrete. *New writers only; one poem from each issue, no longer than 40 lines, no bias; PV Publications is very anti-vanity press, v.p. reversed PV. A Poet's Vigilantes press. One annual copy, issued in Nov. of each year.* Annual; 25p($1)/yr; 1971; 40pp; A5; 200 circ; lo. Reports: return. Pays: one copy. Ads: good causes free, others haggle. Discounts: usual trade. ALP.

NZFCMA BULLETIN, **Ian Baugh,** 21 Ambler Ave., Auckland 7, New Zealand. Articles, photos, reviews, letters, news. *The only independent magazine on marine ferrocement. Material relevant to the do-it-yourselfer and the professional. Practical information, designs, service experience with ferrocement: 100 words to 5000.* 2/mo; $17.20/yr (airmail); single copy: not supplied; free sample; 1972; 58pp; A5; 400 circ; lo. Reports immediately. Pays copies only. Ads: $30($45 U.S.)/p; $15 ($23 U.S.)/½. Discounts: sent airmail for suface rates (sub: $15, U.S.). Back issues: $1.50 (U.S.) while supplies last. Pub'd 11 issues 1973, expects 7 in 1974. COSMEP, COSMEPA.

OASIS, Oasis Books, **Ian Robinson;** assistant eds: **John Stathatos, Anthony Lopez,** 12 Stevenage Rd., London SW6 6ES, UK. Articles, poetry, fiction, art, photos, satire, interviews, criticism, music, letters, longpoems, plays, collages, concrete. *Any length style – no biases except towards the excellent. Translations both prose and poetry. Greece: Seferis, Ritsos, Sinopolous, Alexandrou, Ioannon, Vakalo Sahtounis, Fassianos, Stahatos, Goumas. German: Eisenreich, Heise, Zomack, Schaefer, Bobrowski, Wurm, Werf, Andersh, Meyrink, Bienek. Italy: Buzzati, Betti. UK: Booth, Redgrove, Shuttle, Curtis, Oxley, Thurley, Burgis, Marshfield, Austin, Grubb, Lee, Simpson, Engel, Jaffin, Lambert, Cinicolo, Matthews, Welch, Brown, Tribe, Wiessbort. Poland: Jasienski, Busza. USA: Bonner, DeMasi, Manzo, Arvin, Matteson, Cummins, Fulton. Canada: Green, Svoboda, Kennon, Bowering, Birney, Bullock, Payerle, Thorne, McWhirter, Stedingh. France: Jacob, Demelier, Du Cornet. Brazil: Bandeira, Carvalho, Andrade. Portugal: Pessoa. Mexico: Ehrenberg, Mena.* 4/yr; 80p($4.50)/yr; 20p($1.50)/ea; 1969; 74pp; A5; 500+ circ; off. Reports 2 wks. Pays: copies, so far. Ads: £8/page pro rata. Discounts: 33%. ALMS, ALP.

OCCULT AMERICANA, **Ms. Barbara Mraz,** 3686 Ludgate Rd., Shaker Hts., OH 44120. Articles, interviews, reviews. Bi-monthly; $3/yr; 50 cents/ea; 50 cents/sample; 1971; 18pp; 7x8½; 300 circ; lo. Reports 6 wks. Pays: $10 per. Ads: exchange only; 10 cents per class/wd. Pub'd 6 issues 1973. COSMEP, Occult history.

OCCUM RIDGE REVIEW, **Richard Schaaf,** PO Box 68, S. Willington, CT 06265. Poetry, fiction, longpoems. 2/yr; $1.80/yr; 90 cents/ea; 1973; 40pp; 7x7½; 500 circ; lo. Reports 2-4 wks. No pay; copies only. Ads: $50/p; $25/½; no class/wd. Discounts: 40% to bookstores.

OCCURRENCE, **John Wilson,** 8 S. George St., Mechanicsburg, PA 17055. Poetry. *The magazine will hopefully adjust to its content. Issue One contained poems by (in order of appearance): William Bronk, Toby Olson, J.D. Whitney, Susan Wohlbruck, John Taggart, Ted Hall, Hugh Seidman, Keith Wilson, Theodore Enslin, Donald Bowie, Howard McCord, John Wilson, Russell Edson.* Irreg; $1/issue No.1 (will change); 1973; lp. Pays copies only. Pub'd 1 issue 1973, expects 2 in 1974. COSMEP.

Oddments, **Gerda Mayer,** ed. & publ., 12 Margaret Ave., Chingford, London E4, UK. Poetry. *Oddments Press published* Poet Tree Centaur *(a Walthamstow Poetry Group Anthology) in 1973: contributors were Frank Davies, Andrea Finn, Gerda Mayer, William Oxley, Stanley J. Thomas, etc. No unsolicited mss. please as future plans uncertain. N.B. Oddments is not a mag.* Odd intervals; 5p post./sub; qto; 200 circ; off.

OFF OUR BACKS: a women's news journal, **Off Our Backs Collective,** 1724 20th St., N.W., Washington, DC 20009. Poetry, fiction, articles, art, photos, cartoons, interviews, satire, criticism, reviews, letters, parts-of-novels, longpoems, collages, plays. Monthly; $6/yr U.S.; $7/yr Canada; 45 cents/ea; 45 cents/sample; 1969; 32 pp; 11½x15; 8M circ; lo. Reports 3 mos. No pay. Ads: no full page; $50/¼; class/

word $2/40 wds. Back issues: 25 cents/ea; 20 cents/ea for orders of 10 or more. Pub'd 10 issues 1973, expects 12 in 1974. COSMEP, Women.

THE OHIO REVIEW, W. Dodd, C.G. Thayer, S.W. Lindberg, S. Plumly, S.R. Crowl, Ellis Hall, Ohio Univ., Athens, OH 45701. Poetry, fiction, articles, interviews, criticism, reviews. *Looking for excellence in poetry, fiction, and essays of general humanistic interest that attempt to cross disciplinary lines or view their subjects against a broad intellectual background.* Recent contributors include Robert Bly, Joyce Carol Oates, Mark Strand, Mona Van Duyn, Herbert Gold, Gerald Weales, Donald Hall, Jack Matthews, Carolyn Kizer, Charles Bukowski, Theodore Weiss, Richard Shelton, Galway Kinnell. 3/yr; $5/yr; $2/ea; $2/sample; 1959; 124 pp; 6x9; 900 circ; lo; lp. Reports 10-12 wks. Pays: copies + min. 5 cents/prose wd; min. $5/poem. Ads: $60/p; $40/½; no class/wd. Discounts: rates on request. Back issues: rates on request. Pub'd 3 issues 1973, expects 3 in 1974. COSMEP, CCLM.

OLD FRIENDS, Glebe Press, David Allen, Anne Becker, Kelp Homburg, William Mayville, 3007 Porter St. N.W., Washington, DC 20008. Poetry, fiction, essays, art, photos, cartoons, satire, criticism, parts-of-novels, longpoems, collages, plays, concrete art. *"Our approach is to explore beyond formality in art: we want to reveal the person creating. Writers, graphic artists, and photographers should send 7-10 sample of their work. A substantial selection is necessary to present the wholeness and diversity of the artist's expression."* Some recent contributors have been: David Axlerod, Debbie Berson, Pat Barnes, Jackie Potter, Dolores Neuman. Q; $5/yr; $1.25/ea; sample; 1973; 48pp; 5½x8½; 250 circ. Reports 30 days. Pays copies only. No ads. Discounts: 40% bulk. Back issues: $1.25/ea. Pub'd 2 issues 1973, expects 4 issues 1974 (maybe books also).

THE OLD RED KIMONO, Ken Anderson, PO Box 789, Rome,GA 30161. Poetry, fiction, art, plays. *All submissions must be short.* Q; 1972; 10pp; 8x11; 500 circ; lo. Reports 1 mo. Pays: 2cc; copies only. Pub'd 4 issues 1973, expects 4 in 1974. COSMEP, CCLM.

Oleander Press, Will Marston, U.S.: 210 Fifth Ave., New York, NY 10010; U.K.: 28 Parkfield Crescent, Harrow HA2 6JZ. Poetry, travel, law, language, archaeology, plays. *We have begun an* Oleander Modern Poets *with the exceptional writers only in the Penguin style featuring Hans-Juergen Heise, Philip Ward and Osten Sjostrand. Future volumes will be mainly bilingual texts and translations by well-known writers and translators. Books on minority literatures:* Romagnol *and* Friulan *by D.B. Gregor;* Burmese *by Anna Allott. Write first before submitting.* 3-4/yr; 1965. Reports: send letter first. Pays: by arrangement. No ads. Discounts: 33% booksellers. ALP.

Olivant Press (see WEID)

OMEGA, Sun Press, Sananda, 67 Wildmoor Rd., Shirley, Solihull, Warwickshire, UK. Articles, poetry, art, news items, interviews. *The material is factual communications being received telepathically from the 'Council of the Twelve Lords', 'The Brotherhood of the Seven Rays', 'The Heavenly Host' 'The Solar Space Fleet' 'The Cosmic Hierarchy of God' forming a planetary network of Light under the direction of St. John the Divine, & Jesus-Sananda co-ordinating 'The Suns of Light' 'The Wanderers' 'The Light Workers' 'New Age Groups' for the great plan for Earth, formulating the foundation principles of the 'New Faith' 'The Divine Unity of Faith' the Faithists, in preparation for 'The Golden Age on Earth.' Beat That!* Irreg; £1/sub; 25p/ea; pf/sample; 1970; 32pp; 10x8; 3000 circ; off. Ads: £10/p & pro rata. New Age Material.

OMENS, G.S. Fraser, gen. ed., Sam Brown, John Martin, David Timms, Andy

York, 9 Roundhay Rd., Leicester, UK. Poetry, art, longpoems. *Any reasonable length of poems are considered. The editors have no particular prejudice as to style. The summer issue may take the form of a pamphlet of an individual poet and we are always on the lookout for poets of high calibre who have a good body of work. Recent contributors include Veronica Forrest-Thomson, Beth Cross, Benenice Moore, Nina Steane, Sam Brown, John Martin, Andy York.* 4/yr; 80p/yr; 20p/ea; 1971; 36pp; 6x8"; 500-1000 circ; off. Reports: 12 wks max. Pays: 3 complimentary copies only. Ads: £10/page; £6/½; £5/¼.

Omphalos Press, **Martin Booth, Hugh Lauder,** 15 Keats Way, Rushden, Northants NN10 9BJ, UK. Poetry, longpoems, verse plays. *Length and style immaterial; no biases; some books paperback.* 1973; 48pp; A5; 500-1500 circ; lp. Reports 3 mos. Pays: yes. Discounts: trade. ALP.

The Omphalos Press, **Roy H. Sagarin,** The Chatham Bookstore, Central Sq., Chatham, NY 12037. Poetry, fiction, art, photos, parts-of-novels, plays. *David Kherdian, Nonny Hogrogian, Peter Kane Dufault, Joel Bernstein, Don Moyer, Louis Hammer. Poetry, short fiction, bias toward high quality writing. Looking for real statements of perceptive, creative individuals. Not concrete, not personal shlock unless its really unique. Lean toward naturalism, surrealism, environmentalism, clear thinking, ideational yet creatively composed. (If you believe this garbage send your stuff elsewhere).* 1973; lo; lp. Reports 2-4 wks. Pays copies only. Discounts: 40% trade. Back issues: $1.50. Pub'd 1 issue 1973; 1 book 1973, expects 4 in 1974. COSMEP, NESPA.

ON SITE, Site, Inc., **Alison Sky, Michelle Stone,** 60 Greene St., New York, NY 10012. Articles, art, photos, interviews. On Site – *a publication dealing with new concepts and innovations related to the environmental arts and architecture. Rather than deal with these subjects as traditionally separate categories, On Site functions as an idea catalyst, presenting advanced and revolutionary thought on all aspects of public space.* 3/yr; $7/for 3 issues: No.5,6,7; $2.50/ea; $2.50/sample; 1972; 50pp; 8½x11; 3M circ; lo. Pays copies only. No ads. No discounts except in large quantities. Back issues: $3. Pub'd 2 issues 1973, expects 3 in 1974. COSMEP.

ONE: the writer's magazine of fiction & poetry, Andarth Interrelated Projects, **Paul Freeman,** PO Box 1347, New Brunswick, NJ 08903. *One welcomes fiction and poetry of all lengths and styles. We're especially looking for people stories – strong characters and emotions. One has published science fiction, mystery, and satire as well as "straight" stories. Contributors in recent issues included Lillian E. Carlton, W.S. Doxey, Stan Taikeff, Richard Bastian, Chip Miller, and Gerald Schoenewolf. We definitely do not like "cute, trite, or bullshit" manuscripts. One also publishes a Writer's Bulletin in between regular issues. The Bulletin is free to anyone interested.* 3/yr; $3/yr; $1/ea; $1/sample; 1973; 50pp; 5½x8; 500 circ; lo. Reports 4 wks. Pays: no cash; 3 copies. Ads: $40/p; $20/½; 10 cents class/wd. Back issues: $1.50. Pub'd 3 issues 1973, expects 3 in 1974. COSMEP.

THE ONTARIO REVIEW, **Raymond Smith,** 6000 Riverside Dr. East, Windsor, Ont., Canada N8S 1B6. Poetry, fiction, articles, art, photos, interviews, criticism, reviews, letters, parts-of-novels, longpoems, plays. *A North American journal of the arts, the Review welcomes contributions of all kinds, especially fiction and poetry. The editors are also looking for essays dealing with twentieth-century American and Canadian writers, artists, and thinkers, especially those who have not received much critical attention in the past. Studies bridging the Canadian and American cultures are particularly welcome.* Bi-annual; $5/yr; $2.50/ea; 1974; 100pp; 6x9; lo. Reports 2-3 wks. Pays copies only. Ads: $50/p; $25/½. COSMEP.

THE OPEN CELL, **Milton Loventhal, P. Friedman, J. McDowell,** PO Box 52, Berkeley, CA 94701. Poetry, fiction, art, photos, satire, parts-of-novels, longpoems, plays. *Limit 10 pages prose submissions. Limit 5 poems per submission. Art & photos b&w only. Long poems are fine. Particular interest in work by women, 3rd World, senior citizens, prisoners,* but all *writers' work receives serious consideration. Experimental forms, very internal or "personal" works probably receive favorable bias. A few recent contributors: Glee Knight, Barbara Holland, Richard Latta, Steve Richmond, R.A. Roth* . . . 4/yr; $2/yr; $5/yr instit; 50 cents/ea; free sample with SASE; 1969; 8pp; tabloid (11½x17); lo. Reports vary; attempt swift reply. Pays copies only. Ads: 50 cents class/wd. Discounts: write us. Back issues: Vol.1, Nos.1-3 no longer available; Nos.4-7, $2; Nos.7-15, 50 cents; No.16, 50 cents. Pub'd irreg. due to financial problem now solved; expect 4 issues 1974. Particularly interested in work by Third World, Women, Chicano, Black, American Indian, Gay, G.I., Prison.

OPEN PLACES, **Eleanor M. Bender, Thomas Dillingham, book rev. ed.,** Box 2085, Stephens College, Columbia, MO 65201. Poetry, fiction, reviews. *Open Places has expanded to include short fiction, reviews of small press publications and poetry. I like a variety of writing and published a very diversified magazine.* 2/yr; $3/yr; $1.50/ea; 1966; 64pp; 600 circ; lo. Reports 6 wks. Pays copies only. Ads: $65/p; $35/½. Back issues: $1.50. CCLM.

OPENSPACES, The Laurel Press, **Elizabeth Brown, Robert Brown,** 1409 S. Saltair Ave., Los Angeles, CA 90025.Poetry, prose poems (whatever can be handset which is a lot). *openspaces is a field of poems: play the field. An open space, windowless. A dream concerning the business of imaginations. A game to love; play for keeps. Some recent contributors: Alvaro Cardona-Hine, Holly Prado, Robert Stern, Dudley Laufman, Jarold Ramsey, Ameen Alwan, Barbara Hughes etc. The example of the poet as the complete editorial farmer — imagining, sowing, growing, tending and harvesting the words by hand.* 2-3/yr; $5/yr; $2-$3/ea; free sample as they last; 1973; 44pp; 6½x9; growing to 500 circ; lp. Reports 2-3 wks. Pays: $1 & 1 copy. No ads. Discounts: trade, special, most anything; editions are numbered; limited to 250-500 copies/books & mags. Back issues: $2. Pub'd 1 issue 1973, expects 2-3 issues, 2 books 1974. COSMEP, COSMEPA, Woman & Man.

Open University Press (see SESAME)

Openings Press, **Dom Sylvester Houedard, John Furnival,** Rooksmoor House, Woodchester, Glos., UK. Concrete. *Openings Press is concerened mainly with bringing out poster-poems in unlimited editions and silk-screen prints in limited editions. For financial reasons our operations are rather restricted and we regret that we are unable to accept unsolicited material.* Varies; 15p/ea; 1964; single sheets; varied page size; 500 circ; silk-screen/lp. Pays: copies. Ads: none. Discounts: 33%. ALP.

OPERA, **Harold Rosenthal,** 6 Woodland Rise, London N10 3UH, UK. Articles, criticism. *Up to 2000 words on general subjects appertaining to opera.* 13/yr; 25p each. Pays: by arrangement.

OPINION, Opinion Publications, **Dr. James E. Kurtz, Sue Meyer,** Box 1319, Dodge City, KS 67801. *We prefer the hard-hitting, but well written essay type story on either a sociological, philosophical or theological theme.* Monthly; $5/yr; 50 cents/ea; 50 cents/sample; 1954; no. pages varies; 8½x11; 4M circ. Reports 3-4 wks. Pays copies only. Ads: $30/p; $15/½; 10 cents class/wd. Discounts: yes we extend disc. rates. Pub'd 15 issues in 1973.

Orange Press (see VERSE GAZETTE)

ORBIS, Hub Publications Ltd., **Robin Gregory,** Orbis, Youlgrave, Bakewell, Derbs. UK. Articles, poetry, criticism, letters. *The magazine of the International Poetry Society.* 4/yr; £1.20($5)/yr; 30p($1)/ea; 1969; 48pp; 8x6"; lp. Ads: £15($45)/page; £8($24)/½. Discounts: 33% trade. ALP.

ORCADIAN, Kirkwall Press, **Gerald A. Meyer,** Orcadian Office, Kirkwall, Orkney, UK. 52/yr; £3.38/yr; 3p/ea; 1854; 8pp; 22x15"; 9118 circ; lp. Ads: £77/page; £38.50/½; 10p/line.

Orchard Press (see LYTTON RECORD, WORLD OF H.G. WELLS (Wellsiana))

ORE, Ore Publications, **Eric Ratcliffe,** mang. ed., **Brian Louis Pearce,** adv. ed., 7 Claymores, Stevenage, Herts, UK. *No sick material or* unpatriotic *material. No concrete work. Ideally based on the past of ancient Britain as a faith for the future.* 2-3/yr; 20p/ea; 10p/sample; 1954; 30pp; 650 circ; off. Reports 2 wks. Pays: by arrangement. Ads: 2p/word. Discounts: 33% trade; 12½% libraries. Back issues: 10p. ALP, Occult, White, Arthurian legend/Ancient British, SF.

THE ORIGINAL ART REPORT (TOAR), **Frank Salantrie,** PO Box 1641, Chicago, IL 60690. *Exclusive interest in fine art (visual) in Midwest and elsewhere as it affects the region's art, community, and the people. No standard reviews, previews, profiles, or puffy pieces.* Monthly; $10/12 issues; $1/ea; $1/sample; trial sub: 3 issues/$2; 1967; 4pp; 8½x11; 100-1M circ; lo. Reports: normal. Pays copies only. No ads. No discounts. Back issues: $1.25/ea if available. Pub'd 3 issues 1973, expects 9 in 1974.

ORION: A Bimonthly Anthology, CSA Press, Inc., **David Anthony Kraft,** Lakemont, GA 30552. Poetry, fiction, articles, art, photos, plays. *Interviews, reviews, letters, parts-of-novels must all have a metaphysical slant.* 6/yr; $5/yr; 90 cents/ea; 90 cents/sample; 1955; 96pp; 5x8; 1500 circ. Reports 2 wks to 1 mo. Pays copies only. No ads. Discounts: 1/3 off on packs of 12. Back issues: 50 cents. Pub'd 6 issues 1973, expects 15 in 1974; 10 books in 1973. Metaphysics.

Orphan Press (see EMPTY BELLY)

ORPHIC LUTE, **Viola Gardner,** 3815 Mercier, Kansas City, MO 64111. 2/yr; $5/yr; $1/ea; 1957; 34pp; 8½x5½; 300 circ; mi. Reports at once. Pays prizes, 1 copy. Back issues: $1.

OSGOLDCROSS REVIEW, Poets Press of Osgoldcross, **G. England,** 50 Chiltern Drive, Ackworth, Pontefract WF7 7DW, UK. Poetry. *First issue including Harriet Rose, Diana Hendry, Nicki Jackowska, Henny Kleiner, etc still available. Publication of future issues suspended until further notice.* 5p px/ea; 1973; 12pp; 10x8; 150 circ; mimeo.

OSIRIS, **Andrea Moorhead,** 1065 University Pl., Schenectady, NY 12308. Poetry, fiction, criticism, reviews, music, longpoems, plays, concrete art. *An international journal, publishes work in English, French, Italian. Seeking work in German and Spanish. Welcomes essays on contemporary art/poetics. Recent contributors: Michel Cosem (France), Marina Ceratto (Italy), R. Kostelanetz, R. Federman.* 2/yr; $3/yr; $1.50/ea; 50 cents/sample; 1972; 48pp; 6x9; 500 circ; lo. Reports 3-5 wks. Pays copies only (2). Ads: $50/p; $30/½. Discounts: 40%. Pub'd 2 issues 1973, expects 2 in 1974.

OSTRICH, Erdesdun Pomes, **Keith Armstrong,** 10 Greenhaugh Road, South Wellfield, Whitley Bay, Northumberland, UK. Articles, poetry, art, cartoons, photos, interviews, criticism, letters, longpoems, plays, collages, concrete. *Radical arts mag.*

Examining artist's place in the community and the role of the arts in contributing to social change. Past contributors include: Edwin Morgan, Barry Cole, Michael Chamberlain; Translations of Lorca, Yevtushenko, Gorbanevskaya. Plus articles on political issues of the day. Graphics/photos. Q; 60p/qtr; 15p/ea; pf/sample; 1971; 40pp; quarto; 500 circ; off. Reports: 1 mo. Pays: copy. Ads: free. Discount: 1/3. ALMS, ALP.

OTHER SCENES, **John Wilcox,** BCM/OSCENES, London WC1V 6XX, UK. Irreg; $10/sub; $1/ea; 1966; no. pp varies; circ varies; off. Reports: 48 hrs. Pays: low. COSMEP, Occult.

OUR GENERATION, Black Rose Books, **a collective,** 3934 St. Urbain St., Montreal, Quebec, Canada. Articles, cartoons, criticism, reviews. *Articles vary, up to 40 pages each. We are a radical libertarian socialist journal. All of our articles reflect that bias – all our editorials represent an agreed upon position. Half our material is written by the editors.* 4/yr; $5/yr; $1.50/ea; $1.50/sample; 1961; 96pp; 7¼x9¼; 3M circ; lp. Reports 2 wks. No pay. Ads: $100/p; $50/½; no class/wd. Discounts: 1/3 to bkstores; 6% on sub. to sub. agency. Back issues: Vol.1 thru 6, $163.50. Pub'd 4 issues 1973.

OUT OF SIGHT, **James Mechem,** Box 32, Wichita, KS 67201. *Poetry. Recent contributors include Diane Kruchkow, Gloria Kenison, Blythe Ayne, Ruth Moon Kempher, Michael Joseph Phillips, Ann Menebroker, Glenna Luschei, Alta, Carol Berge, John Stevens Wade, Richard Snyder, George Montgomery, Alan Britt, Steve Sneyd, Duane Ackerson, Joel Deutsch, Lyn Lifshin, Joyce Holland, Albert Drake and John Jacob.* Weekly; $100/yr; free single copy; free sample; 1971; 8pp; 5½x8½; 30 circ. Reports 6 mos. Pays: secret. Pub'd 60 issues 1973, expects 40 in 1974. COSMEP, CCLM.

OUT THERE MAGAZINE, Pedestrian Press, **Stephen M.H. Braitman,** 55 Keystone Way, San Francisco, CA 94127. Poetry, fiction, interviews, satire, criticism, reviews, letters. *Originally a science-fiction oriented publication,* Out There *is now expanding to include first rate prose & poetry without such a rigid bias. The editor's personal tastes run to the weirdly horrifying, shock with meaning and depth, and the unnatural made real. He likes the flesh to cringe with the realization of life's unmerciful glory. Yeah.* Irreg; 75 cents/ea; 75 cents/sample; 1967; 30pp; 8½ x11; 500 circ; mi. Reports: resonable. Pays copies only. Ads: $50/p; $30/½. Back issues: Issue No.3–75 cents; issues No.2 & 1 sold out. Pub'd none 1973, expects 1 issue in 1974.

THE OUTER CIRCLE, Plunkett Press & Art Associates, **Helen L. Thorington,** R.D. No.1, Monroeton, PA 18832. *Publishes stories, poems, articles. Stories and articles should be limited to 1500 words. Has published Ellen Tifft, James Bertolino. Six issues in print.* Q; 20-30pp; 8½x5½; 150 circ and growing. Pays copies. Back issues: $1.25/copy.

OUTPOSTS, Outposts Publications, **Howard Sergeant,** 72 Burwood Road, Walton-on-Thames, Surrey, UK. Articles, poetry, criticism. Outposts *is the oldest independent poetry magazine in the UK. It was founded to provide a satisfactory medium for those poets, recognised or unrecognised, who are concerned with the potentialities of the human spirit, and who are able to visualize the dangers and opportunities which confront the individual and the whole of humanity. Although recent contributors have included famous poets like Ted Hughes, Peter Porter, George MacBeth, Vernon Scannell, Kingsley Amis, Thomas Blackburn etc, the magazine makes a special point of introducing the work of new and unestablished poets to the public.* 4/yr; £1/yr; 25p/ea; 1944; 36pp; demi 8vo; 1500 circ; lp.

Reports 2 wks. Pays: £1/page approx. Ads: £20/page; £12/½; £8/¼. Discounts: 10% Publishers/Series.

Outrigger Publishers Ltd. (see CAVE)

OUTSIDER, **Frank Edwards,** 225 Croydon Road, Caterham, Surrey CR3 6PG, UK. Poetry, fiction, art, criticism, letters, longpoems, collages, concrete. *Recent contributors include Adrian Mitchell, George MacBeth, Mike & Fran Horovitz, Bob Cobbing, Brian Patten, John Best.* Erratic; £1.50/10 issues; 20p/ea; 1969; 40pp; qto; 300 circ; mim. Reports up to 1 yr. Pays: copies. Ads: £5/page, personal ads free. Discounts: 33%. Back issues: 25p.

OUTWORLDS: an Eclectic Journal, Outworlds Productions, **William L. Bowers,** PO Box 148, Wadsworth, OH 44281. Articles, art, photos, cartoons, interviews, satire, criticism, reviews, letters, parts-of-novels, collages. *Associate editors: Stephen E. Fabian & Michael Glicksohn. Columnists: Poul Anderson, Piers Anthony, Greg Benford, Terry Carr, Susan Glicksohn, Robert A.W. Lowndes, Andrew J. Offutt, Jodie Offutt & Ted White. In the early years the emphasis was on the art & graphics; we've kept those ... and added the words.* Outworlds *is basically slanted toward the science fiction community, but not exclusively. We run very little poetry (and that by regulars), and no fiction as such. Main emphasis is on people and things people do, rather than things, though recent topics of discussion have ranged from four letter words in sf through reprint policies of professional magazines ... to the joys of peanut butter.* Outworlds *exists to please the editor, who is Old & Mean ... but he has fun with it. And so do most of the readers.* Q; $4/yr; $1.25/ea; $1/sample; $5/yr library; 1 in 1966, resumed in 1970; 40pp; 8½x11; 1500 circ; lo. Reports 2-4 wks. Pays copies & subs. Ads: rate sheet on request. Discounts: available only from publisher & through sub. agencies. Back issues: $1.25/ea when available. Pub'd 4 issues 1973, expects 4 in 1974. COSMEP.

OVERLAND, **S. Murray-Smith,** GPO Box 98a, Melbourne 3001, Australia. Poetry, fiction, articles, art, photos, cartoons, interviews, satire, criticism, reviews, letters, parts-of-novels, longpoems. *Mainly Australian material. Radical inclinations.* Q; $4 (Aust.)/yr domestic; $6 (Aust.)/yr Europe Asia; $8 (Aust.)/yr Americas; 1954; 64pp; quarto; 3M circ; lp. Pay: by arrangement. Ads: $80 (Aust.)/p; $40 (Aust.)/½. Discounts: 25%. Pub'd 3 issues 1973.

OVERSPILL: for the longer poem, **Eric Harrison,** 3 Grantley Close, Shalford, Surrey, UK. Poetry, criticism, letters, longpoems. *Poems up to 200 lines, prose up to 4 quarto sides. Preferred verse develops new aspects and variations of traditional forms and styles rather than extreme experiments and innovations. Contributors include Gerald England, Hugh McKinley, William Kean Seymour, Rosalind Wade, Vivienne Finch.* 4/yr; £1/yr; 20p/ea; 1972; 20pp; qto; 150 circ; mim. Reports 2 wks. Pays: only by prior arrangement. Ads: none. Discounts: 20%. ALP, ALMS.

Ox Head Press, **Don Olsen,** 414 N. 6th St., Marshall, MN 56258. Poetry, satire. *I'm back at it after a near 2 year lapse. The same format as before — poetry pamphlets by one author of 1 to 5 poems each. Contributors have been John Haines, Robert Bly, H.R. Hays, Donald Hall, Michael Hamburger, John Ridland, James Bertolino, Richard Deutch, Jack Matthews, Stephen Dunn. I'm also going to be doing one or two short (about 15 poems) books a year.* Irreg; $5/10 issues; $1/ea (but varies); 1967; 4x6; 300 circ; lp. Reports mo or so. Pays: $25 plus 25 copies. No ads. Discounts: trade, 50%. Back issues: $1/ea if in print. Pub'd none in 1973; expects 4 issues, 1 book 1974.

Oxford University Press for the University of Leeds (see JOURNAL OF COMMONWEALTH LITERATURE, MUSIC & LETTERS)

P.E.N. NEWSLETTER, English Centre of International P.E.N., 62-63 Glebe Place, London SW3 5JB, UK. Ads: £7.50/page, £.4/½.

Pacific Perceptions, Inc. (see STONECLOUD)

PACIFIC RESEARCH AND WORLD EMPIRE TELEGRAM, 1963 University Ave., E. Palo Alto, CA 94303. Articles, reviews. *Radical political economy and analysis of U.S. foreign policy, emphasizing Asia and the Pacific.* 6/yr; $5/2yrs (individual); $15/yr (institution); 50 cents/ea; free sample; 1969; 24pp; 8½xll; 1M circ; lo. No pay. Discounts: bulk (5 or more) 50%. Agent 10%.

PAGES, **David Briers,** 23 Wellesley Road, Chiswick, London W4 4BU, UK. *The magazine as a gallery: performance art, mail art, new music, outer reaches of visual poetry, Fluxus, jokes, projects, information, very international.* Irreg; £1.00/sub; 25p/ea; postage/sample; 1970; 30pp; A4; 1000 circ; off. Reports: long. Pays: copies. Ads: apply. Discounts: trade 33%. Back issues: pf.

PAID MY DUES, Women's Soul Publishing, Inc. (non-profit), **Dorothy Dean right now, soon to be collective,** PO Box 5476, Milwaukee, WI 53211. Articles, art, photos, cartoons, interviews, criticism, reviews, music, letters. Paid My Dues *is a feminist journal of women and music covering original songs (words and music), articles about musical herstory, women artists, women in broadcasting, announcements of conferences, interviews with women musicians and music lovers, reviews of relevant records and books, etc. Recent contributors: Cambridge-Goddard Women's Music Project, Holly Near, Florence Reece, Betsy Greiner-Schumick, Madeline Davis. No special requirements as to length of articles, etc. Biases: material by women only (except in special cases). Send SASE for return of material.* 4/yr; $4/yr U.S.; $1/ea; $1.50/sample (1st class mail); 1974; 40-48pp; 8½xll; lo. Reports 3 wks. Pays copies only (3). Ads: $40/p; $25/½; no class. yet. Discounts: 35% disc. on 10 or more copies to individual women, women's and alternative bkstores, women's centers. Back issues: none yet. Expects 4 issues in 1974. COSMEP, Women, Women's News Network member.

PAINTBRUSH, a journal of poetry, translations, & letters, B.M. Bennani, Box 3353, University Sta., Laramie, WY 82071. Poetry, articles, interviews, criticism, reviews, letters, translations. Paintbrush publishes established, as well as serious up-and-coming poets, translators, etc. Contributors to the Spring issue include: Richard Eberhart, W.H. Auden, Robert Creeley, Howard McCord, W.M. Ransom, Robert Pack, James Tate, Sonia Raiziss, Joseph Bruchac, Robert Bly, Alfredo de Palchi, and Werner Aspenstrom. Poems must show what Ciardi calls the poet's passionate devotion to (1)rhythm, (2)diction, (3)image, and (4)form. Translations, from any language, must say something in English, and must include biographical notes. Essays, reviews, criticism, must not exceed 10 type-written double-spaced pages. Ex: Paul Mariani's "Williams: The Last Phase" and Richard Eberhart's "W. H. Auden: A Memoir." Mss cannot be returned unless accompanied by SASE. 2/yr; $3.50/yr; $2/ea; $1/sample; 1974; 60-70pp; 6x9; 500 circ; lo; lp. Reports 1-4 wks. Pays copies only. Ads: $150/p; $100/½; class. $15/1x2½ inch box. COSMEP, CCLM, NESPA.

PAINTED BRIDE QUARTERLY, **R. Daniel Evans, Louise Simons,** 527 South St., Philadelphia, PA 19147. Poetry. *We want people with experience in writing poetry-high quality material. We have no particular bias towards style or subject matter, but generally shy away from old fashioned rimed verse. Would like more good women poets. Recent contributors include Tarn, Hollo, Tagliabue, Bluford, Braun, Colten, Mariah, Audre Lorde, Malanga, Major, Bukowski, Dorman, et al.* 4/yr; $4/yr; $1/ea; $1/sample; 1973; 48pp; 6x9; 1M circ. Reports 2 mos. Pays copies only. No ads. Discounts: upon request. Back issues: $1.50 for first 2 issues (these are rare). Pub'd 1 issue 1973, expects 4 in 1974; no booktitles. COSMEP.

EL PALACIO, Museum of New Mexico Press, **Carl E. Rosnek,** PO Box 2087, Santa Fe, NM 87501. 4/yr; $6/yr; $1.50/ea;1913; 48-52pp; 8½x11; 1M circ. Reports 3 to 4 wks. Pay: minimal. No ads. Discounts: 40% on bulk orders to bona fide retailers. Back issues: $1 to $1.50 ($500 for a full set of available back issues). Pub'd 4 issues, 4 books 1973; expects 4 issues 5 books in 1974.

Pale Horse Press (see also REVIEW '74), **Joseph McLaughlin, ed. & publ.,** Box 109 New Philadelphia, OH 44663. *The concept of Pale Horse Press is unique in that the house will lend its imprint to* self-publishing *authors whose work is of sufficient quality. This service includes, if necessary, administrating publication, including securing copyright in the author's name, designing cover, editing and arranging contents, and sub-contracting actual manufacture of the book. We are not a subsidy house. No promotion, other than occasional advertising of an overall listing, is provided. The idea, is to provide the strength of a recognizable umbrella over a collection of individuals. Poetry, fiction, criticism.* 1 book in 1974, expect 2 in 1975.

THE PAN AMERICAN REVIEW, Funch Press, **Seth Wade,** 1100 West Samano, Edinburg, TX 78539. Poetry, fiction, articles, art, interviews, satire, reviews, letters, collages. *A recent Pan American University research grant will help assure one (double) issue this year. After that the mag is expected to come out whenever material, money, and time meet. Heavy emphasis on Latin American work and things related to Latin America. Some contributors: Birney, Stokes, Bonazzi, Lifshin, Fox; as translators, Bly, Pettinella, Oliphant, Seth Wade; poets in translation, Neruda, Huidobro, Parra, Lihn, Paz.* Irreg; $3.50/yr; $2/ea except for double issues; 50 cents/sample; 1970. Reports 1 day to 6 wks. Pays copies only. Discounts: 50% trade. COSMEP.

PANACHE, **R.B. Frank, pub. & ed., Dr. Lenson, poetry issues, ed.,** Box 2214, Princeton, NJ 08540. Poetry, fiction, parts-of-novels. *David Shapiro, Robert Coover, Jay Bail, Keith Cohen, Raymond Federman, Alan Feldman, Robert Fagles, Gary Goss, Mike Finley, James Grabill, Gayl Jones, Arthur Vogelsang, Ken Kwint, J.F. Bory, Marvin Cohen, etc., etc. Prefer fiction under 4000 words but will look at longer. Want good, well-written work, whether traditional or way out.* 2/yr; $1.50/ea; 1965; 64pp; 6x9; of. Reports vary. Pay: some. Pub'd 2 issues 1973, expects 2 in 1974. COSMEP, CCLM.

Pantheon Press (see COSMOPOLITAN CONTACT)

Papa Bach Bookstore (see BACHY)

PAPER PUDDING, **Michael Zucaro,** P.O. Box 30, Villa Grande, CA. 95486. *A quarterly magazine of literature and art.*

Paper Tiger Press, (see SQUEEZEBOX)

THE PAPERMAN, The Paperman Publishing Company, **H. Randall Williams,** 929 South 22nd St., Birmingham, AL 35209. Poetry, fiction, articles, art, photos, cartoons, interviews, satire, criticism, reviews, letters. *3000 word limit, no biases.* Wkly; $4.50/yr; 10 cents/ea; 10 cents/sample; 1973; 12pp; 11x14; 6M circ. Reports 2 wks usual. Pay varies; copies only sometimes. Ads: $200/p; $115/½; 6 cents class/ wd. Back issues: 15 cents/ea + postage. Pub'd 18 issues 1973. COSMEP.

THE PARIS REVIEW, **George A. Plimpton, ed.,** 45-39 171 Place, Flushing, NY 11358

PARNASSIAN, Calder Valley Poets' Society, **Mrs. Maud Fearnley,** 3 Callis Wood Bottom, Charlestown, Hebden Bridge, Yorks, UK. 4/yr; 1915; 8pp; 8x5"; lp.

PARTISAN REVIEW, **William Phillips,** Rutgers Univ., 1 Richardson St., New Brunswick, NJ 08903. Poetry, fiction, articles, interviews, criticism, reviews, parts-of -novels. Q; $7.50/yr; $2/ea; 160pp; 4¼x7 3/8; 9M circ; lp. Reports 3 mos. Pays: 1½ cents per wd; 40 cents per line poetry. Ads: $110/p; $75/½. Discounts: 40% bulk; 25% agent. Back issues: cover price + postage. Pub'd 3 (No.3 double issue) issues 1973, expects 4 in 1974. COSMEP, CCLM.

Pathfinder Press, Inc., **Gus Horowitz,** 410 West St., New York, NY 10014. *Books and pamphlets on labor, history, philosophy, socialism, Third World, women's liberation, the Black and Chicano movements, and other social struggles.* Discounts: books: 1-4/25%, 5-49/40%, 50-99/42%, 100+/45%; panphlets: under 25/25%, 25-199/40%, 200-499/42%, 500+/45%; (single or assorted titles); text discount: 25%.

PATTERNS, (see STONE COUNTRY)

PAX, **The Benedictines,** Prinknash Abbey, Gloucester, UK. 2/yr; 50p/ea; 1904; Pays: none. Monasticism/Liturgy.

PEACE & PIECES REVIEW, Peace & Pieces Press/Foundation, **Grace Harwood, Todd S.J. Lawson, David Hoag, M. Custodio,** Box 99394, San Francisco, CA 94109. Poetry, fiction, articles, interviews, satire, criticism. *We are a quarterly review especially interested in prose & poetry, satire & black & white illustrations (no photos) by women writers, bi-lingual writers who will do their own translations, gay people, Chicanos, atheists, anti-atheists, misc. dingbats, ex-lovers, etc. Short prose. we are especially equipped to handle Chinese, Japanese, Spanish poetry if provided camera-ready copy, but we do not specialize. Italian, French, etc. American writers are encouraged to submit as, of course, English-speaking & writing peoples. Satire very welcome.* 4/yr; $3.50/yr; $1/ea; 69 cents/sample; 1971 38-50pp; 8½x10; 300+ circ. Reports 3 wks. Pays: sub; copies only. Ads: $50/p; $28.50/½; 50 cents per word class/wd. Discounts: libraries $3 per year; poor people: whatever they can afford; prisons: free; others: flexible. Back issues: $5/issue (if available free to poor people). Pub'd 4 issues, 6 books 1973; expects 4 issues, 4 books 1974. COSMEP, Third World, Women, Chicano, Black, American Indian, Gay, Multi-lingual Writers.

PEACE NEWS, **Beale, Clark, Ellwood, Hyatt, Reandon,** 5 Caledonian Road, London N1 9DX, UK. Articles, poetry, cartoons, photos, news items, interviews, criticism, letters. Weekly; £4.94/yr; 7p/ea; 1936; 10pp; 14x10; 4-5000 circ; lp; Reports: 1wk. Pays: low. Ads: classified 2p/word, £1/col. Discounts: 15% annual contract. Back issues: 10p. ALP, Women, Ecology, 3rd World, Black, Gay, Peace/libertarian.

THE PEACEMAKER, **DiAnne Eckman, Tom Harman, Alice Ann Carpenter, John Leininger,** 10208 Sylvan Ave., Cincinnati, OH 45241. Articles, reviews (very few - some books), letters. *Articles from 100 to over 1000 words are usual. We're more a newsletter than a magazine, carry info. on activities we've been involved in related to non-exploitative, simple living, the revolution. There's a definite anarchist leaning, and we are the pacifist organ of a pacifist group (Peacemakers).* Every 3 wks; $3/yr; free sample; 1949; 8pp; 8½x11; 3M circ. Reports: deadline is about 10 days before pub. date. No ads. Discounts: all the work is volunteer, including ours. We very much appreciate contributions. Pub'd 15 issues 1973, expects 15-16 in 1974. Third World, Food/Ecology, Prison. We deal with all types of Peace activites, alternatives.

Pedestrian Press (see OUT THERE MAGAZINE)

PEGASUS, **O.F. Gibb,** Green Island, Ardleigh, Colchester CO7 7SL, UK.

M.E. Pegs & Associates (see A SMUDGE ON THE WINDOW)

PEKING REVIEW, Post Office Registration No. 2-922 Peking. (37), People's Republic of China.

PEMBROKE MAGAZINE, **Norman Macleod,** PO Box 756, Pembroke, NC 28372. *Arthur Gregor, Ray Young Bear, Kay Boyle, Georgia O'Keeffe, R.C. Gorman, Picasso, Daniel Hoffman, Robert McAlmon, David Ignatow, Simon Ortiz, Frank Waters, W.S. Graham, Kregg Spivey, Carl Rakosi, Norman Macleod, Kris Hotvedt, Brom Weber.* Annual; $2/yr; $2/ea; no sample; 1969; 152pp; 6x9; 1500 circ; lo. Reports 4 wks; Pay varies. Ads: $50/p; $25/½. Discounts: Agency & bkstore 40%. Back issues: out of print. Pub'd 1 issue 1973. COSMEP, CCLM, Third World, Black, Am.Indian.

PENETRATION, Jumpin Jack Flash, **Paul Welsh,** 13 Westholm Avenue, Heaton Chapel, Stockport, Cheshire SK4 5BE, **Chris Pickles, assist. ed.,** 17 Chelsea Avenue Southend-on-Sea, Essex, UK. Articles, poetry, fiction, art, cartoons, photos, interviews, music, letters. *American Distribution: Mia, 702 Roosevelt Street, Tempe, Arizona 85281.* 6/yr; 10p, 50 cent/ea; 1974; 16pp; 10x8"; off.

PENNINE PLATFORM, **Mabel Ferrett,** 2 Vernon Road, Heckmondwike, Yorkshire WF169LU, UK. Articles, poetry, art, news items, criticism, letters. *Jon Silkin, Norman Nicholson. Length – short preferred. All styles. No biases bar porn.* 4/yr; £1/yr; 25p/ea; 26pp; 8x5"; 300 circ; off. Reports: varies. Pays: none. Ads: £5/page.

THE PENNY DREADFUL, **Beth Copeland, poetry ed., Tony Ardizzone, fiction ed.,** English Dept., Bowling Green State Univ., Bowling Green OH 43403. Poetry, fiction, art, interviews, criticism, reviews, letters, parts-of-novels, longpoems. *We publish quality fiction and poetry, valuing experimental work yet accepting good traditional stories and poetry. We admire and have published the works of Philip F. O'Connor, Robert Early, Michael Berryhill, Carolyn Forche, Diane Wakoski. Regular feature is interviews, usually done here at Bowling Green, with visiting writers.* 3/yr; $1.50/yr; 50 cents/ea; 50 cents/sample; 1970; 30pp; 8½x11; 700 circ; lo. Reports 2-4 wks. Pays 3 copies. No ads. Back issues: 50 cents (though many not available). Pub'd 3 issues 1973, expects 3 in 1974. CCLM.

PENNY POEMS, Trouser Press, **Nigel Jenkins & E. Von McGregor,** 3 Dale Street, Leamington Spa CV32 5HH, UK. Poetry. *PP is a specifically LOCAL poetry mag covering the Leamington and mid-Warwickshire area so generally we do not use poems by people outside the area unless, as guest poets, they have been specifically asked to contribute. (D.M. Thomas, Connors, Sneyd, Fallon, Pilcher, Land). The main aim is to encourage the reading and writing of poetry in this area, especially among those who, as readers have never taken much interest in poetry or, as writers have been struggling away in isolation, unaware - as are most people - of the available small press outlets for their work. PP is more concerned with emergent talent than with propagating the work of more sure-footed poets.* 5-6/yr; formerly 1p each. We rely on donations now; 1972; 12pp; A4; 700-1000 circ; mim. Reports: 24 hours.

The Pennyworth Press, **David Foy,** 1429 28 St., S.W., Calgary, Alberta, Canada. Poetry. *Intend to publish poetry of finest quality in small editions well printed but not big-money book buff stuff! Or in a semi-periodic series of monographs.*

*Will often rely on editorial services of poets & consider masters. Invite experienced poets to suggest possible publishing ventures. (Not a vanity press but will print for individuals as a specialist commercial printer. Donot disdain stationery, cards, other ephemeral work.)*1973; 1p. Reports 24 hrs for rejects, longer for possibles. Pays: small advance, large royalties. Expects up to 4 books in 1974. Po-biz.

PENUMBRA, **Charles Haseloff,** GPO Box 1501, NYC 10001. Poetry. 1-2/yr; $5/2 yrs; $1.50/ea; $1.50/sample; 1967; 56pp; 5½x8½; 500 circ; lo. Reports 4-8 wks. Pays copies only. COSMEP, CCLM, Poetry.

PEOPLE'S BOOKSELLER NEWSLETTER, **Bob Broedel,** c/o Co-op Books & Records, PO Box 2436, Tallahassee, FL 32304. Articles, interviews, reviews, news. *It will serve as a clearing-house for information useful to progressive bookseller. Emphasis will be placed on left-political resources. Sub-title:* A Newsletter Directed to Progressive Booksellers. Approx. 3/yr; $1 (in 10 cent stamps)/yr; 30 cents/ea; two 10 cent stamps/sample; 1974; 4pp; 8½x14; 1M circ; of. No pay. No ads. Back issues: 30 cents/ea. No issues, books pub'd 1973, expects none in 1974. COSMEP, Third World, Women, Chicano, Black, Food/Ecology, Am.Indian, Gay, G.I., Prison, general left-political.

People's Translation Service, 2490 Channing Way, Berkeley, CA 94704.

PEOPLE'S YELLOW PAGES OF THE SF BAY AREA, **People's Yellow Pages Collective,** PO Box 31291, San Francisco, CA 94131. *A directory of alternative services and products available in the San Francisco Bay Area. Contributions of listings and illustrations gladly accepted.* 1/yr; $1.95 + 30 postage/ea; 1971; 160pp; 8½x11; 25M circ; lo. No pay. No ads available. Discounts: 40% for orders of 10 or more for resellers. Back issues: No.1, $1.25; No.2, $1.75. Pub'd 1 book 1973, expects 1 in 1974. COSMEP, Women.

Peoplesmedia, Inc. (see RAMA, The Peoplesmedia Monthly)

Perivale Press, **Lawrence P. Spingarn,** 13830 Erwin St., Van Nuys, CA 91401. Poetry. *We are planning to specialize in translations of modern poetry, and will pay advances of $150 on manuscripts of 64 to 80 printed pages, original and translation, suitable for paper-back book.* Reports 6-8 wks. Discounts: 40% to trade on books. Expects 1 book 1974. COSMEP.

PERSONAL POETRY BROADCASTS, **David Ross, Marjorie Ross, asst. ed.,** 20400 Frederick Rd. (1-17), Germantown, MD 20767. *Daily radio programs on six stations. Estimated listenership, 3,000,000. Will send sample recording for $3. Certificate of Broadcast Quality, showing poetry used; station airing it. Also awards occasional tape or record for outstanding work. Wants simple, uncomplicated poetry. Acceptable themes are: religion, philosophy, nature, patriotism, hopes, dreams, humor, memories, etc. Grammar, spelling unimportant. "If we feel our listeners can identify with it, we'll probable use it." Word length: 24 lines or less. Nothing handwritten, although clear carbons or copies are okay. Do not contact our stations. It makes unnecessary work (and resentment) for them. No profanity or sick psyche material. Poet retains all rights, during and after broadcast. Since broadcasting is not publishing, copyright is not required. Poetry remains property of poet. Publishes occasional Anthologies,* Best Broadcast Poetry, (year), *irregularly, when enough sufficiently satisfying poetry warrants. Anthology material is copyrighted, for poets' protection. All rights remain with poet. SASE required for correspondence. No poetry returned.* Reports 5-8 wks, except when overwhelmed.

PETERLOO POETS SERIES, **E.J. Morten, publishers,** 4 & 6 Warburton Street,

Didsbury, Manchester 20 UK. *We have published three books of poetry as follows:* The Snowing Globe - *Peter Scupham O 901598 42 9;* Signs of Life - *Stanley Cook 0 901598 41 0;* The Love Horse - *John Mole 0 901598 84 4;* Elswhere - *David Seltzer 0 901598 85 2.*

Phantom Court Press, **A. D. 2200,** c/o Abyss, PO Box C, Somerville, MA 02143.

PHOEBE, the George Mason Review, **Ann Elizabeth Poe, Richard Bausch, James Everhard,** George Mason Univ., 4400 University Dr., Fairfax, VA 22030. Poetry, fiction, art, photos, criticism, reviews, parts-of-novels, longpoems, plays. *We encourage prose. (No novels due to space. Chapters acceptable.) Essays dealing with writers and artists. Regionalism. Local color. Photos and art can only be reproduced in black 'n white. Porno and works of unbending piety have slim chances.* 2/yr; $2/yr; $1/ea; 1972; 80pp; 11x8½; 2400 circ; lo. Reports immediate to 3 mos. Pays copies only (2). No ads. Pub'd 3 issues 1973, expects 2 in 1974.

PHOENIX, **Harry Chambers,** 8 Cavendish Road, Heaton Mersey, Stockport SK4 3DN, UK.

THE PHOENIX, Morning Star Press, **James Cooney. Am.ed. Nidra Poller, Eur. ed.,** The Phoenix, Morning Star Farm, West Whately, RFD Haydenville, MA 01039. *We expect to attain regular quarterly issues this year.* Irreg, 4 numbers per vol; $8/yr; $2.50/ea; $10/yr foreign; 250pp; 5¼x7 5/8; 3100 circ; lp; Reports usually 2-3 wks. Pays copies only. Ads: free to radical causes; also exchange ads; no paid ads. Discounts: agent. Back issues: write for current information; quite a few are out of print.

PHOENIX FIRES, American Mosaic FFCE (Poetry Enterprises), **Constance Adele Henning,** 932 Griggs S.E., Grand Rapids, MI 49507. Poetry, fiction, articles, art, photos, cartoons, interviews, satire, criticism, reviews, music, letters parts-of-novels, longpoems, collages, plays. *Any or all but not color, not over 2-3 pages. Also will do layout and typography for other poets and/or editors. Am constantly upgrading. As subscribers increase, they must remember they have more competition. A separate qualification is used for new and juvenile writers. A firm stand is taken on material that most people would not care to find sons and daughters reading. Some religion – but not a whole raft of it. Variety.* 4/yr; $10/yr; $2.50/ea; $2.50/sample; teachers & students apply, also groups; 1972; 60pp; 8½x11; 250 circ (growing); lo. Reports 2 mos (and decreasing). Pays: Mosaic Book/if ordered. Ads: 'have not done so yet; ½p/$10 if wanted; class./wd 25 wds free to subscribers. Discounts: $5/yr – teacher, student, creative club such as poetry or writers, etc. (over 12). Back issues: not available except Fall issue 1973; others are collector item. Pub'd 4 issues 1973, expects 4 in 1974; expects 2 books in 1974.

PHOENIX THEATRE BROADSHEETS, New Broom Private Press, **Toni Savage and Zeta Alessandra,** 48 Walton Street, Leicester, UK. *Broadsheets printed at irregular intervals - given away free to patrons of the Phoenix Theatre, Leicester.*

PIGIRON (Literary & Art Magazine), **Jim Villani,** PO Box 237, Youngstown, OH 44501. Poetry, fiction, articles, art, photos, cartoons, interviews, satire, criticism, reviews, parts-of-novels, longpoems, collages, plays, concrete art. *Equal emphasis on language forms (fiction, poetry, criticism, articles) and design forms (photography, engravings, pen & ink). We treat each issue of our magazine as a work of art in itself, not as another nugatory journal stilting the compositions of the artists we publish. Any topic or idea can be evolved into a work of art. We emphasize craft, not theme. Comtemporary and experimental forms fare best, but we will publish any form or model if it is flexible and graphic.* 3/yr; $3/yr; $1/ea; $1/

sample; 1973; 64pp; 7x10; 1500 circ; lo. Reports 4-8 wks. Pays 2 copies. No ads. Discounts: on request. Pub'd 1 issue 1973; expects 3 in 1974. COSMEP.

Pigiron Press (see also *PIGIRON, TALES OF THE ENEMY),* **Jim Villani,** ed.-in-chief, PO Box 237, Youngstown, OH 44501. Poetry, fiction, articles, art, photos, cartoons, interviews, satire, criticism, reviews, parts-of-novels, longpoems, collages, plays, concrete art. Pigiron, *literary & art magazine.* Tales of the Enemy, *underground comic. We are especially concerned with regeneration in the arts as the result of new & established artists maturing & mastering their craft. There are no new subjects or themes, but there is a pervasive quality of newness infused in successful works of art. We strive to venerate that newness in the publications of Pigiron Press. We want digestible material: literature & art that will induce our readers to show our magazines to their friends. We call it mutual art; art that is shareable on any level of consciousness.* Lo. Reports 4-8 wks. Pays copies only. Discounts: on request. Back issues: not available. Pub'd 4 issues 1973, expects 7 in 1974. COSMEP.

Pilot Press Books, **Eric Greinke,** PO Box 2662, Grand Rapids, MI 49501. Poetry, fiction, art, longpoems. Pilot Press *publishes full-length books in both hardcover & paperback format. Length varies from 48 to 300 pages. Mainly poetry from the following schools & movements: Dada/Surrealism, Black. Will consider good Gay Lib anthology if anyone has edited one, or Woman's Lib, or Concrete, if it's capable. Royalties paid: 10% Contract. Have published some 30 plus titles since inception in 1972. Have published Kirby Congdon, Ben Tibbs, John Woods, Herbert Martin, Joseph Brennan, Diane Wakoski, Donald Hall, Etheridge Knight, Dudley Randall, & many, many others. Write for free catalog & checklist.* 3-8/yr; 1972; 48-300pp; 300-3M circ; lo. Reports 1-4 wks. Discounts: trade & libraries: 40% no min; 20% disc. to individuals ordering direct from catalog. Pub'd 13 books 1973, expects 3 in 1974. COSMEP.

PLANTAGENET PRODUCTIONS RECORDED LIBRARY OF THE SPOKEN WORD, Plantagenet Productions, **Dorothy Rose Gribble,** Westridge, Highclere, Newbury, Berks.,England, UK. *Spoken word recordings of poetry, philosophy, narrative and light verse on LP, tape, and by arrangement cassette. Special orders undertaken. Recent issues: "Lyrics of Ronsard" translated by Charles Graves and "Poet's Choice" written and read by Edgell Rickword. Next issue: "By Special Permission," twentieth century poetry from Dorothy Rose Gribble's recital "A Pride of Writers."* LPs £ 2.25, £2, £ 1; tapes £ 1.75 plus postage. Spoken word recordings.

PLATFORM, Green Horse Press, **Andrew Cozens,** assisted by **Jim Cozens, Cynthia Corres,** "Avalon," London Road, Stockbridge, Hampshire SO20 6EJ, England, UK. Articles, poetry, art, cartoons, photos, interviews, criticism, letters, longpoems, concrete. Platform *is concerned with what's being written today, with the upholding of critical standards without pretension or pose-taking. Recent contributors wide and varied from world-wide sources. Continue to invite genuine contributions.* 3 pa; 50p for 4; 15p/ea; free sample; 1971; 50pp; 8x5"; 500 (now) circ; litho. Reports: varies, but immediate acknowledgment. Pays: none, at moment. Ads: free listing for small presses. Discounts: by arrangement. Back issues: free for postage. ALMS.

PLOUGHMAN, Fragment Press, **Gary Oliver**, PO Box R.217, Royal Exchange, Sydney, N.S.W., Australia 2070. Poetry, art criticism, reviews, longpoems, collages, concrete art. Ploughman *a magazine of poetry & poets & the things related to both. The only comments I have on material are (i) see what we have already printed by looking at the mag. (ii) as the mag is printed on foolscap paper (lengthwise not up & down) & folded in half, poetry with long lines sometimes presents a problem & arrangements have to be made.* Ploughman *is a little magazine devoted primarily to printing unpublished poems, poetry, visuals, letter-pictures, graphics, drawings together with small press notes and occasional reviews. Contributions are from the U.K., the U.S.A., and New Zealand as well as from Australia.* Q; $4(Aust.)/yr within Aust; $5 (Aust.)/yr overseas; $1 (Aust.)/ea within Aust; $1.50 (Aust.)/ea overseas; no sample; 1973; 24pp; 6½x8½; 500 circ; lo. Reports usually same day. Pays copies only. Ads: under terms of sales tax act mag does not contain any paid ads. Discounts: 20% Trade, Agent. Back issues: No.1 &2 (titled *Ploughman's Lunch)*,$2 (Aust.)/ea in Aust., $3 (Aust.)/ea o/s; Double issue 3/4, $3 (Aust.) in Aust., $4.50 (Aust.) o/s. Pub'd 2 issues 1973, expects 5 in 1974; no books 1973, expects 1 in 1974.

PLOUGHSHARES, **DeWitt Henry, Peter O'Malley & others**, Box 529, Cambridge, MA 02139. Poetry, fiction, articles, art, photos, interviews, reviews, parts-of-novels, longpoems, plays. *Max. length for prose 6000 wds. We're biased towards new writers, towards writers in the Boston & New England area, & towards "rediscovery" of neglected writers of interest to same. Recent contrib: Richard Hugo, Bill Knott, Fanny Howe, Paul Hannigan, Bobbie Louise Hawkins, Russell Banks, Maxine Kumin, Madeline DeFrees, Arthur Vogelsang, Jack Marshall, Barry Spacks, Richard Yates, Brian Moore, Tillie Olsen, George Garrett, James Whitehead, Scott Turow, Tim O'Brien, Thomas J. Cottle, Kathleen Spivak, Bob Kaven, Marge Piercy, Alan Lebowitz, Andre Dubus, J.D. Reed, Michael Ryan, Wm. Doreski.* 3/yr; $8/4 issues; $2/ea; 1971; 128-144 pp; 8½x5½; 1500 circ; lo. Reports 3 mos. max. Pays $5/pg prose (to $50 max.); $10/poem. Ads: $100/p; $60/½. Discounts: trade 40%; agent 25%. Back issues: 1/1 out of print, available by Vol. sub. only; other nos. $2 Pub'd 2 issues 1973, expects 4 in 1974. COSMEP, CCLM, NESPA.

PLUM, Guild of Undergraduates, Liverpool University, **Jane Goulding and Gladys Mary Coles**, c/o York Avenue, West Kirby, Wirral, Cheshire or Students Union, 2 Bedford Street North, Liverpool 3, UK. Articles, poetry, fiction, art, interviews, criticism. *Short pieces mainly; a miscellany of creative writing with bias towards good quality poetry and lively prose.* 2/yr; 10p/ea; 1973; 32pp; 1000circ; off.

Plunkett Press & Art Associates (see THE OUTER CIRCLE)

PM NEWSLETTER, B.B. Books, **Dave Cunliffe**, 1 Spring Bank, Salesbury, Blackburn, Lancs BB1 9EU, UK. *Lists and reviews little magazines, small press books, underground and community newspapers, pamphlets, posters and broadsheets. Alternative and counter-culture documents and publications of all kinds. Distributed with postal subscription copies of* Global Tapestry Journal. 4/yr. ALP.

POCKET POETRY MONTHLY, The Florida Press, **Richard Marsh**, PO Box 134, Key West, FL 33040. Poetry, articles, interviews, criticism, reviews, letters, longpoems. *Purpose of PPM is to extend range of poets published in small journals; also to propagate work of small journals, especially poetry journals. PPM uses reprints only of poems published in English language publications — no original poetry. Will include some book and magazine reviews, criticism, articles, interviews — all relating to current and future trends of poetry. Art wanted for cover. Photos with interviews. Dedicated to discovering the best of current work.* Monthly; $8/yr; 75 cents/ea; 75 cents/sample; 1974; 32-48pp; 4¼x5½; 1M circ; lo; lp; Reports 1 mo or less. Pays: 2 copies to author; 1 copy to mag. Ads: $25/p; $15/½. Expects 1 issue in 1974. COSMEP.

POEM, **Robert L. Welker,** PO Box 1247, West Sta., Huntsville, AL 35807. Poetry 3/yr; $3.50/yr; $1.25/ea; no sample; 1967; 60pp; 500 circ. Reports 2 wks. Pays copies only (2). Back issues: $3 early issues. Pub'd 3 issues 1973, expects 3 in 1974.

POEMS OF SIGNIFICANCE, J.Mark Press Subsidiary, **Anne Walker and volunteer guest editors,** 480-M Union Blvd., Box 122, West Islip, NY 11795. Poetry. Send to 2 poems, 3-16 lines and return env. We care here about the poet, not the editorship. We ask that poems have a personal significance to the poet and he states the significance (under 15 words) in parenthesis under poem; which will appear in print. The extent of editorship is limited to the poems having reasonable literary merit, no profanity or vulgarity. We feel that just as if we could see what was behind Mr. Poe's poems, or Mr. Frost's one day people will enjoy finding a little insight into our lesser-known poets who may eventually be of equal public interest. We suggest you study a sample. Q; $5.95/paper; $8.95/cloth; $3.95/sample; 1974. 50pp; 8½x5½; 3M circ; lo. Reports promptly. Pays: 2 to 10 cents/line. Ads: poetry books: $5/¼page. Discounts: available on request. Pub'd no issues 1973, expects 2 in 1974. COSMEP.

POET & CRITIC, Iowa State Univ. Press, **Richard Gustafson,** Engl. Dept., Iowa State Univ., Ames, IA 50010. Poetry, articles, art, cartoons, satire, criticism, reviews. 3/yr; $1/ea; free sample; 1964; 48pp; 6x9; 500-1M circ; lp; Reports immediately to 8 wks. Pays copies only; $30 prize. COSMEP, CCLM.

POETRY, **Daryl Hine,** 1228 North Dearborn Parkway, Chicage, IL 60610. Poetry reviews. 12/yr; $1.25/ea; 1912; 64pp; 5x9; 10M circ; lo. Reports 6 wks. Pays: prose $10/page; verse $1/line. Back issues: $1.50.

POETRY AND AUDIENCE, School of English, University of Leeds, Leeds, York UK. Poetry, art. 26/yr; 75p/yr; 2p/ea; 1953; 18pp; A5; 500 circ; mim/off. Reports:vary. Pays: none. Ads: none.

POETRY AUSTRALIA, South Head Press, **Grace Perry, ed.,** 350 Lyons Road, Five Dock 2046 NSW, Australia.

POETRY EASTWEST, **Syed Amanuddin,** PO Box 391, Sumter, SC 29150. Poetry Empathizes with world poetry movement. Emphasis on dramatization of experience and freshness of image and phrase. Interested only in unpublished poems and translations under 30 lines. Poems submitted for Poetry Eastwest are also considered for Creative Moment. Guest Editors: Dr. Grace Perry (Australia),Howard Sergeant (England), and Robert Thompson (New Zealand). 1/yr; $2/yr; $1.50/yr individuals; $1/sample; 1967; 44pp; 5½x8½; 500 circ; lo. Reports 6-8 mos. Pays copies only. Discounts: dealer 25-40%; 40% disc. on all orders of 5 or more copies be sent to one address. Back issues: $4. COSMEP, CCLM.

POETRY INFORMATION, **Peter Hodgkiss,** 17 Carlingford Road, London NW3 1RY, UK. Articles, news items, criticism, letters. Reviews of small press material English & other. Poetry Index– list of articles on poetry in newspapers/periodicals. Articles on current developments in this country and abroad- e.g. Laurence Upton on Poland in PI8. List of bookshops. 4/yr; 50p/yr; free sample; 1970; 25 pages; A4; 500 circ; mim. Back issues: 25p/issue. ALMS.

POETRY NATION, **C.B. Cox and Michael Schmidt,** 266 Councillor Lane, Cheadle Hulme, Cheadle, Chesire SK 8 5PN, UK. Articles, poetry, interviews, criticism, longpoems. 2/yr; £ 2.90/yr; £ 1.60/ea; 1973; 144pp; 8½x5½"; 2-3000 circ; lp. Pays: variable. Ads: £ 20/page pro rata.

POETRY NEWS, Birmingham Poetry Centre, **B.P. Hogan,** 175 The Radleys, Marston Green, Birmingham B33 0QP, UK.

POETRY NEWSLETTER, **Richard O'Connell,** Dept. Of English, Temple Univ., Philadelphia, PA 19122. Poetry, interviews, longpoems, plays. *Recent contributors: William Burford, Josephine Jacobsen, Rhoda Gelfond, Anthony Johnson, Arthur Winfield Knight, A.D. Winans.* 12/yr; $2.88/yr; 24 cents by mail/ea; free single; 1971; 12-16pp; 8½x10; 500-1M circ; mi. Reports 1-2 mos. Pays copies only. No ads. Back issues: limited number of bound copies of *Poetry Newsletter,* No. 13-24, available $3 postpaid. Pub'd 12 issues 1973, expects 12 in 1974. COSMEP.

PN3 VERBAL EXPERIMENTATION, Poetry Newsletter, **Wally Depew, Linda Bandt,** 819-17 St., Sacramento, CA 95814. Poetry, fiction, articles, art, photos, cartoons, interviews, music, satire, criticism, reviews, letters, parts-of-novels, longpoems, collages, plays, concrete art; all/any must be verbal experimentation. *All work anonymous.* Irreg; $10/all PN publications; $1/ea; 50 cents/sample; 1968; 3 5/8x4¼; 125 circ; mi; lo; lp; Reports 1 mo. Pays copies only. No ads. Discounts: 25-50%. Back issues: 1-4/$3 ea; others $1. 4 for $3.50.

PN 2 NONVERBAL POETRY, Poetry Newsletter, **Wally Depew, Linda Bandt,** 819-17 St., Sacramento, CA 95814. Poetry, fiction, articles, art, photos, cartoons, interviews, satire, criticism, reviews, music, letters, parts-of-novels, longpoems, collages, plays, concrete art. All/any nonverbal. *All Work anonymous.* Irreg; $10/all PN Publications; $1/ea; 60 cents/sample; 1968; 3 5/8x 4¼; 125 circ; mi; lo; lp; Reports 1 mo. Pays copies only. Discounts: 25-50% Back issues: 1-8/$3 ea. All others $1; 4 for $3.50.

POETRY NEWSLETTER SPECIAL ISSUE, PN, **Wally & Linda Depew,** 819-17 St., Sacramento, CA 95814. Poetry, fiction, articles, art, photos, cartoons, interviews, satire, criticism, reviews, music, letters, parts-of-novels, longpoems, collages, plays, concrete art; all/any. *Recent cont: Gary Elder, Richard Kostelanetz, Jean-Pierre Armeuux.* Irreg; $10/all PN Publications; 50 cents/ea; $1/3 issues; 1964; 12-30pp; 4¼x5½; 150 circ. lo. Reports 1 mo. Pays copies only. No ads. Discounts; 25% to 50%. No back issues.

POETRY NIPPON, The Poets' Society of Japan, **Onsey Nakagawa, Yorifumi Yaguchi, Naoshi Koriyama,** 5-11 Nagaike-cho, Showa-ku, Nagoya 466, Japan. Poetry, articles, art, photos, interviews, criticism, reviews. *Poems about Japan, haiku, tanka, one-line poems and translations of Japanese poems only are accepted from non-members. Essays on poetry and reviews of poetry books are also solicited.* Q; $7/yr; $1.80/ea; free sample; 1967; 40pp; A5; 600 circ; lo. Pays copies only. Ads: $40/p; $20/½. Discounts: 40 to 20 percent depending on quantity. Pub'd 4 issues and 1 book 1973, expects 4 issues, 1 book in 1974.

POETRY NOW, **E.V. Griffith,** 3118 K St. Eureka, Ca 95501. Poetry, photos (of poets). *Poetry Now is a 6-issues-per-year tabloid poetry journal extremely eclectic, featuring new work by arrived and arriving writers. As a special feature, each issue devotes 3 pages to reprinting the "best" poems from other poetry magazines and literary journals. Book reviews are by samples of the best poems from the books considered. Contributors include William Stafford, Edwin Honig, James Tate, Russell Edson, Harold Norse, Charles Bukowski, Marge Piercy— and scores more. Illustrated with photos of the poets.* 6/yr; $5/6issues; $1.25/ea; sample/1 copy free for postage; 1973; 32 tabloid; 12x16; 1M+ circ; lo. Reports 1 day to 1 mo. Pays copies only. Ads: $150/p; $85/½; no class/wd. Discounts: classroom: $4/yr (6 issues), but with min. of 15 copies to one address (instructors office, Dept. of Eng., etc). Pub'd 1 issue 1973, expects 6 in 1974. CCLM.

POETRY OF OUR TIME, J. Mark Press, **Barbara Fischer,** Box 2057-M, North Babylon, NY 11703. Poetry. *Send 1 or 2 line poems, 3-16 lines. Aesthetic, contemporary poetry that interacts with the reader. (No vulgarity, profanity, devoutly religious or light or humourous.) Don't imitate or try to be outlandishly different. Be yourself. Enclose return env. Send one submission to this editor and wait for reply. After ten years, we find we've published scores of today's popular poets. Being partial to everything we accept, we'd have to list 5000 names to be fair, so we won't give any. We suggest, you study a sample: any of our titles will present a clear picture of what we look for.* Q.; $5.95/paper; $8.95/cloth; $3.95/sample; 1963; 50pp; 8½x5½; 3M circ; lo. Reports promptly. Pays: 2 to 10 cents/line. Ads: commercial $5,000 runs 4 issues; class/wd: poets' books: $5/30 wds. Discounts: quoted on request. Back issues: $50@ clothbound prior to 1973; most numbers completely sold out. Pub'd 4 issues, 2 books 1973; expects 20 issues, 10 books in 1974. COSMEP, Suffolk City Legislature, Cultural Affairs.

POETRY OF THE CIRCLE IN THE SQUARE, Bristol Arts Centre, **Bill Pickard,** Bristol Arts Centre, 4/5 King Square, Bristol 2, UK. Poetry. 2/yr; 10p/ea; 1966; 20pp; 10x8; mim; Reports: members only.

POETRY OF THE YEAR, J. Mark Press, **Barbara Fischer,** Box 2057-M, North Babylon, NY 11703. Poetry. *Send 1 or 2 poems, 3-16 lines. Aesthetic, contemporary poetry that interacts with the reader. (No vulgarity, profanity, devoutly religious or light or humorous.) Don't imitate or try to be outlandishly different. Be yourself. Enclose return env. Send one submission to this editor and wait for reply. After ten years, we find we've published scores of today's popular poets. Being partial to everything we accept, we'd have to list 5000 names to be fair, so we won't give any. We suggest, you study a sample: any of our titles will present a clear picture of what we look for.* Q; $5.95/paper; $8.95/cloth; $3.95/sample; 1963; 50pp; 8½x5½; 3M circ; lo. Reports promptly. Pays: 2 to 10 cents/line. Ads: commercial $5,000 runs 4 issues; class/wd: poets' books: $5/30wds. Discounts: quoted on request. Back issues: $50 @ clothbound prior to 1973; most numbers completely sold out. Pub'd 4 issues, 2 books 1973; expects 20 issues, 10 books in 1974. COSMEP, Suffolk City Legislature, Cultural Affairs.

POETRY PEOPLE, R.V.K. Publishing Co., **S.P.Stavrakis,** PO Box 264du, Menomonee Falls, WI 53051. Poetry, photos, line-art. Poetry People, *a publication which stresses a wide spectrum of experimental poetry. . .a response to the current trend on the part of small publishers to create elitist, cliquish attitudes and narrow editorial margins in their poetry things. Poetry is a people's art, and no one should be excluded because his style doesn't exactly match the editor's or his name isn't well known.* 2/yr; $10/yr; $6.25/ea; 1972; lo. Reports 2-6 wks, if you include post., possibly never if you don't. Info on request with two stamps. Pays over $100 cash awards and prizes each issue. For photos and line art, cash for those used. All contributing authors, artists get discounts on copies. $15/yr all publications.

POETRY REVIEW, The Poetry Society, **Eric Mottram,** National Poetry Centre, 21 Earls Court Square, London SW5, UK.

POETRY VIEW, (Half-page), Appleton Post-Crescent (View Sun. Mag. Sec.), **Dorothy Dalton,** 1125 Valley Rd., Manasha, WI 54952. Poetry. *Serious poetry to 20 lines— light verse 4 to 8 lines. Free verse preferred, fresh use of language— no religious, no overly sentimental. Enclose SASE with submissions. Recent contributors: Eve Triem, Richard Latta, Alan Britt, Joyce Odam, Charles R. Cantrell, Lee Avery Reed, Sarah Ryder. A tearsheet is sent to out-of-town contributors.* Weekly; 1970; ½p; 50M circ. Reports 2-3 mos. Pays $3 per poem, month following publication. Pub'd 52 issues 1973, expects 52 in 1974.

POETRY WALES, Christopher Davies Ltd., **Meic Stephens**, Llandybie, Ammanford, Carmarthenshire. Articles, poetry, interviews, criticism, letters, longpoems. 4/yr; £ 1.52/yr; 38p/ea; 1965; 120pp; 5½x8½"; 1000 circ; lp; Reports: 2-3 wks. Pays: by arrangement.

POETRY WORKSHOP, Poetry Workshop Press, **Stephen Morris**, Faculty of Art & Design, The Polytechnic, Wolverhampton, Staffs, England, UK. *Recent contributors: Adrian Henri, William Wantling, Martin Booth, Yevgeny Yevtushenko, Pete Morgan. Poetry.* 3/yr; 50p/yr; 25p/ea; free sample; 1967; 30pp; 8x6"; 500 circ; lp; Reports: 1 month. Pays: 2 copies.

POETS & POETRY, Poetry Press, **Michael Gettisburg**, 6a Culver Street, Colchester, Essex, UK. Poetry, interviews, criticism, letters. *Poets and Poetry will only publish work of a high standard both in poetry and critical essays. No restriction regarding length of material. The aim of the magazine is to publish more essays on poets and poetry than just publishing poems, and capture a very large audience.* 4/yr; 80p/yr; 20p px/ea; 1973; 40pp; 720 circ; off/mim. Reports: 2-3 wks. Pays: £ 1.50 + free sub/Essays only. Back issues: 15p.

Poets & Writers, Inc. (see A DIRECTORY OF AMERICAN POETS)

Poets Press of Osgoldcross (see also OSGOLDCROSS REVIEW), 50 Chiltern Drive, Ackworth, Pontefract WF7 7DW, UK. Poetry. *Only publications to date:* For Her Volume One *by Gerald England (100 numbered copies) and* Osgoldcross Review No. 1 *(150 numbered copies).* 5p each + postage. No plans to publish any new titles in 1974. Sample/5p px; 1972; 8pp; 10x8; 100+ circ; mim.

The Poets' Society of Japan (see POETRY NIPPON)

POETS—WHY PAY TO PUBLISH?, P.V. Publications, **Malc Payne**, 4 Wealden Close, Crowborough, Sussex, UK. *Instructional handbook containing information for aspiring poets. Sponsored by members of PV; warns of vanity presses & gives other means of publication- mainly advocating the small presses and need to support same; hints on presentation; SAEs; editors &c. Supplied free to schools, universities, libraries on receipt of s.a.e(4p). First edition 1000 copies; following editions, revised and brought up to date,* 1 *of 3000 at any one time.* 50p pf/ea; 1974; 30pp; A5; off. Ads: on application. Discounts: usual trade. ALP.

THE POINT, "Raw Power Press for the People," **Raye X,** PO Box 1001, El Cerrito, Ca 94530. Fiction, articles, art, photos, cartoons, interviews, satire, criticism, reviews, music, letters, parts-of-novels, political poetry. *Jerry Elmer, Brian Cullman, Robot Hull, Lester Bangs; some material crude, raw, salty— all aimed at the young (16-25) or at people who enjoy getting a message in an unusual way. Much music and humor in some issues; down to business in others.* Monthly; $4/yr; 35 cents/ea; 50 cents/sample (includes postage); 1971; 8-12-24pp; tab; 1-5M circ; lo. Reports 14 days. No pay. Ads: no advertising accepted except free to causes; classified: $1 per line to business, free to people. Discounts: trade only; free exchange. Back issues: 50 cents/ea plus mailing. Pub'd 8 issues 1973. COSMEP, Third World, Women, Chicano, Black, Food/Ecology, American Indian, Gay, G.I. Prison, Music/Theatre.

Polaris Press (see also ALGOL), **Andrew Porter,** PO Box 4175, NewYork, NY 10017. Articles, art, interviews, criticism. *Polaris Press will be reprinting material from* Algol: A Magazine About Science Fiction, *for wider circulation and sales to libraries and individuals. Original material may be published in the future. First titles expected in June 1974.* 5½x8½; lo. Discounts: 40% to booksellers. COSMEP, FAPA.

The Pomegranate Press, **Jeffrey Katz,** 1713 Mass. Ave., Cambridge, MA 02138. *We are a small press in Cambridge, Massachusetts, publishing illustrated American Poets Broadsides and chapbooks of poetry, short fiction and essays.*

Poni Press, **Tom Buchan, Emma Chapman,** 10 Pittville Street, Edinburgh, EH15 2BY, UK. Poetry, fiction, satire, longpoems, plays. lp. ALP.

The Popular Press (see JOURNAL OF POPULAR CULTURE)

PORT TOWNSEND JOURNAL, The Woolman Press, **Jack Cady, William Penn, Cheryl Van Dyke,** 933 Tyler St., Port Townsend, WA 98368. Poetry, fiction, articles, interviews, satire, criticism, reviews, parts-of-novels, longpoems, plays. *Length of material can vary. We have published chapbooks, etc., within the Journal. Have no biases as to style or content, but insist only on quality. The editors have varying tastes and backgrounds, so quality can be our only bias. The journal was begun by writers for writers. We have found that a standard of excellence does not always mean that our contributors have published elsewhere. The staff of the Journal has a small but established writing community that is nowhere near a major university. Recent contributors include Frank Maloney, Richard Blessing, David Wilson, W.M. Ransom, Ernest Hekkanen, Steven Jaech, Peter Hays.* Semi-annual; $3/yr; $2/ea; $1.40/sample; 1973; 75pp; 8½x 11; 400 circ; mi. Reports 3 wks. Pays copies only. Ads: $25/p; $15/½. Back issues: Vol.1, No.2: $1.25; Vol.1, No.1: gone. Pub'd 2 issues 1973, expects 4 in 1974. COSMEP.

Bern Porter (press), **Bern Porter, Eudine Porter,** 22 Salmond Rd. Box 209, Belfast, ME 04915. Poetry, fiction, art, longpoems, plays, concrete art. *Avant-guard experimental expression of highly literary quality and on order of distinct breakthroughs in letters. Books only.* lp; Reports 60 days. Pays 10% retail. COSMEP, NESPA, COSMEPA.

Portfolio Press, **Ken Arnold,** ed., 1912 Fairband Rd., Baltimore, MD 21209.

POT-HOOKS & HANGERS, **J.Patton, J. Brand,** PO Box 718, Old Chelsea Sta., New York, NY 10011. Poetry, longpoems, concrete art. *Poems— any length, any style.* 2/yr; $1.50/ea; $3/yr; $1.50/sample; 1973; 48pp; 6x9; 550 circ; lo. Reports 2 wks-3mos. Pays 2 copies. No ads. Discounts: trade 40%; institution 20%. Back issues: none as yet.. Pub'd 1 issue 1973, expects 2 in 1974. COSMEP.

POWDER MAGAZINE, Light, Powder and Construction Works, 350 Victoria St., North Melbourne, Victoria, Australia. Monthly; $5/yr-indiv; $10/yr-inst; 50cents/ea.

Prairie Poet Books (see AMERICAN POET)

PRAIRIE SCHOONER, **Bernice Slote,** 201B Andrews, City Campus, Lincoln, NB 68508. *Recent contributors include Carole Oles, Anais Nin, Roland Tharp, Joyce Carol Oates, Jon Dressel, Jack Ledbetter.* Q; $4.50/yr; $1.50/ea; free sample; 1927; 100pp; 32x48pi; 1200 circ; lo. Reports 3 mos. Pays copies only. Ads: $50/p; $35/½; Discounts: Agency: $3/yr; schools: $3.60/yr. Back issues: $2. Published 4 issues in 1973, expects 4 in 1974.

Press O Zero, **Thomas Fitzsimmons,** English Dept., Oakland Univ., Rochester, MI 48063 (until mid'75: English Dept., Tokyo Univ. of Education, Bunuyo-ku, Tokyo, Japan.) Poetry, longpoems, plays, concrete art. *Broke for the "moment" but will return.* COSMEP.

Pressdram Ltd. (see PRIVATE EYE)

Pressed Curtains (see CURTAINS)

PREVENTION—The Magazine for Better Health, Rodale Press, **Ed-in-Chief Robert Rodale, Ed. Dir. Keith Etson, Mang. Ed. Nancy Butler,** Potten End, Berkhamsted, Herts, UK. Articles, art, cartoons, news items, letters. *We prefer authors to query first. Prevention has its own philosophy for healthful living and it is sometimes difficult for writers outside the staff to "pick up" our style. We base our reputation on the accuracy with whichwe draw from medical references. Therefore, we require full references to support articles- all of which are aimed at the general public. Topics of bias: health, health cure, vitamins, natural living "success" stories, fitness, organic gardening, and farming, ecology, natural beauty methods, slimming, nutrition— theme important throughout.* Monthly; £2.20/yr; 15p/ea; free sample; 1942; 100pp; 8½x5¼..; 1,200,000 worldwide, 65,000 UK; off. Reports: 4-6wks. Pays: £ 10/1000 words+up. Ads: £ 80/page, £ 42/½, £ 22/¼. Discounts: 15% agency. Women, Ecology, Health/organic Gardening/Fitness.

PRISM INTERNATIONAL, **Michael Bullock,** Creative Writing Dept., Univ. of British Columbia, Vancouver, BC, Canada V6T 1W5. 3/yr; $5/yr; $1.75/ea. no sample; 1959; 152pp;6x9; 750-1M circ; lp; Reports 1 wk. Pays $5 per pg. Pub'd 3 issues 1973, expects 3 in 1974.

*PRIVATE EYE, Pressdram Ltd.,***Richard Ingrams,** 34 Greek Street, London W1 UK. Cartoons, photos, satire, news items. Fortnightly; £ 3.25/yr; 12p/ea; free sample; 1961; 28pp; 110,000 circ; off. Ads: £ 200/page pro rata. Discounts: negotiable.

ProActive Press, **James H. Craig & Marge Craig,** PO Box 296, Berkeley, CA 94701. *Our puopose in establishing the ProActive Press is to assist in the co-creation of a caring society through humanistic politics. We are eager to share what skills we have with anyone who has a good, readable manuscript that offers a promising pro life, pro-active program for humanizing social change. (We're not interested in more re-actions to the horrors we see and sense all about us.) Our* Synergic Power: Beyond Domination and Permissiveness *shows the kind of manuscript we're interested in.* 1973; lo. Discounts: 40% trade, 20%/text- in both cases for orders of 5 or more books. Expects 2 books in 1974. COSMEP, Humanistic, Politics.

*PROFILE, Anvil Press, Liverpool,***Susan P.Place,** 1st floor, 5 Cases Street, Liverpool L1 1HW, UK. Articles, cartoons, photos, criticism. *Profile is an unusual small mag- though attractive, with tinted papers & 2 color gloss cover, it is a giveaway (subsidised by ads) for the lst year student. Articles on the city, entertainments, arts etc., with rundowns and surveys of transport, social aspects, accomodations, hassles, consumerism, etc., Many illustrations and photos and some bits of local poetry and art. Two separate editions- Liverpool and Manchester.* Annual; 8p pf/each; 1971; 40pp; A5; 8000 circ; off. Ads: £ 37.50/page, £ 20/½, £ 11/¼. ALP.

Progettare INPIU', Via Ripanmonti 89, 20139 Milano, Italy.

PROMONTORY, Headland Publications, **Gerald England,** 745 Abbeydale Road, Sheffield S7 2BG (Business:56 Blakes Lane, New Malden KT3 6NX) UK. Poetry. *High-quality poetry only required. Contributors include Penelope Shuttle, Anna Adams, Harriet Rose, Patricia Martland Colin Simms, and Eugeno Montale (translated by Stanley Thomas). Unsolicited MSS arriving without s.a.e. or IRCs are destroyed.* 3/yr; 50p, $2/yr; 15p px/ea; 1974; 12pp; A5; 250 circ; lp. Reports 1 month. Pays: under review.

*PROSPICE, Aquila Publishing Co., Ltd.,***J.C. R. Green, Michael Edwards, Martin Booth,** 18 Atherstone Close, Shirley, Solihull, Warwickshire B90 1AU, UK. Articles, poetry, fiction, art, photos, satire, interviews, criticism, letters, longpoems, concrete. *Trade Discounts: orders over £3=35%; orders under £3=25%; orders under £1=20%; all pf. U.S. Agents wanted: 60% U.S. prices. Magazine concerned with poetics, translation etc. Many Top Critics write for the magazine. Issue 1 contains Cid Corman (on Olson), Gabriel Josidouci etc. Poems from Robert Bly, Carl Rakosi, Adrian Henri, George MacBeth, Douglas Dunn, George Seferis, and others. Also poems in Italian, with translations etc.* 3/yr; £2/yr; 60p/ea; 30p/sample; 1973; 96pp; 8¼x5½; 1000 circ; off/lp. Reports vary. Pays: by agreement; Normally only copies. Ads: £12.50/page; £7.50/½. Discounts: 10% agency/ALP/ or COSMEP. Occult, Ecology, ALP, ALMS, COSMEP.

PROTEUS, **Frank & Cathy Gatling,** 1004 N. Jefferson St., Arlington, VA 22205. Poetry, fiction, art, photos, criticism, reviews, parts-of-novels, plays. *Will be doing about 90% prose. Will use a very few highly objective, strictly-controlled, imagistic poems. But chiefly fiction. Outrageous as you please if you do it skillfully.* Q; $3.50/yr; $1/ea; 50 cents/sample; 1972; 80pp; 6x8½; 600 circ; lo. Reports 1-6 wks. Pays copies only. Pub'd 2 issues 1973, expects 3 in 1974. COSMEP, CCLM.

THE PROVIDENCE REVIEW, **Mark Halliday, L. Laird Holby, David H. Cashman,** 64 Elmgrove Ave., Providence, RI 02906. Poetry, fiction, articles, satire, criticism, reviews. *We are trying to build a local identity for our magazine. Therefore we limit our contributors almost exclusively to residents of Rhode Island.* Monthly; $5/yr; 50 cents/ea; 1973; 20pp; 8½x11; 200 circ; lo. Reports 1 mo. Pays: $1 plus 2 copies. Pub'd 10 issues 1973, expects 10 in 1974. COSMEP.

THE PTA MAGAZINE, National Congress of Parents and Teachers, **Donal Mahoney,** 700 North Rush St., Chicago, IL 60611. Poetry, fiction, articles, art, photos, interviews, criticism, reviews. *Short stories: $150. Poems: $10. Reports or articles on "issues of the day" (1,500 words): $100-$150. Highest quality only criterion. Free sample on request and contributor's copies. Writers: query or submit to Donal Mahoney, ed. Artists and photographers: write to Grazyna Girdvainis, Art Director.* 10/yr; $3.50/yr; 50 cents/ea; free sample; 1920's; 44pp; 8x11½; 80M circ; lo. Reports: small staff, varies. Pays copies in addition to money. Ads: under revision; no class/wd. Back issues: first copy free. General interest.

Puckerbrush Press, **Constance Hunting,** 76 Main St., Orono, ME 04473. Poetry, fiction, criticism. 2 bks/yr; $2.25/ea, paperback; 1971; 80pp; 7x10. Reports 1 mo. Pays: 10% royalties. Pub'd 2 issues 1973: *An Old Pub Near The Angel,* and *Dorando,* by Boswell. NESPA.

PUERTO DEL SOL, Dept. of English, New Mexico State Univ., Las Cruces, NM 88001.

Pulp Press (see 3¢ PULP)

Pulse-Finger Press, Box 16697, Philadelphia, PA 19139.

Pushcart Book Press, **Bill & Nancy Henderson,** PO Box 845, Yonkers, NY 10701. Pushcart *publishes* The Publish-It-Youself Handbook: Literary Tradition and How-To, *edited by Bill Henderson, a complete guide on publishing without the assistance of vanity or commercial publishers, including essays by Anais Nin, Stewart Brand, Alan Swallow, Leonard Woolf, Richard Kostelanetz, Dick Higgins, Gordon Lish (plus 20 others). Complete bibliography and how-to section.* $5/paper; $10/cloth; 300pp; 5½x8½; lo. Pub'd 2 books 1973. COSMEP.

PV Publications (see NUCLEUS, POETS—WHY PAY FOR PUBLICATION?, RADIX)

PYRAMID, Hellric Publications, **Ottone M. Riccio,** Hellric House, 39 Eliot St., Jamaica Plain, MA 02130. Poetry, fiction, articles, art, cartoons, interviews, satire, criticism, reviews, music, parts-of-novels, longpoems, plays. *Overstocked — not accepting new materials until 1975.* Irreg; $5/4 issues; $1.50/ea; 1968; 78pp; 8½x 5½; 500 circ; lo. Reports: days to months. Pays: $3–20/page plus copies and 4 issue sub. No ads. Discounts: 50% on orders for 20 or more copies or subs. Back issues: No.6, $3; Nos.1-5,7+, $1.50/ea. Pub'd 1 issue 1973, expects 4 in 1974. Independent.

Quaker Fellowship of the Arts (see REYNARD)

QUARTERLY REVIEW OF LITERATURE, **T. Weiss, R. Weiss,** 26 Haslet Ave., Princeton, NJ 08540. Poetry, fiction. *Vol.XIX will be a special 30th Anniversary celebration. Culled from the best of* QRL's *long past as an international literary magazine, these volumes constitute an anthology and history of* QRL *as well as a retrospective of the literary scene over the last thirty years. No new material will be considered.* 2/yr; $10/yr; $5/ea; 1943; 500pp. Discounts: 10%. COSMEP, CCLM.

Quarto Press, **B.L. Pearce, J.B. Easson, publ.,** 69 Swan Road, Feltham, Middx TW13 6PE, UK. Poetry. *Business manager: E. Cottrell. New series of pamphlets featuring the verse of outstanding new writers. Previously unpublished poets preferred, but veterans considered. Mss. and inquiries invited.* 2-3/yr; 40p/ea; 16pp; A5; lp. Reports 1 mo. Pays: by negotiation. Discounts: 25% trade & bulk.

QUEST, Spook Enterprises, **Marian Green,** 38 Woodfield Ave., London W5 1PA, UK. Articles, news items, interviews, criticism, letters. *Articles 2000 words — Western Mystery Tradition, Hermetic, Magic, and all* practical *aspects of Modern Western occultism. Recent authors: Cottie Burland, E.A. St. George, Stewart Farrar, Francoise Strachan plus others who are experienced in their own speciality.* 4/yr; 90p/yr; 25p/ea; 1970; 38pp; qto; 1000+ circ; off. Reports 2-3 wks. Pays: nil. Ads: small exchange ads only. Discounts: 33% trade. Back Issues: 6/£1. Occult.

QUETZAL: A Journal of Native American Arts, Quetzal/Vihio Press, **Randall Ackley,** (Ricardo Sanchez, Simon Ortiz, Howard McCord), Many Farms RPO Box 68, Chinle, AZ 86503. Poetry, articles, art, photos, interviews, reviews, letters, longpoems. *Ethnic and regional only. Almost all material by invitation; seeking poetry, stories, art by Indians, Chicanos, Mexicanos, & special SW work by Anglos who are of the place. Issues in cycles: SWPC, Chicano, Indian, Mt. & River Anglos of SW, . . . co-editors for these Red Bird, Ricardo Sanchez, Simon Ortiz,* . . . 3/yr; $7.50/yr; $3/ea; $3/sample; 1970; 50+pp; 8½x11; 250 circ. Reports: much worse than it should be. Pay: varies; copies only usually. Ads: $50/p; $30/½; no class/wd. Discounts: 25% if ordered before publication. Back issues: $5 when available, we usually ship all printed. Suspended publ. 1973, expects 4 issues 1974; expects 1 book 1974. COSMEP, UPS, CCLM, Third World, Chicano, American Indian.

Tony Quinn (Garbage) Publications, **Tony Quinn,** Flat 2, 26 Waterloo Road, Bedford, UK. Articles, poetry, fiction, cartoons, satire, criticism, letters. *Most articles less than three pages. Editor/publisher contributes most of the material. Guest contributors welcome but space limited. Romantic anarchist, anti-authoritarian bias. Special interests: bizarre short fiction, drug experiences changing social attitudes & sub-cultures.* Irreg; 10p/ea (average); 13p pf/sample; 1973; 20+pp; A4; 500 circ; dup. Reports: 2-3 wks. Pays: small. Ads: none carried. Discounts: 3p/copy on 5 or more copies.

QUIXOTE, 1014 Williamson St., Madison, WI 53703.

RLC'S MUSEUM GAZETTE, Richard L. Coulton, **Richard L. Coulton,** Bentley, Alberta, Canada TOC OJO. *Material should be short & concise (200 wds average). Deals with little-known aspects of, summaries of, new developments in: Earth & Life Sciences, history, transportation, geography, etc. 'information in a nutshell.'* 3-4/yr; 50 cents/4 issues; free samples; 1966; 4pp; 8½x14; mi. Reports 2-4 wks in most cases. Pays copies only. Ads: 1 cent/word.

R.V.K. Publishing Company (see POETRY PEOPLE)

RACE TODAY, Russell Press, **Darcus Howe,** 184 Kings Cross Road, London WC1 UK. Articles, art, cartoons, photos, news items, interviews, criticism, letters. *We are interested in all material relating to the struggle against racism both in the U.K. and abroad. That includes first-hand reporting, features and review material.* Monthly; £2/yr; 15p/ea; 1969; 32pp; A4; 4500 circ; off. Reports: 14 days. Pays: negotiable. Ads: £24/page; £14/½. Discounts: 10% pub/agents. Back issues: 20p. Third World, Black.

RADICAL AMERICA, 5 Upland Rd., Cambridge, MA 02140. *A non-sectarian Marxist journal edited by a group of 12 independent socialists in the Boston area includes articles on the history and current condition of the working class in North America and Western Europe; shop floor and community organizing; the history and politics of women's liberation; contemporary socialist theory and practice; popular culture and poetry (eg. by surrealists, feminists, socialist workers, and black prisoners); advertising on an exchange basis; discounts available for bulk orders and consignment sales; institutional subs. double regular rate. Free catalogue of back issues and pamphlets available.* $5/yr; $10/yr with special pamphlet mailings; $1/ea; 1967; 96-192pp; 4½x6; 2M circ; photo offset by Detroit Printing Co-op I.W.W. I.U. 450.

RADICAL PHILOSOPHY, **Richard Norman, Sean Sayers,** University of Kent, Canterbury, UK. Articles, cartoons, satire, criticism. 4/yr; £1.25/yr; 25p/ea; 1971; 34pp; A4; 2000 circ; off.

RADICAL SOFTWARE, Gordon & Breach, **Ira Schneider, Beryl Rorot,** c/o Gordon & Breach, One Park Ave., New York, NY 10016. Poetry, fiction, articles, art, photos, interviews, satire, criticism, reviews. *Radical Software is the magazine of video. Material usually relates in some way to video equipment, cable TV, technology assessments, etc.* 9 times per vol; $12.50/yr; $1.95/ea; no sample; 1970; 64pp; 8½x11; 10M circ; lo. Ads: $300/p; $175/½. Discounts: 50% to distributors (min. order 50); 40% to bookstore (min. order 10); 10% to sub. agencies. Back issues: $3. COSMEP.

RADICAL—TRADITIONALIST PAPERS, Cokaygne Press, 1 Jesus Terrace, New Square, Cambridge, UK. *An occasional series of political broadsides delivered in the traditional nineteenth-century manner — have proved highly popular with London economists and politicians.* 2/yr; 15p pf/ea; 1972; 16-20pp; 7x5"; 1500-3000 circ; off. Ecology, Occult, Politics.

RADIX, PV Publications, **Malc Payne; co-eds: Brian Moses, Bill Kent,** 4 Wealden Close, Crowborough, Sussex, UK. Poetry, fiction, art, news items, concrete. *Unbiased: no love for epic poems. Oxley, MacCaigh, McGough, Connors, Sneyd, Nixon, Salway, Moses, McNeil, Mao, Mia Albright, MacKinley, Lloyd Gold, Margaret George, Margaret Pain, Juanita Pierse, Mayer, Joyce Kahn, John Rice, Vaish, lijima. 3 issues 1973 — 3 expected '74; unsolicited mss received without SAE/IRC to WPB.* 3/yr; 75p($3)/yr; 25p($1)/ea; 1972; 30pp; A5; 500 circ; lo. Reports: return. Pays: 1 copy. Ads: haggles invited. Discounts: usual trade. Back issues: funny — we seem to sell out. ALP.

Ragnarok Press, **Rochelle Holt, D.H. Stefanson,** 311 Memphis St., Holly Springs, MS 38635. Poetry, fiction, art, photos, parts-of-novels. *Anais Nin contributed a 1971 unpublished Diary entry for hardbound* Eidolons. *Sharon Spencer, another member of the modern circle wrote introduction for* Children of the Poet, *an anthology containing Erica Jong, Uli Bita, Deena Metzger & other women poets. Feb. 1974 appeared Lynn Sukenick's 2nd book of poems,* Water Astonishing. *Judo poems titled,* The Gentle Way *by Carole Van Wyngarden available as broadside.* Wing Span of an Albatross *& other books by Rochelle Holt.* Often; 1970; lp. Discounts: 20% disc. bulk or classroom; will also trade certain issues. Back issues: $5 for *Eidolons* which includes Anais Nin 1971 Diary entry. Pub'd 3 issues 1973: *(Children of the Moon,* Women poets; *A Ballet of Oscillations* by Rochelle Holt; *A Peaceful Intent,* photos & haiku); expects 3 issues 1974. Women.

The Rainbow Bridge, distributors & publishers, PO Box 40208, San Francisco, CA 94140. *Free mail order & wholesale catalogue representing over 50 publishers — many foreign mostly small — all spiritual. Over 500 titles.* Pub'd 3 books 1973, expects 2 in 1974. Spiritual.

rainbow resin (see TH UINTA GARGOYL (TUG))

RAINCOAST CHRONICLES, Harbour Publishing, **Howard White, Peter Trower,** Box 119, Madeira Park, BC, Canada VON 2HO. Poetry, fiction, articles, art, reviews, parts-of-novels. *The magazine's prime concern is the history and culture of the British Columbia coast. We publish mainly articles on coast history, with the occasional poem or short story. Literary merit is at least as important as historical accuracy. Recent contributors have been Peter Trower, Pat Lane, John Kelly, Scott Lawrence, and many writers never published before.* Q; $5/yr; $1.75/ea; $1.75/sample; 1972; 56pp; 7½x10½; 8M circ; lo. Reports 4 wks. Pay: dependent on length & quality. Discounts: schools & libraries 20% off; bkstores 40% off; distributors 50%. Back issues: none. Pub'd 2 issues 1973, expects 4 issues, 3 books in 1974.

RAMA, The Peoplesmedia Monthly, Peoplesmedia, Inc., **Charles A. Raisch,** Project One, 1380 Howard, San FRancisco, CA 94103. *We are interested in feature journalism pieces — exposes with a historical & political perspective. Articles on alternatives or new experiences in food, social change, awareness of body, oppression and liberation.* 8/yr; $10/yr instit; $5/yr individuals; 65 cents/ea; 65 cents/sample; 1970;56pp; 8½x11; 42,500 circ; lo. Reports 1 mo. Pays: $5/p. Ads: $310/p; $160/½; $9 per inch class/wd. Discounts: trade, agents, bulk, 15% flat. Back issues: $2. Pub'd 8 issues 1973.

Randall (see CONCEPTS: A Magazine of Positive Poetry, INDIGO: The Voice of American Poets)

Rannoch Gillamoor Poets (see STRATH)

RAPPORT, The Slow Loris Press, Patricia and Tony Petrosky, 95 Rand Ave., Buffalo, NY 14216. Poetry, fiction, interviews, reviews, longpoems. Recent contributors: James Wright, David Ignatow, Michael Casey, Ted Kooser, Tom Johnson, Norman Russell, Martha Dickey, Jane Bailey, Charles Baxter, Shreela Ray. Bi-annual; $3.50/yr; $2/ea; $2/sample; 1971; 60-70pp; 9x6; 750 circ; lo. Reports 2-3 mos. Pays: 3 copies. Ads: $60/p; $30/½. Discounts: 40% to trade; 60% to classroom. Back issues: Rapport 1=$5; 2&3=$1; 4=$1.50; 5&6=$2. Pub'd 2 issues 1973, expects 2 in 1974. CCLM.

Rationalist Press Association (see NEW HUMANIST)

Raven Books, Anvil Press (Liverpool), **Susan P. Place, J. Ben Coker,** 1st Floor, 5 Cases St., Liverpool L1 1HW, UK. Anvil Press (Liverpool), *a small partnership, incorporates the Raven Books imprint, a small publisher dealing with primarily local work in editions from 500 to 8000. We record memories of old Liverpool, publish novels about it, guide books to presentday Liverpool and work by its best poets and humorists.* ALP.

"Raw Power Press for the People" (see THE POINT)

REACH OUT, Reach Out Enterprises, **Miss R. Lee Rader,** 204 Rome-Hilliard Rd., Columbus, OH 43228. Poetry, art, music. Q; $5/yr; $1.25/ea; $1/sample; 1970; 50 pp; 4x6; 200 circ; lo. Reports 2 wks. Pays: copies only. Ads: 4x6/$50. No discounts. Back issues: $1. Expects 4 issues 1974. COSMEP, Poetry.

Real Free Press Insider No.1, Real Free Press (Foundation) INT, **R. Olaf Stoop,** Oude Nieuwstraat 10, Amsterdam, Netherlands. Articles, art, cartoons, satire, reviews, parts-of-novels. RFP Publication: *"Real Free Press (Int.), Illustratie No.1,2, 3,4,5,6 (Spring '74)," no pulp-paper! Tabloid 24. "Kleine Nemo in Dromenland" by Winsor McKay, 36pp; "Powerhouse Pepper" by Basil Wolverton, 28pp; "Armadillo No.3" by Jim Franklin, 28pp; "World of Wizard King" by W. Wood, 20pp, 1974; "Krazy Kat No.1" by G. Herriman, 48pp, 1974.* Lo. No ads. Discounts: 30% discount on 7 copies of one title. Published 6 books in 1973, expects 6 in 1974. UPS.

Real Resources Group (see AMERICAN COLLECTOR)

REALITY, Redemptorist Publications, Orwell Road, Dublin 6, Eire, UK. Articles, fiction, photos. *Illustrated articles especially welcome. Articles and short stories, 1000-1500 words, on all aspects of modern life, including family, youth, religion, leisure.* Monthly; 5p/ea; 1966. Pays: £5/1000 words average. Christian living.

Reality Studio Arts (see BLIMP/REALIT)

REASON MAGAZINE, Reason Enterprises, **Robert Poole Jr., Manuel Klausner, Lynn Kinsky, Tibor Machan,** PO Box 6151, Santa Barbara, CA 93111. Articles, photos, cartoons, interviews, reviews, letters. *Reason is a libertarian magazine, stressing both individual liberty and economic freedom. Generally anti-State, anti-Establishment, pro-Free-market. Recent contributors: Murray Rothbard, Yale Brozen, Paul Anderson, Thomas Szasz, Edith Efron.* Monthly; $9/yr; $1/ea; $1/sample; 1968; 52pp; 8½x11; 10M circ; lo. Reports 2-3 mos. Pays: $10; 1 yr sub plus 10 copies. Ads: $200/p; $125/½; class/wd 15 cents. Discounts: quantity rates on request. Back issues: on request. Pub'd 12 issues 1973, expects 12 in 1974.

Rebel Press, **Ronald Duncan,** 2 Derby St., London W1, UK. Poetry, criticism, long-poems; also: Welcombe Bideford, UK. *Prints works of literary or scientific interest.*

Rebis Press, **Betsy Davids, Jim Petrillo,** 5806 Lawton Ave., Oakland, CA 94618. Poetry, fiction, art, photos, cartoons, interviews, satire, music, letters, parts-of-novels, longpoems, collages, plays, concrete art. *We do mostly books that are handcrafted art objects in themselves. Recent and forthcoming books by Betsy Davids, Ed Moore, Carole Peel, Allie Light, Harriet Herman, Jim Petrillo and John Wehrle.* 1973; lo/lp. Reports: quick. Pay varies. Pub'd 1 book in 1973, expects 10 in 1974. COSMEP, Women, Food/Ecology.

RECON, Recon Publications, **Chris Robinson,** copy ed., **Lewis Bellis,** bus. mngr., PO Box 14602, Philadelphia, PA 19134. Articles. *A monthly publication on military affairs: Pentagon Planning, Strategy & Tactics, GI Movement, 3rd World*

Struggles, and Anti-Militarist Movement. Articles should be less than 1250 words. Monthly; $10/yr libraries & other instit; $5/yr foreign sea mail; $8/yr air mail; $3/yr reg. sub; 25 cents/ea; 25 cents/sample; 1973; 12pp; 8½x11; 1500 circ; lo. No pay. Ads: $30/p; $15/½; 25 cents per line class/wd. Discounts: 40% on orders of 5 or more. Back issues: 25 cents/copy. Pub'd 7 issues 1973, expects 12 in 1974. COSMEP, Third World, G.I., Anti-militarist.

Red Dust, Inc., **Joanna Gunderson,** 218 E. 81st St., New York, NY 10028. Poetry, fiction, art, plays. *New fiction by new writers. Also general, (film, autobiography) and art. Recent titles: Castras Tahrsis,* Third Wedding; Red Dust 1 *and* 2, *anthology of short experimental or new works.* 2-4 bks/yr; 200pp; 1500 circ; lo. Reports 1 mo. Pays: $300 against royalties. Discounts:30% single copy; 40% 2 and over; 20% libraries. Pub'd 2 books 1973, expects 4 in 1974. COSMEP.

Red Fox Publications, **N.S. Thompson,** c/o 38a Longsight Rd., Holcombe Brook, Bury, Lancs., UK. *Published so far: 1) "One day the Bubble Machine will die and pop your everyday with it." 2) "Poems, Delhi 1972." 3) "Yes Cosmo's Cants and the Mad Monk Show." 4) "Blue Shadows on Snow," mini poetry poster. Expected: "Blue Shadows on Snow" print. + one more book and several mini posters.* 1971. ALP.

RED FOX REVIEW, **James Coleman, et. al.,** Mohegan Community College, Norwich, CT 06360. Poetry, fiction, photos. *New magazine connected to poetry contest open to all residents of Connecticut. Also will publish fiction, poetry and photos, primarily from S.E. Connecticut region.* Annual; free with entry to poetry contest; 1974; 80pp; 5½x8; 1M circ; lo. Reports: not soliciting currently. COSMEP.

Red Hill Press, Los Angeles & Fairfax (see also *INVISIBLE CITY),* **John McBride, Paul Vangelisti,** 6 San Gabriel Dr., Fairfax, CA 94930. *Publishes* Invisible City *and individual volumes, both original and translated, including works of: Artaud, Vittorio Sereni, Vallejo, Rene Depestre, John Thomas and Luisa Pasamanik. Recent books by L.A. basin poets: Stuart Z. Perkoff, Alvaro Cardona-Hine, and Robert Peters. Doing more.* RHP books are distributed by Serendipity Books.

Red Maple Corp. Publishing Co. (see THIS MAGAZINE)

RED PLANET EARTH, **Craig Strete, David Trout Staddon, asst. ed.,** 140 Meyer Ave., Dayton, OH 45431, summer address: RR1, Box 208, Celina, OH 45822. Fiction, articles, art, cartoons, satire, letters. *Prints science fiction and fantasy written by Indians. Does look at material by whites. Reports on submissions in 5 days for SASE material. Same standards as major circulation sci-fi mags. This is an inter-tribal effort to help Indian writers. No mainstream.* 6/yr; price/yr varies; 50 cents/ea; 25 cents/sample; 1974; 30pp; 8x11; 600 circ; mi (some). Reports 5 days if SASE. Pays: 1-3 cents/wd. Ads: depends on space availability — mostly AIM related. No discounts. No issues pub'd 1973, expects 6-8 in 1974; expects 1 book in 1974. American Indian, sci-fi.

RED RAG, **Red Rag Collective,** 9 Stratford Villas, London NW1, UK. Articles, poetry, cartoons, photos, news items, interviews, criticism. *Journal of Women's Liberation.* 4/yr; 50p/yr; 10p/ea; 1972; 24pp; A4; 3-4000 circ; off. Women.

Redaction Bibliotheque Humanisme et Renaissance, **Librarie DROZ S.A.,** 11, rue Massot, Geneve, Switzerland. 3/yr; $22/yr; 1934; print. Discounts: 70% to the booksellers. Pub'd 3 issues 1973, expects 3 in 1974.

Redemptorist Publications (see REALITY)

THE REED, **Dennis Shelley, Ray Pitts,** c/o Dept. of Eng., San Jose State Univ., San Jose, CA 95114. Poetry, fiction, art, parts-of-novels, longpoems (sometimes). *Tastes change from year to year with rotating editorship, but in general fiction should be under 5,000 words, poetry under 60 lines. Formerly an undergraduate annual,* The Reed *moved to quarterly format, began accepting outside contributors, and occasionally awarding cash prizes to manuscripts under the recent editorships of Merritt Clifton, Tom McCarty, Bill Swanson, and Tom Suddick, all of whom moved on to* The Berkeley Samisdat Review *and several other related presses. Besides Shelley, Pitts, Clifton, McCarty, Swanson, and Suddick, recent issues include Harold Norse, Nils Peterson, Robert Burdette Sweet, Janice Hays, Jan Zaleski, Tom Halloran, Katherine Gibson, Michael Rizzolo, Fred Hansfield, Ellen Murray, Jo Anne Churchill, Denise K. Taylor, Naomi Clark, Lynda Shearin, Lynda Riese, Rob Swigart, and Suzanne Juhasz, with art by Chris Caughey.* 4/yr (usually in two 100pp double issues); $2/yr; $1/ea; $1/sample; 1948; 100pp; 8½x7; 500 circ; lo. Reports vary from days to mos. Pays copies only, unless a manuscript wins a prize. No ads. Discounts are available on Spring 1973, and 1970 and 1965 issues; others are out of print. Pub'd 3 issues 1973, expects 4 in 1974.

Regent Press (see LEEDS STUDENT)

THE REGINALD A FESSENDEN MEMORIAL RADIO TIMES   , Dildo Press, **Lorenzo W. Milam,** 5 University Ave., Los Gatos, CA 95030. Poetry, fiction, articles, satire, criticism, letters, longpoems. The Radio Times *concentrates on articles of interest in communication and alternative broadcasting, on Federal Communications Commission decisions and dockets of importance, and on general aesthetic views of McLuhanesque transmission.* Monthly; $3/yr; single copy free; 1970; 20-24pp; tabloid; 3M circ; lo. Reports 1 mo. Pays free sub and copies. Ads: $5000/p; $3000/½. No discounts. Back issues: $10 for all previous issues. Pub'd 24 issues, 1 book 1973; expects 24 issues, 3 books in 1974. COSMEP.

Release Press (see also *SOME),* **Larry Zirlin,** gen. ed., **Michael Andre, Harry Greenberg, Alan Ziegler,** co-eds., 478 Seventh St., Brooklyn, NY 11215. Poetry, art, collages. *Not looking at unsolicited manuscripts unless inquiry precedes.* Discount: open to offers. Pub'd 4 books 1973, expects 4 in 1974.

THE REMINGTON REVIEW, Joseph A. Barbato, fiction, **Dean Maskevich,** poetry, 505 Westfield Ave., Elizabeth, NJ 07208. Poetry, fiction, art, photos, parts-of-novels. *We are looking for quality fiction and poetry of any school. Xerox copies and carbons will be returned unread. We also invite submissions of drawings, photographs, and other graphics but do not accept responsibility for damage to such material in the mails. Although our contributors have included Stephen Dixon, Joyce Carol Oates, Alvin Greenberg, John Tagliabue, and Douglas Blazek, we are very interested in new writers. Fiction should be 1500 to 10,000 words in length. Poems should not exceed 100 lines. Submissions must be addressed to appropriate editor and be accompanied by an SASE.* 2/yr; $2/yr; $1/ea; $5/3 yrs; 1972; 80pp; 5x7; 500 circ; lo. Reports 2-3 mos. Pays 2 copies. Pub'd 2 issues 1973, expects 2 in 1974. COSMEP.

RENAISSANCE and MODERN STUDIES, **James T. Bolton, Richard S. Smith,** c/o Sisson and Parker Ltd., Wheeler Gate, Nottingham, UK. Articles, criticism. *Longer scholarly articles in all fields of the humanities. Contributions mainly from University of Nottingham, by whom journal is sponsored.* Annual; £1.75/yr; 1957; 150pp; 400 circ; lp. Reports 2-3 months. Discounts: 20%.

RENASCENCE: Essays on Values in Literature, **John D. McCabe,** Marquette Univ., Milwaukee, WI 53233. Q; $6/yr; $1.75/ea; $1.75/sample; 1949; 800 circ; lp. Reports 2-4 mos. Pays copies only (5). No ads. Discounts: 10% for agents. Back issues: varies, up to $3 per issue. Pub'd 4 issues 1973.

REPARTEE, **Milbish Pute,** PO Box 3232-A, Birmingham, AL 35205. Irreg; donation; 1971; 5pp; 4-600 circ; mi. Reports 2 mos. Pays: at times cash, usually copies. Ads: $1 per col. inch. No discounts. Back issues: if we have any we'll give them away. COSMEP.

Resource Publications (see FOLK MASS AND MODERN LITURGY)

RESOURCES, **Richard Gardner,** Box 490, Somerville, MA 02144. *Newsletter about changing needs/aspirations, new ideas, products, and services, and the people, groups, and organizations that are changing and creating.* Monthly; $5/yr.

RESURGENCE, **Satish Kumar,** 39 Alma St., London NW5, UK. Articles, poetry, cartoons, photos, interviews, criticism, letters. 6/yr; £1.80/yr; 25p/ea; 1966; 30pp; A4; 2000+ circ; off. Pays: nil. Ads: £50/page; £30/½; £20/¼; 5p/word. Decentralized Politics.

REVIEW '74, Pale Horse Press, **Joseph McLaughlin,** Box 109, New Philadelphia, OH 44663. Poetry, fiction, articles, art, photos, interviews, criticism, reviews, long-poems, plays. *Contributors to* Review '74 *include James Magner, William Heyen, Duane Locke, Mimi Albert, John Morgan, Ann Deagon, Thomas Milligan, and Ray DiPalma. Lyric intensity; contemporary language; excellence. Submissions for* Review '75 *will be accepted after Sept. 15, 1974; subscriptions anytime.* Annual; $2/yr; $2/ea; 1974; 48pp; 5x7; 200 circ; lo. Reports immediately. Pays copies only (2). Ads: $20/p; $10/½; $5/¼. Discounts: 40% trade; 50% distributors; 10% agent; free to selected classrooms and libraries after March 1, 1975; inquire. Expects 1 issue 1974 and 1 book 1974.

REYNARD, Quaker Fellowship of the Arts, **Charles Kohler,** Pathways, West Humble, Dorking, **Fred J. Nicholson, asst. ed.,** 91 Sedbergh Road, Kendal, Westmorland, UK. Articles, poetry, art, cartoons, photos, criticism. *Publish occasional poetry etc. Recent contributors include Clive Sansom, Laurence Lerner.* Reynard *is the magazine of the Quaker Fellowship of the Arts (QFA). It is largely a vehicle for members' own work but would not say "No" to contributions of quality. Quakers can be very catholic.* 1/yr; 75p/membership; 25p/ea; free sample; 1954; 32pp; 8½x5½"; 500 circ; off. Reports 1 wk. No pay. Ads: by negotiation. No discounts. Back issues: 25p.

RIPPLE, Leicester University Students Union, **Ric Rogers,** c/o Students Union, Leicester, UK. Articles, poetry, cartoons, photos, satire, news items, interviews, criticism, letters. Fortnightly during terms=11/yr; 4p/ea; 1958; 16pp; 10½x15"; 1800 circ; off. Reports 10 days. Ads: £85/page; £45/½. Student.

RIPPLES, **Jim & Karen Schaefer,** PO Box 52, Ann Arbor, MI 48107. *Unique publishing venture for developing poet and short fiction writer, as the first 3 issues are printed as newsletters of material being worked on, then final issue of year printed in formal format.* Q; $3/yr; no samples; 1973; 20pp; 500 circ; lo. Reports 1 day. Pays copies only. Ads: rates available for formal magazine only. Discounts: considered. *Eclectic poetry not desired, but are interested in natural, organic images of daily life around the perceiver.* COSMEP.

RIVERSIDE QUARTERLY, **Leland Sapiro,** Box 14451 Univ. Sta., Gainesville, FL 32604, **David Lunde, poetry ed.,** 1179 Central Ave., Dunkirk, NY 14048. Poetry, fiction, articles, art, satire, criticism, reviews, letters. *There's no question of "slant" here:* RQ's *job is that of any other critical journal: to increase the reader's enjoy-*

ment by pointing out relationships that might not have been perceived otherwise. My only bias is against articles that don't accomplish this. The scope of the mag is best indicated by some recent titles: "Science=Fiction and the Symbolist Tradition," "The Prudish Prurience of H. Rider Haggard and Edgar Rice Burroughs," "Motifs and Sources for Lord of the Rings." With respect to fiction, max. length is 4,500 words – but such contributors should read a few copies of the magazine before sending in any mss.* Irreg; $2/yr; 60 cents/ea; 60 cents/sample; 1964; 80pp; 8½x5½; 1400 circ; lo. Reports 10 days. Pays copies only. Discounts: $1.50. Back issues: 60 cents/ea all back issues; discount rate 50 cents. Pub'd 2 issues 1973, expects 2 in 1974. COSMEP.

ROAR, Lionhead Publishing, **Martin J. Rosenblum,** 3016 West Michigan St., Milwaukee, WI 53208. Poetry, fiction, articles, interviews, criticism, reviews, letters, parts-of-novels, longpoems, plays. *Lionhead Publishing is currently publishing a series of poetry broadsides by Tom Montag, Toby Olson, Mike Tarachow, Karl Young; and more are planned as are chapbooks. Roar is a post-projectivist annual collection of poetry, experimental prose and criticism, still in the planning stage due to lack of money.* Yearly. Reports 1 mo. Pays copies only. COSMEP.

Roberton Publications, **Kenneth Roberton,** The Windmill, Wendover, Aylesbury, Bucks, UK. Music. *All types of standard and educational music, no pop or jazz, bias towards choral works of all kinds.* Off. Reports 2 mos. Pays: 10% royalty on retail sp.

ROCHDALE'S ALTERNATIVE PAPER (RAP), **David Bartlett,** 230 Spotland Rd., Rochdale, **John Walker,** 555 Prestbury, Ashfield Valley, Rochdale, UK. Articles, cartoons, photos, satire, news items, letters. Monthly; £1/yr; 5p/ea; 1971; 16pp; 15x9; 4,250 circ; off/litho.

ROCKY MOUNTAIN REVIEW, AtLATL Press, Leonard Bird, L. Doran-Maurer, Wayne Johnston, Marianna, Box 1848, Durango, CO 81301. Poetry, fiction, art, photos (black & white), longpoems. Will accept any strongly-felt, hard-crafted material that excites the diverse biases of the editors. From 1/3 to 1/2 of each issue – depending upon quality: reflects Rocky Mountain and desert Southwest. Tri-annual; $4/yr; $1.50/ea; $1.50/sample; 1973; 48pp; 5½x9; 400 circ; lo. Reports 2-6 wks. Pays copies only. Ads: $75/p; $37.50/½; $19/¼. Discounts: trade, bulk, classroom, 40%. Back issues: $1.50/ea. Pub'd 1 issue 1973, expects 3 issues, 2 books in 1974. COSMEP.

Rodale Press   (see PREVENTION)

Rodale Press   (see THEATRE CRAFTS)

ROLLING STONE, St. Arrow Publishers, **U.S.: Jann Wennes, U.K.: Andrew Bailey, mang. ed.,** 25 Newman St., London W1P 3HA. Articles, poetry, fiction, art, cartoons, photos, satire, news items, interviews, criticism, music, letters. *1500-500 words, West Coast style (punchy).* No biases: Tom Wolfe, Anthony Haydn-Guest, Hunter S. Thompson, Ralph Steadman, Richard Goodman. Bi-weekly; £5/yr; 25p/ea; 1967; 48pp; 35,000 circ; off. Ads: £175/page; £95/½; £50/¼; £2.50 per col. inch. Discounts: 5%; 7%; 12%. Cultural Political & Rock.

Rollins College Press   (see EPOS)

Romar Press, **D.M. Bennett,** Fountainhall, Stow, Midlothian, Scotland, UK. Poetry, fiction, cartoons, satire, longpoems. 1972; off. SF.

Rondo Publications Ltd.   (see MERIDIAN)

ROOPVATI (The Nymph), Navyug, Delhi, India, **Mrs. Kailash Puri,** "Bucklands,' 36 Merrilocks Road, Blundellsands, Liverpool 23, UK. Articles, poetry, fiction, art, cartoons, photos, satire, news items, interviews, criticism, letters, longpoems, plays. *The only bilingual monthly in English and Punjabi. Length of material 2-5 pages otherwise serial issues. Style-humorous. Biases - Non-political. Recent contributors: Apa Pant, High Commissioner of India, Adrian Henri, Spencer Leigh, Norman Williams J.P., Professor Mohar Singh, Professor Gopal Puri, Gurmukh Supl Musafir M.P., S.S. Kalra M.A.* Monthly; £3 libraries; 20p/ea; 1956; 64pp; 20x15cm 5000 circ; lp/off. Reports: 1 month. Pays: half advance as is arranged monthly. Ads: £120/page, £65/½, £35/¼, £18/eighth. Discounts: 10% agency. Back issues: 50% extra. Women, Ecology, Occult, 3rd World, Black Asian Immigrants.

ROOTS, 6 Lonsdale Terrace, Edinburgh 3, UK. Articles, poetry, photos, news items, interviews, criticism, letters. 12/yr; £1/yr; 6p/ea; 1971; 20p; 7x9"; 1000 circ; off. Reports: varies. Pays: copies usually. Ads: £12/page pro rata. lp/word. Community.

ROOTS, Roots Publications, **Anton Stewart,** 30 Basegreen Avenue, Sheffield S12 3FA, UK. Articles, poetry, fiction, art, satire, criticism, letters. *Roots is tired of receiving poetry from people who have not seen the magazine and whose sole interest appears to lie in having their poems published in as many magazines as possible.We will send a sample copy of the mag to anyone who is interested. We are interested in your ideas, however expressed. We particularly welcome constructive letters and articles. Roots, in addition to being a literary magazine, is a forum for the discussion of all things relevant to human existance.* 5/yr; 50p, $2/yr; 12½p/ each; free sample; 1972; 28pp; A5; 200 circ; mim. Reports: 3 mos. Pays: copies only. Ads: by arrangement.

Bertram Rota (Publishing) Ltd., 4,5 & 6 Savile Row, London W1X 2LN, UK.

ROUGH TIMES, edited collectively, P.O. Box 89, W. Somerville, MA 02144. Poetry, articles, art, criticism, reviews. *We consider ourselves a political journal, so that's one of our biases. Material should relate to mental health.* 8/yr; $6/yr individual, $12/yr institution; 75 cents/ea; 50 cents/sample; 1970; 24pp; tabloid; 6M circ; lo. Reports 1 month. Pays copies only. No ads. Discounts: 1/3 off on orders of over 10 copies. Back issues: write us. Pub'd 6 issues, 1 book in 1973, expects 8 issues, 1 book in 1974. COSMEP.

ROUND UP, **Lawrence Upton,** c/o 18 Clairview Road, Streatham, London SW16, **J.C.R. Green,** 18 Atherstone Close. Shirley, Solihull, Warks, UK. Articles, news items, interviews, criticism, letters. *The only regular mag giving info on poetry and experimental writing publications and gigs in UK.* 6/yr; 50p px/yr; 10p px/ea; 1974: 25pp; 10x8"; 200 circ; mim/off. Reports: 2-3 wks. Pays: 1 copy for substantial contributions. Ads: on application to London address. Discounts: 33%.

Roundhouse Press, (see STOOGE)

Royal Society of St. George (see ENGLAND)

The Rudinger Foundation, Inc. (see FIRELANDS ARTS REVIEW)

THE RUFUS, Gyst Publications, **Patricia Ann Bunin,** P.O. Box 75982, Los Angeles, CA 90075. Poetry, poetry articles, poetry interviews, poetry reviews. *Exists primarily to provide a forum for new and established poets. Solicit material of any length, subject matter, form or writing style, as long as standards of excellence are met. Features editorials, letters to ed., articles on new developments, book reviews, awards. Cash payments to award winners. Uses graphics and photography to illus-*

trate some poems. Recent contributors: Irving Layton (Canada), Michael Harper (Brown Univ.), Lori Petri (Calif.). We critique all submissions. 3/yr; $5/yr domestic; $6/yr overseas; $2/ea; free sample to libraries only; 70pp; 8½x5½; 300 circ; mi/lo. Reports 6 wks to 2 mos. Pays contributors copies. No ads. Discounts: 45% to agents and bookstores. Back issues: $1.50 for 1972 quarterly issues. Pub'd 4 issues in 1973, expects 3 in 1974. UAP.

Runa Press, **Eithne Strong,** Monkstown, Co. Dublin, Eire, UK. Poetry. Occasional; £1.50 average/ea; 1944; 60-70pp. Reports: 14-21 days. Poetry, Philosophy.

Running Press, **Lawrence Teacher, Stuart Teacher,** 38 South 19th Street, Philadelphia, PA 19103. *We publish only non-fiction, quality (large format), softcover books. Books that tell people how to make things, build things, get things etc. Two of our current publications are ongoing:* The Dome Builder's Handbook and Energy Book No.1/Alternative Sources & Backyard Applications. *By ongoing we mean that we are dependent upon contributors for the bulk of info exchange, dependent to the point that without them there is no publication. Both the* Dome Book and Energy Book No.1 *will be published annually and bi-annually respectively, so contributions can be submitted at any time. Contributions range from full scale plans and lengthy articles to short thoughts or fantasies.* Lo. Pub'd 6 books in 1973, expects 7 in 1974. COSMEP.

Russell Press (see RACE TODAY)

S Press Edition, **Angela Kohler, Klaus Einhorn, Michael Kohler,** d-432 Hattingen-Blankenstein, Marktplatz 2, West Germany. Poetry, fiction, music, concrete art. *We publish exclusively sound poetry on tapes, ie poetry to be performed and heard as opposed to poetry designed primarily to be read. Two editorial principles are observed: 1. poets themselves perform their work and/or supervise production; 2. the scope of the series is international. So far we have published mainly European authors, among others: Otto Nebel, Raoul Hausmann, Helmut HeiBenbuttel, Gerhard Ruhm, Henri Chopin, Arno Holz, Eugene Gomringer, Bernard Heidsiek, and John Cage. Starting this year we will publish American poets: Charles Olson, Robert Creely, Gary Snyder, Edward Dorn, Jerome Rothenberg, John Giorno, to begin with.* Annual; price varies; 1970; open reel tape cassettes. Reports 1 month. Pays royalties. All tapes still available. Published 5 tapes in 1973, expects 5 in 1974.

S.A.T.R.A. and Churches of St. Ann's (see NEW CHASE CHAT)

G. Sack Press, **Olivia Concholar, Lloyd Roth, Rick Smith,** Box 2762-D, Pasadena, CA 91105. Poetry, longpoems. *To date, only one title: Exhibition Game (Rick Smith). Future books will probably include an anthology of prison poetry. Not presently soliciting manuscripts.* Irreg; $2/ea; 60pp; 5¼x7 3/4; lo. Discounts: 40% to stores plus 50% to anyone who orders more than 15. Published 1 book in 1973, expects 1 book in 1974. COSMEP.

SADAKICHI HARTMANN NEWSLETTER, **Richard Tuerk, chief ed., George Knox, Harry Lawton, Michael Elderman, Wisteria Hartmann Linton,** Dept. of Literature and Languages, East Texas State Univ., Commerce, TX 75428. Poetry, articles, art, photos, cartoons, criticism, reviews. *Usually short articles, ranging up to about 10 typewritten pages; longer articles are usually broken into parts to be run in subsequent issues. We tend to follow the MLA Style Sheet for articles needing documentation. However, because our audience is very diverse, we prefer to have articles written in nontechnical prose with limited documentation. Recent contributors include Hans-Peter Breuer, George Knox, Harry Lawton, Edward Hagemann, Roger Hull, and Saburo Ota. We also publish reminiscences of Hartmann, pictures of and about Hartmann, and poems by and about Hartmann.* 3/yr;

$2.50/yr; $1/ea; free sample; 1969; 8pp; 8½x11; 200 circ; lp. Reports few wks. Pays copies only (2). No ads. No discounts. Back issues free on demand while the supply lasts. Pub'd 3 issues 1973, expects 3 in 1974.

Sage Publications Ltd. (see URBAN LIFE & CULTURE)

SAILING THE ROAD CLEAR, Lake Grove Printing, **Jane Creighton,** 2107 Marine Dr., Boulder, CO. 80302. Poetry. *Poetry because this is what we know best, interested in good longpoems, hopefully escaping biases toward one or another style (avoiding schools in turn for good poems) – perhaps reviews in the near future. Magazine quite young yet to know* everything *about its personality. Recent contributors: John Newlove, Bobby Byrd, Rochelle Owens, Keith Wilson, Theodore Enslin, Joan Larkin, – And highly excited about recent Canadian work.* 3-4/yr; $3/4 issues; 75 cents/ea; 1973; 40pp; 6x8; 400 copies circ; lo. Reports 3 wks. Pays copies only. Discounts: not that far yet. Back issues: 75 cents. Pub'd 1 issue 1973, expects 3 in 1974. COSMEP.

ST. ANDREWS REVIEW, **Ronald H. Bayes,** Execu. ed., **Malcolm Doubles, Manag. ed.,** St. Andrews College, Laurinburg, NC 28352. Poetry, fiction, articles, art, photos, interviews, criticism, reviews, music, parts-of-novels, longpoems. *Contributors have included: James Laughlin, Carolyn Kizer, R. Buckminster Fuller, Kobo Abe, Ykio Mishima, Senator Sam J. Ervin, Senator Hugh Scott and others.* 2/yr; $3.50/yr; $2/ea; 1970; 75pp; 6½x9¼; 650 circ; lp.

St. Arrow Publishers (see ROLLING STONE)

ST. CROIX REVIEW (formerly RELIGION & SOCIETY), **Angus MacDonald,** Box 244, Stillwater, MN 55082. *Chicago Manual of Style. Bias classical liberalism, most contributors are professors. We favor a market economy and limited government role, though an important government role.* Bi-monthly; $10/yr; $2/ea; sample; 1968; 48pp; 6x9; 2500 circ; lo. Reports 2 wks. Pays copies only. Ads: $200/p. No discounts. Back issues: available at current price. Pub'd 6 issues 1973, expects 6 in 1974.

ST. LOUIS JOURNALISM REVIEW, Focus/Midwest Publ. Co., Inc. **Editorial Board,** PO Box 3086, St. Louis, MO 63130. Articles, interviews, criticism, letters, *Only if they apply to St. Louis metropolitan area – possible Missouri.* Bi-monthly; $5/yr; 50 cents/ea; sample; 1970; 16pp; tabloid; 4M circ; lo. Reports 4-6 wks. Pays copies only. Discounts: 20%. Back issues: $1. Pub'd 6 issues 1973, expects 6 in 1974.

SALT, Tegwar Press, **Robert Currie,** 1119–13th Ave., N.W., Moose Jaw, Sask., Canada. Poetry, reviews. *The movie* Bang The Drum Slowly *may have helped a larger audience to guess that poetry is* the exciting game without any rules. *However,* Salt *prefers poems that are short, specific, vivid and not obscure. Still, any poem can lead to a love affair.* 2/yr; $1/yr; 50 cents/ea; 50 cents/sample; $2/5 issues; 1969; 26pp; 8½x11; 350 circ; mi. Reports 1 mo. Pays copies only. Back issues $1/ea. Pub'd 2 issues 1973, expects 2 in 1974.

SALT CREEK READER (see NEW SALT CREEK READER)

SALT LICK, Salt Lick Press, **James Haining, Daniel Castelaz,** PO Box 1064, Quincy, IL 62301. Poetry, fiction, articles, art, photos, cartoons, interviews, satire, criticism, reviews, music, letters, parts-of-novels, longpoems, collages, plays, concrete art, correspondance art. *Gerald Burns, Michael Lally, Robert Trammell, Ron Silliman, David Searcy, Bruce Andrews, Wilton David, Ann Darr, Robert Slater, Albert Drake, Stephen-Leggett, Wm. Hart, Robert Mejer, Lee DeJasu, Castelaz, Victor*

Contoski, more. Irreg; $3/yr; $1.50/ea; $1.50/sample; 1969; 68pp; 10½x8½; 1200 circ; lo; hand additions. Reports 10-30 days. Pay: if available; always copies. Pub'd 1 issue 1973, expects 1 in 1974; expects 2 books 1974. COSMEP, CCLM, Correspondence Artists.

SALTED FEATHERS, **Dick Bakken,** 932 S.E. 40th, Portland, OR 97214 (tele: 234-1160 unlisted). Poetry, poet photos, poet interviews, poetry documentary. *Send no more manuscripts ever: current 400-page Allen Ginsberg book is the terminal issue of* Salted Feathers. *Complete original* Salted Feathers *backsets (1964-1967) available to libraries and collectors.* Irreg: $5/yr; 1964; 40pp; 8½x11; 500 circ; mi; lo.

SALTED IN THE SHELL, **Gary Lawless,** c/o 40 High St., Belfast, ME 04915. Poetry, interviews, letters, longpoems. *Travelling, not much time to read & collect mail – so accepting no more submissions – gathering them as I travel.* 3-6/yr; $2.50/yr; 50 cents/ea; 50 cents/sample; 1972; 15pp; 8½x11; 400-500 circ; mi. Reports 1 wk to 1 yr. Pays copies only. Discounts: $10/100. Back issues: Nos. 1-13 without No.4=$7.50. Pub'd 6 issues 1973, expects 1 book 1974. NESPA.

SALTHOUSE, **D. Clinton,** English Dept., Bowling Green State Univ., Bowling Green, OH 43403 *(this address will change summer '75).* Poetry, articles, letters. *This is the first announcement of* Salthouse *and with it I'm looking for exciting, incredible and startling poems. Premiere issue is hopefully March, 1975. Editor is co-founder of* The Ark River Review *(1971), former coordinator of the Poetry in the Schools Projects for the Kansas Arts Commission and former poetry editor of* The New Newspaper *of Wichita, KS. Hopefully a semi-annual. A year before production, size and paper weight is a little foggy. Please do not send anything that is too serious or anything near that category. I simply want to provide a forum for knock-out poems – the kind you can go back again and again and enjoy. SASE only.* 2/yr; $1.50/yr; 75 cents/ea; 50 cents/sample; 1975; 300 circ; lo. Reports under 1 mo. at first. Pays 2 copies. Ads: negot., very interested; 20 cents/wd class/ wd. Discounts: send correspondence and we can work something out, I'm sure. Back issues: no back issues/premiere issue probably March, 1975. Expects 2 issues 1975.

SALTILLO, **J.C. Wilson,** 201 Andrews Hall, Univ. of Nebraska, Lincoln, NB 68508. Poetry, fiction, articles, reviews. 3/yr; $3/yr; $1/ea; 1971; 52pp; 6x9; 400 circ; lo. Reports 1 mo. Pays copies only. Back issues: $2/ea. Pub'd 3 issues 1973, expects 3 in 1974. COSMEP.

Samisdat Associates (see BERKELEY SAMISDAT REVIEW)

SAMPHIRE – New Poetry, **Michael Butler & Kemble Williams,** 45 Westfields, Catshill, Bromsgrove and Heronshaw, Holbrook, Ipswich, UK. Poetry. *Reviews used. Mag should be studied first.* 4/yr; 65p/yr; 15p/ea; 700 circ; off. Reports 6-8 wks. Pays: £1/poem/page. Ads: by arrangement. Poetry.

San Marcos Press, **Ernest Tedlock,** P.O. Box 53, Cerrillos, NM 87010.

SAND DOLLAR, **Jack Shoemaker,** 650 Colusa, Berkeley, CA 94700.

SANDWICHES (Excello and Bollard), Excello and Bollard, **Paul 'Kid Clam' Lamprill, Graeme 'Brinsley' Carter,** 66b Whitstable Road, Canterbury, Kent CT2 8EB, UK. Poetry, fiction, satire, criticism, letters, longpoems, concrete. *Humorous accent. Nothing offensive in rude terms. Magazine totally reflects the editors. It is ours and we share it with others, rather than being tools of criticism.* 4/yr; 60p/yr; 15p/ea; 1973; 18/20pp; A4; mim. Reports: 2-4 wks. Back issues: 10p. ALP.

Sangre de Cristo (see JANUS–SCTH)

SANITY, **Zoe Fairbairns,** 14 Grays Inn Road, London WC1, UK. Articles, cartoons, photos, satire, news items, interviews, criticism, letters. 8/yr; £1/yr; 5p/ea; 3½p/sample; 8pp; 15xll; 5000 circ; off. Pays: none. Ads: £1/col.inch, 2½p/wd. Discounts: Enquire. Peace.

SANTIAGO, Revista Santiago, Universidad de Oriente, Direccion de Extension Universitaria, Santiago de Cuba, Republica de Cuba.

SAPPHO, Sappho Publications Ltd., **Jacqueline Forster,** BCM/Petrel, London WC1V 6XX, UK. Articles, poetry, fiction, art, cartoons, photos, satire, news items, interviews, criticism, letters. Sappho *is published by homosexual women for all women.* Sappho *is the only Lesbian magazine in Europe. The contents are contributed by readers and subscribers about womens rights, Bi-sexual/Homosexual/ Heterosexual, Single and Married Women. Contributors include Maureen Duffy, Ronald Searle, Ian Harvey, Harriette Frances.* Monthly; £3/yr; 25p px/ea; 1972; 24-32pp; 6 mo; 1000 circ; off. Reports: 1 month. No pay. Ads: £20/page, £12/½; £8/¼. Discounts: varies. Back issues: £1/5 copies pf. Women, Gay.

SATIS, **Matthew Mead,** 14 Greenhill Place, Edinburgh 10, UK. Poetry. Varies/ea; 30p, $1/sample; 1960; 250 circ. Discounts: 33% trade.

THE SATURDAY CLUB BOOK OF POETRY, The Saturday Centre, **Patricia Laird,** Box 140, P.O. Cammeray, N.S.W., Australia 2062. Poetry, art, photos, cartoons, longpoems, collages, concrete art. *All styles accepted. Recent contributors: Judith Wright, Ian Mudie, Louis Johnson, Rac Desmond Jones, Joanne Burns, Ross Fitzgerald, Peter Skrzynecki, Stefanie Bennett.* 4/yr; $5.50 (Aust.)/yr; $1.70 (Aust.)/ea; $1.50/Poets' Series; 1972; 44pp; A4; 400 circ; of. Reports 3 mos. Pays: from $2.50 per page + comp. copy. No ads. Discounts: available to agents for $1.03 per copy if 6 or more purchased. Also sub. disc. Back issues: 1st & 2nd issues no longer available. Pub'd 4 issues 1973, expects 4 in 1974; 3 books 1973, expects 5 in 1974. Also publish *The Saturday Centre Poets' Series.*

SAVACOU, **Edward Brathwaite, Kenneth Ramcaand, Andrew Salkey,** P.O. Box 170, Kingston 7, Jamaica. Poetry, fiction, articles, art, interviews, satire, criticism, reviews, parts-of-novels, plays. SAVACOU *is a literary/academic journal of the Caribbean Artists Movement. There are 4 issues per subscription but these are not necessarily 4 each year.* Q; $6/yr; $2/ea; 1970; 120pp; 4000 circ; lp. Ads: J$100/p; J$50/½. Discounts: 20% to bookshops on order of over 12. Published one double issue in 1973, expects 2 issues in 1974. Third World (West Indies).

SCENE, 62 High Street, Harpenden, Herts, UK. *The medium for people seeking people.* 35p/ea.

The Sceptre Press, **Martin Booth,** 15 Keats Way, Rushden, Northants NN10 9BJ, England, UK. Poetry, longpoems. *Length immaterial: style wider than insular British poetry; no biases towards schools of technique etc., recent contributors include Robert Bly, Cid Corman, Ed Mycue, David Grubb, Peter Redgrove, Harry Guest, Elaine Feinstein, Hugh Lauder, Stephen Sossaman, Lawrence 'Good Elf' Upton, Nick Malone; unknown poets encouraged to submit - we publish approx 2 unknowns to every known poet: SAE essential for reply. The aim is to publish what's good in any school of thought, as long as we've the money to do it, in booklet and broadsheet form.* 24/yr; varies/sub; SAE/sample; 1968; 8pp; varies/size; 150 (limited editions)/circ; lp. Reports: 4 wks. Pays: always copies; sometimes cash as well. Ads: we circulate other press's leaflets with our own. Discounts: 25%. ALP

SCHISM, Donald L. Rice, 1109 W. Vine St., Mt. Vernon, OH 43050. Poetry, articles, art, cartoons, interviews, satire, criticism, reviews, letters. We use 20 or more articles and 12 cartoons in each issue — but only if they have appeared in other small press periodicals. We do not solicit manuscripts nor would we use unsolicited. We do encourage exchange subscriptions with any other periodical. We reprint from both Left and Right and try to give an unprejudiced overview of the material available. (95% of our circulation is among libraries). When using an article, we give full credit to the source including subscription information and, if provided, the periodical's philosophy. Sources are as diverse as People's World and The Racialist, The Western Socialist and Christian Crusade Weekly. Writers are as diverse as Strom Thurmond and Allen Ginsberg, Angela Davis and Henry Hazlitt. However, most writers are unknown to the general public. Q; $7.50/yr; $2/ea; $1/sample; 1969; 64pp; 8½xll; 1100 circ; lo. Discounts: 10 or more copies of one issue to one address (schools only) $1/ea. Back issues: $2 (Vol.I, Nos.1&2 o/p). COSMEP.

SCHIST, A Journal of Poetry and Graphics, **Sandy Dorbin**, PO Box 257, Willimantic, CT 06226. Poetry, art, photos, reviews, music. Schist *is open and non-sectarian. Expect rigidity to set in in another year however. Tired of so much cynicism. Poetry is still news that stays news.* Irreg; $8/4 issues libraries; $7.50/4 issues individuals; $2/ea; $2/sample as available; 1973; 52-64pp; 6x9; 500 circ. Reports vary, try to be fast. Pays copies only (2). Back issues: none available. Pub'd 1 issue 1973, expects 2 in 1974. COSMEP.

SCHMUCK ANTHOLOGICAL, Beau Geste Press/Libros Accion Libre, **Felipe Ehrenberg (for Latin America),** Jose de Teresa 52, Mexico 20, D.F. Mexico, and **David Mayor,** Langford Court South, Cullompton, Devon EX15 1SQ, UK. Articles, poetry, fiction, art, cartoons, photos, satire, news items, interviews, criticism, music, letters, collages, concrete. *Please - no poetry (haven't you heard mama, dada dies every day. . .) length now up to 12 miles. biases: to looking out the window and walking under ladders. Recent contributors; Hungarians, Czechoslovaks, Poles (short or long), Frenchies, Germans, Jugoslaves, Latin Americans, sometimes even the exoctic English, and very occasionally the Americans. No Martians.* 3-4/year; £4/yr; varies/ea; review/exchange/sample; 1972; 60pp; A4; circ. going uppp; mim/off/lp/screen. Reports: up to 2 yrs. Pays: copies. Ads: £20.50/page pro rata. Back issues: sells out too fast.COSMEP, ALP, Women, Ecology, 3rd World, Black, Gay.

School of Scottish Studies, University of Edinburgh (see TOCHER)

SCIENCE FOR THE PEOPLE, 9 Walden St., Jamaica Plain, MA 02130. Articles, art, photos, cartoons, criticism, reviews, letters. Science for the People *is the publication of Scientists and Engineers for Social and Political Action, a group which seeks to organize scientists, to seminate and disseminate scientific information, and to present a critique of the scientific estate from a radical, socially conscious viewpoint.* 6/yr; $12/yr (or less if impoverished); 75 cents/ea; free sample; 1969; 42pp; 8½xll; 6M circ; lo. Reports 2 mos. No pay. No ads accepted except movement publications and activities. Discounts: will exchange with other publications; 40% discount for bookstore bulk orders. Back issues: 50 cents. Pub'd 6 issues 1973, expects 6 in 1974. Science.

SCILLONIAN MAGAZINE, **Clive Mumford,** c/o Newsageant, St.Mary's, Isles of Scilly, Cornwall, UK. Articles, poetry, photos, news items. *A voluntary local magazine run entirely for the islands - shall leave some printed history and record.* 4/yr; £1.60 pf/yr; 40p pf/ea; 1925; 100pp; 8½x5½"; 2000 circ. No pay. Ads: £10 per page. £6/½. No discounts.

The Scopcraeft Press (see also THE MAINSTREETER), **Antony Oldknow,** 1118

Cherry St., Grand Forks, ND 58201. *Founded 1966. Has published* Scopcraeft Magazine *1966-71;* The Fifth Horseman *1967-68;* The Mainstreeter *1971-present. Also a variety of books and anthologies: most recent:* Crossing Into The Prairies *by Bruce Severy, the poet-teacher whose text books were burned in Drake, North Dakota – price $1.50.*

SCOTIA REVIEW (for the Scottish Muse & Nation), Scotia, **David Morrison,** 33a Huddart Street, Wick, Caithness, Scotland, UK. Articles, poetry, fiction, photos, criticism, letters, longpoems. *Short stories to 3500 words. Poetry in Scots, English and Gaelic (with translations into Scots or English). Scottish orientated magazine with nationalist bias. Recent contributors: Alan Bold, Tom Scott, Frank Thompson, John Herdman, Sydney Goodsir Smith, John L. Broom, Robert Mac Lellan. T.S. Caw.* 3/yr; £1 pf/yr; 25p px/ea; 1972; 60pp; 5 3/4x8¼; 450 circ; off. Reports: 3 months. Pays: small pay or copies. Ads: £10/page pro rata. Discounts: 33 1/3%. Scottish literature.

Scottish Arts Council, 19 Charlotte Square, Edinburgh EH2 4DF, UK.

SCOTTISH INTERNATIONAL, **Tom Buchan,** 23 George Square, Edinburgh EH8 9LD, UK. Articles, poetry, fiction, art, cartoons, photos, satire, news items, interviews, criticism, music. Monthly, £2.00/yr 20p/ea; 20p/sample; 1968; 44pp; A4; 5000 circ; off. Reports: 3-4 wks. Pays: on publication. Ads: £75/page, £40/½, £25/¼. Discounts: 10% on series of 5. Back issues: £1.00. Ecology.

SCREE, Duck Down Press. **Kirk Robertson, Bette Gilleland, J. Warren Hockaday,** P.O. Box 478, Trinidad, CA 95570. Poetry, fiction, art, photos, cartoons, interviews, satire, reviews, letters, collages, concrete art. *Open to anything really but especially like collages (suitable for black/white reproduction), prosepoems, humor, farts and assholes as well as summer breezes but nothing really(?) long.* Scree *anticipates a change of locale summer '74 so stay tuned. Contributors: Locklin, Koertge, Lifshin, Nations, Winans, Crews, etc.* Q; $4/yr; $1.50/ea; sample/exchange; 1973; 40-60pp; 8½x11; 300-500 circ; mi,lo. Reports 1-2 wks. Pays 2-5 copies. No issues in 1973, expects 4 in 1974.

SCREEN, *Society for Education in Film and Television,* **Sam Rohdie,** 63 Old Compton Street, London W1V 5PN, UK. Articles, interviews, criticism. *Usual length articles is between 3000-6000 words. Subscription to* Screen *is part of* Seft. 4/yr; £2.25/yr; 60p/ea; 1969; 128pp; 8½x5½"; 3000 circ; lp. Reports: at least 1 month. Pays: £15/article. Ads: £30/page, £16/½, £9/¼. Discounts: 10%. Back issues: 70p. SF, Film and Television Theory & Aesthetics.

SCREEN DOOR REVIEW, *Arbitrary Closet Press,* **Richard Neva,** Box 54, Onondaga, MI 49264. Poetry, art, photos, letters, plays. *Street variety - confrontation. Impeach Nixon then no president again. Elect a poet. Highly arbitrary graphic biases range from the obscure to the bizarre. No mss. returned without SASE.* Irreg; price/yr vague; 1972; lo;lp. Reports immediately. Pays copies only. No ads. Discounts: free libraries. Back issues: when I get one I'll be glad to share. Pub'd none 1973, expects 1 at a time in 1974.

SCREEN EDUCATION NOTES, *Society for Education in Film & Television,* **Edward Buscombe,** 63 Old Compton Street, London W1V 5PN, UK. Articles, criticism. *Articles generally 3000 words.* SEN *is available as part of membership of* Seft *and is received together with* Screen *(q.v.)*. 4/yr; £2.25/yr; 20p/ea; 1971; 40pp; 9½x8½"; 2000 circ; off. Reports: 1 mo. Ads: £30/page, £16.50/½; £9/¼; Discounts: 10%. Film & Television Education.

Scrimshaw Press, **Fred Mitchell,** 149 9th St., San Francisco, CA 94103.

SCRIPT—The magazine on Alternative Radio, Script Publications, **Nik Oakley,** (Miss), 35 Glenmore Road, London NW3 4 DA, UK. *Articles, cartoons, photos, satire, news items, interviews, criticism, letters. 500-1000 words per article on alternative radio/commercial radio. Mainly for listener interest rather than technical. Recent contributors include Nigel Turner, David Hobbs.* 24/yr; £1/yr; 15p/ea; 1972; 28pp; 10x8; 5000 circ; off. Ads: £40/page & pro rata, class.: 4p/wd. Discounts: 10% 3 issues (series). Alternative radio.

SCROTUM (see also GONE SOFT), Balls Press, **John C. Currier, Jr.,** 25 Roslyn St., No 3, Salem, MA 01970. Poetry, fiction, art, cartoons, interviews, satire, parts-of-novels, longpoems. *SCROTUM is not at present looking at any new contributions. The magazine is working with a vast backlog of material incl. Arvin, Steikunas, Light, Phillips, Griffin, the Knights, Locklin, etc.* Infreq; $1/ea; 1970; 50pp; 8x11; 100 circ; mi. Pays copies. Back issue (no 1) is unavailable. Published no issues in 1973, expects 2 in 1974.

Scrub Pine Studios/Tangential Bivalve Corporation (see EAST END INDEPENDENT)

Sean Dorman Manuscript Society (see WRITING)

SEARCH FOR TOMORROW, Blue Wind Press, **George Mattingly,** 820 O'Farrell No 309, San Francisco, CA 94109. Poetry, fiction, art, photos, cartoons, satire, reviews, collages, concrete art. *The editorial policy is to have none, i.e., no "fixed" biases. Henceforth S.F.T. will not print less than 4 poems or 2 pages of prose by each author, so send a good chunk of work. Recent contributors: Josephine Clare, Charles Potts, Russell Edson, Anselm Hollo, Sheila Heldenbrand, Lewis MacAdams . . .* Irreg; $3/4 issues; $1/ea; 1970; 60pp; 6x9; 1500 circ; lo, lp. Reports 2-4 wks. Pays copies only. Ads: $50/p; $30/½. Discounts: Trade - 40% bulk (25+) - 45%; wholesale - 50%; institution - 0%; mag sub agency - 20%. Back issues: No.1 - n/a; No.2 - $10; No.3 - $5; No. 4/5 - $5. Published 1 issue in 1973, expects 2 in 1974; pub'd 2 books 1973, expects 2 in 1974. COSMEP, CCLM.

SECOND AEON, Second Aeon Publications, **Peter Finch,** 3 Maplewood Court, Maplewood Avenue, Llandaff North, Cardiff CF4 2NB, UK. Articles, poetry, fiction, art, cartoons, photos, criticism, letters, longpoems, plays, collages, concrete. *An attempt at the best poetry from both sides of the Atlantic, from traditional works to concrete plus poetry in translation, fiction, articles based around the functioning of the creative process plus "the small press scene" the largest round up of comment on recent activity being printed in the UK. Recent contributors: Robert Bly, John Wain, Peter Redgrove, Wm. Burroughs, Wm. Wantling, Gary Snyder, Peter Porter etc.* 3/yr; £1/yr; 32p/ea; 1967; 150pp; 8x5"; 2000 circ; off. Reports: 2 wk. Pays: copies only. Ads: £10/page, £6/½. Discounts: 24% sale or return, 33% bookshops. COSMEP, ALP.

Second Aeon Publications, **Peter Finch,** 3 Maplewood Court, Llandaff North, Cardiff CF4 2NB, UK. Poetry, art, longpoems, collages, concrete. *Books and booklets that grew from extension of the magazine* Second Aeon *providing outlet for good modern poetry in both traditional and experimental forms. Recently concentrating on some of the more experimental items that need an airing. Book, booklet and folder form. Numerous anthologies, mainly concerned with experimental poetry published.* 12/yr, £2/yr; no sample; 1967; 300-5000 circ; off. Reports: 2 wks. Pays: by arrangement. Ads: none. Discounts: 25% sale or return, 33% cash.

SECOND COMING, **A.D. Winans,** PO Box 31246, San Francisco, CA 94131. Poetry, fiction, articles, art, photos, interviews, satire, criticism, reviews, letters, longpoems. *Open to any school of poetry as long as the poet is honest, has something to say and a means of expressing it. Experimental and Avant Garde work is not only welcome but openly sought. No length restrictions on poetry. Tends to use short, short fiction ranging from 500 to 1500 words. Occs. uses a longer piece but here too the work must be exceptional in order to stand a chance. If you've been rejected by other small lit markets of similar reputation you're probably wasting your time here as well.Credit lists do not impress the editor, the quality of the work does. Recent contributors have included Ben Hiatt, Jack Micheline, Harold Norse, Charles Bukowski, Joyce Mason, Gerald Locklin, Linda King, Harley Elliot, Peter Wild, etc.* 3/yr; $3.50/yr public; $5.75/yr libraries; $1 to $1.50/ea; 75 cents/sample; 1972; 72pp; 5½x8½ to 6x9; 1000-1500 circ; photo of. Reports 1-6 wks. Pays copies only. Ads: $80/p; $40/½; class./wd. 10 cents. Discounts: 40% 10 copies or more; 50% cash, 10 copies or more; Trade disc. Back issues: No.1 - $20; No.2 - $1.25; No.3 - $1.25; No.4&5 - $5; No.6 - $2. Pub'd 2 issues 1973; 1book 1973; expects 2 in 1974. COSMEP.

SEED—The Journal of Organic Living, Seed Publications, **Nigel Wilson,** 269 Portobello Road, London W11, UK. Articles, art, cartoons, photos, recipes, interviews, criticism, letters. *Articles 1000-2000 words. Seed is about natural foods and natural living. Incredible bias against processed foods, and all energy-and-capital- intensive activities! We try to take a humorous approach. Articles range from science to mysticism, from well-reasoned sensible articles to unsubstantiated mystical wishy-washy rubbish! (fairies etc!)* Monthly; £2.40/yr; 20p/ea; 1972; 32pp; 30x21cm; 5000 circ; off. Reports: immediate. Pays: £3/1000 wds. Ads: £55/page pro rata. Back issues: Vol. 1 (1972) 10p, Vol. 2 (1973) 15p. Ecology, Occult, Natural foods & Natural Living.

SENECA REVIEW, **Ira Sadoff, James Crenner,** Hobart & William Smith Colleges, Geneva, NY 14456. Poetry, fiction, art, interviews, reviews. *We print the best material we get, tend toward poems where the image is more central than the idea, although we try to remain reasonably eclectic. We solicit our own artwork. We also use a number of translations: Neruda, Vallejo, Elvard, Desnos, etc. Recent contributors include: Bly, Merwin, Tate, Stafford, Wagoner, Greg Orr, Edson, Dobyns, Jong, Ignatow, R.V. Cassill, Shelton, Busch, Seidman, Klappert, Justice.* 2/yr; $2/yr; $1.25/ea; 1970; 80pp; 5½x8½; 1M circ; lp. Reports 2 to 6 weeks. Pays: $5/page of poetry, $25/short story. Discounts: 30% discount, agencies, none to libraries. Two issues pub'd in 1973. Expects 2 in 1974. COSMEP.

SEQUOIA, UP Press, **Marie Willardson,** Storke Publications Bldg., Stanford, CA 94305. *Editorial policy is to accept only contributions from Stanford students, staff, associates. We publish poetry, short fiction, artwork.* 3/yr; $3/yr; $1/ea; 1891; 40-50pp; 9x6; 1,000 circ; lo. Reports 3 wks. Ads: $80/p; $40/½. Back issues: 50 cents ea. Pub'd 3 issues in 1973, expects 3 in 1974.

SESAME, Open University Press, **Les Holloway,** Sesame, The Open University, Walton Hall, Milton Keynes MK7 6AA, UK. Articles, cartoons, photos, satire, news items, interviews, criticism, letters. *Sesame is published to link the students and staff of the Open University throughout the UK. Its contents are almost wholly devoted to University matters and to related higher education topics.* 9/yr; £1/yr; free/ea; 1972; 12pp; A3; 45,000 circ; off. Reports: 1 month. Pays: nil. Ads: £150/page, £2/col. inch, 2p/word. Student.

Sesheta Press, **Richard Downing,** 32 Pinfold Lane, Skerton, Lancaster LA1 2BJ, Lancs, UK. Poetry, fiction, art, interviews, longpoems. *From early in 1974 Sesheta will not appear in magazine anthology form. Instead we will publish, at irregular intervals, collections by individual authors. These will normally be solicited. Intend to retain mixture of U.K. and U.S. writers as in magazine. In need of generous patron.*

Irreg; £1.50,$4.50/sub; 50p, $1.50/ea; 1971; 86pp; 20x14cm; 250 circ; off. Reports: 3 wks. Pays: single copy. Discounts: 33% bookshops. Back issues: still remain at pub price.

Seven Square Press (see BOX 749)

Seven Woods Press, **George Koppelman,** PO Box 32 Village sta., NYC 10014. Poetry, longpoems. *Our two most recent books have both been book-length longpoems:* Transitions *by Nathan Whiting and* Opticks *by Albert Goldbarth. We would tend to favor similar length manuscripts, though not exclusively.* 1972; lo. Pays: 10%. Discount: trade. Published 1 book in 1973, expects 1 in 1974. COSMEP.

THE SEVENTIES, The Seventies Press, (formerly The Sixties Press), **Robert Bly,** Odin House, Madison, MN 56256. Poetry. *Greg Orr, Bill Knott, Thomas Transtromer, Gary Snyder, Tom Pickard, Allen Ginsberg, Robert Bly, Douglas Lowder.* Irreg; $4/yr; $1/ea; 1958 (as The Fifties); 82 pp; 5½x8½; 3M circ; lp. Reports long. Pays: $10/page. No ads. Discounts: Distrib by Book People. Back issues: 75 cents/ea.

Seventy Five Press (see THE SPICY MEATBALL)

THE SEWANEE REVIEW, **George Core,** University of the South, Sewanee, TN 37375. Poetry, fiction, articles, criticism, reviews, parts-of-novels, longpoems, plays. *Recent contributors: Robert Penn Warren, Janet Lewis (Mrs. Yvor Winters), John Hall Wheelock, Robert Hollander, Thomas H. Landess, John T. Irwin, Caroline Gordon, Howard Baker, Harry Morris, M.E. Bradford, Ashley Brown, Russel Kirk, Sally Wood, Jack Matthews, Howard Nemerov, Cleanth Brooks, Louise Cowan, Albert J. Guerard, B.H. Haggin, Kathleen Raine, Peter Taylor, John William Corrington.* Q; $7/yr; $2/ea; 1892; 185pp; 6x9; 3800 circ; lp. Reports 2 wks - 2 months. Pays: fiction & essays $12 per printed page; reviews $10; verse 60 cents per line. Ads: $120/p; $75/½. No discounts. Back issues: 1964 to present $3/copy. Prior to 1964 $4/copy. Four issues pub'd in 1973. Expects 4 in 1974. COSMEP, UPS, CCLM.

S.F.COMMENTARY, **Bruce R. Gillespie,** GPO Box 5195AA, Melbourne, Victoria 3001, Australia. Articles, interviews, criticism, reviews, letters. S.F. Commentary *is a critical journal about "speculative fiction," particularly science fiction, and fantasy. Preferred types of articles: (1) long, in-depth reviews of important books in the field (2) personal material about s.f. authors or readers (3) Studies of particular authors or styles.* SFC *aims also to keep up with the news of the s.f. world — those writers and fans who are most closely connected with the social and international aspects of s.f. Recent contributors: Stanislawlem (Poland's top s.f. writer), George Turner (a leading Australian critic), Darko Suvin (Canadian critic and academician), Philip Dick (leading s.f. writer), etc.* 6/yr; $6(U.S)/yr; $1(U.S.)/ea; $1(U.S.) sample; 1969; 50pp; quarto; 400+ circ; mi. Reports 6 wks. Pays: copies only. Ads: $10(U.S.) / p; $5(U.S.) / ½. Pub'd 8 issues 1973, expects 6 in 1974.

SHADES OF LIGHT, **Editorial Collective - students,** Crete-Monee High School, W. Exchange St., Crete, IL 60417. Poetry, fiction, art, photos, cartoons. SHADES OF LIGHT *is a high school literary-creative arts publication. Contributions are open to the entire student body of Crete-Monee High School.* 2/yr; 75 cents/ea; sample free; 1972; 60pp; 8½x7; 600 circ; lo. Pub'd 2 in 1973, expects 2 in 1974.

THE SHAKESPEARE NEWSLETTER, **Louis Marder,** University of Illinois at Chicago, IL 60680. Poetry, articles, criticism. *Brevity is the soul of wit. Col. articles - 800 words. Write in advance with ideas.* Q; $2/yr; 50 cents/ea; free sample. Reports vary. Pays copies only. Ads: $254/p; $137/½. No discounts. 6 issues pub'd in 1973.

expects 6 in 1974. Literature - Shakespeare.

SHAMAN, **Dora Sherwood,** 47 Fletcher St., Kennebunk, ME 04043. Poetry, photos. 2/yr; $2/yr; $1.25/ea; 1973; 80pp; Reports 4-6 wks. Pays $5/p. Pub'd 1 issue in 1973, expects 2 in 1974. COSMEP, NESPA, Poetry.

Shambhala Booksellers (see CODEX SHAMBHALA)

SHAMELESS HUSSY REVIEW (formerly REMEMBER OUR FIRE), **Alta,** Box 424, San Lorenzo, CA 94580. Poetry. *Good poetry (that is, poetry I like) keeps me rejuvenated. leapleap.* 1/yr; 75 cents/ea; 1969; 40pp; 8½x11; 1M circ; of. Reports depends on how crappy my life is, 1-12 months. Pays 2 copies. Ads: $10/page; $5/½. Discounts: institutions pay $1. Bookstores 50 cents. Back issues: $7/ea. One issue pub'd in 1973. COSMEP, Women, Gay, Children.

SHAVIAN (Journal of the Shaw Society), High Orchard, **Robert Clare (Gen),** **Eric F.J. Ford (Exec),** 125 Markyate Road, Dagenham, Essex RM8 2LB, UK. All types of material used. *Bias — life/work/times/influences on and from Bernard Shaw (1856-1950). Promotion of Bernard Shaw scholarship.* 2/yr; £2.00/yr; 75p/ea; 60p/sample; 1953; 24pp; A5; 600 circ; off. Reports 3 mos. Pays: varies — normally copies. Ads: £15/page pro rata. Discounts: 20%. Back issues: 60p. Literary/Cultural Heritage.

SHEEP IN FOG, **Marylou Lewandowski,** c/o Dept. of English, San Jose State Univ., San Jose, CA 95114. *Material by invitation only. Recent numbers include John DuBois, J.R. Hampton, Donald Riccomini, the editor, and five or six others.* Bi-annual; free for SASE while they last; 1972; 8pp; 8½x7; 150 circ; mi. No submissions please.

Shelters Press (see WISCONSIN'S IMPACT)

SHENANDOAH, Washington & Lee Journalism Laboratory Press, **James Boatwright, Dabney Stuart, poetry ed.,** PO Box 722, Lexington, VA 24450. Poetry, fiction, interviews, reviews, essays. Q; $4/yr; $1.25 ea; sample; 1950; 95pp; 5½x9; 1M circ. Pays by arrangement. Ads: $60/page single issue; $35/½. Discounts: 20% agency disc.; 50% bulk disc. Back issues: $1.75. Pub'd 4 issues 1973, CCLM.

Shining Waters Press (see RIPPLES MAGAZINE)

Shiva Publications, 66 Polmuir Road, Aberdeen, UK. *Small scale publishers specialising in religious philosophy/mysticism (not occult). Please write first before sending MS.*

SHOCKS, 123 Ord St., San Francisco, CA 94114.

THE SHORE REVIEW, Shore Press, **Kenn Kwint,** 2931 S. 57 St., Milwaukee, WI 53219. *Recent contributors include: James Tate, Denise Levertov, Buk, Russell Edson, Al Goldbarth, Harley Elliott, Gerald Burnes, Hugh Fox, Joseph Bruchac, Doug Blazek, Philip Dacey, Duane Ackerson, Richard Kostelanetz and others.* $5.50/yr; $1.50/ea; $1.50/sample; 1968; 52pp; 2500 circ; lo. Reports 3 wks. Pays copies only. No ads. No discounts. Back issues: $1.50/ea. Pub'd 4 issues 1973, expects 4 in 1974; 2 books 1973, expects 4 in 1974. COSMEP.

SIGNAL, **Miroljub Todorovich,** Dobrinjska 3, 11000 Belgrade, Yugoslavia. Poetry, art, photos, criticism, collages, concrete art. 2/yr; $3/yr; $1, $5/ea; 1970; lo. Pub'd 1 issue in 1973.

THE SILENT PICTURE, First Media Press, **Anthony Slide,** 6 East 39th St., New York, NY 10016. Articles, interviews, criticism, reviews, letters. *Accept only material related to silent films. The magazine is called "the only serious quarterly devoted entirely to the art and history of the silent motion picture."* 4/yr; $4/yr; $1/ea; $1/sample; 1968; 60pp; 8x10; 1200 circ; lo. Reports 1 mo. Pays copies only. Ads: $50/p; $30/½. Discounts: trade 35%; agent 25%. Pub'd 2 issues 1973, expects 4 in 1974. COSMEP.

SING OUT! – The Folk Song Magazine, **Bob Norman,** Sing Out!, 106 W. 28th St., New York, NY 10001. Poetry, articles, art, photos, interviews, reviews, music. *Traditional, contemporary, topical songs and musicians. Articles: 1000-1500 wds. Record reviews: 200 wds maximum. Book reviews: 500 wds maximum.* Bi-mo; $6/yr; $1/ea; free sample; 1950; 48-52pp; 7x10; 10M circ; lo. Reports vary. Pays copies only. Ads: $400/p; $235/½; 50 cents class/wd; Special Folk Market Place ad section: reduced rates for small advertisers. Discounts: agency disc. only: 12½%. Back issues: $1. Pub'd 6 issues 1973, expects 6 in 1974. Folk Music.

SINTER, **D.E. Steward,** Jurastrasse 18, 4053 Basel, Switzerland. Poetry, fiction, art, photos, satire. *Sinter uses photocopy technology in samizdat form. Comments, contributions (those of any reasonable length may be published), books, advice are all welcome. Circulation is circumspect. Request copies of any issue as needed. Money to pay postage is also welcome. Bias against dogma and dogmatists of all sorts. Recent contributors: Marie-Claire Blais, Mary Meigs, Pedro Montez, Frank Solomon, Diana Wells.* 3/yr; no sub. fee or price; 1973; 3pp; mss. 175 circ. Reports immediately. Pays copies only (10). No ads. Discounts: no charge so no disc. Back issues: no charge. Pub'd 3 issues 1973, expects 3 in 1974.

SIPAPU, Konocti Books, **Noel Peattie,** Rt.1, Box 216, Winters, CA 95694. Articles, interviews, reviews. *A newsletter for librarians, editors, collectors and others interested in Third World Studies, the counter-culture, and the alternative press. Konocti Books will try to reflect these themes. We interview people like Len Fulton.* 2/yr; $2/yr; $1/ea; $1/sample; 1970; 20pp; 8x11; 450 circ. Reports 3 wks. Pays by arrangement. No ads. No discounts. Pub'd 2 issues 1973, expects 2 in 1974; 1 book 1973. COSMEP.

SISTERS, Daughters of Bilitis, **Sisters Collective,** 1005 Market St., No.402, San Francisco, CA 94103. Poetry, fiction, articles, art, photos, cartoons, interviews, reviews. *Submissions must be by women, relating somehow to women's movement or lesbianism. We prefer personal stories, no poems unless original and less than 100 lines.* Monthly; $5/yr; 50 cents/ea; 50 cents/sample; 1970; 32pp; 8½x5½; 900 circ; lo. Reports 1 mo. Pays 1 free mag. Ads: $50/p; $25/½; class. $1/line. Discounts: 30 cents/ea for lots of 10. Pub'd 12 issues 1973, expects 12 in 1974. Women.

Site, Inc. (see ON SITE)

SIXPACK, Pierre Joris, 19 Deal Rd., London SW17 9JW, UK; W.R. Prescott, Box 158, Lake Toxaway, NC 28747. Poetry, fiction, articles, art, photos, interviews, criticism, reviews, music, letters, parts-of-novels, longpoems, collages, plays. *Poetry to Joris in London, fiction to Prescott in NC. Please read the magazine before submitting. Include SAE. Particularly interested in receiving innovative &/ experimental fictions, biases toward linguistic and structural experiments rather than visual-conceptual concretions for narrative. : : :How to dance sitting down. Recent contributors: Antin, Ted Berrigan, Blackburn, Burroughs, Cid Corman, Enslin, Eshleman, Ginsberg, Giorno, Grossinger, Lee Harwood, Jack Hirschman, Lindy Hough, Anselm Hollo, Robt. Kelly, Kerouac, Mac Low, Eric Mottram, Joel Oppenheimer, Rochelle Owens, George Quasha, Tom Pickard.* 3/yr; $6/£3/y₁,

$2.50/£1/ea; 1972; 150pp; 8x10; 1500 circ; lo. Reports 1-2 mos. Pays: $25 + 2 copies. Discounts: 40% to trade. Back issues: No.1, $10; No.2, $5; all others, $2.50. Pub'd 3 issues 1973 (one double issue), expects 3 in 1974. COSMEP.

Derek G. Skinn (see FANTASY ADVERTISER INTERNATIONAL)

SKYWRITING, *Blue Mountain Press,* **Martin Grossman, Scott M. Walker,** Business address: PO Box 203, Gig Harbor, WA 98335, Mss. to either Gig Harbor address or 730 Whites Rd., Kalamazoo, MI 49008. Poetry, fiction, art, photos, interviews, criticism, reviews, letters, longpoems. Skywriting *attempts to remain as open as possible, so there are no real biases concerning style. We are interested in quality poetry, and fiction as it presents itself, and have in the past published work by Haines, Merwin, Charles Wright, Paul Zweig, Paul Nelson, Ira Sadoff, Stokes, Goldbarth, Matthews and others. From our fifth issue on, we will 'feature' a poet, and present critical articles, interviews, more personal views, as well as the poet's newest work. We're expanding.* 2-3/yr; $4/3 issues; $1.50/ea; $1.50/sample; 1971; 60-80pp; 9x6; 500-750 circ; lp. Reports 2 wks. Pays copies only. Ads: $60/p; $35/½. Discounts: 40%; payable 30 days. Pub'd 2 issues 1973. COSMEP.

The Slow Loris Press (see RAPPORT)

THE SMALL POND MAG OF LITERATURE, **Napoleon St. Cyr,** 10 Overland Dr., Stratford, CT 06497. 3/yr; $2.50/yr; $1/ea; $1/sample; 1964; 40pp; 5½x8; 275 circ; lo. Reports 1-15 days. Pays copies only (2). Ads: $30/p; $18/½; no class/wd. Discounts: inquire. Back issues: 75 cents to $5 (inquire). Pub'd 3 issues 1973, expects 3 in 1974. COSMEP, CCLM, NESPA.

The Small Press Book Club, Box 1906, San Pedro, CA 90733.

SMALL PRESS REVIEW, *Dustbooks,* **Len Fulton, Ellen Ferber,** PO Box 1056, Paradise, CA 95969. Articles, photos, criticism, reviews, letters. SPR seeks to study and promulgate little magazines and small presses worldwide. It was started in 1966 as part of Dustbooks' skein of small mag/press information publications which include, among other things, this Directory you're reading. The first issue was an "In Memoriam" issue (Alan Swallow). Other special issues have included Women (11), Small Press Orgs (12), Canadian Small Presses (15), Bukowski (16), African Presses (20). A list of reviewers and reviewed on request, fall '74. We've published reviews/essays by hundreds of writers on hundreds of writers. Some recent contributors: D.S. Long, Charles Tidler, Hugh Fox, Andrew Curry, Gene Detro, Doug Blazek, Foster Robertson, Anne Pride, Diane Kruchkow, Alta, Lita Hornick, C.M. Stanbury, and a multitude of others. News and reviews relevant to world small press movement welcome. Most major pieces are solicited — but it's not hard to get on that list! We use more than 50% of the unsolicited copy we get. We don't belong in anyone's critical ashcan — we stand alone, mean, kiss no asses, and put bigots of ALL kinds on a fast horse to nowhere. 6/yr; $5/yr; $1/ea; 1966; 32-64pp; 8½x11; 2,000 circ; lo. Reports 1 month. Pays by arrangement — though we're trying for 1 cent/word. Ads: $45/p; $25/½; 7 cents/word/class. Discounts: 40% to bookstores. Back issues: $1/ea (all available, though the No.12 Org issue is about gone). Pub'd 6 issues 1973, expects 6 in 1974. COSMEP, CCLM, ALP, ALMS, Mean.

THE SMITH, *The Generalist Assn., Inc.,* **Harry Smith, Sidney Bernard,** 5 Beekman St., New York, NY 10038. The Smith *is a function of The Generalist Association, Inc., as is* The Newsletter of The State of The Culture. *Joint imprint projects include* The Scene/New Egypt Books (*with* Gnosis), SPR *books and the* Per/Se Award Plays. *The most general mag; no pet esthetic theories, no arbitrary tests set before experience of the work itself. The enemy of civilization: anti-conven-*

tional; questions the given values. Anything goes as long as it's good. 3 book-sized issues, plus occasional supplements; $7/yr; $3/ea; free sample; 1964; 192pp; 6x9 but variant formats are used; 2500 circ; lp. Reports variable. Pays: $5, $10, & up. No ads. Discounts: 1-2 copies, 20%; 3-6 copies, 30%; 7 or more copies, 40%. Back issues: catalog sent on request. Pub'd 8 issues, 3 books 1973; expects 5 issues, 3 books in 1974. COSMEP, CCLM.

Ted Smith Graphics (see GRAPHIKTRAKT)

Smoking Mirror Press (see JOURNAL 31)

Smoothie Publications (see also *DATR),* **John Noyse,** 62 Vere Road, Brighton, Sussex, England, UK. Articles, poetry, art, cartoons. *Mainly bibliographical material on the alternative press eg.* Directory of Alternative Periodicals *(3rd ed. 1974)* Alternative Press in Britain. *SAE for list.* 1970; mim. Discounts: 25% to trade.

A SMUDGE ON THE WINDOW, M.E. Pegs & Associates, **Douglas Mumm, Hank Shankerbolt, Zurt Beefpie,** 33069 Grennada, Livonia, MI 48154. Poetry, fiction, articles, art, photos, cartoons, interviews, satire, criticism, reviews, music, letters, parts-of-novels, longpoems, collages, plays, concrete art. *All variable. Recent contributors: Kurt Nimmo, Dean Creighton, Lance Jackson, Lenard Guardino, Chris Jambor, Burt Burtoli, Rose Hiller, Judith Johnson, Randy Stegmeyer, Dunc Jambor, Margaret Gonzales, June Cicciarelli, Gary Lucchetti, Lisa Burell, Brown Bazemore.* Q, varies; $4/yr; $1/ea; $1/sample; 1969; 20pp; page size varies; lo. Reports vary. Pays copies only, one per work. No ads. Discounts: classroom only: 30 for $15. Back issues: not applicable. Pub'd approx. 10 "pieces" in 1973.

Smyrna Press, **Dan Georgakas,** Box 841 Stuyv. Sta., NYC 10009. *Getting back into production after a few years layoff. We are looking for people who combine awareness of the latest literary innovations with a conviction for anarcho-communist revolution. This doesn't mean every poem has to be "political."* Irreg; $1.50/ea usually; 25 cents to writers; 1968; 50pp; 6x9; 1M circ minimum; lo. Reports 1 mo maximum. Pays copies only. Discounts: by arrangement. Pub'd no books in 1973, expects 2 in 1974. COSMEP.

SNAKEROOTS, **Tobin Simon + student editor(s),** Pratt Institute/Humanities Bldg., Brooklyn, NY 11205. Poetry, fiction, satire, parts-of-novels, longpoems, short plays. *Open to known & unknown writers. Will publish anything written that is good. Space limited (64pp/issue), so shorter pieces would be better, some long prose alright. We're new so we're still quite open to any style. Want it to have some magic to it. Recent contributors: Ron Padgett, Ned O'Gorman, Richard Perry, Marilyn Coffey.* 2/yr; free sample (send postage); 1973; 64pp; 5½x8½; 1M circ; lo. Reports 1 day to 1 mo. Pays 2 copies. No ads. No back issues. Pub'd 1 issue in 1973, expects 2 in 1974. COSMEP.

SNARF, Kitchen Sink Enterprises, **Denis Kitchen,** PO Box 5699, Milwaukee, WI 53211. Cartoons, comic strips. *No poetry. Comic book format. Stories range from 1-10 pages. Machine-gun attack on cultural & political absurdities. Recent contributors: Will Eisner, Harvey Kurtzman, Evert Geradts, Peter Poplaski, Denis Kitchen.* Q; $2.50/yr; 65 cents/pp ea; no sample; 1972; 36pp; 6¾x9¾; of. Reports 2 wks. Pays $30 page per 20M copies sold. No ads. Discounts: 40% off for 50 or more. Back issues: 80 cents.

SNOWY EGRET, **Humphrey A. Olsen, Alan Seaburg (poetry), Wm. T. Hamilton (fiction),** 205 South Ninth St., Williamsburg, KY 40769. Poetry, fiction, articles, art (limited), satire, criticism, reviews, parts-of-novels, longpoems. *Emphasis on man in relation to natural history, philosophical and historical natural history.*

Prose generally not more than 3,000 words, but use up to 10,000; poetry generally less than a page. Payment on publication; receives contributor's copy and can get add'l copies at 50 cents ea. Originality of material or treatment, and literary quality important. Recent contributors include Lucien Stryk, Emilie Glen, Gary Elder, Daniel McKinley, John Eastman. 2/yr; $1.50/yr; 75 cents/ea; 50 cents/sample; 1921; 40pp; 8½x11; 250 circ; mi. Reports 6 wks. Pays: $2/page prose; $2/ minimum for poetry, $4/page. No discounts. Back issues: $1 when available. Published 2 issues 1973, expects 2 in 1974. COSMEP, CCLM, Man and Nature.

SOCCER AMERICA, **Tom Mertens,** PO Box 23704. Oakland, CA 94623. *Articles, art, photos, cartoons, interviews, reviews — all related to soccer.* Weekly; $9.50/yr; 35 cents/ea; 1971; 20pp; 8½x11; 3,500 circ; lo. Pays 50 cents/inch. Ads: $138/p; $69/½. Discounts: 20% to agents. Back issues: 35 cents/ea. Pub'd 52 in 1973, expects 52 in 1974. Sports.

SOCIALIST WORKER, Cambridge Works, Corbridge Crescent, London E2 9DS, UK. *Articles, photos, news items, letters.* Weekly; £4/yr; 5p/ea; 16pp; A3; 40,000 circ; off. Ads: classified 1p per word/display; £3, sci. Discounts: other socialist groups.

Society for Cultural Relations with USSR (see ANGLO-SOVIET JOURNAL)

Society for Education in Film and Television (see SCREEN & SCREEN EDUCATION NOTES)

Society for Education Through Art (see ATHENE)

Society for Women Writers and Journalists (see THE WOMAN JOURNALIST)

Society of Authors (see AUTHOR)

Society of Umbra (see UMBRA PRODUCTIONS)

SOFT NEED, Expanded Media Editions, **Udo Breger & Martin Bubenzer,** D-34 Gottingen, Gronerlandstr. 21, West Germany. *Soft Need was thought out to give us a facility to use material, sent to us by the authors of e.m.e. program i.e. a letter may be accompanied by a poem or short piece of text, photos and the like. Thus becoming a mag that includes all sorts of material from very known authors as well as younger ones. More and more it should become a sort of mag that fights suppression of every kind, without getting financially engaged. Nr 8 is the first issue, Nr 9 will be coming out in Oct. 74 incl Burroughs, Pelieu, Demattio, Dowden, Mary Beach, Kolonah, maybe Ginsberg, a.o.* 2/yr; DM6.80/ea; 1973; 40-60pp; 14 x19cm; 500 circ; lo. Ads: DM250/p; DM180/½. Discounts: single 25%, 5Ex. 30%, 10 Ex. 33%, from 25-50%. Pub'd 1 issue, 7 books 1973, expects 1 issue, 8 books in 1974.

Soft Press (see CLOUD NINE/"Vancouver Island Poems")

SOFT STONE, **Karl C. Wang,** 102-40 62nd Ave., Apt. 6C, Forest Hills, NY 11375. *Poetry, fiction, articles, art, photos, cartoons, interviews, satire, criticism, reviews, music, letters, parts-of-novels, longpoems, collages, plays, concrete art, translations. No restriction on the length of material. Any style; no biases. Contributors for the 1st issue: Anne Waldman, Joseph Bruchac, Greg Kuzma, Jonathan Baumbach, Murat Namet-Nejat, Clarence Major, Susan Schaffer, and others.* 3/yr; $3/3 issues; $1/ ea; $1/sample; 1973; 100pp; 7x9; 1M circ; lo. Reports 2 wks-1 mo. Pays: 2-3 copies. Ads: $80/p; $40/½; 10 cents/wd/class. No issues pub'd 1973, expects 3 in 1974. COSMEP.

Sojourner Press Collective, **Vicki Gabriner,** Box 7684, Atlanta, GA 30309. Fiction. Sleeping Beauty: A Lesbian Fairy Tale. *Original drawings, hand calligraphy, purple & yellow paper. Make checks out to Vicki.* 70 cents/ea. Women.

SOL, Sol Publications, **Malcolm Wright,** 6 Kings Road, Westcliff-on-Sea, Essex SSO 8BH, UK. Articles, poetry, fiction, art, cartoons, satire, letters, longpoems. *Any length considered up to 3000 words, or serials. Beautiful, avant-garde, personal. Contributors: G.E. Messoud, Ian Langhead, Antonio Claudio Carvalho, Gordon Grange, Roger McGough, Alison Tcharny, Stephen Morris, Phil Webb, Andrew Darlington.* 2/yr; 15p/ea; 1969; 16 or 20pp; qto; 750 circ; off. Reports 1 mo. No pay. Ads: 10p/10 words. Back issues: No's 1-6 @ 70p; 1-5 @ 60p etc. or 15p/ea. Gay, SF.

Sol Press, **R. Bruce Allison,** 107 Minneola St., Hinsdale, IL 60521. None pub'd in 1973, expects 3 books in 1974.

Solar Age Press, Jack Frazier, Box 53022, New Orleans, LA 70160. Presently doing research on strip mining and plan a book to be called: Earthrape, Inc. Already published: The Marijuana Farmers, Hemp Cults and Cultures. $2.95/each. Library and wholesale discounts on request. Published one book in 1973, expects one book in 1974. COSMEP. Food/Ecology.

The Solo Press (see CAFE SOLO)

SOME, Release Press (see separate listing), **Alan Ziegler, Larry Zirlin, Harry Greenberg,** 311 West 91st St., NYC 10024. Poetry, fiction, art, cartoons, interviews, criticism, reviews, music, letters, parts-of-novels, longpoems, collages. *Recent contributors include Tate, Simic, Lux, Ignatow, Piercy, Malanga, Stokes, Sherwin, Edson, Bly, Veitch, Violi, Hannigan + special Bill Knott section in Number 4.* 2/yr + broadsides; $3/yr; $1/ea; 1972; 72pp; 8½x5; 1M circ; lo. Reports: erratic. Pays copies only. Back issues: $10 for Nos. 1 & 3, $5 for No.2. Pub'd 2 issues in 1973, COSMEP, CCLM.

Some Of Us Press, **Terry Winch, Lee Lally, Ed Cox, Michael Lally, Tina Darragh, Ed Zahniser,** 4110 Emery Place, N.W., Washington, DC 20016. Poetry. *We publish one 20-40 page chapbook per month. We are non-profit and sell all books for one dollar each. We organized for the purpose of publishing good poetry that the larger, commercial presses ignore.* 12/yr; $1/ea; 1972; 20-40pp; 5½x8½; 500 circ; lo. Reports a mo; if possible please send four copies of manuscript for faster reading by editorial board. Pays copies. Discounts: 40/60 usual. Back issues: $1. Pub'd 12 issues 1973, expects 12 in 1974. *Send one dollar for sample book and free list of titles in print. Have published Bruce Andrews, Susan Baker, Ed Cox, Gabrielle Simon Edgcomb, Tim Dlugos, Margaret Gibson, William Holland, P. Inman, Beth Joselow, Simon Schuchat, Leonard Randolph, Lee Lally, Michael Lally, Terry Winch, Ed Zahniser.* COSMEP.

SOMETHING ELSE NEWSLETTER, **Dick Higgins,** PO Box 26, W. Glover, VT 05875.

SONOMA REVIEW, **Joe Jeremy,** PO Box 1016, Petaluma, CA 94952. Poetry, fiction, articles, art, photos, cartoons, interviews, satire, criticism, reviews, letters, parts-of-novels, plays. *Should be fairly short.* 4/yr; $4/yr; $1.50/ea; 1974; 30-50 pp; 8½x5½; 250 circ; lo. Reports 2-3 wks. Pays copies only (for right now). No ads (plan to within next 2 yrs). COSMEP, UPS, ALP, CCLM, NESPA, COSMEPA, Third World, Women, Chicano, Black, Food/Ecology, Am. Indian, G.I., Prison.

Sonus Press (see WAVE)

SOS (Save on Shopping) Directory, PO Box 96, Dearborn, MI 48121. COSMEP.

SOUNDINGS, **Peter Garland,** The Athenian School, Danville, CA 94526. Music. *I'm going to end the press, as of June 1974. The 2 books* Soundings *has (and will) published:* Music is Dangerous *(essays by surrealists Andre Breton and Paul Nouge on music, 48pp) and* Ives, Ruggles Varise: A Critical Anthology *(essays by Lou Harrison, Philip Corner and James Tenney and others).* Soundings *also features work by older Amer. music. including one issue (No.5) devoted solely to 2 Mexican composers (Julian Carrillo and Silvestre Revueltas).* Q; $7/yr; $3/ea; sample; 1972; 128pp; 8½x11; lo. Reports irreg. Pays copies only (3-6). No ads. Discounts: 40% for bookstores; others have never come up. Back issues: No.1, $3; No.2, $3; No.3-4, $4. Pub'd 4 issues 1973, expects 2 in 1974; 1 book 1973, expects 1 in 1974.

SOUTH CAROLINA REVIEW, **Robert Hill, Richard Calhoun, William Koon,** Dept. of English, Clemson Univ., Clemson, SC 29631. Poetry, fiction, articles, interviews, criticism, reviews. 2/yr; $2/yr; $1.50/ea; 1965; 84pp; 6x9; 650 circ; lp. Reports 2-6 wks. Pays copies only. Discounts: agents 20%. Back issues: $1.50/ea.

SOUTH DAKOTA REVIEW, Dakota Press, Box 111, Univ. Exchange, Vermillion, SD 57069. **John R. Milton.**

South Head Press (see POETRY AUSTRALIA)

Southern Arts Association, 78 High St., Winchester, UK.

SOUTHERN POETRY REVIEW, **Guy Owen, Mary C. Williams,** Dept. of English, North Carolina State Univ., Raleigh, NC 27607. SPR *is not a regional mag — though we have a special interest in young Southern talent. We lean toward short poems in "the modern mode." No light verse, no nature poems. Book reviews are assigned. (We do not consider poems during the summer months.)* 3/yr; $3/yr; $1.50/ea, 50 cents/sample; 1958; 60pp; 700-1M circ. Reports 1 wk to 1 mo. Pays $3 a poem plus contrib. copy. No ads. Discounts: 30%. Back issues: $1. COSMEP, CCLM.

SOUTHERN REVIEW, English Dept., Univ. of Adelaide, South Australia 5000.

THE SOUTHERN REVIEW, **Donald E. Stanford, Lewis P. Simpson,** Drawer D, Univ. Sta., Louisiana State Univ., Baton Rouge, LA 70803.

SOUTHWEST REVIEW, SMU Press, **Margaret L. Hartley, Charlotte T. Whaley, asst. ed.,** Southern Methodist Univ., Dallas, TX 75275. Poetry, fiction, articles, interviews, criticism, reviews. *For stories and articles, we prefer 3-5000 words. Poems may be any length, but we are looking especially for those 18 lines or less. In spite of the name of our sheltering institution, we are not looking for religious material, especially not devotional verse. Some recent contributors: Joyce Carol Oates, Abraham Rothberg, H.E. Francis, William Goyen, Marion Montgomery, H.L. Van Brunt, Harold Witt.* Q; $5/yr; $1.50/ea; free sample if available; 1915; 120pp; 6x9 trim; 1M circ; lp. Reports 3 mos. max. Pays: ½ cent /wd; $5/poem. Ads: $60/p one time; $50/p 4 times; $32.50/½ one time; $27.50/½ 4 times. Discounts: agency commission 15% on ads; agency disc. 25% of sub. Back issues: vary according to availability, please query. Pub'd 4 issues 1973.

THE SOU'WESTER, **David H. Rathbun,** Dept. of English, Southern Illinois Univ., Edwardsville, IL 62025. Poetry, fiction, reviews, parts-of-novels, longpoems, plays. *Contributors have been X.J. Kennedy, David Ignatow, Allen Tate, Richard Eberhart, Robert Penn Warren, William Stafford, Laurence Lieberman, Albert Goldbarth, Harvey Shapiro, Robert Bly, others.* 3/yr; $3/yr; $1/ea; 1960; 65pp; 6x9;

500 circ; lp. Reports 3 wks. Pays 2 copies plus one of following issue. Back issues: $1.25/ea. Pub'd 3 issues 1973, expects 3 in 1974. COSMEP.

SPAFASWAP, **Lois J. Long,** 1070 Ahern Dr., La Puente, CA 91746. Poetry, fiction, articles, art, cartoons, longpoems. *No restrictions as to type of material, but will not consider pornographic stuff. Emphasis is on poetry, but we do use one short short and one short short non-fiction. Payment is generally in copy, but we are just beginning to pay on a limited basis ($1 for short poems and fillers, $5 for fiction, non-fiction, longer poems) to a few selected entries in each issue. Writers are encouraged to sponsor their own material.* 6/yr; $4/yr; 50 cents/ea; 1969; 32 pp; 5½x8½; 200 circ; lo. Reports within 2 wks. Ads: $2 per ad (so far we have not had to limit the length of ad). Back issues: 50 cents. Pub'd 6 issues 1973, expects 6 in 1974.

SPARE RIB, **Rose Ades, Rosie Boycott, Marion Fudger, Rosie Parker, Marsha Rowe, Rose Verney,** 9 Newburgh St., London W1A 4XS, UK. 12/yr; £3/yr; 20p/ea. Women.

SPARROW (monthly chapbook), Black Sparrow Press, **John Martin,** PO Box 25603, Los Angeles, CA 90025. Poetry, fiction. 15-20 books/yr; 1968; of; lp. Reports 30-60 days. Pays: 10% royalty. COSMEP.

SPEAKOUT, **Christine Root, Betty Kemmer,** PO Box 6165, Quail Sta., Albany, NY 12206. Poetry, fiction, articles, art, interviews, reviews, letters, news. *Feminist bias. Reason for being – to provide a place in print for women of upstate New York – to keep women informed especially on legislative issues and the women's movement on every level locally, statewide, nationally and in the sisterhood of the world.* Monthly; $3.50/yr; 30 cents/ea; free sample; 1972; 20pp; 8½x11; 600 circ; mi. Reports: need by 1st of each mo. Ads: $20/½; class/wd free to women. Discounts: bookstores receive 30% commission. Pub'd 11 issues (July-Aug. was a joint issue) in 1973. COSMEP, Women.

"Special Song" Press (see TWEED)

Spectre Press (see also *BALTHUS),* **Jon M. Harvey,** 18 Cefn Rd., Mynachdy, Cardiff CF4 3HS, UK. Articles, poetry, fiction, art, satire, interviews, criticism, longpoems. *Apart from Balthus, most publications will be collections of articles and/or fiction upon certain aspects of fantasy. Also one author collections of prose and/or poetry with a Fantasy aspect. Projected publications are "Dreams of a Dark Hue," "Doorways into Fantasy," a publication on Wizards, Warlocks etc. and one on Atlantis. Recent contributors: Martin Booth, Bruton Connors, Eddy C. Bertin, Gregory Fitzgerald, George Cairncross. Length of material; anything short of novel length.* 1974; off. Reports 1 mo. Pays copy only. Discounts: 25% on 10 or more. Fantasy.

SPECTRUM, **Terry Schwartz,** PO Box 14800 UCSB, Santa Barbara, CA 93107. Poetry, fiction, criticism. Spectrum, *published by the University of California at Santa Barbara. Awarded 1st place prize, collegiate magazine, by CCLM 1972, 1973. Recent contributors include Samuel Beckett, Robert Creeley, Hugh Kenner.* Annual; $2.50/yr; $1.50/ea; no sample; index; 1957; 100pp; 9x6; 250 circ; lp. Reports 2 wks. Pays copies only (2). Back issues: $1.50 per number. Pub'd 1 issue 1973, expects 1 in 1974. CCLM.

THE SPICY MEATBALL, Seventy Five Press, **Ms. Sue Willis,** 236 Clinton St., Brooklyn, NY 11201. Poetry, fiction, articles, art, cartoons, etc. – anything in black & white by kids. *Mostly for our mag we use work by kids at P.S. 75 in Manhattan. The press is more open. We are dedicated to the discovery of the artist and* *artistic insight in all human animals. Children being most accessible.* 2/yr; $3/yr; $2/ea; 1972; 64-100pp; 1M circ; mi; lo. Back issues: S.M. No.1/$3; S.M. No.2/ $2.50; *A Huge Lion of a Book* by Alisa Sheckley,$3; *The Time Machine*, $3. Pub'd 2 issues, 3 books 1973, expects 2 issues, 3 books in 1974. Kids.

Spiritual Community Publications (NEW SPIRITUAL COMMUNITY GUIDE, 1974-76, and *A PILGRIM'S GUIDE TO PLANET EARTH 1975-76),* Box 1080, San Rafael, CA 94902.

SPIT IN THE OCEAN, Intrepid Trips Information Service, Ken Kesey, Ken Babbs, Kathryn Wagner, David Butkovitch, Rt.8, Box 477, Pleasant Hill, OR 97401. Poetry, fiction, articles, art, photos, cartoons, interviews, satire, parts-of-novels. Irreg; $2/ea; 128pp; 6x9; 1M circ; lo. Reports 2 wks. No ads. Discounts: $1.25/ea. Back issues: $2/ea. COSMEP.

THE SPOKESWOMAN, **Karen Wellisch,** 5464 S. Shore Dr., Chicago, IL 60615. Articles, interviews, reviews. Monthly; $7/yr indiv; $12/yr instit; $1/ea; sample free; 1970; 12pp; 8½x11; 7M circ; lo. Ads: "Help wanted only." Pub'd 12 issues 1973. COSMEP, Women.

Spook Enterprises· (see QUEST)

Spring Church/ Quixote Books, **Morris Edelson (Quixote), Ed Ochester (Spring Church),** PO Box 127, Spring Church, PA 15686. Spring Church *is as of this listing not soliciting mss. Recent books:* Natives: An Anthology of Contemporary American Poetry *(Erica Jong, Marge Piercy, Dave Etter, Tom Clark, Pete Winslow, Victor Contoski, and others) $1.50;* Ed Ochester, The Third Express, *$1. Though we hope to expand our publishing operations in the future, as of this writing The Spring Church Book Co. is primarily a discount retailer of books from all publishers. We specialize in children's books, food/ecology and poetry.* 1972; lo. Discount: Spring Church/Quixote Books: 33 1/3%, 5 or more; retail lists: 25% (average). Pub'd 2 books 1973. Food/Ecology, Poetry, Children's books.

SPRING RAIN, **Karen Sollid, John Sollid,** PO Box 15319, Seattle, WA 98115. Poetry. *We publish unsentimental lyric poetry. Any length.* 4/yr; $4/yr; $1.25/ea; $1.25/sample; 1971; 50pp; 8½x5½; 400+ circ; lp. Reports 2 mos. Pays copies only (2). No ads. Discounts: 40% trade, 20% libraries, 33% distributors. Pub'd 4 issues 1973, expects 4 in 1974; 1 book 1973, expects 1 in 1974. COSMEP.

SQUEEZEBOX, Paper Tiger Press, **Margaret Freeman, James Mechem,** 334 N. Vassar, Wichita, KS 67208. Poetry, fiction. Squeezebox *makes pressing sounds: some lyrical some actual some surreal some stick & some slide. We want coherence, clear images, and some movement. Can you say it with* Squeezebox? 4/yr; $2.50/ yr; 1973; 45pp; lo. Reports 6 wks. Pays copies only. Ads: $8/p; $4.50/½. Back issues: $1/ea. Pub'd 1 issue 1973. COSMEP, Women (not limited to).

STAGE 1, 21 Theobalds Road, LondonWC1X 8SL, UK. *Concentrating much more on broadly 'home' issues – important strikes, community organising, the workings of capitalism in Britain/Europe and the struggles to overthrow it, etc. but still putting out some books on 3rd world areas of revolutionary struggle.* 1968. Third World.

STAND, **Jon Silkin, Lorna Tracy, Dave Heal,** 58 Queens Road, Newcastle-on-Tyne, NE2 2PR, UK. 4/yr; £1.25/yr; 40p/ea; 1952; 80pp; 6½x8¼"; 2500 circ; lp. Reports 1-2 mos. Pays: £5/poem; £6/1000 words prose. Ads: £33/page pro rata. CCLM.

STANLEY, Cepheid Variable Press, **John-Tim Cowden,** PO Box 5475, TAMU, College Station, TX 77844. Poetry, fiction, articles, art, cartoons, interviews, satire, criticism, reviews, letters. *Stanley is free for a contribution and this is preferred. It is science fiction in material but it is more a magazine of Texas A&M Sci-Fi Fandom. Style varies, biases vary, I vary. You'd vary too, it you were doing this.* Recent contributors: Joe Pumilia, Steven Utley, Darrel Schweitzer. 8/yr; $1/yr?; 10 cents/ea?; free sample; 1971; 7pp; 8½x11; 300 circ; lo. Reports variable. No pay. Ads: ? Discounts: will trade 'zines. Back issues: free if available. Pub'd 2 issues 1973, expects 8 in 1974.

STAR-WEB PAPER, All This And Less Publishers, **Thomas Michael Fisher, Richard Blair, corresponding ed.** Poetry, fiction, articles, essays, photos, cartoons, interviews, satire, criticism, reviews, music, letters, parts-of-novels, haiku, collage, drama, concrete art, bibliographies. *Born 1/14/73. First year happy: 4 issues, book by David Wade, tape of Hugh Fox giving his fourth life-time reading. More projects on the way. Most of the stuff in SWP is "experimental," "avant-garde"... but we're open to tradition — anything in fact that will lie flat on the page and fit our eccentric definition of art. Send along blueprints, journal excerpts, scientific essays. Don't let our list of first-year contributors scare you off; we've published many people who had no other work in print. We try to be human, not uptight. Esp. dig visuals & have printed great artwork alongside great cartoons; see? Go ahead & send us some stuff — we're going through the mill too, and know what promptness and consideration are. Publishers: send us your flyers and we'll stick them in our outgoing mail, as one way of saying thanks to the small press community which has given so much help and made us feel so good about our first year. Can also get into plain correspondence about nothing. Wide open to submissions, length doesn't matter, and hopefully we'll be doing some books next year, and tapes via cassette, that's another medium. We've published work by Dorn, Bowering, Bertolino, Olson, Creeley, J. Williams, Cage, A.D. Winans, John Burnett Payne, Al Drake, Gerald Lange, Emilie Glen, Michael Joseph Phillips, Brother Dimitrios, Kenneth Beaudoin, Hugh Fox, Lyn Lifshin, Ann Menebroker, Bethene Baldridge, Joyce Mason, George Montgomery, Anselm Hollo, Helen Luster, Len Fulton, David Lyle, Randall Ackley, David Meltzer, F.A. Nettelbeck, Richard Blair, Richard Snyder, Steve Richmond, R.H. Bayes, Fredric Koeppel, John Bennett, Thomas Johnson, Peter Wild, Ben Hiatt, and others. We want to participate in magazine exchanges.* Back issues of Nos. 2 and 3 are $1/ea, the Hugh Fox tape is $5, and a special 88 page Black Mountain College issue with Creeley, Olson, Dorn, J. Williams and John Cage is $3. Freq: 60 cycles per second. $5/5 issues (a bargain); $10/5 issues for libraries; single/sample: $1 cash or stamps or exchange; 40pp; 8½x11; circ by osmosis; mi, of, xerox, pen & pencil. Reports 2 wks. Pays copies. Ads: by arrangement. Discounts: arrangement. Pub'd 4 issues in 1973-74. COSMEP.

STAR WEST, Star West Library, **Leon Spiro, Chev. Lit. Fr.,** PO Box 731, Sausalito, CA 94965. Poetry, articles, art, photos, cartoons, satire, reviews, concrete art. *Short, dynamic, multi-lingual + Black English. Stephen Morris, Bryan Walters, Felix Leon, Laureat, Rigby Graham, Jean-Paul Flament, Suzanne Kristen, Gordon Curzon, Etel Adnan, Thomas Danisi, Louis Lippens, Marg—Campbell, Cleone Montgomery.* $6.60/yr; $1/ea; no sample; 1963; 4-6pp; newspaper; 5M circ; lo. Reports 2 wks. Pays copies only. No ads. Discounts: 30%. Back issues: out of print. Pub'd 1 master issue plus 11 mini-editions (8½x11 double pages!) in 1973. Independent.

STARDANCE, Blue Dragon Press, **Marek Urbanowicz,** 40 Coombe Lane West, Norbiton, Surrey, UK. Poetry, longpoems. *As yet only one magazine has come out; next publication will be a children's story — out this April (The Adventures of Hobold) 15p pf. After that 'Nascent' — much larger mag. long poem sequence plus prose; also friend's poems.* Irreg; 10p/ea; 1972; 7pp; off. ALMS, ALP.

STEPPENWOLF, **Philip Boatright, Jean Shannon**, PO Box 55045, Omaha, NB 68155. Poetry, articles, criticism, reviews. *Especially interested in the longer poem, translations (must be accompanied by a copy of the work in its original language), articles and critical comment. Request no more unsolicited mss. until further notice.* 1/yr; $2/yr; 1965; 70pp; 8½x5½; 500 circ; lp. Reports 1-2 wks. Pays copies only. COSMEP, CCLM.

STEREO HEADPHONES: Magazine of the New Poetries, **Nicholas Zurbrugg**, "Church Steps," Kersey, near Ipswich, Suffolk, England, UK. Articles, poetry, art, photos, interviews, criticism, letters, collages, concrete. *Stereo Headphones publishes work from the international art and poetry avant-garde. Issue 4: Anthology of Sound Poets' Work and comments 30p pf. Issue 5: Anthology of Japanese Experimental Poets and more sound poets. 45p pf. Issue 6: Over 70 pages by poets and artists who "treat texts" with Tom Phillips, Ed Ruscha, Raoul Hausmann, Hans Richter, Ian Hamilton Finlay, D.S.H., Edwin Morgan, Thomas A. Clark, Bob Cobbing and much more 70p pf + Book and magazine reviews.* Annual; price/ea varies; 45p pf/sample; 1969; 50pp; 6x9"; 500 circ; off. Reports: ages. Pays: free copies. Discounts: 33% (6 or more). Back issues: issues 1,2,3 sold out. ALMS, Experimental poetry.

STINKTREE, **Thomas Johnson**, PO Box 14762, Memphis, TN 38114 (until Sept. 1, 1974); after that: c/o Dept. of English, 252 Goldwin Smith Hall, Cornell Univ., Ithaca, NY 14850. Poetry, art, interviews, criticism, reviews. *Favor the poem which relies on muscular language, intuitive antennae and whose bedrock is the felt image. Recent contributors: Sonia Raiziss, Douglas Blazek, Joseph Bruchac, William Witherup, James Bertolino, G.S. Sharat Chandra. Translations of Cocteau, Bernardo Bertolucci, Pasolini.* Occasional; $3.50/2 issues; $2/ea; 1971; 48pp; 5½ x8½; 300 circ; lo. Reports 2 wks to 1 mo. Ads: free to selected presses. Discounts: straight one third. Back issues: No.1 unavailable; No.2, $3; No.3, $2. Pub'd 1 issue, 2 books 1973; expects 2 issues, 2 books in 1974.

THE STONE, magazine of the arts, The Stone Press, **R. Jorgensen**, mag. 115 Eddy St., Ithaca, NY 14850, **G.P. Skratz**, press a 'j' p.c. fr. the void, RFD 3, Box 153, Norwich, CT 06360. Poetry, fiction, art, photos, cartoons, music, letters, parts-of-novels, longpoems. *Current:* Stone No.10, *an Ithaca anthology, A Place Among Hills. "An Oar in the Old Water" by Wm. Matthews, chpbk 2. Dave Kelly, Lyn Lifshin, Bob Morgan, Bill Matthews, Hash Flash, Bill Witherup, Peter Wild.* Annual; $1/ea; 1967; 64pp; 5½x8½; 1M circ; lo. Reports 1 wk to 1 yr. Pays 2 copies. Discounts: 40%. Pub'd 1 issue 1973, expects 1 in 1974; 1 book 1973, expects 3 in 1974. COSMEP.

STONE COUNTRY (formerly PATTERNS), **Judy Neeld, ed. & publ.**, 20 Lorraine Rd., Madison, NJ 07940. Poetry, art, letters. *Criticism, reviews staff-written. Stone Country has metamorphosed from Patterns. It now appears regularly instead of irregularly with a partially revamped editorial board. Otherwise, format remains similar to the original publication. We publish mature poetry from poets of all ages, in styles from the traditional to the experimental and anywhere in between. However even traditional verse should be handled as contemporary literature. We look for creativity and insight from our poets and tend to turn down poems that depend on Anglo-Saxonisms for so-called shock value. Not shocked at all, merely bored, we find A-Sisms are trite and uncreative. Recent contributors include: Judson Crews, Elizabeth Bartlett, Colette Inez, Ken Kwint, Forrest Anderson. Poems should generally be 35 lines or less, though will consider longer. Need small/professional pen & ink drawings — 4x4 or 3x4 inches.* 3/yr; $3.50/yr; $1.25/ea; $1/sample; 1970; 36pp; 8½x5½; 400 circ; lo. Reports within a mo. Pays copies only (1). Ads: $10/p; $7/½; class/wd 5 cents (20 wd min.); $4/¼. Discounts:

schedule available on inquiry. Back issues: $1 for back issues of *Patterns* while they last. Pub'd 2 issues 1973, expects 3 in 1974. COSMEP.

Stone-Marrow Press, **James Bertolino,** Dept. of English, Univ. of Cincinnati, Cincinnati, OH 45221. Poetry, art, photos. *Most work used is solicited. Books range from 16 to 56 pages. Not interested in Kayak neo-surrealism and other fashionable modes. Poems which define kinds of psychic space, and work as vehicles for travel are of particular interest. Recent books by Howard McCord, Thomas Johnson, Diane Ackerman, Nancy Steele, James Sprouse, Floyce Alexander, Bertolino.* Distributed by Serendipity Books. 3/yr; $1/sample; 1970; page size varies; 300-700 circ; lo. Reports 1-3 mos. Pays copies only. Pub'd 3 chapbooks 1973, expects 2 in 1974.

Stone Press (see also HAPPINESS HOLDING TANK), **Albert and Barbara Drake,** PO Box 227, Okemos, MI 48864. 1968. Small books and pamphlets. Pub'd 3 in 1973, expects 3 in 1974. *Books in '73 by Peter Nye, Judith Root, Barbara Drake. Also publish posters: Richard Kostelanetz, Harley Elliott, William Stafford, Earle Birney, etc.* 6 posters for $1.25.

The Stone Press, **G.P. Skratz,** RFD 3, Box 153, Norwich, CT 06360. Poetry, fiction, articles, art, photos, cartoons, interviews, satire, music, letters, parts-of-novels, longpoems, collages, plays, concrete art. *Books by Peter Wild, Bill Matthews, Doug Blazek and Dave Kelly. Broadsides by Kurt Schwitters and Michael Andre. Send money. Send great stuff.* Irreg; 1967; 500 circ; lo; lp. Reports: varies. Pays: "lotsa copies." Discounts: 40%, 50%, whatever's necessary. Pub'd 1 book in 1973, expects 2 books in 1974. COSMEP, NESPA.

STONE SOUP, a journal of children's literature, **William Rubel, Gerry Mandel, Richard Hof, Gretchen Rendler, Darryl Reveaux, Laura Garcia,** Box 83, Santa Cruz, CA 95063. Poetry, fiction, art, reviews, plays. *Stone Soup is the only children's literary magazine in the country. The journal prints a wide range of stories, poems, plays, games, book reviews, and illustrations by children under 13 from all over the United States and Canada. Creative and critical work by adults for children is also included. All manuscripts should be accompanied by a SASE.* 3/yr; $4.50/yr; $2/ea; 1973; 80pp; 5 7/8x8¾; 1M circ (growing 200 per mo. min.); lo. Reports 1-3 wks. Pays 1 copy. No ads. Discounts: available upon request. Back issues: $2.50. Pub'd 2 issues no books in 1973. Children's lit.

*STONECLOUD, Pacific Perceptions, Inc.,***Dan Ilves,** ed-in-chief; **Autumn Stanley, Howard Aaron, Vee Gleason, Nick Warner,** main address: 1906 Parnell Ave., Los Angeles, CA 90025. Poetry, fiction, articles, art, photos, interviews, satire, criticism, music, letters, parts-of-novels, longpoems, plays. *A project of Pacific Perceptions, Inc. a non-profit corporation with educational and literary status. Briefly and generally devoted to bettering ourselves and towards the improvement of selves and things primarily through the arts, but not exclusively through them. Stonecloud is not a college lit mag – but a college-based journal of artistic and literary effort. Not limited to the arts – interviews with scientists, articles by psychologists, free thinkers, etc . . .* Bi-annual; $6.75/3 issues; $10/5 issues; $2.50/ea; $1.75/sample; 1971; 150pp; 8½x11; 3M circ; lo. Reports 2 mos, but give notices of receipt of material. Pays: copies, depends on what & how long. No ads perse but have sponsors & a directory (just starting it). Discounts: 20-25% on purchases of 10 or more. Back issues: $2. Pub'd 1 issue 1973, expects 3 in 1974. COSMEP.

STONEY LONESOME, Nosferatu Press, **Richard Pflum and David Wade;** mascot: **Steinway J. Blotto,** 420 N. Washington, Bloomington, IN 47401. Poetry, photos, collages, concrete art. *Will take some medium-long poems (about three to four typewritten pages). Pflum spends too much time with Steinway J. Blotto. Wade's* *still trying to define Subrealism with help of Brother Dimitrios; perhaps it's not worth defining, not even mentioning; maybe it's just a joke, maybe not. Love good Concrete poems. Still eclectic and proud of it. All elites should be self-destructive (immediately!). (Love to all, and give Shithooski my regards, D. Wade).* 1/yr; $2/yr; $2/ea; 1969; 100pp; 8¾x7; 300 circ; lo. Reports 2-4 mos. or less. Pays 1 copy mag. No ads. No discounts. Back issues: $5/ea for remaining copies of No.2 and No.4; all others sold out. Pub'd 1 issue (300 copies) in 1973-74; no books yet. Eclectic.

STOOGE, Roundhouse, **Geoffrey Young, Laura Chester,** 4063 Petit Rd., Oconomowoc Lake, WI 53066. *Some contributors: Howard McCord, Tom Clark, Kathleen Fraser, Tom Raworth, A. Gold, Lyn Lifshin, Judy Grahn, Stan Rice, Erica Jong, Guy Williams, Clayton Eshleman, Marie Harris, Russell Edson, Margaret Atwood, Joe Brainard, Kenward Elmslie. We are open to short prose, experimental forms in poetry and fiction/prose-poems/tightly written journal accounts. We print known and unknown writers; works that are pushing the limits outwards. We hold to no one "school" or style, but respond to the honest, original voice. We are receptive to women writers, but steer clear of political jargon in our selections. Try us, submit.* Bi-annual; $3/yr; price/ea varies; $1.50/sample; 1967; 70pp; 500 circ; lo. Reports: prompt. Pays: $5 a piece; 2 copies also. Discounts: 40% off to bookstores. Back issues: Stooge No.1=$20; No.2=$20; No.3=$5; No.4=$100; No.5=$5; No.6=$10; No.7=$1.50; No.8=$1.50; No.9=$1.50; No.10=$3; No.11=$1.50. Pub'd 2 issues 1973, expects 3 issues, 3+ books 1974. COSMEP, CCLM, Women & Men.

STRAIGHT, **John Townson,** 50 Upper Brow Rd., Huddersfield HD1 4UP, UK.

STRATH, Rannoch Gillamoor Poets, **Michael Park and Neil McNeil,** 1 Buttermere Close, Bletchley, Milton Keynes MK2 3DG, UK. Poetry, criticism. *Will consider all types of poetry, preferably short length, from new poets as well as established poets. Only biased towards good poetry!* 4/yr; 60p/yr; 15p pf/ea; 1972; 20pp; ½A4; 150-250 circ; mim. Reports 1 wk. Pays: nil. Ads: none at present. Discounts: nil.

STREET CRIES, Whispers Press, **Robbie Woliver, Patricia Velazquez,** Box 210, Room C-009, Old Westbury, NY 11568. Poetry, fiction, articles, art, photos, cartoons, satire, criticism, music, parts-of-novels, longpoems, collages, plays, concrete art. Yearly award for outstanding literary work (cash award). Our magazine is dedicated to the socially, economically, politically & sexually bypassed. 3/yr; $1/ea; 1973; 75pp; 5½x8½; 5M circ; lo. Reports 3 or 4 mos. Pays copies only. No ads. No discounts. Back issues: issue 3, $2. Pub'd 3 issues, 1 book 1973; expects 3 issues, ? books 1974. COSMEP, CCLM, Third World, Women, Black, American Indian, Gay, G.I., Prison, Spanish & English writing, Men's Movement.

Street Editions, Wendy Mulford, 31 Panton St., Cambridge, Cambs, UK. Poetry. John James: Letters from Sarah. Andrew Crozier: Printed Circuit. J.H. Prynne: Wound Response. Douglas Oliver: In the Cave of Suicession. 1973; off/lp. Reports quick. Discounts: booktrade. ALP, Modern British Poetry.

STREET RESEARCH BULLETIN, Street Research, **Ted T. Wrangler, J. Wally Sprout,** 86 Railton Rd., London SE24 OLD, UK. Articles, cartoons, photos, letters. ½/yr; 15p px/ea; 1972; 40pp; off. Discounts: 33 1/3%.

Streetword Press, 8 Findhorn Ave., Hayes, Middx, UK. ALP

STUDIA CELTICA, University of Wales Press, **J.E. Caerwyn Williams,** University of Wales Press, Merthyr House, James St., Cardiff, UK. *Devoted mainly to philosophical and linguistic studies of the Celtic languages with some contributions on*

Celtic archeaology and early Celtic history. Annual; £1.50; Dbl-vol (1973-74) £3.

STUDIO INTERNATIONAL, Peter Townsend, 37 Museum Street, London WCl, UK. *An international magazine dealing with contemporary fine arts. Only illustrated articles and notes accepted. Reproductions of paintings, sculpture, drawings, engravings, applied art etc. Intending contributors should send a preliminary letter.* Monthly; 87p/ea; 1893. Pays: by arrangement. Fine Arts.

SUCCESS, Kate Dean, 17 Andrews Crescent, Paston Ridings, Peterborough PE4 6XL, UK. Articles, poetry, interviews, criticism, letters. *100-500 words on all aspects of writing. Recent contributors: Brian Aldiss, Margery Hilton, J.C. Meredith Scott, Julia Watson, Andrew Cozens, Diane Pearson, Pamela Beattie, Catherine Cookson,* 6/yr; £1.50/yr; 25p/ea; 1968; 28pp; 8x5; 200 circ; Reports: immediately. Pays: 1 copy + reviews. Ads: £2/page, £1/½, 2½p/word. Back issues: 10p. Literary.

SUCTION, Suction Press, Darrell Gray, 9828 Lawlor St., Oakland CA 94506. Poetry, fiction, art, cartoons, interviews, criticism, reviews, longpoems. *Suction prefers to print sizeable groups of poems by poets, poem-sequences, or single longpoems. We are also looking for vigorous, non-indulgent prose – short stories (4-12 pgs) and critical articles and essays concerning everything from "aesthetics" (ie. particularly poetic field theory) to cybernetics and structural analysis.* Bi-annual; $2.50/yr; $1.50/ea; 1969; 60-80pp; 8½x11; 1000 circ;mim; Reports: 1-2 wks; Pays: copies only; no ads; Discounts 40%; Back issues: No.1/$10.00, No.2-present/$2 Pub'd 2 in 1973, expects 2,1974. COSMEP.

SUMMER BULLETIN, Yorkshire Dialect Society, John Waddington Feather, "Fair View," Old Coppice, Lyth Bank, Shrewsbury SY3 0BW, UK. Articles, poetry, news items, *Summer Bulletin is the mid-year publication of the YDS. Transactions is the year-end publication, usually more academic in content.* Annual; 50p per yr; 50p/ea; 1954; 40pp; 8x6"; 1000+ circ; off. Reports: usually return. Pays: nil. Ads: nil. Discounts: nil. Dialect.

THE SUN, Sun Publishing Co., Skip Whitson, c/o The Sun, PO Box 4383, Albuquerque, NM 87106. Poetry, articles, art, photos, cartoons, interviews, reviews, music. *Justin Stone, Paul Reps, Gary Snyder, Art Kleps, Allen Cohen, H.C. Monteith, etc.* Monthly; $5/8 issues; 50 cents/ea; 1974; 32pp; 10x14; 5,000 circ; lo. Reports 2 months. Pays: $1 per typed page. Ads: $200/p; $100/½; 10 cents class/wd ($2 minimum). No discounts. Back issues: $1 each. Published no issues, 1 book in 1973; expects 10 issues, 8 books in 1974.

Sun Press (see OMEGA)

SUN TAN, Sun Tan Press, Salvatore Farinella, ed., 3 Sussex Street, Boston, MASS

02120. Poetry, art, interviews, reviews, longpoems. SUN TAN wants poems that stop the breath, flash recognition of the human condition, are not afraid to take chances. Recent contributors: Bill Knott, Kathleen Spivack, John Wieners, Tom Lux, Paul Mariah, Ian Young, Charlie Shively, Joyce Mansour, etc. Q; $4/yr; $1/ea; 1973; 54pp; 7½x8½; 250 circ; lo. Reports: 1 month. Pays: copies only. No ads. Discounts: none. Pub'd none in 1973, expects 4 issues in 1974. COSMEP, CCLM, NES-PA.

SUNDAY CLOTHES: A Magazine of the Arts, Lame Johnny Press, L.M. Hasselstrom (fiction), Daniel Lusk (poetry), Ray Shermoe (art), 51 Sherman St., Deadwood, South Dakota 57732. Poetry, fiction, articles, art, photos, interviews, criticism, reviews, parts-of-novels. *We want visual art of all types, sent to us as black and white photos for reproductional fiction, poetry plays, book reviews, criticism- whole spectrum of verbal arts. MUST be accompanied by SASE. We'd like to encourage, enhance especially Midwestern region- -which we interpret broadly, and we accept work from everywhere. All our recent contributors are important to us, not just the names you'd recognize.* Q; $7.50/yr; $2.50/ea; $1.50+ postage/sample; 1971; 48pp; 8½x11; 1500 circ; lo. Reports: 10 days fiction—3 wks. others. Pays: 1 copy + 1 yr. sub.. Ads: $100/p, $50/½. Discounts: $6/yr class., institutions. Back issues: $1.50+ postage/ea. Pub'd 4 issues in 1973, expects 4 issues, 1 book in 1974. COSMEP, CCLM,

SUNTEMPLES, a quarterly journal of poetry, art & photography, Inca Press, Phil Silva, PO Box 769, La Jolla, CA 92037. Volume 1, No.1 printed in Feb., 1974. Will publish mostly poetry, art and photography, but will consider short-short prose. Will also consider some interviews, reviews, letters, cartoons, and articles. Starting with the February, 1975 issue, a $25 Annual Writing Award will be given to the writer deemed most worthy who's been published in preceeding four issues. Award given for best poem or short-short prose piece. Within the foreseeable future, Suntemples will do a Women's Poetry Issue, a Chicano Poetry Issue, Black Poetry Issue, and a Prison Poetry Issue. Contributors include Gary Snyder, Gallo Kirack, Ken Kwint, Arthur & Glee Knight & others. 4/yr; $4/yr; $1/ea; $1/sample; 1974; 32pp; 8½x7; 1M circ; lo. Reports 1-4 wks. Pays 1 copy; cash maybe. Ads: $15 per ad (display), business-card size; class/wd 10 cents/wd. Discounts: 25% (price per copy: 75 cents) on orders of 10 to 25 copies; 30% (price per copy: 70 cents) on orders of 26-50 copies; 50% for 51-100 copy orders; 50% for orders exceeding 100 copies. Back issues: none as yet. Expects 4 issues 1974; 1 book 1973, expects 8 in 1974. COSMEP, Women, Chicano, Black, Food/Ecology, Am.Indian, Prison.

SURFSIDE POETRY REVIEW, (formerly EGG- - A Lit Quarterly), William Linehan, George Betar, Theodora Jankowski (Paris), Mike Routh (Texas A&M). P.O. Box 289, Surfside, CA 90743. Poetry, fiction, articles, art, photos, satire, criticism, reviews, letters, parts-of-novels, longpoems, plays. *Our only standard is quality: decent, mature work that has something important to say and realizes it in an interesting mahner. We shall undoubtedly print some work we should not and reject some work we should. For this human failure, we apologize beforehand. All points of view are encouraged.* 4/yr; $3.50/yr; $1/ea; 50 cents/sample; 1972; 52pp; 5½x 8½; 500 circ; Reports: 1-2 mos.. Pays: 1 copy only. No ads. Discounts: Query. Back issues: $1/when available. Pub'd 4 issues in 1973, expects 4 issues in 1974. COSMEP.

SURREALIST TRANSFORMACTION, Transformaction, John Lyle, Harpford, Sidmouth, Devon EX10 ONH, UK. Articles, poetry, fiction, art, cartoons, satire, interviews, criticism, letters, longpoems, plays, collages. *Material of any length. Concerned entirely with the international surrealist movement. In addition to printing unpublished work by Breton, Magritte, Nougé , et al, contributors cur-*

rently include: Scutenaire, Ken Smith, Soanberg, J.H. Matthews, Mariën, Ted Joans, A. Earnshaw, Pierre Dhainaut, Mariö Césaring, Cabanel, Arnost, Budik, Vancrevel, John Lyle, Ian Breakwell, Leo Garet. 50p/ea; 1967; 56pp; 1000 circ; off. No ads & no discounts. Surrealism.

SUZANNE, Exeter College, Exeter, **J. Harrison,** 28 Okehampton Road, Exter, Devon, UK. Articles, poetry, fiction, art. *Local poetry/art/prose/articles, but mainly poetry.* Monthly; 15p/ea; 1971; 20pp; 12x9; 300 circ; off. Poetry.

The Swallow Press, **Durrett Wagner,** 1139 S. Wabash Ave., Chicago, ILL 60605. *We're doing less poetry this year and next. We're stacked up to here with back/ accepted/unpublished mss. and must get ourselves cleared up. Michael Anania is no longer poetry editor.*

Swan House Publishing Co., **Alexi Zweig,** P.O. Box 170, Bklyn, NY 11223. Mss. on health, spiritual and physical.

Sydon, Inc., **Sy Kahn, Don Gray,** 451 So. Regent St., Stockton, CA 95204. Poetry. *No books published in last several years—* not *currently seeking mss.* Pub'd/as possible; 1965; 1p; Pays: 10% royalties. No ads. No issues pub'd in 1973. COSMEP.

Tahmahnawis Publishers, 1329 S.W. 14th, Portland, OR 97201.

TALES OF THE ENEMY, Pigiron Press, **Joe Zabel,** P.O. Box 237, Youngstown, OH 44501. Cartoons, satire, comic strips. *Comic book format. 4-10 page stories preferred, as well as one-pagers. Sophisticated execution and depth are essential. Page size is proportional to 5x8 inches. Interested in surreal, experimental, underground & satirical comix stories. No mimics of commercial pulp & humor, please. The megalomaniac blueprint buried in the vaults of* PIGIRON PRESS *calls for the elevation of pulp art to a high art form. Emphasis on character development. Complex, but readable stories desirable.* 4/yr; $1/yr; 30 cents/ea; 25 cents/sample; 1972; 32pp; 5½x8½; 1M circ; lo. Reports 4-8 weeks. Pays 4 copies. No ads. Discounts: schedule on request. Back issues not available. Pub'd 3 issues in 1973, expects 4 in 1974. COSMEP.

TALISMAN, **Blythe Ayne,** Box 80713, Lincoln, NB 68501. Poetry, fiction, art, photos. $2.50/6 issues; 39 cents/ea; lo. COSMEP, Magic.

TANGENT POETRY QUARTERLY, Estuary Press, **Robert D. West,** 9075 River Styx Rd., Wadsworth, OH 44281. Poetry. *Our first book can now be ordered:* No One Noticed When God Died, *500 copies limited, signed edition, hardcover — $5 post paid, by our editor, Robert D. West. 64 pages. All poetry.* Estuary Press: *We plan one book a year.* Q; 1966; 32pp; 5½x8½; 120 circ; of. Reports 6-8 wks. Pays copies only. Back issues: Vols. 2,3,4 are available at 50 cents each.

TANTALUS, Tantalus Press, Robert Lamansky, Leonard Kubo, P.O. Box 9331, Honolulu, HI 96820. **Poetry, fiction, articles, art, interviews, reviews, letters, parts-of-novels, longpoems. All types considered, the only requirement that it be of high literary quality. No limit on length, but we will not publish book-length manuscripts, i.e. novels.** Q; $4/yr; $1/ea; $1/sample; 1974; 24pp; 5½x8½; 500 circ; lo. Reports 2-3 weeks. Pays 5 copies on publication. Ads: $40/p; $25/½. **Discounts: 40% on orders of 25 or more, 25% on all other trade orders. Expects 4 issues in 1974. COSMEP.**

The Tantivy Press (see FOCUS ON FILM)

TAR RIVER POETS, East Carolina Univ. Poetry Forum Press, **Vernon Ward,** P.O. Box 2707, Greenville, NC 27834. Poetry, art, photos, reviews, longpoems, collages. *Normally publishes work of ECU Poetry Forum members. Features one guest poet of note each issue (150-200 lines). John Woods, Julia Fields, and William Stafford have been featured recently.* Irreg; price varies; 1967; 64pp; 6x9; 1M circ; lo. Reports, inquire first. Pay varies. Discounts: 40% to trade. Back issues: as published in each issue. Pub'd 2 issues in 1973, expects 2 in 1974. Poetry.

TARGET (NEWBALD), **Roy Saunders,** 16 South Newbald Road, North Newbald, York YO4 3SX, UK. Articles, poetry, fiction, art, cartoons, photos, satire, news items, criticism, letters. *Average length of article 200-300 words on mainly local topics. Articles on seasonal themes always welcome especially if of interest to a mainly rural community. "Chatty" style required.* Nothing *Esoteric. Cover art and design always welcome. Page lay-out ready for heat copying or offset work welcomed.* 6Yr; 60p/yr; 6p/ea; free sample; 1973; 12pp; ½A4; 200 circ; mim/off. Reports: month. Pays: none (unless by special arrangement). Ads: by arrangement. Community.

TASTE IT, John Herrmann, 1511 Elvado Dr., Simi Valley, CA 93065. Poetry, fiction, articles, art, photos, cartoons, interviews, satire, favorable reviews, music, letters, collages. We are an anti-bummer, intergalactic publication. We are interested in the pursuit of happiness, self-determination, sensual pleasures, alternative lifestyles, people, UFO'S and living. Every 4-6 weeks; $8/yr; 75 cents/ea; 75 cents/sample; 1974; 50-80pp; 8x10; lo. Pay:open . Ads: $200/p, $105/½; 25 cents/word for the first 25 words, 20 cents word thereafter/class. Discounts: will be considered by ability to pay and number of insertions. Loose Folks.

Tau Delta Phi Press, **Ray Pitts, Merritt Clifton, Tom Gallardo, J. Michael Gonzalez,** Box T, San Jose State Univ., San Jose, CA 95114. *Material by invitation only.* Tau Delta Phi's *principle project is biennial publication of* The Tower List, *a guide and directory to the faculty of San Jose State University. All writing and editing is done by the brothers of* Tau Delta Phi, Men's Honorary Scholastic Fraternity. *Recently, however,* Tau Delta Phi *has launched a literary series with* The Tower Anthology of The San Jose Movement in Fiction, *produced in cooperation with* The Berkeley Samisdat Review *and* The Reed. *108 pages,* The Tower Anthology *includes, besides members Merritt Clifton, Ray Pitts, and Nils Peterson, outside authors Tom Suddick, Dennis Shelley, Robert Burdette Sweet, Stella Zamvil, Thomas Livingston, Fred Hansfield, Dale C. Dalton, Richard Amyx, Marylou Lewandowski, and Ron Vinyard.* The Tower Anthology *is $1.25; 10% off on orders of 10 or more. Founded 1916.*

Taurus Press of Willow Dene, **Paul Peter Piech,** 2 Willow Dene, Bushey Heath, Herts WD2 IPS, UK. Articles, poetry, art, satire, longpoems, lp. *Publish some 5-10 new titles a year.* ALP, 3rd World, Black.

Tavistock, Inc. Box 302, Kennebunkport, ME 04046.

TAWTÉ, A Journal of Texas Culture, **James Cody,** 1612 Cambridge St., Cambridge, MA 02138, **Paul Foreman,** 2311-C Woolsey, Berkeley, CA 94705. Poetry, fiction, articles, art, photos, cartoons, interviews, satire, criticism, reviews, music, letters, (small) parts-of-novels, longpoems, collages, plays. *A journal of Texas culture of, by and for Texas Artists, Writers and Thinkers in Exile. Return postage requested with submissions. The aim is to examine the uniqueness of Texas in its Anglo, Mexican, Indian, and Black art, poetry and general culture. Contributors need not be native-born Texans, but should have lived there at one time or another, long enough to have been touched by the Texas sun and landscape. Issue 1 has gone to* press. Issue 2 in Fall, 1974 (Sept. 1 deadline), will be a special on Texas Indian lore and will be published on the 100th sun remembrance of the battle of the Leaves of the Yellow Moon in Palo Duro Canyon. 2/yr; $5/yr; $2/ea; $2/sample; 1974; 40-60pp; 6x9; 1M circ; lo. Reports 3-6 mos. Pays copies only. Ads: $40/p; $20/½. Discounts: 40% trade, 50% 20 copies or more. COSMEP.

Tegwar Press (see SALT)

THE TEILHARD REVIEW, Teilhard Centre for the Future of Man, **Dr. John Newson,** Christ Church College, Canterbury, Kent, UK. Articles, interviews, criticism, letters. *An International Journal of Integrative Studies concerned with the Future of a Humanity increasingly responsible for its own Evolution. Contributors include Ian Ramsey, Ewart Cousins, Donald Gray, Stafford Beer, the Duke of Edinburgh, Margaret Mead, John Robinson and many others.* 3/yr; £1.50/yr; 50p/ea; 1966; 32+pp, 8 colour paper; Quarto; 3-4000 circ; lp. Ads: On request from Hon Sec, Teilhard Centre, 3 Cromwell Place, London SW7 2Je. Discounts: none except bulk order for over 100 copies as we are a Charity. Back issues: 50p, all back copies available.

TELEPHONE, Telephone Books, **Maureen Owen,** 412 W. 110th, No.42, NYC 10025. Poetry, fiction, cartoons, parts-of-novels, longpoems, collages, plays, concrete art. *Works usually don't exceed 7 pages or thereabout. Poetry is the primary concern. Many unknown writers esp. have appeared but more known contributors are: Ron Padgett, Peter Schjeldahl, Anne Waldman, Ron Silliman, Tom Veitch, Michael Brownstein, John Giorno, Pat Nolan, Kenward Elmslie, Joe Brainard, Philip Lopate, Johnny Stanton, Tony Towle.* 3/yr; $3/yr; $1/ea; free sample; 1971; 75pp; 8½x14; of. Reports directly. Pays copies only. Back issues: $4/issue. Pub'd 2 issues, 2 books 1973, expects 2 issues in 1974. COSMEP.

TELOS, **Paul Piccone, A.Arato, J. Cohen, P. Breines, D. Howard,** Washington Univ., Sociology Dept., St. Louis, MO 63130. Articles, interviews, criticism, reviews. *Articles may range from brief critical comments to lengthy monographs.* Telos *has published mostly work dealing with a critical, theoretically-sophisticated approach to social and political theory. Our press has recently released* Towards a New Marxism *(ed. Piccone & Grahl) and* Marx & Engels on Literature & Art *(ed. Baxandall & Morawski).* 4/yr; $8/yr; $2/ea; $2/sample; 1968; 160pp; 6x9; 2M circ; lo. Reports 6-8 mos. No pay. Discounts Bkstores & other bulk orders: 30% net. Agents for subscribers: 10%. Pub'd 4 issues 1973, expects 4 in 1974; 2 books 1973, expects 3 in 1974.

Temporary Gymnasium Press (see THE GOODFELLOW CATALOG OF WONDERFUL THINGS, THE GOODFELLOW NEWSLETTER)

Tendon Press (see THE NORTH STONE REVIEW)

TENNYSON RESEARCH BULLETIN, Tennyson Society, **Tennyson Society Publications Board,** Tennyson Research Centre, Free School Lane, Lincoln LN2 1EZ, UK. Articles, criticism, letters. £ 2/yr subs (£1.50 *to individuals)*, $6 ($4.50) in*cludes all publications issued in the year. Includes all notes and queries relating to Tennyson and select articles up to 5000 words. A cumulative index covering 1967 to 71 (Vol.1) has now been issued and is available.* 1/yr; 1967; 36pp; 12.5x13.7cm; 500 circ; lp. Discounts: 25% trade. Back issues: some available.

TERRAN— —A Journal of Natural Religion & Magic, **Rod Frye,** Box 7374, Hampton, VA 23666. Poetry, articles, interviews, satire, criticism. *1000 words max. Was:* X--Underground Journal of Occult, *this title did not get point across. . . we are not*

Black Magic or Satanism. Is: Earth Religion, Paganism, Wicca, Magic. . .a natural feeling of oneness with the Universe. $5/6 issues; $1/ea; $1/sample; 16-24pp; 8½xll; 200-l000 circ; mi. Reports: couple weeks to year. Pays copies only. Ads: 25 cents/class. word. Discounts: Past issues (1 and 2) 50%. Back issues: $1/ea. Pub'd 3 issues in 1973, expects 2-3 in 1974. Pagan, Wicca, Occult.

Territorial Press (see DACOTAH TERRITORY)

Tetralith Books, 2 Lancaster Grove, London NW3, UK.

Thales Microuniversity Press, **Chris Humphrey**, Box 241, Stillwater, OK 74074. *Academic, counterculture and occult/spiritual book manuscripts, preferably no longer than 200 pages. Photos, line-drawing and calligraphy desirable.* 1973; 128-256pp; 5 3/8x7; 2M circ; lo (web). Reports 1 mo. Pay: co-op. Discounts: 40% b bookstores, 45% wholesalers, 55% distributors. Back issues: WHOLE-EARTH, INNER SPACE 99 cents. Pub'd 1 book in 1973, expects 1 in 1974. COSMEP.

Thames & Hudson Ltd. (see BRITISH JOURNAL OF AESTHETICS)

THEATA, Eskimo, Indian and Aleut Printing Company, **Russell Carrier, Sarah Islo**, Student Orientation Services, Univ. of Alaska, Fairbanks, AK 99701. Articles, art, photos. *Articles and art provided by Native students at the University of Alaska. Only photos are bought from outside contributors and pay for them is nominal. Photos bought have all been black and white Alaskan wilderness scenes or scenes of rural Alaska. Articles deal with Native experience in Alaska. Sample titles: "Skin Masks of Anaktuvuk Pass," "Eskimo Dancing," "Sought Luxury-Gained Pride." Title stands for Tlingit, Haida, Eskimo, Athabascan, Tsimshian, Aleut – all the Native groups in Alaska.* Yearly; $3.50/yr; $3.50/ea; 1973; 135pp; 8½xll; 4M circ; lo. Reports in May only. Pays $5/photo. Discounts: 10 or more copies $2.10/ea. Back issues: $2.50. Pub'd 1 issue 1973, expects 1 in 1974. Am. Indian.

THEATRE CRAFTS, Rodale Press, **C. Ray Smith, Patricia J. MacKay, assoc.ed.**, 250 W. 57th St., New York, NY 11019. Articles, photos. 6/yr; $6/yr; $1/ea; 1967; 48pp; 8½xll; 25M circ; of. Reports 6 mos. Ads: $730/pg; $450/½; $845/cover 2 or 3; $1745/center spread; (these prices for ads run one time). Pub'd 6 issues in 1973, expects 6 in 1974.

THEATRE DESIGN AND TECHNOLOGY, U.S. Institute for Theatre Technology, Pub., **Tom Watson**, 1 Hillside Rd., Newark, DE 19711. Articles, photos, interviews, reviews. *Articles on theatre architecture, engineering, and other production related topics.* Q; $12.50/yr libraries only, free to members of USITT; $3/ea; 1965; 40pp; 8½x11; 1800 circ; lo. Reports 1-3 mos. Pays copies only. Ads: $250/pg; $300/covers; $150/½; no class/wd. Back issues: $3.75. Pub'd 4 issues 1973.

THEATER NOW, Theater Now, Inc., **Marie J. Kilker**, 303 Eason Dr., Carbondale, IL 62901. Articles, photos, interviews, criticism, reviews, letters. *Ceased publication.* Bi-annual; $1/yr; 75cents/ea; 75 cents/sample; 1972; lo. No ads. No discounts. No issues pub'd in 1973, expects none in 1974.

THEATRE QUARTERLY, TQ Publications Ltd., **Roger Hudson, Catherine Itzin, Simon Trussler**, 39 Goodge Street, London W1P 1FD, UK. Articles, photos, interviews. *3000-10,000 words. Emphasis on examination of theatre and plays (past and present) from the point of view of performance both in techniques and impact on audience - against literary criticism of plays. Leaning towards popular theatre. Practical records of rehersal process, etc.* 4/yr; £3/yr; 80p/ea; 1971; 104pp;

7¼x9¾; 4000 circ; off. Reports: varies. Pays: £15-35/article. Ads: £45/page.

THEATREFACTS, TQ Publications Ltd., **Roger Hudson, Catherine Itzin, Simon Trussler,** 39 Goodge Street, London W1P 1FD, UK. Information - Factual & Bibliographic. Theatre *Checklists on outstanding playwrights, directors and performers considered from outside contributors (see magazine for form required). Other features (Current Bibliography & International Theatrediary) provided from existing sources.* 4/yr; £1.50/yr; 50p/ea; sample; 1974; 40pp; A5; circ. not yet known; off. Reports: varies. Pays: £10-20/feature. Ads: £25/page.

THEOLOGY, **Rev. G.R. Dunstan,** King's College, The Strand, London WC2R 2LS, UK. *Mss should not exceed 3500 words. Greek, Hebrew etc. should be transliterated.* £3.50/sub; 25p/ea; 56pp.

THE THIRD THING, Tolphus Books, **Shaun Farragher,** PO Box 248, Edgewater, NJ 07020. Poetry, fiction, art, photos, interviews, reviews, letters, longpoems. Tolphus books *and* THE THIRD THING *are a part of Poets in Focus, a reading series, and poetry workshops at the Focus II coffee house/Community Center at 163 W. 74th St., NYC. Open and scheduled poetry readings occur each Thursday evening at 8:30 p.m.* THE THIRD THING *is especially interested in parts of longpoems and English language poetry from outside America. We will consider the publication of translations if the original is sent with the translation. Recent contributors include: Joel Oppenheimer, Barbara Holland, Konstantinos Lardas, Brian Swann, and Kathleen Chodor.* 4/yr; $3/yr; $1/ea; free sample with SASE; 1974; 64pp; 8½x11; 500 circ; lo. Reports 1 week - 1 month. No ads. Discounts: free to alternate schools, prisoners, out of work persons. Back issues: No 1 - $2.50 after Jan. 1975. Expects 4 issues, 2 books in 1974.

THIRD WORLD, Fabian Society, **John Hatch. Assist. ed. Carole Evans,** 11 Dartmouth Street, London SW1H 9BN, UK. *A forum for the problems of developing peoples.* 10/yr; £3 pf, $8.50 (air $13.50)/yr; 30p, $1/ea; 1971; 16pp; off. Ads: 25p/line. 3rd World.

Third World Press, 7850 South Ellis Ave, Chicago, IL 60619

Third World Publications, 67 College Road, Birmingham B13 9LR, UK. *UK agents for the Tanzanian Publishing House. Specialise in pamphlets - expanding to carry a range of publications which include children's books written in Third World, which in places like London, Birmingham, Manchester etc. should be used in schools. Mail-order firm - though welcome people dropping in. Details of all publications/ sale or return service/etc. available on request. Non-profit making - seeking to get across factual information about exploitation etc. preferably avoiding tedious political cliches.* 3rd World.

THIRD WORLD REPORTS, **Peter Hellyer,** 282 Park Road, London N8, UK. Articles, news items, interviews. *Airmail subs £12 (students £7). Material between 400 and 2500 words on "liberation movements" and progressive governments in Third World, and on opposition to them. Mainly political/military. Recent interviews with leaders from Cuba, Somalia, Palestine, South Yemen, Namibia, etc.* Monthly; £5/sub; free sample; 1970; 16pp; A4; 500 circ; students £3.50/sub; off. Reports: 3 wks. Pays: variable. Ads: £20/page pro rata. Back issues: 50p/ea where available. 3rd World.

13th MOON, **Ellen Marie Bissert,** 30 Seaman Ave., NYC 10034. Poetry, fiction, articles, art, photos, cartoons, interviews, criticism, reviews, parts-of-novels, longpoems, concrete art. *We are interested in publishing work by women whoever and whatever those women choose to be.* 2/yr; $2/yr domestic, $3/yr foreign, $4/yr institutions/libraries; $1/ea; $1/sample; 1973; 64pp; 6x9; 1M circ. Reports vary. Pays copies only (2). Ads: $50/page; $25/½; class/wd 5 cents. Discounts: 40% to bkstores and agents. Back issues: 1st issue $5. Pub'd 2 issues 1973, expects 2 in 1974. COSMEP, Women, Gay.

THIS IS NOT THE TITANIC, Folk/Frog Press, **C. S. Crowther,** PO Box 15407, Salt Lake City, UT 84115. Poetry, reviews. *No editorial bounds placed upon work submitted. Would like to publish approx. 10 pages per poet. Recent contributors: Hugh Fox, John Oliver Simon, Karen Waring, Lyn Lifshin, Charles Potts, Douglas Blazek, Al Maserik, Paul Vangelisti, Charles Bukowski, . . . others.* 2/yr; $5/yr; $3/ea; $2.50/sample; 1973; 140pp; 5½x8; 1M circ; of. Reports 1 - 2 mos. Pays copies only. No ads. Discounts: 40% to booksellers. will work exchange with other mags. Back issues: $2. 1st issue March 1974. Expects 2 issues, 4 books in 1974. COSMEP.

*THIS MAGAZINE (*formerly *This Magazine is About Schools), Red Maple Corp. Publishing Co.,* Satu Repo, mng. ed., George Martell, John Lang, Rick Salutin, John Saul, Daniel Drache, 56 Esplanade St. E., Suite 407, Toronto, Ont., Canada M5E 1A8. Poetry, articles, art, photos, cartoons, interviews, satire, criticism, reviews, letters. *Articles on education, culture, politics, dealing with Canada and Canadians and the Canadian nationalist movement. Recent contributors: Margaret Atwood, Bob Davis, Loren Lind, Claire Culhane, Satu Repo.* Bi-monthly; $3.50/yr U.S.; 50 cents/ea; 50 cents/sample; $5 institutions; 1966; 32pp; 9x14; 9M circ; lo. Reports 2 mos. No pay. Ads: $250/page; $150/½; class/wd $10 per column inch 14 pica column. Discounts: agency 10%. Back issues: $1. Pub'd 4 issues 1973, expects 6 in 1974.

THOMAS HARDY YEAR BOOK, Toucan Press, **J & G Stevens Cox,** Mt. Durant, St. Peter Port, Guernsey, C.I. Articles, poetry, photos. news items. interviews. criticism, letters. *Articles 1000 - 3000 words.* Annual; 60p/yr; 60p/ea; 1970; 100 pp; Quarto; 3000 circ; lp. Reports: 1 month Pays by arrangement. Ads. £10/page. Back issues: £1.00.

Thorp Springs Press (see HYPERION)

3¢ PULP, Pulp Press, Box 8806 Sta. H, Vancouver 5, B.C. Canada. Poetry, fiction, articles, art, photos, cartoons, interviews, satire, criticism, reviews, music, letters, parts-of-novels, longpoems, collages, plays, concrete art. *We exist in order to see that any writing worth printing can be published. We are an outlet for people who do not have some other means. So our contributors are 99.9% uncelebrated. We have no biases re. content or form. "Short" mss go into 3¢ PULP. Longer ones appear in book or booklet form. 24 issues now available at special reduced rate - $5.00 annum - to bring the 3¢ magazine into the privacy of yr own home.* 26/yr; $5/yr; 3¢ ea; free sample; 4pp; 5¼x8½; 1M circ; lo. Reports average 2 weeks. Pays copies only. No ads. Discounts: we give 3¢ Pulp to bookstores who then sell it for 3¢. Classroom, about $20 for 40 copies of each no. for the year. Inst. $10. Back issues: we only print 1000 copies. All numbers are rare but available in subscription.

304 Publications (see THE GODDARD JOURNAL)

THREE RIVERS POETRY JOURNAL, **Gerald Costanzo,** PO Box 21, Carnegie-Mellon University, Pittsburgh, PA 15213. Poetry, articles, interviews. *Prefer short lyric poems with emphasis on figurative language. Reviews are invited from previous contributors. In current issue (3–4): Collette Inez, Lloyd Davis, T. Alan Broughton,*

Russell Edson, Russell Steinke, Paula Rankin, Albert Goldbarth, David Steingass, a short feature section of poems by Harold Witt. And we're still trying to print as much good work by new poets as we can find. Semi-annual; $4/4 issues; $1.25/ea; $1/sample; 1972; 40pp; 8½x5½; 500 circ; lo/lp. Reports 2 weeks - 1 month except summer. Pays copies. Exchange ads only. Discounts: 40% trade, libraries $4 for 4 issues. All back issues o.o.p. Pub'd 2 issues, 5 books in 1973, expects 3 issues in 19

Three Rivers Press, PO Box 21, Carnegie–Mellon University, Pittsburgh, PA 15213. *All titles are hand set letterpress cover, offset text. In 1974 Three Rivers Press published:* BY BREATHING IN AND OUT, *Albert Drake, 12pp. $1.25;* THE OBED– IENCE SCHOOL, *Greg Kuzma, 12pp. $1.25;* ELECTION, *William L. Fox, 12pp. $1.25.* TONIGHT IS THE NIGHT OF THE PROM, *Mark Jarman, 20pp. $1.50 is currently at press.*

TIME OUT, **Tony Elliott,** 374 Grays Inn Road, London WC1X 8BB, UK.

TIMESTREAM, Tube Inc., **Richard Coady,** 32 Coventry Road, Strathfield 2135 (or Box S3 Strathfield 2136) NSW Australia. Poetry, art, photos, collages. *Usually poems short enough for ½ quarto page size. I adventure through the* Nation Review *for poetry etc., so that the widest selection of poems are represented. I usually pick poems that are readable and have something to say.* 6/yr; $1/3 issues; $.30 ea; 16pp; ½ quarto; 300 circ; lo. Pays 3 copies per poem. Pub'd 3 issues (offset) and 3 issues (Gestetner, before June) in 1973, expects 5 in 1974.

TITMOUSE REVIEW, Titmouse International Press, **Avron Hoffman, Richard Harper, Linda Hoffman, (Richard Snyder),** 720 W. 19th Ave., Vancouver 9, B.C., Canada. Poetry, fiction, cartoons, satire, collages, concrete art. *Specializing in the FAR–out, the hard-to-digest, the easy-to-read.* 3/yr; $3/yr; $1/ea; sample; 1922; 64pp; 12x40; 500 circ; lo. Reports vary. Pays copies only. Pub'd 3 issues in 1973 COSMEP.

TOCHER, (published by: School of Scottish Studies, University of Edinburgh), **Alan Bruford,** School of Scottish Studies, 27 George Square, Edinburgh EH8 9LD, UK. Poetry, interviews, music. *All contents taken from archives of the School of Scottish Studies, mostly from tape recordings but including some MS. donations, covering Scots and Gaelic traditional tales, songs and other lore or memories. Regular features on notable folksingers or storytellers (e.g. Jeannie Robertson), and on subjects such as witchcraft, tall tales, or illicit distilling. English translation with all Gaelic material, staff music with all songs.* Qtrly; 60p/yr; 15p/ea; sample/ free to trade; 1971; 36pp; A8; c.1000 circ; off/litho. Reports: **no** outside contributions used or paid for. Ads: none. Discounts: usual: 1/3 to trade & bulk orders. Back issues: no special prices. Folklore.

TOLAR CREEK SYNDICATE, **Bill Thompson,** PO Box 471, Mountainair, NM, 87036. Poetry. Tolar Creek *is deeply rooted in the Earth, fed by the Sky, nutured by the Moon. Spirit mainly Southwest. Major influences: Wilson, Snyder, Enslin.* Irreg; $2/yr; 1967; 20pp; 8½x11; 200 circ; mi. Reports 3 mos. Pays copies only. Pub'd 1 issue 1973, expects 3 in 1974; 1 book in 1973, expects 1 in 1974.

Tolphus Books (see THE THIRD THING)

Toothpaste Press, **Allan Kornblum,** PO Box 546, West Branch, IA 52358. Poetry. *Committed until Spring '75, to* Scattered Brains *by Darrell Gray,* Not So Much Love of Flowers *by Allan Appel, &* Hazel *by John Sjoberg.* Mi; lp. Discounts: trade, distributor, bulk, bulk classroom 40%. Back issues: *Toothpaste Magazine,* $25 complete set. Pub'd 2 books in 1973, expects 3 in 1974. COSMEP, CCLM.

TOTTEL'S, **Ron Silliman,** 235 Missouri, San Francisco, CA 94107. Poetry, long-poems, concrete art. *Issue No. 11 was Clark Coolidge's work; No. 12 will be Ray Di Palma; No. 13 David Melnick; No. 14 Bruce Andrews; No. 15 Larry Eigner.* Irreg; 1 yr sub free; no single copy; no sample; 1970; 20pp; 8½x11; 150 circ; lo. Reports 1 day to 5 mos. Pays copies only (10). No ads. No discounts. Back issues: Xerox copies of No 1-10 in a ring binding: $100. Pub'd 2 issues 1973, expects 3 in 1974.

Toucan Press (see THOMAS HARDY YEARBOOK)

Toulouse Press, **Sylvia Hikins,** 14 Harringay Avenue, Liverpool L18 1JE, UK. Poetry, art, photos, satire. *Toulouse Press is affiliated to the Merseyside Arts Association. It publishes poetry books and booklets. Its aim is to publish high quality books at the lowest possible price.* 4/yr; varies/ea; 1972. Pays: negotiable. Discounts: 33% retailers. ALP, Poetry.

THE TOWN FORUM, INC., **Prof. Chas. Dedeurwaerder, Asla,** 1600 N.W. Van Buren, Corvallis, OR 97330. Articles, photos, interviews, reviews, letters. *THE TOWN FORUM is a participatory publication for researching & fostering new human-centered communities in harmony w/nature. Present work is concentrated on a 1,000 acre site near Eugene where members are building a new town for 2,500.* 4/yr; $5/yr; $2/ea; 1972; 40pp; 8½x11; 5M circ; lo. No ads. Discounts: $1/ea for 5 or more; 50 cents/ea for 10; 25 cents/ea for 100.

TQ Publications Ltd. (see THEATRE QUARTERLY, THEATREFACTS)

TRANSACTIONS OF THE YORKSHIRE DIALECT SOCIETY, **Stanley Ellis,** School of English, University of Leeds, UK Articles, poetry. *Society also publishes anthologies of dialect verse and prose, also booklets of academic and scholarly value on dialect.* Annual; 50p/yr; 50p/ea; 1897; 64pp. Octavo; 750 circ; off. Reports: 18 mo. Ads: none. Discounts: none. Dialect & Language.

TRANSATLANTIC REVIEW, **J.F. McCrindle,** 33 Ennismore Gardens, London SW7 1AF and Box 3348, Grand Central Station, New York, NY 10017. Fiction, art, interviews. *Fiction: must not be over 5000 words. Interviews: usually film and theatre. Art: line drawings. Our policy is to encourage young writers.* 3/yr; 85p, $3/yr; 25p, $1/ea; 1959; 176pp; 8x6"; 3000 circ; off. Reports: 2 mos. Pays: by arrangement. Ads: $75, £20/page pro rata. Discounts: retail/33%, ad discounts to ALMS members. Back issues: these vary, see magazine. ALMS, Literary.

Transformaction (see SURREALIST TRANSFORMACTION)

Transgravity Press, **Paul Brown, Gen., Peter Nijmeijer, Translation,** 47 Northwall Road, Deal, Kent CT14 6PW, UK. Articles, poetry, fiction, art, cartoons, photos, satire, news items, interviews, music, letters, longpoems, plays, collages, concrete. *Press has its own letterpress on which is produced its TGPress Editions. Other work handled under the New Selection title. Will publish whatever we can or want* 1971. ALP.

Traumwald Press, **Helen Bugbee,** 3550 Lake Shore Dr., Chicago, IL 60657. Poetry, fiction.

Treacle Press (see NONE)

TREE, Tree Books, **David Meltzer,** PO Box 9005, Berkeley, CA 94709. Poetry, articles. *Each issue devoted to a central theme. No.5,* The Snake, The Apple; *No.6.* Messiah; *No.7,* Golem; *No.8,* The Angel Tree *attempts to present new works* *alongside with translations of texts from the* Kabbalah *in hopes of elucidating a continuity in these inward traditions of creation. Though the range of material utilized is wide, all works must address themselves to the issue's thematic focus. Recent contributors: Peter Marin, Anthony Rudolf, Zalman M. Schacter, Paul Celan, Joachim Neugroschel, Jack Hirschman, Stan Brakhage, Kathy Acker, Sharon Nelson, Rose Drachler, Andrei Codrescu, Nathaniel Tarn, Carlos Suares, Emmanuel Pereire, etc.* Bi-annual; $8/yr; $4/ea; $4/sample; 1970; 150pp; page size varies; 1M circ. Reports 2-3 wks. Pays copies only. Discounts: distributed by book people. Pub'd 1 issue 1973, expects 2 in 1974; 2 books 1973, expects 4 in 1974. CCLM.

TRELLIS, The Trellis Press Association, **Margaret Anderson, Winston Fuller, Irene McKinney,** PO Box 656, Morgantown, WV 26505. Poetry, articles, criticism. *No.1 all solicited work, but submissions welcome for supplement. Supplement is a place for readers to respond to issue, with comment, reprints, extrapolations. Some contributors: Wm. Matthews, Greg Orr, Richard Grossinger, Ron Padgett, Albert Goldbarth. TRELLIS is a poetry magazine for use.* Q; $8/yr; $2.50/supplement; 1973; 100pp; lo. Reports 4-6 weeks. Pays copies only. No ads. COSMEP.

TRIANGLES BULLETIN, 235 Finchley Road, Hampstead, London NW3 6LS; Case Postale 31, 1 rue de Varembe (3e), 1211 Geneva 20, Switzerland; and 866 United Nations Plaza, Suite 566-7, New York, NY 10017. *From the centre which we call the race of men, Let the Plan of Love and Light work out, and may it seal the door where evil dwells.* Free sample.

Trigram Press, Blue Tile House, Stibbard, Fakenham, Norfolk, UK. ALP.

TRIQUARTERLY, **Charles Newman, Laurence Gonzales,** University Hall 101, Northwestern University, Evanston, IL 60201.

TRIVIUM, University of Wales Press, **Carl Lofmark,** Department of German, St. David's University College, Lampeter, Cards, UK. Articles, criticism. Annual; £3/ea; 1966; 160pp; 9x6"; 300 circ; lp.

TROLL (see also BRIDGE, A POETRY QUARTERLY), Bridge Publications, **Nanlee Haston Pitts,** 3726 Hibiscus St., Coconut Grove, FL 33133. *Annual collection of experimental, traditional poems and short plays, pen/ink drawings; deadline: December 31st. No prose. No ads. Pays comp. copies; 1yr. sub.; $ prizes.* For additional information see listing for *BRIDGE.*

Trouser Press (see PENNY POEMS)

TRUCK, **David Wilk,** PO Box 86, Carrboro, NC 27510. Poetry, fiction, articles, art, photos, cartoons, reviews, letters, parts-of-novels, longpoems. *Not looking for unsolic. material;* read *a copy before sending anything. Biased toward the unliterary; the content is what matters. Information, specifics, accuracy of vision; to extend perception & not to extol personal emotionalism. I will read anything that comes this way, but usually will use very little of it. Influences are Olson, Duncan, Creeley, Dorn, Spicer, Lew Welch, Grossinger. Recent contribs: Tarn, Metcalf, Elmslie, Bialy, Grossinger, Hough, Enslin, Levi-Strauss, Carruth, Arrowsmith, Olson. Any length, any style but it's the work I measure by: how to live in this place, how to make it home, where the heart is.* 3/yr; $7.50/yr; libraries; $4.50/yr individuals; $2.50/ea; no sample; 1970; 128pp; 6x9; 750 circ; lo. Reports 1 day to 1 yr. Pays copies only (3). Ads: $50/p; $30/½; no class/wd. Discounts: 40% trade; 50% bulk (25 or more); 50% to any legitimate cooperative. Back issues: No.12/ $2; No.11/$2; No.10/$1; previous issues rare or o.p., write for list. Pub'd 2 issues

1973, expects 3 in 1974; no books 1973, expects 1 in 1974. COSMEP, CCLM, NESPA, Natural History.

Truck Press (see also TRUCK), **David Wilk,** PO Box 86, Carrboro, NC 27510. *Publishes* Truck Magazine, *occasionally broadsides; for instance early 1974,* Cold Mountain Sheets, 6 poems: *by Lindy Hough, David Wilk, John Moritz, Paul Mariah, Pierre Joris & Harvey Bialy. Free to subscribers, $3 the set unsigned, $10 the set signed. An edition of 110 of which 10 are signed by the authors & numbered. Others planned for the coming year. Am planning to start publishing pamphlets this year, of particularly fine but relatively unknown & unpublished poets. Am not accepting mss. for this project. Would welcome inquiries from a distributor tho. Usual discounts apply to the broadsides & will also to the books when they appear.*

Tube Inc. *(see TIMESTREAM)*

TUVOTI Books *(see THE UNSPEAKABLE VISIONS OF THE INDIVIDUAL)*

MARK TWAIN JOURNAL, **Cyril Clemens,** Kirkwood, MO 63122. *Some recent contributors: Truman Capote, James Farrell, Robert Graves, Stephen Spender.* 2/yr; $3/4 issues; $1/ea; 1936; 24pp; lo. Reports 2 wks. No pay. Ads: $100/p; $50/½; no class/wd. Pub'd 2 issues 1973, expects 2 in 1974.

TWEED, "Special Song" Press, **Janice M. Bostok,** PO Box 304, Murwillubmah, N.S.W. 2484, Australia, **S.L. Poulter,** Box 5168, Milwaukee, WI 53204. Poetry, articles, reviews, letters. *No restrictions.* Tweed *began to satisfy a need for the haiku enthusiast in Australia. However, it soon developed into a regular poetry magazine with a large percentage of haiku and articles on haiku accepted. Has published haiku by most of the "name" haiku poets of today with articles by William J. Higginson, (ed.* American Haiku Magazine*) and Michael McClintock, (assoc. ed.* Modern Haiku). *General poetry by new and established poets, none considered more worthy than the other, but some names will be recognized, e.g. Sara Rath, Hans Juergensen, S.L. Poulter and other "prison poets."* Q; $4/yr; $1/ea; free sample; 1972; 40pp; 5½x8½; 200 circ; mi. Reports 6 wks. No pay. Ads: no approach as yet. Discounts: negotiable. Back issues: for complete volume, half price. Pub'd 4 issues 1973, expects 4 in 1974.

Small Press Record of Books

This volume lists small press books and pamphlets published throughout the world. Listings are alphabetical by author and include title, publisher, height and width, number of pages, type of cover, print process, date, price and descriptive comment. Also carries a separate list of publishers and addresses.

First Edition (lists books for 1966-68) $2.00
Second Edition (1969-71) $2.50
Third Edition (1972-73) $3.50
Fourth Edition (1974) appears early 1975 . . . . $3.50

DUSTbooks / DRAWER EE
PARADISE, CA. 95969 $11.00/4 issue subscription

23 CLUB SERIES (formerly BUFFALO COLD SPRING), Intrepid Press, **Allen De-Loach,** PO Box 1423, Buffalo, NY 14214. *Experimental prose.* Irreg; price/ea varies; 1971; no. of pages varies; 8½x11; lo. Reports: by request. Pays copies only. No ads. No discounts. Back issues: not available. No issues pub'd 1973. COSMEP.

TWIGS, Pikeville College Press, **Leonard Roberts,** gen. ed., **Lillie D. Chaffin,** poetry ed., College Box 2, Pikeville College, Pikeville, KY 41501. *Lillie D. Chaffin receives her mail at Box 42, Meta Sta., Pikeville, KY 41501.* 2/yr; $5.30/yr; $3/ea; $1.50/sample; 1965; 128pp; 5¾x8; 200 circ; of. Reports 3-6 wks. Pays: four $25 awards and copies. No ads. Discounts: 20%. Back issues: $3. Pub'd 2 issues, 2 books 1973; expects 1 issue in 1974.

Twin Oaks Publications (see LEAVES OF TWIN OAKS)

Twowindows Press/Effie's Books, **Don Gray, Bonnie L. Carpenter,** 2644 Fulton St., Berkeley, CA 94704. Poetry. *Generally hand set type printed on fine papers. Please do not send slight material.* Effie's Books – *exclusively women writers. Exclusive distributor – Serendipity Books.* Occasional; 1967; page no. and size vary; lp. Reports vary. Pays copies only. Pub'd 3 books 1973, expects 10 in 1974. COSMEP, Women.

Tyndall Creek Press, **David Beecher,** 17 Ashford St., Allston, MA 02134. Poetry. *We publish only books of poetry. For financial, and other reasons, our editions to date have been poems by members of our own editorial circle. We have not solicited mss on the outside. As to preferences, too much modern poetry is simply dull. There should be style and/or meaning. The experimental should be deliberate so knowledge of forms is important, but not essential.* 1970.

TZADDIKIM, House of Love and Prayer Publications, **Steven L. Maimes,** 224 Judah St., No.1, San Francisco, CA 94122. Criticism, reviews. *Tzaddikim is a catalogue-bibliography of Chassidic, Kabbalistic and selected Judaic books. Books are available by mail order.* 2/yr; $1/yr; 25 cents/ea; free sample; 1972; 16pp; 8½x 5½; 1500 circ; lo. Ads: inquire for rates. Discounts: 15 cents/ea. Back issues: free if available. Pub'd 2 issues 1973, expects 2 in 1974. COSMEP.

TH UINTA GARGOYL (TUG), rainbow resin, **Karl Kempton,** c/o 574 3rd Ave., Salt Lake City, UT 87103 *(sacramento bi juli 74).* Poetry, art, interviews, reviews, longpoems. *issu no.1 feetures DJackson bi jack hirschman. ilustrated bi elaine glenn whoz to b feetured in no.2. im mainlee interestd in th long poem, 6-9 pages, but hav mi i open for anee work, inkluding konkret, which iza charged field talisman of xtremlee hi vibratoree power.* th uinta gargoyl *iza 10 page talisman whoz energies reshape th reeders neuron konekshuns retuning em for mandala resepshun. 3 books frum* rr: th trubador anthology, *15 poets frum trubador poet fest. 8 slc 7 west ofden ver (andy clausen, geno sky clays, charlet george, charles potts) (1.50).* waiting in blud *by charles potts (2.00) &* matriorakle, *a slc womans anthologee of poetry art & revus.* Irreg; $2/yr; $1/ea; no sample; 1974; 10pp; letter; 5-600 circ; mi. Reports: idealee 1-2 wks. Pays: kommunal share. Ads: $1,000/p; $750/½; $10 class/wd. Discounts: 40% trade; 10% bulk. Back issues: suppli & demand. Pub'd no issues (born in 74), 3 books 1973; expects 4 issues, ? books 1974. resin.

UMBRA PRODUCTIONS, Society of Umbra, **David Henderson,** Box 4338, Sather Gate Sta., Berkeley, CA 94704. Poetry, fiction, art, photos, cartoons, interviews, criticism, parts-of-novels, longpoems, collages, plays. *Available* Blackworks Anthology. *includes full-length Novella "Diet Book For Junkies" by Hart-Leroi Bibbs. Poetry by: Langston Hughes, Ishmael Reed, Nikki Giovanni, Larry Neal, Imamu Baraka (LeRoi Jones), Cecil M. Brown, Toni Cade (criticism: "The Plays of Ed*

Bullins"), Al Young, Jay Wright, Victor Hernandez Cruz (fiction), Bob Kaufman, Calvin C. Hernton, Ron Welburn, Quincy Troupe, Tom Weatherly. Drawings by Glenn Myles and Joe Overstreet. 1/yr; $3/yr; $1/$3/ea; 1961; 50-100pp; page size varies; 3M circ; lo. Reports: long time. Pays copies only. Ads: $1,000/p. Discount: great disc. on anthology quoted above. Back issues: ½ price. Expects 1 issue 1974.

Umbridge University Press, **Roger Airey**, Slug Hall, Shoreham, Sevenoaks, Kent, UK. Poetry. *The set of three books, "The Sex War," "Luv-Man-Ship" and "Songs without words" cost 50p pf, 2 signed by the author. Single copies 20p.* Annual; 64pp; 8x5"; 5000 circ; off.

UNDER THE SIGN OF PISCES: Anais Nin and Her Circle, The Ohio State Univ. Libraries, **Richard R. Centing**, 1858 Neil Ave., Ohio State Univ., Columbus, OH 43210. Articles, art, photos, interviews, criticism, reviews. Q; $2/yr; 75 cents/ea; 1970; 16pp; 5½x8½; 500 circ; lo. Reports 1 mo. Pays 1 copy. Ads: inquire, no charge. Back issues: same as regular sub., $3/yr. Pub'd 4 issues 1973, expects 4 in 1974.

UNDERCURRENTS, Undercurrents Ltd., **Godfrey Boyle**, 275 Finchley Road, London NW3, UK. Articles, photos, news items, interviews, criticism, letters. *Features, 1-4000 words. News items, 100-500 words.* 6/yr; £2($5)/yr; 35p(85 cents)/ea; 1972; 56pp; A4; 3000 circ; off. Reports 1 mo. Pays: £5($13)/1000 words (nominal). Ads: 1p/word. Ecology, 3rd World, SF, Radical Science.

Underground/Alternative Press Service/Europe (see MAGIC INK)

UNICORN: a miscellaneous journal, **Karen S. Rockow**, ed., **Stuart J. Silverman**, assoc. ed., 1153 E. 26 St., Brooklyn, NY 11210. Poetry, fiction, articles, art, photos, cartoons, interviews, satire, criticism, reviews, letters, collages, concrete art. *We are looking for all types of material, particularly lively articles and reviews (serious and whimsical) on all topics. We favor well-written pieces on the more offbeat and fun aspects of popular culture, folklore and literature; use MLA style for any footnotes. Please — no intellectualose, studied incomprehensibility or pomposity. We pay $10 for front covers; $5 for back covers.* 3/yr; $2.50/yr individual; $3.50/yr library; $1/ea indiv; $1.50/ea library; 1967; 32-36pp; 700 circ. Reports 3-4 wks (longer during summer). Pays: $5 honorarium for essays + copies & offprints; copies & offprints to other contributors; sometimes other fringe benefits. Ads: write for rate card. Discounts: 30% disc. on orders of 10 copies or more. Back issues: $1 for indiv; $1.50 for libraries. Pub'd 3 issues 1973, expects 3 in 1974. COSMEP, CCLM.

UNICORN: The Graphic Fantasy Magazine, Unicorn Comics, **Mike Higgs, Phil Clarke**, 221 Appleton Ave., Birmingham B43 5QE, UK. Articles, art, cartoons, photos, interviews, letters. *Articles must be well illustrated and cover the subject completely. We are not interested in short "outline" articles. Illustrations would be reproductions in line or ½tone of the work of a particular cartoonist, fantasy artist — Comic book covers or photos of a particular artist. We are interested in original comic strips — we suggest a preliminary letter before submissions of mss. Free copies of the magazine are sent to contributors of the issue in which their work appears. Contents also include reprints of Vintage Comic Strips or portfolios of a particular artists work. We cover items associated with Comics, Fantasy Art, etc.* Irreg; price/ea varies; 30p/sample; 1970; 40pp min; qto; 500 circ; off. Reports 1 or 2 wks. Pays: none (except under special circumstances). No ads. No discount. SF, Comics.

Unicorn Bookshop, **Bill Butler, Malcolm Smith, Tony Bennett, Michael Hughes**,

Mark Broad, Nantgwilw, Llanfynydd, Carmathenshire, Wales, UK. *Interested in publishing short books that because of their subject matter or design or for other reasons cannot be done by 'straight' publishers. Interested also in material designed to change the consciousness of the reader (or the author) by its content, by its design or by its existence. Idea being that if something can be done once it can be done again, better.* 1967; lo. Reports to 2 mos. Pays: royalty. ALP, Women, Ecology, Occult, 3rd Word, Black, Gay, SF, Change.

UNICORN JOURNAL, **Teo Savory,** PO Box 3307, Greensboro, NC 27402. Poetry, fiction, articles, art, photos, parts-of-novels, longpoems, plays. *Journal V next issue (1974), is all "booked up" – sorry!* 1/yr; $2/yr; 1966; 128pp; 6x9; 3M circ; lp. Reports 3 mos. min. Pays: $5/p plus 2 copies. Ads: $125/p; $75/½. Discounts: trade 40%. Back issues: all back issues available at $2 list price. COSMEP, CCLM, NESPA.

United Front Press, PO Box 40099, San Francisco, CA 94140. *United Front Press publishes pamphlets aimed at providing accurate information on the true history and current struggles of the American people. Some of our recent publications include photo-histories of working women in America, and the Chinese–Americans; analyses of the food price situation, and the energy crisis – both done through a combination of text and comics; and the story of the successful Farah strike handled in both English & Spanish. We are non-profit. We do no printing ourselves.* Discounts: people interested should write for free catalog.

U.S. Institute for Theatre Technology, Pub. (see *THEATRE DESIGN AND TECHNOLOGY)*

Unity Press, **Stephen Levine,** PO Box 1037, Santa Cruz, CA 95061. *Unity Press is a publishing group dedicated to the convergence of various spiritual and worldly paths which lead toward the same high awareness. It is our purpose in book publishing, as in life, to discover lenses through which we might focus on our essential nature to allow a clearer vision of the world we all share.* 1971; lo. Pub'd 2 books 1973, expects 6 in 1974. COSMEP.

UNIVERSITY OF WINDSOR REVIEW, **Dr. Eugene McNamara,** Sunset Ave., Windsor 11, Ont., Canada. Poetry, fiction, articles, art, criticism, reviews, music, letters, general. *Mss. should be no more than 5000 words, reviews should not exceed 1500. No U.S. Stamps. Canadian and international coupons only.* 2/yr; $2.50/yr; $1.25/ea; no samples; 1965; 100pp; 6x9; 200 circ; lp. Reports 3-4 mos. No pay. COSMEP.

UNMUZZLED OX, **Michael Andre,** Box 374, Planetarium Sta., New York, NY 10024. Poetry. Q; $4/yr; $1/ea; 1971; 80pp; 5½x8; 1600 circ; lo. Discounts: 40%. Book People is distributor for *Unmuzzled Ox.* Back issues: No.1, $12; No.2, $10; No.3, $5; No.4, $2.50 (signed $12). COSMEP, CCLM.

Unpublished Editions, **Dick Higgins,** PO Box 26, West Glover, VT 05875. *The Unpublished Editions Press was founded in 1973. It consists mainly of works by Dick Higgins, theatrical works, poetry, essays etcetera. The editions are small, 300 copies per book, and a small series of deluxe editions, signed and numbered. These books are not available in bookstores and should be ordered directly from* Unpublished Editions *in Vermont.* COSMEP, CCLM, NESPA.

THE UNSPEAKABLE VISIONS OF THE INDIVIDUAL, TUVOTI Books, **Arthur Winfield Knight, Glee Knight,** PO Box 439, California, PA 15419. Poetry, fiction, articles, art, photos, cartoons, interviews, satire, criticism, reviews, music, letters, parts-of-novels, longpoems, collages, plays, concrete art. *Herbert Gold, Jack Kerouac, Allen Ginsberg, Herbert Huncke, Carl Solomon, Peter Orlovsky, Gregory Corso, Neal Cassady, Carolyn Cassady, John Clellon Holmes, Michael McClure, Larry Rivers, Robert La Vigne.* 1 Vol/yr; $5/yr; $5/ea; 1971; 200pp; 8½x11; 2M circ; lo. Reports 1 mo. Pays copies only. Ads: inquire; no class/wd. Discounts: inquire. Back issues: Vol.1 (Nos.1,2,3)/$50; Vol.2 (Nos.4,5,6)/$25; Vol.3 (Nos.7/8, 9)/$10. Pub'd 2 issues (one a "double") in 1973, expects 1 Vol. in 1974; 1 book 1973, expects 1 in 1974. COSMEP, CCLM.

UP AGAINST THE LAW, **U.A.T.L. Collective,** c/o 1 Elgin Ave., London W9, UK. Cartoons, photos, satire, news items. 1/yr; 15p/yr; 1971; 30pp; 7000 circ; off. Discounts: 33 1/3%. Radical Law.

UP Press (see SEQUOIA)

URBAN LIFE AND CULTURE, Sage Publications Ltd., **Head of editorial board: John Lofland (Univ. of California),** 44 Hatton Garden, London EC1N 8ER, UK. *New studies in urban ethnography. Emphasizes participant observation and intensive qualitative interviewing and includes annotation of significant current books and articles.* 4/yr; £4.70/individuals; £7/institutions; 1972.

Urion Press, **A.H. Rosenus, L.L. Wynne, John Pittman,** Box 2244, Eugene, OR 97402. Fiction, reprints. *In our view, the West has stood for the beauty of the world, for Being over concept, for the unified man as opposed to the specialized man, for the natural over the industrial. If we take our readers deep into nature and the psychic life it contains, it is not because we are unaware of the irrelevance of nature to the industrial path; but because the industrial path, as it exists today, does not teach the soul, nor can its literatures. Our objective is to publish staples: books that will be as likely to be read thirty years from today as they are now. We especially invite suggestions for reprints in the area of California history and related works by native Americans. Recent titles include a reprint by Joaquin Miller and an original novel by David Middlebrook.* 1972; lo; lp. Reports 2-3 mos. Discounts: bookstores: 40% on orders over 3; jobbers: 50% on orders over 10; 20% disc. to libraries. Pub'd 1 book 1973, expects 2 in 1974. COSMEP.

UT REVIEW, **Duane Locke,** Univ. of Tampa, Tampa, FL 33602. Poetry. *We are looking for poems of acute and direct observation through the altered consciousness that fuses the subject and object into a new substantial linguistic reality freed from the illusions of facts and conceptual thought — the immanentist poem.* Recent contributors are *Alan Britt, Paul Roth, Steve Barfield, Silvia Scheibli, Nico Suarez, James MacQueen, Charles Hayes.* 4/yr; $2.50/yr; 75 cents/ea; 32pp; 500 circ; lp. Reports 1 day on. Pays copies only. No ads. Discounts: 40%. Pub'd 4 issues 1973. COSMEP, CCLM, NESPA.

VAGABOND, **John Bennett,** PO Box 879, Ellensburg, WA 98926. Poetry, fiction, articles, art, interviews, letters, parts-of-novels, longpoems. Irreg; $3/yr; $1/ea;

1966; 72pp; 8½x7; 500 circ. Reports fast. Pays copies only. Ads: $100/p; $45/½; class/wd 10 cents. Discounts: write for info. Back issues: $1. Pub'd 3 issues, 3 books 1973; expects 4 issues, 4 books 1974. COSMEP.

TOM VEITCH MAGAZINE, Grape Press, **Tom Veitch,** 461 Wilde St., San Francisco, CA 94134. Poetry, fiction, articles, art, photos, cartoons, interviews, satire, criticism, reviews, music, letters, parts-of-novels, longpoems, collages, plays, concrete art. *This magazine is Tom Veitch's personal ego-blast. It doesn't accept submissions but does print collaborations between the editor & his buddies. Also prints "letters to the editor."* No submissions. Ads: $10/p; $5/½. Discounts: 40% on orders of 5 or more copies (plus postage). Back issues: set of 1-5: $10.

Ventura Press, **Raymond Barrio,** PO Box 2268, Sunnyvale, CA 94087. *Private press. Self-publishing only. Books (no mag). No submissions. Books in print by Barrio: "Quartet," four $1 art booklets; "Experiments in Modern Art," $5.95; "The Plum Plum Pickers," farm workers novel, $2.45.* Lo.

VER POETS VOICES/BROADSHEETS/POETRY POST, Ver Poets, **May Badman, May Ivimy,** 61-63 Chiswell Green Lane, St. Albans, UK. Poetry. *Our members, whose work only we use, are some of them published poets – Mole, Gurney, Jaffin, Ivimy, Owen, Mitchell, Clark, etc. Others are beginners or have not had any breaks. All types of work acceptable if in our opinion it works in one way or another.* 6/yr; £1.20/yr; 10 or 20p/ea; 1966; 20-40pp; 6½x8"; 300 circ; mim. Reports: immediate. Discounts: 10% shops. Poetry.

VERSE GAZETTE, The Orange Press, **Paul Werner, Ellen Quackenbos,** c/o Werner, 850 Amsterdam Ave., NYC 10025. Poetry, art, music, concrete art. *Poster-poems & calligraphy. We encourage writers & others to submit their own layout, & to join in the printing when possible. One book in 1973: "Ya-Trang & The Magic Pearl: A Vietnamese Folk-Tale" ($2.50, all proceeds to medical aid for Indochina).* 4/yr; $5/yr institutions (flexible); sample/send postage; 1973; 8pp; 11x17; 500 circ; lo. Reports 1 wk. Pays: $5 plus copies. No ads. Discounts: 35 cents per poster. Back issues: 50 cents per poster. Pub'd 3 issues, 1 book 1973; expects 4 issues, 2 books 1974. COSMEP.

VIEWPOINT AQUARIUS, **Mrs. Jean Coulsting and Rex Dutta,** c/o Fish Tanks Ltd., 49 Blandford St., London W1, UK. Articles, news items, interviews, criticism, letters. *Flying saucers. Key to Theosophy. Yoga/Meditation.* Monthly; donation/sub; e.g. 20p/ea; free sample; 1972; 30pp; foolscap; mim. Reports: short. Pays: voluntary. Occult.

VIEWS & REVIEWS, **Jon & Ruth Tuska,** 633 W. Wisconsin, Milwaukee, WI 53203. Articles, art, photos, cartoons, interviews, reviews, music, letters. 4/yr; $5/yr; $1.50 /ea; sample; 1968; 48pp; 9x6; 6M circ; lp. Reports: ? fast rejects. Pay: depends. Ads: inflating. Discounts: 10 copies bulk order on yearly basis: $30/yr; agents: $4 /yr. Back issues: $2. Pub'd 4 issues 1973, expects 4 in 1974.

VILLAGE REVIEW, New Port Press, **Quenten Lane,** Lapboards, Newport, Essex, UK.

THE VINEYARD, Daniel Gorham, 8 Ravenna St., Asheville, NC 28803. We need short articles of background material on whats wrong with the current organization and outlook of the Christian churchs – especially Eastern Orthodox, Roman Catholic, Episcopalian and Luthern – who runs things, why they run them and should they do so? What can a Christian or a church group do in todays political world – can we influence the political movements? Want short, sweet, hard hitting material that tells it like it is — we need lots of art work —. Monthly; $3/yr; 50 cents/ea; 1970; 8pp; page size/legal; 10M circ; lo. Reports 3 mos. Pays: $5 to $50; copies only/poetry. Ads: $48/p; $29/½; class/wd 12 cents. Discounts: 10%. Back issues: none at present time. Pub'd 14 issues 1973, expects 18 in 1974. Free Religious.

VOICES OF NORTH DEVON, 107 Pilton St., Pilton, Barnstaple, North Devon, UK. Tel. Barnstaple 5665. Articles, poetry, fiction, art, cartoons, satire, news items, interviews, criticism, music, letters, longpoems. *No restriction on length, style, biases. Recent contributors are local people — plus contributions from people in other areas and abroad who support our work. Local artists, including John Hurford and Thomas James, members of local councils, children, poets, compilers of crosswords, etc, etc, etc.* Monthly; £1/yr; 5p/ea; 1972; 12pp; 10x8"; 500 circ; mim. Reports: varies. Ads: free, but donations accepted. Discounts: 33%. Back issues: 3p/ea px. Community Magazine.

A WAKE NEWSLETTER: Studies of James Joyce's Finnegans Wake, **Clive Hart, Fritz Senn,** Dept. of Literature, Univ. of Essex, Wivenhoe Park, Colchester, Essex CO4 3SQ, UK. Articles, criticism. *Articles on Joyce's* Finnegans Wake, *with occassional notes and articles on other books by Joyce. No other material normally included. Short articles preferred. The bias is exegetical rather than critical.* 6/yr; £2/yr; 35p/ea; free sample; 1962; 24pp; A5; 700 circ; off. Reports: 24 hrs. Pay: nil. No ads. Discounts: nil. Back issues: £1.25 p.a.; 30p single copies.

Walden Press (see also HURON REVIEW), 423 South Franklin Ave., Flint, MI 48503. *Try for 2 books per year. Letterpress. ¾ poetry; ¼ novels. Short press run: 500. Most of sales to libraries. Since 1965.*

WASHINGTON SCENE, **Robert England,** 5884 Leesburg Pike, Falls Church, VA 22041. Articles, art, photos, cartoons, interviews, satire, criticism, reviews, music, letters. *Reviews 750-1000 words; features 2000-2500 words. Like personable writing — also analytical, critical writing. Highly literate, unstilted writing preferred. We need writers who understand how to entertain and provoke readers.* Monthly; $3.50/yr; 30 cents/ea; 1973; 20pp; 11x16; 45M circ; lo. Reports 30-60 days. Pays: $40-$60 for features; $20-$25 for reviews. Ads: $475/p local; $588/p national; $237.50/½ local; $294/½ national; 90 cents class/line. Discounts: write for specific information; rates are generally low. Back issues: 50 cents. Pub'd 5 issues 1973, expects 12 in 1974.

WASHINGTON WATCH NEWSLETTER, **Tristram Coffin,** 5601 Warwick Place, Chevy Chase, MD 20015. *The newsletter is an attempt to coherently present news and facts from Washington, by quotes from leading newspapers in the U.S. and abroad.* 2/mo; $12/yr; no single copy; free sample; 1971; 4pp; 8½x11; 9M circ; Reports 2 wks. Pay: negotiable. No ads. Discounts: classroom: 10 or more for $6/ea; agent: $10/ea. Back issues: 50 cents/ea. Pub'd 24 issues in 1973.

WAVE, Sonus Press, **Edwin Tarling,** 3 Bewick Grove, Preston Road, Hull, East Yorks, UK. Poetry.

Peter Way Ltd. (see GREAT NEWSPAPERS REPRINTED)

WAYSIDE BULLETIN, The Wayside Press, **Joan Atwater, Mary Radcliffe,** PO Box 333, St. Helena, CA 94574. Poetry, articles, art. *We are interested in any serious questioning or probing of the meaning of life, relationship, or any really serious matter of living. Articles may be written in the form of letters. Serious and nature poems. Drawings.* Monthly; free sub; 1972; 28pp; 5½x8½; 250 circ; mi. Reports 1 wk. Pays copies only. No ads. Pub'd 12 issues, 10 books 1973, expects 12 issues, 5 books 1974. COSMEP.

WEBSTER REVIEW, **Nancy Schapiro, Harry Cargas,** Webster College, Webster Groves, MO 63119. Poetry, fiction, interviews, criticism. Q; $5/yr; $1.25/ea; 1974; 80pp; 5 7/8x8 3/7; lo. Reports 3 wks. Pays free copies. Expects 4 issues in 1974. COSMEP.

WEID, PO Drawer 1409, Homestead, FL 33030. Poetry, fiction, articles, art, photos, cartoons, interviews, satire, criticism, reviews, music, letters, parts-of-novels, longpoems, collages, plays, concrete art. Every 4th month; $5/yr; $2/ea. CCLM.

WEIRD TRIPS MAGAZINE, Kitchen Sink Enterprises, **Denis Kitchen,** PO Box 5699, Milwaukee, WI 53211. Fiction, articles, art, photos, cartoons, interviews, satire. *We do not use poems. Potential contributors are urged to obtain back issue to get feel of unusual format.* Back issues: 80 cents.

Wellcome Institution for the History of Medicine (see MEDICAL HISTORY)

Welsh Arts Council/Cyngor Celfyddydau Cymru, **Meic Stephens,** Museum Place, Cardiff, UK. Poetry, art. *The literature dept. has published for re-sale an illustrated catalogue of the Dylan Thomas exhibition titled "Welsh Dylan" available @ 50p + 10p postage together with a fine edition poster poem of "Fern HILL" @ 55p + 10p postage. A further series of 10 posterpoems of famous Welsh and Anglo-Welsh poems are due to be published in 1974. Details on application. Unsolicited mss are not required.*

WEST COAST POETRY REVIEW, **Wm. Fox, Bruce McAllister, W.M. Ransom,** 1127 Codel Way, Reno, NV 89503. Poetry, interviews, criticism, reviews, letters, longpoems, collages, concrete art. *No length limit. Prefer intelligent and extensive critical articles over reviews. Looking for sophisticated concrete poems, computer art and experimental unclassifiables, as well as excellent conventional poems. Contributors: Meyers, Stafford, Blazek, Elvard, Follain, Goldbarth, Johnson, Kuzma, Matthews, Wilbur, Witt, Wright, Yevtushenko, I.H. Finlay, Emmett Williams, Peter Finch. Very few translations.* Q; $5/yr; $1.50/ea; 1971; 72pp; 6¼x9¼; 500 circ; lo. Reports 1 wk. Pays copies only. Ads: exchange, but we're picky. Discounts: 40% trades. Back issues: $1.50. Pub'd 4 issues, 4 books 1973; expects 4 issues, 4 books 1974. COSMEP, CCLM.

West Coast Poetry Review Press, **Wm. Fox, Bruce McAllister, W.M. Ransom,** 1127 Codel Way, Reno, NV 89503. *Four books a year, mss. by invitation only. Duane Ackerson,* Weathering, *38pp, $2;* A Problem of High Water, *Greg Kuzma, 46pp, $2 are typical. The Meyers translation of Francois Dodat's* Lord of the Village, *a bestiary;* Costanzo/ Massman/ McAllister, *a tri-thology;* Leaves and Ashes, *John Haines, co-published with Kayak Press. Forthcoming: books by William Stafford, Thomas Johnson, D.S. Long and Isabel Reade's translation of fables by Enrique Anderson Imbert. Some concrete poetry titles being talked about for 1975.*

WEST COAST REVIEW, West Coast Review Publishing Society, **Frederick H. Candelaria,** Eng. Dept., Simon Fraser Univ., Burnaby 2, BC, Canada. 4/yr; $6/yr; $1.50/ea; 1966; 64pp; folio; 500 circ; lp. Reports vary. Pays: $5/ca. Ads: $50/p; $25/½. Discounts: trade $4.80. Back issues: available through Kraus Reprint Corp. Pub'd 4 issues 1973.

WEST END, **John F. Crawford,** Box 354 Jerome Ave. Sta., Bronx, NY 10468. Poetry, articles, interviews, criticism, reviews, longpoems. *Marxist orientation means sensitivity to objective forces in one's life. Look for sensitivity to the world in general. No sexism, ego-trips, in-group stuff, please. Contributors range from Levertov* *to Lifshin. Any subject OK within guidelines above. Print many young writers. Give me idea of what you're into. (By the way, Old Left orientations are encouraged if you're writing politics).* 4/yr; $2.50/yr; 50 cents/ea; no sample; 1971; 48 pp; 7x8½; 500 circ; lo. Reports 3 mos. Pays copies only. No ads. Discounts: 60/ 40 consignment to all but movement bkstrs, free to them. Subs. $5/yr to libraries. Back issues: Vol.1/$15; Vol.1, No.1 almost o.p. Pub'd 4 issues 1973, expects 3 in 1974; expects 1 book 1974. COSMEP, CCLM, Marxist Orientation.

WEST HIGHLAND FREE PRESS, West Highland Publishing Co. Ltd., **Brian D.H. Wilson,** Kyleakin, Isle of Skye, Scotland, UK. Articles, poetry, cartoons, photos, news items, letters. Weekly; £4.50/yr; 5p/ea; 1972; 8pp; 7000 circ; off. Pays: negotiable. Ads: 60p/col. inch. Discounts: 10%.

John Westburg Assoc., Publishers (see NORTH AMERICAN MENTOR MAGAZINE)

WESTERLY, **Editorial Committee,** Dept. of English, Univ. of Western Australia, Nedlands, W.A. 6009, Australia. Poetry, fiction, articles. Q; $4.80/yr posted; $1.10/ea.

WESTERN HUMANITIES REVIEW, University of Utah Press, **Jack Garlington, Franklin Fisher, assoc. ed.,** Univ. of Utah, Salt Lake City, UT 84112. Poetry, fiction, articles, interviews, satire, criticism, reviews, music, letters, parts-of-novels, longpoems, plays, concrete art. *No biases, we hope, except toward good writing. Some recent contributors: Roberta Kalechofsky, Laurel Trivelpiece, William Stafford, Jorge Luis Borges, Joyce Carol Oates, Leon Rooke, Jack Matthews, Ira Sadoff, Clarice Short, Martin Booth.* Q; $5/yr; $1.50/ea; sample; 1947, 96pp; 6¾x10; 1M circ; lp. Reports about 1 mo. Pays: $100 per story and article; $35 per poem. Ads: $100/p; $50/½. Back issue prices depend on issue. Pub'd 4 issues 1973. COSMEP, CCLM.

WESTERN WORLD REVIEW, **Robert F. Sagehorn,** PO Box 2714, Culver City, CA 90230. Articles, reviews, criticism, essays. *Good non-fiction on politics, economics, media, philosophy or most anything.* Q; $2/yr; 50 cents/ea; 1965; 40pp; 8½x7; under 500 circ; lo. Reports 2 wks. Pays copies only. COSMEP.

WETLANDS, **Thomas S. Zawyrucha, Carl A. Starace Jr., photo ed., Peter Bieling, art ed., Paul Silverman, sci. ed.,** Box 252, West Islip, NY 11795. Poetry, fiction, articles, art, photos, cartoons, interviews, satire, reviews, letters, longpoems. *All accepted prose and poetry is environmentally oriented, and usually less than 5 typewritten pages in length. Our pure environment articles and interviews are metropolitan New York in nature.* Q; $3/yr; 75 cents/ea; 1971; 32pp; 8½x11; 1M circ; lo. Reports 1 wk. Pays copies only. Ads: $75/p; $40/½; no class/wd. Discounts: lower rates for repeats of ads, i.e. full page for 1 year $200 (4 issues). Back issues: 75 cents; the Spring 1972, Vol.1, No.1 and the Spring 1973, Vol.2, No.1 are not available. COSMEP.

WEYFARERS, Guildford Poets Press, **Eric Harrison, John Emuss, Julian Nangle, Peter Pwtram, David Colbeck,** 10 Ashcroft, Shalford, Surrey, UK. Poetry, criticism, letters. *Short poems, averaging one per page. Wide variety of traditional and experimental. Contributors include Brian Petten, Martin Booth, Michael Horovitz, Leonard Clark.* 3/yr; £1/yr; 35p/ea; 30p/sample; 1972; 30pp; 8x5½"; 150 circ; off. Reports: 4 wks. Pays: none except by prior arrangement. No ads. Discounts: 20%. ALMS, ALP.

WHEELS, **Harriet Rose,** 53 Blenheim Gardens, London NW2, UK. Poetry. *An occasional publication. Will put out an issue when enough really excellent material comes in to make it worth the work involved. Great poems make it worth doing. Good poems fill an issue, but there are never enough of the first category available. Bias toward highly charged memetic poetry, but have taken particularly excellent compression poems and will again. Will use long poems but only if they're much better than the acceptable quality for shorter work due to space limitations. Have published Gavin Ewart, Anne Beresford; Barbara Holland, Norman Hidden, Stanley Thomas, B.C. Leale, Daphne Gloag, Victor West, etc.* 30p/ea; 1973; 30pp; off. Discounts: 30% bookstores.

WHISPER & SHOUT, c/o 84 Bisley Road, Stroud, Glos, UK. Articles, poetry, photos, interviews, collages. *Recent contributors H.D. Thoreau, Kenneth Patchen, Henry Miller. Bias-anarchist & anti-military philosophy. Style-free. No.2- collection of poems called* Redruth Days. *also contains photographs and engravings.* Every 6 yrs; 25p/ea; 1968; 32pp; 8x5"; 2000circ; off/lp.

Whispers Press (see STREET CRIES)

WHITE ARMS MAGAZINE, **Jim Jordan,** c/o Dana Wichern, 10215 Hickory Valley Drive, Fort Wayne, IN 46815. Poetry, fiction, articles, art, cartoons, interviews, criticism, reviews, letters, longpoems, collages, concrete art. *Anything enclosing* space. *The words are so nice to hear and look at. Big words and little words. Words alone and together. Also pictures are a relief. Grandma Moses and Andy Warhol are the best of course. Also interviews, diaries, reviews, journals, letters. People are funny. Things that travel as a whole from page to page are after all what a magazine is about. Issue One(derful) April 1974 contains: interview with Mary Ellen Solt (and two poems), 3 original silkscreens, poems by Tom Fisher, Judson Crews, Stephen Leggett, Lyn Lifshin, Bianca Schwartz's Journal.* 3/yr; $3.50/yr; $1/ea; Sample: exchange; 1974; 55pp; 8½x11; 250+ circ; lo. Reports: immediately. Pays: two copies only. Ads: will list nice ones free. Expects 3 issues 1974.

White Bones Press (see BONES)

White Mountain Publishing House, **R. Alaine Everts,** PO Box 5571, Madison, WI 53705.

White Urp Press (see ABBEY)

WALT WHITMAN REVIEW, Wayne State University Press, **William White and Charles E. Feinberg,** Business matters: Wayne State Univ. Press, Detroit 48202; Editorial: William White, Dir., Journalism Program, Oakland University, Rochester, MI 48063. Articles, criticism, reviews. *We publish only articles dealing with Walt Whitman and his works, reviews of books about Whitman, and new editions of Whitman's writings.* 4/yr; $4/yr; $1/ea; 1955; 32pp; 9x6"; 700 circ.; lp. Reports: within a few days. Pays: copies only. Ads: none. Back issues: $4/vol.; $1/issue. Pub'd 4 issues 1973, expects 4 issues 1974.

Whitson Publishing Company (see STUDIES IN THE TWENTIETH CENTURY in additional listings)

WICA NEWSLETTER, **Dr. Leo Louis Martello,** 153 West 80th St., New York, NY 10024. *Writers must be well-versed in* Witchcraft: The Old Religion *as outlined in book of same name by Dr. Martello. Has nothing to do with Judeo-Christian defined "witchcraft" and no connection with devil-worship, Black Masses etc. Recent contributor was Patricia Crowther, author of* "Witch Blood: Diary of a Witch

High Priestess" *from England.* 10/yr; $4/yr; 50 cents/ea; 1970; 24030pp; 8½x11; 3500 circ; of. Pays up to $10 &/or copies. Ads: $150/pg; $75/½; class/ed 25 cents /wd. Discounts: Less than 10 is 40%; 10 or more is 50%. Pub'd 10 issues 1073; 3 books 1073, expects 2 in 1974. COSMEP, Witches Liberation.

WILD FENNEL, P.W. Frames, Pub., **Pauline Palmer, Ed.,** 105 Grand Avenue, Bellingham, WA 98225. Poetry, fiction, articles, art, cartoons, interviews, satire, criticism, reviews, letters. *Especially interested in humor, fantasy, science fiction. Fiction should be fairly short (not longer than 2500 words in most cases). Style is basically informal but we're flexible. Art work and cartoons should be line drawings, black ink on white paper. We encourage active reader participation through letters of comment and contributions.* Irreg; 50 cents/ea; Sample: 10 cent stamp; 1970; 18-24pp; 8x10; 200-500 circ; lo. Reports: 2-3 wks. Pays: copies only. Discounts: trade. Back issues: Nos. 1-7 out of print; issue no. 8 available at 25 cents/copy. Pub'd 1 issue 1973, expects 2-3 in 1974.

Wilderness Press, **Thomas Winnett,** 2440 Bancroft Way, Berkeley, CA 94704. *Trail guides, outdoor how-to books, outdoor adventures.* Lo. Reports: 7 days. Pays: 8-10% royalty. Ads: none. Discounts: 40% trade. Pub'd 5 books 1973. Expects 7 books 1974.

WIN MAGAZINE, Win Publishing Empire, **Maris Cakars,** Box 547, Rifton, NY 12471. Poetry, articles, art, photos, cartoons, interviews, reviews, letters. *Recent contributors: Murray Bookchin, Allen Ginsberg, Robert Bly, Martin Jezer, Barbara Deming, Phil Berrigan, Dan Berrigan.* Weekly; $7/yr; 20 cents/ea; Sample: free; 1966; 24pp; 8½x11; 8000 circ; lo. Reports: 1 mo. Pays: copies only. Ads: $75/pg; $50/½; $1/10 wds. Discounts: 10 copies or more: 10 cents /ea. Pub'd 44 issues 1973 . COSMEP, UPS, Peace and Justice.

WIND MAGAZINE, Quentin R. Howard, R.F.D. Rt. No.1, Box 810, Pikeville, KY 41501. Poetry, fiction, reviews, one-act plays. No taboos, editor will establish his own taboos on reading each manuscript. Any length poems, fiction, reviews. Recent contributors: Josephine Jacobson, John Unterecker, Peter Wild, Philip Dacey, Kay Boyle, Bruce Bennett Brown, Eve Triem, Eve Merriam, Larry Rubin, George Scarbrough, Lewis Turco, Philip Appleman, May Sarton & others. Q; $4/yr indiv; $5/yr insti; $1.25/ea; no sample; 1971; 64pp; 5½x8½; 250 circ. Reports 10 days hopefully. Pays copies only. Ads: haven't taken any as yet. No discounts.

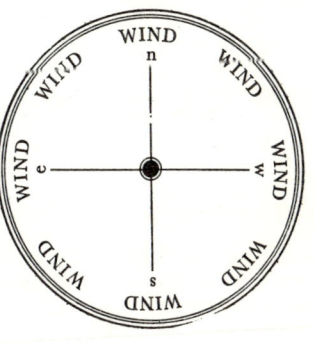

Back issues: all of past volumes $5.50. Published 4 issues 1973, expects 4 in 1974. COSMEP, CCLM, Kentucky Arts Commission, The Academy of American Poets.

Windflower Press (see THE SALT CREEK READER)

THE WINDLESS ORCHARD: a quarterly magazine of photography and contemporary poetry, **Robert Novak,** Section of Eng., Purdue Univ., Fort Wayne, IN 46805. Poetry, articles, art, photos, criticism, reviews. *Only poetry with contemporary or avant-garde techniques.* Q; $3.75/yr; $1/ea; $10/3 yrs; 1970; 50pp; 8½x 11; 300 circ; lo. Reports 1-6 wks. Pays 2 copies. No ads. Back issues: $1/ea. Pub'd 4 issues 1973. COSMEP.

Winston-Paramount Books (see BEST POETS OF THE 20th CENTURY ,NOTABLE AMERICAN POETS)

WISCONSIN PATRIOT, Wisconsin Alliance Press, Inc., **Bob Peterson, D.A. Weimer,** 1014 Williamson, Madison, WI 53715. Articles, photos, cartoons, interviews, reviews. Newspaper of the Wisconsin Alliance party. Monthly; $3/yr individual, $5 /yr institutions; 25cents/ea; free sample; 1971; 12pp; tabloid; 1800 circ; of. Reports 1 mo. No ads. No discounts. Pub'd 11 issues 1973.

WISCONSIN REVIEW, Univ. of Wisconsin Press, **Marilyn Weller, Gary Busha,** Box 177, Dempsey Hall, UW-O, Oshkosh, WI 54901. Poetry, fiction, art, photos, interviews, satire, reviews, parts-of-novels, plays. *Prefer poems to be no more than 2pp. single-spaced; fiction to be 4000-5000 words at maximum. We will consider anything good by anybody.* Q; $3/yr; $1/ea; 50 cents/sample; 1965; 60pp; 7x8½; 500 circ; lo. Reports: 6-8wks. Pays copies only; Back issues: 75 cents/issue. Pub'd 4 issues 1973, expects 4 issues 1974.COSMEP.

WISCONSIN'S IMPACT, Shelters Press, **S.L. Poulter,** PO Box 5168, Milwaukee, WI 53204. Poetry, fiction, articles, art, photos, interviews, satire, criticism, reviews, letters, parts-of-novels, longpoems, collages. *Length: up to 100 or so lines will be considered... modern, contemporary work in all art fields. No biases except for an obvious lack of talent/creativity... recent contributors include Lyn Lifshin, Hans Juergensen, Robert Fitzgerald, Edith Kaltovich, E.T. Caldwell, Sara Rath, etc.* Q; $5/yr; $1.50/ ea; $1/sample; 1973; 40-48pp; 5x8; 300 circ; lo. Reports within 30 days. Pays one copy. Ads: $50/pg; $30/½; 10 cents/wd. Discounts: 30% to agents /bookstores; Institutions: $10/yr. Back issues: Vol. 1, No. 1: $5. Pub'd 1 issue 1973, expects 4 issues 1974.

WITCHCRAFT DIGEST, **Dr. Leo Louis Martello,** 153 West 80th St., New York, NY 10024. *Writers must be well-versed in*Witchcraft: The Old Religion *as outlined in book of same name by Dr. Martello. Has nothing to do with Judeo-Christian defined "witchcraft" and no connection with devil-worship, Black Masses, etc. Recent contributor was Patricia Crowther, author of* "Witch Blood: Diary of a Witch High Priestess" *from England.* Annual; $1.20/copy; 1970; 24-30pp; 8½x11; 3500 circ; lo. Pays up to $10 &/or copies. Ads: $150/p; $75/½; class/wd 25 cents/wd. Discounts: 40%/less than 10; 50%/10 or more. Back issues: $1.20/ea. Pub'd 1 issue 1973, expects 2 in 1974. COSMEP, Witches Liberation.

Wolf House Books (see THE LONDON COLLECTOR)

THE WOMAN JOURNALIST, Society of Women Writers & Journalists, **Pat Garrod,** 45 Basildon Court, Devonshire Street, London W1N 1RF, UK. Single copy/free to members; 1894, No payment.

WOMAN'S CHOICE, PO Box 320, Botanic Road, Glasnevin, Dublin 2, Eire, UK. *Short stories, true-life stories, fashion news, beauty, serious features.* Weekly; 6p/ each; 1968. Women.

Woman's Soul Publishing, Inc. (see PAID MY DUES)

WOMEN: A JOURNAL OF LIBERATION, Collective of 8 women— rotating responsibilities, 3028 Greenmount Ave., Baltimore, MD 21218. Poetry, fiction, articles, art, photos, cartoons, interviews, satire, reviews, collages. We follow a general thematic format but welcome any material that reflects a women's consciousness. Articles should be limited to 5000 words or less & accompanied by SASE to insure being returned— we are unable to pay for material published. Irreg; $4/yr individual, $5/yr Canadian, $10/yr institution; $1/ea; no free sample; 1969; 72pp; 8½x11; 20M circ; lo. Ads: $200/pg; $100/½; $50/¼; $25/1/8; no class/wd. Discounts: Bulk: 5 or more of same issue–@85 cents consignment, @ 75 cents prepaid. Pub'd 2 issues 1973, expects 1 or 2 in 1974. COSMEP, Women.

WOMEN & FILM, Siew Hwa Beh, Saunie Salyer, 2802 Arizona Ave., Santa Monica, CA 90404. Articles, photos, interviews, criticism, reviews, letters. *W & F is a feminist publication concerned with the image & treatment of women in film & the development of a critical & theoretical foundation for non-Chauvinist film study.* 3/yr; $3/yr individuals, $5.50/yr institutions; $1/ea; $1/sample; 1972; 80pp; 8½x11; 5M circ; lo. Reports 2 mos. Pays copies only. Ads: $99/pg; $59/½ $35/¼. Discounts: Agent 25%. Back issues: no.1/$1; No. 2 out of print. Pub'd 3 issues 1973. COSMEP, Third World, Women.

WOMEN IN STRUGGLE (newsletter), **J.C. Taylor,** Box 324, Winneconne, WI 54986. Bi-monthly; sample free with SASE; 1970; 8pp; 8½x11; under 500 circ; lo. Pub'd 5 issues 1973. COSMEP, Women.

WOMEN OF LA RAZA, Concilio Mujeres/Communicaciones, **Dorinda Moreno,** 2588 Mission St., Rm 201, San Francisco, CA 94110. Poetry, articles, art, photos, interviews, criticism, reviews, music, longpoems, collages, plays, concrete art. *We have 4 newsletters: (1) Journal Writings Anthology, "La Mujer-En Pie de Lucha," D. Moreno, ed., Espina del Norte, publisher. (2) Chicana, "La Razon Mestiza." (3) Womens movement, "Advocates for Women," (we do not put out, but contribute work & input). (4) Teatro, "Me voy pi Teotihuacan," Chicano theatre.* Monthly; 1974; mixed no. of pg; pg size: legal; lo. Back issues $8/book, 325 pg, 5x8. Pub'd 500 copies of "En Pie de Lucha" in 1973, expects 2M in 1974. Third World, Women, Chicano, Am. Indian.

WOMEN STUDIES ABSTRACTS, **Sara Stauffer Whaley & Karen Caviglia,** PO Box 1, Rush, NY 14543. Bibliographies, reviews. *Bibliographic articles accepted. Recent contributors include: Martha Wilson and Margrit Eichler (in essay with one editor).* Q; $8.50/yr indiv, $12/yr instit, $7/Yr, students; $3/ea; 1972; 96pp; 6x8½; 1200 circ; lo. Reports 1 mo. Pays 25 copies. Discounts: $1.50 bulk. Back issues: same as current. Pub'd 4 issues 1973.Women.

WOMEN'S HISTORY RESEARCH CENTER, **Laura X,** 2325 Oak, Berkeley, CA 94708. *Two magazines: 1)* Films By and About Women 2) Female Artists Past and Present. *Our material is directories & Bibliographies.* COSMEP, UPS, Women.

Women's Press Collective, 5251 Broadway, Oakland, CA 94618. Woman to Woman, *anthology, $1.50 (bulk $1.10);* Eating Artichokes *by Willyce Kim, poetry, $1 (bulk $.60);* Rape Journal *by Dell Richardson, poetry, $.75 (bulk $.45);* Yesterday's Lessons *by Sharon Isabell, novel, $2.50 (bulk $1.50); By Judy Grahn:* Edward The Dyke, *poetry, $1.25 (bulk $.90);* The Common Woman, *poetry, $.25 (bulk $.15);* Elephant Poem Coloring Book, *$.85 (bulk $.50);* A Woman is Talking to Death, *$1.25 (bulk $.75); By Pat Parker:* Child of Myself, *poetry, $1 (bulk $.60);* Pit Stop, *poetry, $1 (bulk $.60).* 1970; lo. Pub'd 4 in 1973, expects 15 in 1974. Third World, Women, Chicano, Black, Gay, Lesbian, G.I., Prison, White Trash, Children, Jewish.

WOMEN'S REPORT, Womens Report Collective, 75 Albert Place Mansions, Lurline Gardens, London SW11, UK. Articles, photos, news items, criticism. *Short (c.200 word) items, plus two-page features. Essentially a news magazine for women- who are unable to find information on law, health, social security, women's aid centres, feminist publications etc., etc., adequately covered elsewhere. Also acts as a clearinghouse for names and addresses for people interested in specific* subjects- e.g. history, health, psychiatry, etc., etc. Bi-monthly; £1 or £2/yr; 17p/ each; 1972; 20pp; A4; 1500 circ; lo. No ads. Women.

WOMEN'S STUDIES NEWSLETTER (see The Feminist Press)

WOOD IBIS, **James Cody,** c/o Flowers Books, 186 Hampshire St., Cambridge, MA 02139.(until June 1, 1974); 4703 York Hill Drive, Austin, TX 78723 (after June 1, 1974). Poetry, fiction, articles, art, criticism, reviews, music. *A subtitle might be, "A Journal of Contemporary Shamanism." Emphasis on the revival of the ceremonial in the passage of the seasons, of the earth and life; sense of place; of the vision quest (hanblechia) and dream vision; encouraging tribalism. The poem as a shamanic act; the provision of new feeling, new direction for peoples. Respect for nature and animals as our brothers and sisters, grandmother and grandfather. Particularly interested in the Americas. Also Africa, Australia, Oceania. Europe, too, but skeptical. Emphasis on contemporary, living writers. No archaeology or anthropology unless you're pretty sure we'd be interested. Return to the land. Closing Black Elk's Hoop. No distinction between primitive and civilized. Will accept strong general and urban poetry. Articles, essays and reviews of pertinent materials. Black and white line drawings. First issue coming together. Tentatively will have material by Paul Foreman, Gene Fowler, Barbara Holland, Jim Cody, Norm Moser, others.*1-2/yr; $2/yr; $2/ea; 1974. Reports 2 wks. to 6 mos. Pays copies only. Ads: $40/pg, $20/½; class/wd 5 cents/wd. Discounts: normal 40%. Expects to publish 1 issue in 1974. COSMEP, Third World, Women, Chicano, Black, Ecology, Am. Indian, Third World Whites, Everything.

Wooden Needle Press (see WORDS)

VIRGINIA WOOLF QUARTERLY, **Dr. Suzanne Henig and Dr. Florence Talamantes,** 6762 Cibola Road, San Diego, CA 92120. Poetry, fiction, art, articles, photos, interviews, satire, criticism, reviews, letters, parts-of-novels, longpoems, collages, plays, concrete art. *VWQ is published for the purpose of studying, documenting, appreciating, and perpetuating the memory of Virginia Woolf as artist and feminist, the Bloomsbury group, their friends, associates, acquaintances and the times in which they lived. We also publish translations of creative work, original poetry and fiction with a strong feminist bias. However, excellence is what we strive for. Recent issues included works by John Lehmann, Germaine Bree, Francoise Gilot, Hope Morrlees, and an interview withDurrell, as well as an unpublished letter by T.S. Eliot and an unpublished novel by Virginia Woolf.* Q; $10/yr; $2.50/ea; $2.50/sample; 1972; 85-150pp; 8½x11; 1000+ circ; lo. Reports 6 mos.-1 yr.Pays copies only. Ads: $100/pg; $50/½, class/wd 25 cents each. Discounts: 20%. Back issues $2.50. Pub'd 4 issues in 1973, expects 4 in 1974. Women, Conference of Learned Journals.

The Woolman Press (see PORT TOWNSEND JOURNAL)

Word and Action (Press) (see CHESIL)

WORDS, Wooden Needle Press, **R.C. Morse,** 355 Marlborough St., Boston, MA 02115. Poetry, fiction, art, interviews, criticism, reviews, longpoems. *Terry Stokes, Greg Orr, Bill Knott, Bill Matthews, Peter Davison, Kenn Kwint, Richard Morris, David Wilk, Ray Amorosi, Etc, etc, etc.* Bi-monthly for now; 1972; 32pp; 5½x8½; 400-1M circ; lo. Reports soon enough. Pays copies only. Ads: $100/pg; $50/½. Back issues: none available. Pub'd 7, 8 issues 1973, expects 5 in 1974. COSMEP.

WORDS BROADSHEETS, Words Press, **Julian Nangle,** 11 Sol-y-vista, Frith Hill Road, Godalming, Surrey, UK. Poetry, fiction, art, collages. *Most poems must be not longer than 50 lines. Recent contributors include Brian Patten, James Kirkup, John Pudney, Eric W. White, Martin Booth, Denton Welch, Peter Redgrove, Char-*

les Causely and Harry Guest. In 1974 we are hoping to publish a series of ten broadsheets devoted to the work of Denton Welch. Limited edition of each broadsheet, printed on Glastonbury Antique Laid Paper. 25 copies signed by poets. 10/ year; £2.50, £10 signed/yr; 25p, £1 signed/ea; 1973; 4pp; 8x5; 100 circ; lp; Reports: immediate. Pays: £2.50/poem or v.short story + 1 signed copy. Discounts: 25% trade. Back issues: double price. ALP.

WORKERS' POWER, I.S. Publishing Company, 15131 Woodward Ave., 3rd Fl., Highland Park, MI 48203.

WORKSHOP NEW POETRY, Workshop Press, **Norman Hidden,** 2 Culham Court, Granville Road, London N4 4JB, UK. Articles, poetry, criticism, *Recent contributors have included W.H. Auden, Dannie Abse, George Barker, Alan Brownjohn, Bob Cobbing, Jeni Couzyn, D.J. Enright, Thom Gunn, Michael Hamburger, Seamus Heany, Adrian Henri, Ted Hughes, Elizabeth Jennings, Laurence Lerner, Peter Porter, Louis Simpson, Jon Stallworthy, Louis Zukovsky. Submissions: solicited; unsolicited, subscribers only.* 4/yr; £1.80/yr; 40p/ea; 1967; 40pp; 8x5"; 2000 circ; lp; Pays: by arrangement if solicited. Ads: £21/page, £11/½. Discounts: 25% Back issues: 35p/copy.

THE WORLD OF H.G. WELLS (WELLSIANA), Orchard Press, **Royston King,** c/o 125 Markyate Road, Dagenham, Essex RM8 2LB, UK. Articles, poetry, fiction, art, cartoons, photos, satire, news items, interviews, criticism, music,letters. *Worldwide dissemination of works/life/times/influences on & from H.G. Wells (1866-1946).* 1/yr; £1/yr; 50p/ea; 1970; 40pp; A5; 100 circ; off. Reports: 3 mos. Pays: copies. Ads: £15/page. Discounts: 20% agents. Literary & sociological.

THE WORMWOOD REVIEW, **Marvin Malone,** PO Box 8840, Stockton, CA 95204. Poetry, art, interviews, satire, reviews, letters, parts-of-novels, longpoems, collages, plays, concrete art. *Poetry and prose-poems to 300+ lines reflecting the temper and depth of present human scene. All types and schools from traditional-economical through concrete, dada and extreme avant-garde. Special fondness for prose poems/fables. Each issue has yellow-page section devoted to one poet or topic (e.g. Bukowski, Wantling, Jon Webb, Micheline, Crews, Locklin, Koertge, Dick Higgins, Ian Hamilton Finlay, Steve Richmond, John Currier, Wm. Burroughs, etc).* Q; $3.50/yr individ., $5.50/yr institu.; $1.50/ea; 1959; 44pp; 5½x8½; 800 circ; lo. Reports 2-7 wks. Pays 3-7 copies/or cash equival. Discounts: institu/ agents: reg. issues $5.50/yr; agency cost $4.50/yr. Reg. $11/2 yr, agency cost $9/ 2 yrs. Back issues: $1.50 per issues 12-45. Pub'd 4 issues 1973. COSMEP, Scientist X, CCLM.

THE WRITER, Bond Street Publishers Ltd., **Mrs. H. Johnson,** 124 New Bond St., London W1A 4LJ, UK. Articles, interviews, criticism, letters. *All articles submitted must be really practical, offering sound advice and information. Articles 300-1200 words.* 12/yr; £3/yr; 25p/ea; 1921; 48pp; A5; off. Reports: 5 wks. Pays: by arrangement, usually £5/1000 words. Ads: £20/page pro rata, 5p/word. Back issues: 10p.

Writers and Scholars International Ltd. (see INDEX ON CENSORSHIP)

WRITERS' ARTS REVIEW, 1926 N. Kenmore Ave., Apt. 105, Los Angeles, CA 90027. Writers' Arts Review *has scheduled its first issue for February 1974. It will be a quarterly for novelists, poets, screenwriters and playwrights meant to draw together the writing arts by critiquing works of established writers from the standpoint of artistic construction and expression of the artist's intent. We'll also publish original poetry, have an interview and run a calendar of upcoming literary events in each issue.*

Writers Forum, (see also KROKLOK and AND), **Bob Cobbing & John Rowan,** 262 Randolph Avenue, London W9, UK. Poetry, art, music, longpoems, concrete. *Mainly publishes members and those associated in some way with* Writers Forum. *15 items published in 1973, plus 9 reprints. 107 items since 1963.* Varies; Varies/each; 1963; size varies; mim/off. Pays: copies. Discounts: trade 33%, 40% on large orders. ALP.

WRITING, Sean Dorman Manuscript Society, **Sean Dorman; Assoc. ed. Fred Altfield,** 4 Union Place, Fowey, Cornwall PL23 1 BY, UK. Articles, poetry. *Articles: 300/350 words on subjects of interest to authors and journalists. Poems: 8 to 20 lines (of quality, in any style). Style: literary.* 2/yr; 50p/yr; 30p/ea; No samples; 1959; 60pp; 8x6½; 1000 circ; off. Reports: 2 wks. Pays: $5/article or poem. Ads: $10/page, $6.25/½, 12 cents/word; ads exchanged. No discounts. No back issues.

WYVERN, **Chris Talbot & John Keane,** Student Council, Essex University, Wivenhoe Park, Colchester CO4 3SQ, UK. Articles, poetry, fiction, art, cartoons, photos, satire, news items, interviews, criticism, music, letters. *Average article/story=600. words. Bias= 1)left-wing 2) student/youth orientated.* 8/yr; 40p/yr; 5p/ea; 1964; 16-20pp; A4; 2000+ circ; off. Reports: 3 wks. No pay. Ads: £30/page, £16/½, £9/¼, £1.35/col. inch.

Y Lolfa, Y Lolfa, Talybont, Ceredigion (Cardiganshire) SY24 5ER, Wales. Tel. Talybont 304. *Prop; Robat Gruffudd. Printers and publishers interested in anything that will help the Welsh Revolution (Free Wales-Welsh Wales!). We do posters, paperbacks, funny cards, music, poetry, plays, "Cymraeg" stickers and of course that awful magazine* Lol *(see under "Lol"). Send for free 16pp catalogue!*

Yardbird Press   (see MUSHROOM)

Years Press   (see CENTERING: A Magazine of Poetry)

YELLOW BRICK ROAD, Emerald City Press, **Robert Matte,** 1025 E. Orange St., No. 31, Tempe, AZ 85281. Poetry, fiction, art. *Prefer poetry under thirty lines. Will consider anything of quality but prefer work with an absurdist tinge. Accept "short short" fiction— off the wall stuff. Art should be surreal, no bowls of fruit.* 3/yr; $3/yr; $1/ea; 75 cents/sample; 1974; 30pp; 8½x11; 300 circ; lo. Reports 2 wks.-1 mo. Pays: 2 copies. No ads. Expects 2 issues, 1 book in 1974.

YELLOW BUTTERFLY, **Laurence & Guadalupe Fallis,** Box 3 BD Univ. Park, Las Cruces, NM 88003. *Seeking a wide range of materials and styles. Query before submission for list of current projects. Recent emphasis upon broadsides and one poet issues.* Irreg; $2/yr; 75 cents/ea; 75 cents/sample if available; 1972; 100 circ; mi; lo. Reports 2-4 wks. Pays copies. No ads. Back issues: 75 cents. Pub'd 1 issue 1973, expects 5 in 1974.

YES (A Magazine of Poetry), **Virginia Elson, Beverlee Hughes,** Smith Pond Rd., Avoca RD 1, New York, NY 14809. Poetry. *Interviews with Adrien Stoutenburg, David Slavitt, Colette Inez, David Wagoner, Maxine Kumin. Poetry by Stoutenburg, Slavitt, Inez, Goldbarth, Swann, Dacey, Glen, Tagliabue, Oles, Witt etc.* 3/yr; $4/yr; $1.50/ea; $1/sample; 1970; 48pp; 5½x8; 400 circ; lp; Reports 2-3 wks. Pays copies only. Back issues: Vols 1-3/$2 per issue; complete set (all issues) $50. Pub'd 3 issues 1973, expects 3 in 1974. COSMEP, CCLM.

Yorkshire Arts Association, Glyde House, Glydegate, Bradford BD5 0BQ, UK.

Yorkshire Dialect Society   (see SUMMER BULLETIN)

Yorkshire Poets' Association (see INTAK')

Young Publications, **Lincoln B. Young,** 69 West Main St., Appalachia, VA 24216. Poetry, longpoems. *We publish collections of poems in book form only. No magazines. We will accept any type of poem that appeals to us, regardless of length, style, etc. We accept poems from beginners as well as well known poets. Some recent contributors are: Stella Craft Tremble, Mildred Moon Howell, J.R. LeMaster, and Louis Ginsburg.* Lo. Reports up to 6 months. No payment. Pub'd 1 book in 1972, expects 1 in 1973.

Young Virgin Weasel Enterprises (see HEART)

Youth Liberation Press (see FPS: the Youth Liberation News Service)

Z MAGAZINE (Aberdeen Arts and Entertainments Guide), Rainbow Enterprises, 177 Victoria Rd., Torry, Aberdeen, **Mike Scott,** 1 St. Peters Place, Old Aberdeen, Aberdeen AB2 3JZ, Scotland, UK. Articles, art, cartoons, photos, news items, interviews, criticism, music. *Reviews of forthcoming events in Aberdeen with comments and longer articles on related topics. Recent interviews with Alexander Gibson (Scottish National Orchestra) and John McGrath (playwright). Specimen copy free to anyone mentioning your directory.* Fortnightly; £1.10/10 issues; 10p /ea (inc. post.); free sample; 1971; 20pp; 17½x24½cm; 900 circ; off/lo. Reports: Copy date: 1 wk. before publication. No pay. Ads: £10/page, £5.50/½, £3/¼. Discounts: for 3 or more insertions. Back issues: 10p/issue (inc.post). Arts Guide.

ZAHIR, **Diane Kruchkow,** Sunset Drive, Plum Island, Newbury, MA 01950. Poetry, fiction, articles, cartoons, interviews, criticism, reviews, letters. 2/yr; $2/yr; $1 /ea; 1970; 60pp; 700 circ; lo. Reports 2-4 wks. Pays 2 copies. Ads: $50/pg; $25/½. Discounts: will work out. Back issues: No. 1/$10; No.3/$2. COSMEP, NESPA, CCLM.

ZAMISDAT, Bonefold Imprint, **Bernard Joseph Kelly,** 68 Parkhill Road, London NW3, UK. Poetry, satire, news items, letters, plays. *Shall probably do a compendium issue in 74 (late) of much stuff piled up over 3 years with reprints too. Work on the Ad-Hoc Poetry Steering Committee and Total Creative Plunge (an event procedure). Compendium issue is likely to be large-40pp of poems and articles. Issues: Sonnet Brushes (McCarthy & Kelly) Wolf Net, McLure; Maymag 72 Allude (English & Spanish- Kelly) Coinhaulers (McCarthy, Dorbie, Kelly) Zamisdat Newsletter, etc.* 4/yr; £1.30/yr; 15-30p/ea; 1968; 10-20pp; A4; 200 circ; off/mim. Reports: week. ALP.

ZEPHYR, **Trevor Hughes,** 9 Britannia Road, Liscard, Wallasey, Cheshire L45 4RN, UK. Articles, fiction, art, music, letters. *Art by U.S. Professional comic artists. Specialises in old/rare U.S. comics, particularly Marvels/D.L.s/E.C.s.* Bi-monthly; £1/yr; 15p/ea; 1972; 48pp; 8x6½"; 500 circ; off. Ads: £1/page; Comics, SF.

ZERO ONE, Dancing Patch Press, **Arthur Moyse, Jan Witte,** 39 Minford Gardens, West Kensington, London W14 0AP, UK. *An elitist magazine. Anarchist orientated. Ill mannered and unappologetic. Will use any material without permission. Will willingly read and return material with a stamped returned envelope but all Zero One published material is either commissioned (unpaid) or simply stolen.* 3/yr; £3/yr; £1/ea; No samples; 1970; 300pp; 8x10"; 350 circ; off. Reports: commissioned work only. No pay. No ads. No discounts. Anarchist.

ZERONE, **Lawrence Upton,** c/o 18 Clairview Road, Streatham, London SW16 and **Liam Maguire,** 65a Trinity Road, Tooting Bec, London SW17, UK. Poetry. *Poetry produced by members of the "Bec Poets" workshops.* 2/yr; 10p px/ea; 1971; 26 pp; 8x7"; 250 circ; mim. Reports: 2 wks. Pays: 1 copy. Ads: on application Discounts: 33%. Back issues: at original price.

ZIGGURAT ANTHOLOGY OF THE FINE ARTS, Ziggurat Publications, **Joshua,** 5685 North Shore Dr., Milwaukee, WI 53217. Poetry, fiction, articles, art, photos, cartoons, interviews, satire, criticism, reviews, music, letters, collages, plays, concrete art. *Accepts nothing more than 5 pages long. Anything relating to the fine arts, no biases involving style. Criterion is the editor's pleasure. Will not give editorial comments on submissions. No returns without SASE. Comes out irregularly, but tries to maintain as close to annual release as feasable. No subscriptions, direct sales ohly. Will exchange with other publishers of small-press magazines and books.* Annual; no sub; $2/ea; no samples; 1966; no. pgs. variable; 8½x11; 1M circ. Reports 2-3 mos. Pays 2 copies. Discounts: 25%. Back issues' $1.00. No issues, 3 books pub'd 1973, expects 10 issues, 10 books in 1974. COSMEP.

ZIGZAG, **Connor McKnight,** 70 Old Compton Street, London W1V 5PA, UK. Articles, interviews, music. Monthly; £2/yr; 15p/ea; 1969; 48pp; A4; 15000 circ; off;.Reports: 3-4 wks. Pays: negotiable. Ads: £80/page, £40/½ + 10% if not camera-ready. Back issues: 20p. Progressive Rock Music.

ZIMRI, **Lisa Conesa,** 54 Manley Road, Whalley Range, Manchester M16 8HP, UK. Articles, poetry, fiction, art, cartoons, satire, interviews, criticism, music, letters, longpoems, concrete. *Speculative fiction and poetry.* 4/yr; 20p/sub; 20p/ea; free sample; 1971; 54+pp; A4; 250 + circ; off/mim. Reports: 2 wks. Pays: copy only.

new poetry

Workshop *New Poetry* magazine was founded by Norman Hidden in 1967. Its guest editors have included John Pudney, Jon Stallworthy, Ivor Cutler, Philip Toynbee, Edward Lucie-Smith, G.S. Fraser, John Horder, Antony Rudolph, Charles Osborne, William Plomer.

Poets who have published in its pages include: W.H. Auden, Dannie Abse, George Barker, Patricia Beer, Alan Brownjohn, Bob Cobbing, Jeni Couzyn, D.J. Enright, Thom Gunn, Michael Hamburger, Seamus Heaney, John Heath-Stubbs, Adrian Henri, Ted Hughes, James Kirkup, Elizabeth Jennings, Laurence Lerner, Peter Levi, Roger McGough, George MacBeth, Barry MacSweeney, Leslie Norris, Brian Patten, William Plomer, Peter Porter, John Pudney, Louis Simpson, Jon Stallworthy, Ted Walker, and Louis Zukowsky.

WORKSHOP PRESS LTD., 2 Culham Court, Granville Road London N4 4JB

$5.00 for a year's subscription to Workshop *New Poetry*

ADDITIONAL LISTINGS

AFRICA TODAY, Africa Today Associates, **Edward A. Hawley, exec. ed., George W. Shepherd, Jr., Ezekiel Mphamlele, Tilden J. LeMelle,** c/o Graduate School of International Studies, Univ. of Denver, Denver, CO 80210. Poetry, articles, art, reviews, letters. Q; $8/yr indiv; $12/yr instit; $2.50/ea; bulk & multiple year available; 1954; 104pp; 2700 circ; lo. Reports 2 mos. No pay. Ads: $140/p; $75/½; $40/¼; no class/wd. Discounts: bulk, institution, agent, etc. Pub'd 4 issues 1973, expects 4 in 1974. Third World.

AFRICAN LITERATURE TODAY, Dept. of English, Univ. of Sierra Leone, Sierra Leone, Africa.

AGENDA, Agenda Editions, **Wiiliam Cookson, Peter Dale (assoc. ed.),** 5 Cranbourne Court, Albert Bridge Rd., London SW11 4PE, UK. Articles, poetry, photos, satire, interviews, criticism, longpoems. *Poetry must be in recognizable contemporary English. No 'concrete' or sound poetry considered.* £2($6)/sub; 45p/ea; 1959; 96pp; 2000 circ. Reports 1 mo. Pays: £1/page poetry. Ads: £30/p; £15/½. Discounts: 33%.

Alice In Wonderland (see OTHER VOICES)

ALTERNATIVE FEATURES SERVICE, **John Berger, Jeanne Lance, David Dunaway, Andrew Ross,** PO Box 2250, Berkeley, CA 94710. Articles, art, photos, cartoons, interviews, reviews. Weekly; price/yr varies; free sample; 1971; 18pp; 8½x 14; 100 circ, to newspapers or radio stations only; mi. Reports 10 days. Pays: $40 for an illustrated feature of 1,000 words. No ads. Pub'd 8 issues 1973, expects ? issues 1974. UPS.

American-Canadian Publishers, Inc. (see also LLANO) celebrates the 20th anniversary of the poem-prose meta-language of new-narrative: grammarless, anti-linear, ideographic, post-haiku-cubistic, para-fictional and fourth dimensional (space-time), with: A First Book of the Neo-Narrative, by Arlene Zekowski & Stanley Berne. American-Canadian's Archives of Post-Modern Literature series, launched in 1973 (advancing the AML series of Wittenborn) with: The Age of Iron (Zekowski) and The New Rubaiyat (Berne), $4 ea., continues with: An "Anthology" of Post-Modern (in preparation/contributions welcome/25pp maximum/SASE/advanced, open, exploratory investigative new structures, new textures, new styles, new forms of consciousness, multi-dimensional, all media, including innovative literary criticism: See Sir Herbert Read's Preface: "The resurrection of the Word" in Zekowski's Abraxas and in Berne's Multiple Modern Gods (American-Canadian), for the theme and scope of the "Anthology.") Also forthcoming: A Second Book of the New-Narrative (will feature new work, plus out of print works by Zekowski and Berne/ also literary criticism, reviews, commentary, also foreign translations, all langs., of Zekowski and Berne works, chaps. selections/ contributions welcome). Also forthcoming, the epics: Histories and Dynasties by Zekowski, and The Great American Empire by Berne. Queries welcome: American-Canadian Publishers, Inc., Drawer 2078, Portales, NM 88130.

BACK ROADS (formerly PAPER PUDDING), Next to Nothing Press, **Stella Nathan, Judith Abrahms, Marcy Page,** Box 543, Cotati, CA 94928. Poetry, fiction, articles, art, photos, cartoons, interviews, satire, criticism, reviews, collages, concrete art. *Modes that reveal contemporary processes; where we are now, how we got here, who we are to each other; not sentiment, but expression. Better yet, creation.* 2/yr; $2/4 issues; 50 cents/ea; 1971; 100pp; 5½x8½; 1M circ; lo. Reports 2 mos. Pays copies only. Ads: $40/p; $21/½; $11/¼. Back issues: $2/copy. Pub'd 2 issues 1973, expects 2 in 1974.

BIG DEAL, **Barbara Baracks,** c/o 141 New Hempstead Rd., New City, NY 10956. Poetry, fiction, articles, art, photos, interviews (?), criticism, reviews, music, parts- of novels, longpoems, concrete art. *Interested in a wide range of styles, unifying criterion a commitment to clear expression. "Expression" itself a debatable word! Long & short works. Poetry and prose (not necessarily fiction), reviews & criticism, reproducible artwork & photos. Experimental. Recent contributors include: Lucy R. Lippard, Jackson MacLow, Ron Silliman, Kathy Acker, Larry Eigner, Bernadette Mayer, Dave Morice, Clark Coolidge, Michael Lally, Alan Sondheim.* 2/yr; $3/yr; $1.50/ea; 1973; 70+pp; 8½x11; 400+ circ; lo; lp. Reports 2-3 wks. Pays copies only. Discounts: negotiable. Back issues: negotiable. Pub'd 1 issue 1973, expects 2 in 1974.

BOOKVIEWS, **Alan Caruba,** Box 157, Maplewood, NJ 07040. *A syndicated weekly column.*

CHE BULLETIN, 28 Kennedy Street, Manchester 2, UK.

CREATIVE MOMENT, Poetry Eastwest, **Syed Amanuddin,** PO Box 391, Sumter, SC 29150. Poetry, notes and articles on/by poets, and reviews of poetry books published by non-commercial publishers. *Particularly interested in world poetry written in English. Poems submitted for* Poetry Eastwest *are also considered for* Creative Moment *and the contributors are urged to send all poetry to* Poetry Eastwest *on the same address. Please query before sending articles and reviews.* 2/yr; $3/yr; $1.50/ea; $1/sample; 1972; 40pp; 5½x8½; 500 circ; lo. Reports 6-8 mos. Pays 1 copy. Ads: $60/p; $30/½; camera-ready copy only. Discounts: dealer discount 25-40%.

Cupola Productions, **Stan Nodvick,** PO Box 558, Havertown, PA 19083.

DAMASCUS ROAD, **Charles Shahoud Hanna,** 6271 Hill Dr., Wescosville, PA 18106. *Barbara Holland, David Ignatow, Colette Inez, Jackson MacLow, Grace Schulman, Michael Heller.* 1/2 yrs; $1.95/ea; no sample; 1959; 70pp; 5½x8½; 500 circ; lp. Pays copies. Discounts: 40% consign; 50% cash; 15% distributor. Back issues: 1st four issues: $7.50. Pub'd no issues in 1973, expects 1 book in 1975 (*The Doctor Generosity Poets: New York).* COSMEP, CCLM.

Decadent Press (see MOONGOOSE)

GAY SUNSHINE: A Journal of Gay Liberation, **Winston Leyland,** PO Box 40397, San Francisco, CA 94140, Tel. (415) 824-3184. Poetry, fiction, articles, art, photos, cartoons, interviews, satire, criticism, reviews, letters. Gay Sunshine, *a Journal of the Gay Liberation Movement, is a literary/political publication. Recent contributors include William Burroughs, Christopher Isherwood, Harold Norse, Gerard Malanga, Allen Ginsberg. We also sponsor a Gay Liberation Book Service. Free list available on request. We need good material. Manuscripts should be doubled spaced and less than 10 pages.* Q; $6/12 issues ($8 overseas); 60 cents/ea; 75 cents/ sample; free to prisoners; 1970; 24pp; 17½x11¼; 10M circ. Reports 2-5 wks. Pay: negotiable or copies. Ads: $200/p; $100/½; 50 cents/line/class. Discounts: 50% off retail for 100 copies or over; regular disc. to distributors & bookstores. Back issues: Nos. 9-12; 14-15; 17-23: 60 cents/ea. Nos. 2; 4-8; 13; 16; 22: $1/ea. Pub'd 4 issues 1973, expects 4 in 1974. COSMEP, UPS, CCLM, Gay.

Ghana Publishing Corporation, Ghana Univ. Press, Accra-Tema, Ghana, Africa.

HIGH TIMES MAGAZINE, **Ed Dwyer,** Box 386 Cooper Sta., New York, NY 10003. Articles, art, photos, interviews, criticism, reviews. High Times *is dedicated to exploring in a tasteful and intelligent manner the psycho-cultural implications of soft drug use around the world.* Q; $10/yr; $1/ea; $1/sample; 1974; 60pp; 8¼ x11; 25M circ; lo. Reports 1 mo. Pays: $25-$100. Ads: $400/p; $225/½; $1/line/ class. Discounts: retailers 50 cents per copy; distributors 35 cents per copy.

INFORMACION MERIDIANA, **A. Piazza,** Rodriguez Pena 754, Buenos Aires, Argentina.

LLANO (Literature Letters Art News Omnibus), American-Canadian Publishers, Inc., Arthur Goodson (director), Arlene Zekowski, Stanley Berne, contrib. eds., Drawer 2078, Portales, NM 88130. Poetry, fiction, articles, art, photos, cartoons, interviews, satire, criticism, reviews, music, letters, parts-of-novels, longpoems, collages, plays, concrete art. All volumes published are art works of literature with exclusively original illustrations of an unusual nature. Please note: the LLANO Newsletter has been temporarily superceded and enlarged by the "Anthology" (to incorporate submissions to LLANO – see American-Canadian Publishers, Inc.) on post-modern multi-dimensional writing. New descriptive American-Canadian catalog and price list of books, first editions, available free. Queries welcome. Lo; lp. Reports 3 mos. Pays: perhaps; copies. Ads: $85/p; $60/½. Discounts: 40% to bookstores; no other. Back issues: books and holographs; buyers, book collectors, libraries, see our latest catalog. Pub'd 2 books 1973, expects 2-3 in 1974. COSMEP, NESPA.

L.A. JOURNAL OF SOUND, **Gary Lauher,** c/o Randy Tenan, Apt. No.7, 1400 East Cotati Ave., Rohnert Park, CA 94928.

MEXICO QUARTERLY REVIEW, Apto. 15, Santa Catarina Martin, Puebla, Mexico.

MIRROR NORTHWEST, **Carl Waluconis** *(substitute for* **Randy Johnson** *– 1 year sabbat.),* Humanities Division, Bellevue Community College, Bellevue, WA 98007. Poetry, fiction, art, photos. 1/yr; $1.50/yr; $1.50/ea; 1971; 96pp; lo. Reports 1 wk to 2 mos. Pays copies only. No ads. Back issues: $1.50 (only issue 4 available).

MOONGOOSE, Decadent Press, **Ralph Alfonso,** 5252 Borden, Montreal, Quebec, Canada H4V 2T1. Poetry. *Will trade with other mags. Will distribute your fliers with* Moongoose *for free. We've undergone format changes and want only poetry. Emphasis on the sensual, and poems about citylife + etc.* Yearly; $1/yr; $1/ea; 1971; 30-50pp; 8½x11; 300 circ; mi. Reports 3 wks (SASE). Pays copies only (1). Ads: $20/p (printed offset); $10/½; no class/wd. Discounts: 75 cents for 3 or more; 20 copies for 50 cents each. Back issues: No.3: 75 cents; everything else is sold out. Pub'd none in 1973, expects 1 issue, 1 book in 1974.

MOTHER EARTH NEWS, Box 38, Madison, OH 44057.

MOTHER'S HEN, 1424 Gough St., San Francisco, CA 94109.

THE MT. ALVERNO REVIEW, PO Box 5143, Ocean Park Sta., CA 90405.

NEW AMERICAN REVIEW, 630 Fifth Ave., New York, NY 10020.

New Hogtown Press, 12 Hart House Circle, Univ. of Toronto, Toronto, Canada.

THE NEWSLETTER, 5 Beekman St., New York, NY 10038.

Next to Nothing Press (see BACK ROADS)

NORTH COUNTRY ANVIL, North Country Alternatives, Box 252, Millville, MN 55957.

Nwamife Publishers, Enugu, Nigeria, Africa.

OTHER VOICES, Alice in Wonderland, **Jane Johnson,** 100 Duchess Ave., London, Canada N6C IN6. Poetry, reviews. *Prefer poems no more than 20 L. No poetry or reviews accepted unless by a subscriber. (An independent poetry mag must be supported.) Any style / any form / but* Good. 2/yr; $3/yr; $1.50/ea; $1/sample; 1965; 18-24pp; 8x10; mi. Reports 2 wks. Pays copies only. No ads. Discounts: none, save for sample, free. Back issues: $2 except when rare. Pub'd 3 issues 1973, expects 3 in 1974.

Out of the Ashes Press, **Norman Solomon, Walt Curtis,** PO Box 42384. Portland, OR 97242. *Poetry, Essays, Fiction. We want to print what speaks real!* Variable; 1970; lo. Reports: variable. Pays copies only. Pub'd 3 books 1973, expects 4 in 1974. COSMEP, Radical.

PEOPLE'S BOOKSELLER NEWSLETTER, **Bob Brodel,** c/o Co-op Bks. & Records, PO Box 2436, Tallahassee, FL 32304.

RITA NOTES, Rita Act, D-69 Heidelberg, Marstallstr 11 A, West Germany. Poetry, articles, photos, cartoons, satire (?), letters. As often as necessary & possible: ca 100/yr; $30/25 issues; 1967; 1-60pp; 1-25M circ; mi; lo; lp (?); other. Reports: whenever have time – long! Pays: 0 + exchanges. Ads: (?). Back issues: $30/25 issues – open notes only. Pub'd 290-393 (?) issues 1973, expects 100 (?) in 1974. G.I., Prison.

Story-Lit Press, **Claude Tiller,** 17417 Woodingham Ave., Detroit, MI 48221. 1972.

STUDIES IN THE TWENTIETH CENTURY, Whitston Publishing Company, **Stephen Goode,** PO Box 12, Troy, NY 12181. Scholarly articles, interviews, criticism, reviews, letters. *Art and literature movements of the 20th century; especially the philosophies from which they ensued.* 2/yr; $4/yr; $2/ea; 1968; 100pp; 6x9; 300 circ; lo. Reports 2 wks +. Pays: 3 copies + 250 offprints. Ads: $50/p. Back issues: $3/ea. Pub'd 2 issues in 1973.

SUNBURST ANTHOLOGY MAGAZINE, **Clarence Poulin,** 87 High St., Penacook, NH 03301. Poetry. *Poem: traditional forms, 3-30 lines, plus a brief biography of the author. Recent contributors: Eleanor Vinton, Poet Laureate of NH, Margaret J. Heinrich, Judson Dicks, Elvira Vitoritto, Vera La Claustra, Alice MacKenzie Swaim, Alice Lemieux-Levesque, Rosaire Dion-Levesque.* Annual; $1.50/ea; 1970; 40pp; 8½x5½; 250 circ; mi. Reports 2 wks. No pay. Ads: $5/½p. Discounts: 4 copies of issue in which a poet is featured is $5; 10 copies $10. Pub'd 2 issues, 3 books 1973, expects 1 issue in 1974. NESPA.

TOUCHSTONE, **Michael Jervis A.C.I.S., John Price A.C.A.,** 19 Portree Dr., Rise Park, Nottingham, UK. Articles, poetry, news items, interviews, criticism, letters.

Monthly; £1.20/yr; 10p/ea; 1973; 25pp; 8x6½; 500+ circ; off. Ads: £4/page pro rata. Back issues: 5p. Occult.

WOMEN CAN (formerly THE PEDESTAL), **Edited Collectively,** 804 Richards St., Vancouver 3, BC, Canada. Articles, cartoons, interviews, criticism. *All fiction–poems must be Canadian in origin. Other material should be of significance + interest to Canadian women. It's a feminist newspaper so we only use material by women and our bias is that we prefer positive feminist material, social/political analysis, experiences of women at work, etc. Length up to 2,000 words.* Monthly (now); $3/yr USA & Canada; $10/yr instit; 25 cents/ea; free sample; 1968; 16pp; 17x11; 1500 circ; lo. Reports: send it when it's done. Pays: just fame; you get a copy! Ads: $5/3 column inches. Discounts: 10% or so for agents, bulk rates 15 cents a copy plus postage individuals + stores only, not to mention women centres. Back issues: some out of print, rates available, on microfilm. Pub'd 6 issues (every 2 mos) 1973, expects 12 in 1974. Women.

UNCLASSIFIED ADS

"HERE ARE MY SWEET LEMONS" poetry by Jane R. Card $3.00. "Poetry Markets" up-to-date market letter $3.00. Hummingbird Press, Box 392, Brea, CA 92621.

YOUR magazine printed, delivered postpaid. Free sample, details. Hummingbird Press Box 392 Brea CA 92621.

KIL-KAAS-GIT records fading Haida and Tlinget lifestyles. Write Craig, Alaska.

NEW WORLDS UNLIMITED, Sal St. John Buttaci, P.O. Box 556, Saddle Brook, N.J. 07662. Poetry. Send 1-5 poems, 2-14 lines. Enclose S.A.S.E. Any form or subject.

NORTHWOODS PRESS publishes 5 ways — one of which is right for you and your book — send long SASE for free booklet — Northwoods Press, Box 24, Bigfork, MN 56628.

THE ORIGINAL ART REPORT (TOAR), fine art newsletter by an artist about art condition in Midwest. Trial subscription: 3 issues: $2.00 to P.O. Box 1641, Chicago, IL 60690. See listing.

20 TIMES . . . Santa Barbara Anthology, $3.50 from PAINTED CAVE BOOKS, 362 Storke Road, Goleta, CA 93017.

SPOKEN WORD RECORDINGS FOR DISCRIMINATING COLLECTORS: Plantagenet Productions, Westridge, Highclere, Newbury, Berks, England.

QUETZAL — a bi-lingual book of poems for public performance from the San Francisco Mission Barrio, by Amilcar Lobos and Leland Mellott, with drawings by Rolando Castellon and Carlos Perez. (Co-published by Glide Publications and Casa Editorial). $3.50. Write Casa Editorial, 362 Capp Street, San Francisco, CA 94110.

Read YOGA – RELAXATION – MEDITATION by Dr. Gopal Puri, Ph.D – £1.05(p.p.) Roopvati Publications, Bucklands, Blundellsands, Liverpool 23 to ease tension, depression; cure nervousness, headaches, insomnia, phobias; to stop smoking and for relaxed living.

See SALTHOUSE listing on page 154.

25% DISCOUNT most Books in Print titles, $3.95 up. 30 cents/book postage. Pennsylvanians: 6% tax. Free organic/homesteading, children's lists. Spring Church Books, Box 127D, Spring Church, Pennsylvania 15686.

WITCH CRAFT, OLD RELIGION BOOK LIST : Stamped Envelope: MARTELLO, 153/West 80 St; New York, N.Y. 10024.

ZAHIR!

The Arts
Council of Great Britain

105 Piccadilly London W1V 0AU

Telephone 01-629 9495
Telegrams Amec London W1

Chairman Patrick Gibson
Secretary-General Sir Hugh Willatt

This is a library of modern poetry covering the period from 1930 to the present. The emphasis is on English poetry since the early 1950's, but American, Australian and translated European and Latin American poets are also represented.
The library is open to the public. Membership is free. Books are available for reference and loan. A catalogue of books in stock is available on request.
The library is open from 10 am until 5 pm on Monday, Tuesday, Wednesday and Friday, and until 7 pm on Thursday. It is closed from 12.30 to 1.30.

THE DOME BUILDER'S HANDBOOK

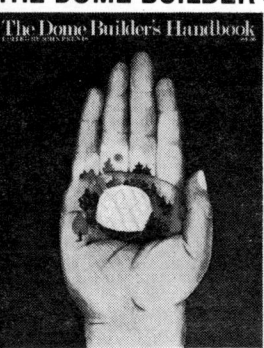

112 pages, illustrated, 4.00 paper 9.80 lib. binding

Twenty contributors explain how they coped with aspects of constructing their own domes. Prenis provides the opening guide to the basic types and techniques with illustrations that clearly convey the stages of complexity. The surface materials vary widely--plastics, canvas, cedar shingle, plywood, polyurethane foam--and almost all contributors include detailed plans along with a photograph of the completed structure. Information and advice, which is almost invariably enthusiastic, range from elaborate to just a few suggestions. Where shown, the cost are from $20 to $2,000. The greatest appeal will be to young people out of their teens. Suitable for pamphlet file as well as shelf

A.L.A. Booklist/ December 15, 1973, Classified books, 500 Pure Science & 600 Technology

THE SENSUOUS GADGETEER;
Bringing Tools & Materials To Life

112 pages, 3.95 paper 9.80 lib. binding

Addressed to the amateur, the concise guide avoids a how-to-do-it recitation in order to emphasize understanding of the functions of basic tools and materials. Illustrated with instructive line drawings. The manual begins with such simple aids as nails, hammers, files, wrenches, and other tools to be used with different woods. Succeeding chapters cover use of adhesives, abrasives, and plastics in molds and for casting sculpture; efficiency of manual techniques is reviewed in conclusion. A brief annotated bibliography is appended.

A.L.A. Booklist/ December 1, 1974, Classified books, 500 Pure Science & 600 Technology

JONATHON ERVIN'S LEATHER NOTEBOOK;
Making Sandals, Belts & Bags

117 pages, 3.95 paper 9.80 lib. binding

A beautifully designed and illustrated how to do it book that has nothing ordinary about it. Mr. Ervin writes clearly and concisely in his instructions and his attention to detail is uncanny. The printing format is styled as a handwritten communication with hand drawn complete illustrations.

A.L.A. Booklist/ March 1, 1974, Classified books, 700 The Arts

The Illustrated *Running Press* Edition of the American Classic
GRAY'S ANATOMY

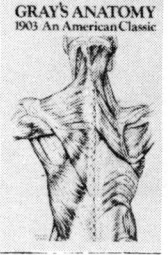

This is the first paperback edition of the classic Gray's Anatomy. The human anatomy is unchanging and this reproduction of the 1903 edition contains the diagrams and illustrations that make this the granddaddy of all anatomy books. The market for this book is every art student, every physician and anyone with an interest in the human body.

1200 pages, over 700 illustrations, 6.95 paper 12.95 cloth

Publication date May 16, 1974

COMPLETE ENCYCLOPEDIA OF NEEDLEWORK

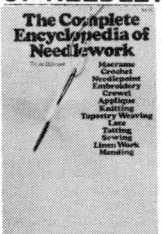

At last! France's needlework "bible" is in paperback! In large format, and for only $4.95! Believe the title; it has it all, carefully written, with clear precise diagramming and instructions even to needle size, thread weight, and how to modify designs. It's old-fashioned and pretty and it works.

Harper's/ April 1974

800 pages, 8 full color plates, 4.95 paper 9.90 lib. binding

LEARNING FROM THE INDIANS;
Wharton James 1908

269 pages, illustrated, 2.95 paper 9.80 lib. binding

Written in 1908 as "What the White Race May Learn From the Indians," this is a quaint and chatty volume by a dedicated outdoorsman who is indignant over the way Indians have been treated and admiring of many things about the way they live. Its tone is a little like those of the old Boy Scout Handbooks, but much more conversational, also more daring, as the author advocates nudity for children, breast-feeding and other such natural actions. It is not a how-to book, but does go into some detail about Indian methods of breathing, food preparation and such. There are lots of photos of a number of different tribes. Interesting to read this would make a good gift book.

Publisher's Weekly FORCASTS/ October 15, 1973

RUNNING PRESS
38 South Nineteenth Street, Philadelphia, Pennsylvania 19103

Announcing...

Poetry NOW

E.V. GRIFFITH, whose continuing poetry magazine, HEARSE, has been called "classic" and "one of the better edited, more important little poetry magazines in America", has launched a new poetry tabloid...**Poetry NOW**. One critic calls it "quite handsome and solid", another hails it as "The best thing that's happened to poetry all year."

Your subscription is invited ($5.00 for 6 issues, $9.00 for 12 issues). Or an "introductory" copy will be sent free to anyone sending 20c postage.

Poetry Now
3118 K Street
Eureka, CA 95501

6 Issues $5
12 Issues $9

Please enter my ... issue subscription. Payment enclosed herewith.

Name...

Street..

City...................... State............... Zip.....

The Smith

Ten Years Ahead

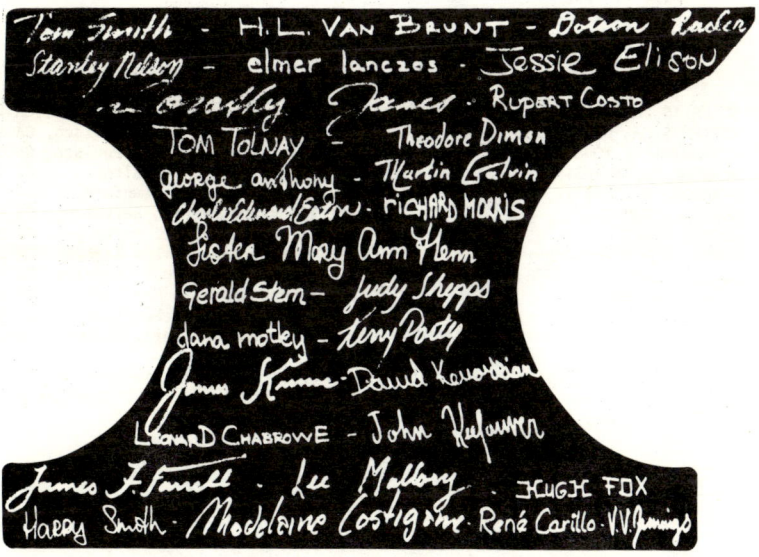

HIGH-VOLTAGE PHOTOGRAPHY

H. S. Dakin, 3456 Jackson Street, San Francisco, CA 94118. Published February, 1974. Library of Congress Catalog No. 74-77233. 65 pp., 8-1/2 x 11 in. paperback. Price $5.00 plus shipping costs (see below).

ABSTRACT

High-voltage photography--known also as Kirlian photography or electrography--is a method of making photographic prints or visual observations of objects using as a light source the luminous corona discharge which appears around electrically conductive objects in a high-voltage, high-frequency electric field.

Living organisms can be made luminous by this method. Tissue damage and electric shock hazard are minimized by the use of high-frequencies and low currents, and by careful design of experimental apparatus.

High-voltage power supplies as used by N. Tesla (1891) and later improvements using electromechanical vibrators and transistors, are described with schematic diagrams. Two circuits especially recommended for high-voltage photographic experiments are shown in detail as construction projects.

Interpretation of previously published observations of apparent "phantom" and psycholuminescent effects is hindered by the inherent instability of some widely used power supplies, and inadequate controls in some experimental work. Further studies with improved apparatus and experimental conditions are needed before previous work can be properly evaluated.

A concluding section discusses other methods, both practical and impractical, of showing physiological conditions and apparent psychophysical energy interactions as visible images or as physically measureable quantities (electrovision, thermovision, sonovision, auravision, plant bioelectrical measurements).

REVIEWERS' COMMENTS

A MASTERFUL PRESENTATION... ESPECIALLY USEFUL.

Stanley Krippner, Ph. D.
California State College, Sonoma

SHOULD BE VERY HELPFUL TO MANY EXPERIMENTERS.

William A. Tiller, Ph. D.
Stanford University

AVAILABLE FROM

STACEY'S BOOKS, MEDICAL DEPARTMENT*	581 Market Street, San Francisco, CA 94105
METAPHYSICAL CENTER BOOKSTORE*	420 Sutter Street, San Francisco, CA 94108
METAPHYSICAL TOWNHALL BOOKSHOP	345 Mason Street, San Francisco, CA 94102
ACADEMY OF PARAPSYCHOLOGY & MEDICINE*	314 Second Street, Los Altos, CA 94022
STANFORD UNIVERSITY BOOKSTORE	Stanford University, Stanford, CA 94305
SHAMBALA BOOKS	2482 Telegraph Avenue, Berkeley, CA 94704
CODY'S BOOKS	2454 Telegraph Avenue, Berkeley, CA 94704
BODHI TREE BOOKSTORE	8585 Melrose Avenue, Los Angeles, CA 90069
ZEITLIN AND VER BRUGGE	815 No. LaCienega Blvd. Los Angeles, CA 90069
SAMUEL WEISER, INC.	734 Broadway, New York, NY 10003
WITKIN GALLERY, INC.	243 East 60 Street, New York, NY 10022
THE SOCIETY OF METAPHYSICIANS	Archers Court, Hastings, Sussex, England

* Mail orders accepted. Add $1.00 (U. S. first class postage or U. P. S.) or $2.00 (foreign A-O rate air mail) per copy for shipping costs. Contact publisher for 40% discount on orders for 5 or more copies.

A harried and often comic journey across the turbulent America of the late 60s. The first (and last?) novel about the small presses.

NOBODY'S PERFECT

By Curt Johnson

Since 1962, Curt Johnson has published the little magazine *December*.

$6.00
Illus., paper, 236 p.p.

CARPENTER PRESS
Route #4
Pomeroy, Ohio 45769

"Along with being long, we find it a little long-winded."—Theodore Solotaroff, Simon & Schuster, Inc.

NOBODY'S PERFECT

ISBN 0—914140—01—9   LC No: 73—87508

MARGINS

MARGINS is a bi-monthly journal reviewing in-depth the little magazine/small press scene as it appears today. Each issue focuses on a topic relevant to small publishing, presents essays on important ideas, books, & magazines, & reviews recent small press/little magazine publications.

Past issues have included: 'On Being a Publisher' by Jay Bail; 'The Little Magger as Librarian' by Felix Pollak; 'Seven Women Poets' by Diane Kruchkow; 'Ten Anthologies: focus & purpose' by Tom Montag; 'Concrete Poetry' by Kathleen Wiegner; 'Toby Olson' by Martin J. Rosenblum; 'Richard Shelton' by Victor Contoski & by Tom Montag; 'New Zealand Scene' by D. S. Long; 'Four Views of Women's Writing' by Marge Piercy, Kathryn Ruby, Honor Moore, & Prudence Juris; 'Inside Aphra' by Elizabeth Fisher; 'Anger, Vision & Love: Two Anthologies of Women's Poetry' by Angela Peckenpaugh; and 'Open Letter: Its Concerns' by John Shannon. Contributing editor Karl Young examines 'narrative from small presses' in his column 'The Story Continues' in each issue.

Past issues have also included reviews by Terrance Ames, Jeffery Woodward, John Jacob, Robert Peters, Dave Buege, Kathryn Whitford, John Leax, and others.

Margins is published 8.5" x 10.5" on newsprint and is saddle-stitched. Issue size has been 40pp., though the size will shortly be increasing to 60pp.

Editor: Tom Montag. Contributing editors: Dave Buege, Martin J. Rosenblum, John Shannon, & Karl Young.

Subscription rates: $3.50/6 issues (one year); $6.00/12 issues (two years). Sample copy: 60 cents.

Special subscription rates to small press editors & publishers: $3/12 issues.

Advertising rates to small presses & little magazines: $20/full page; $12/half page; $7/quarter page; $4/eighth page. Write Margins for composition particulars.

Margins circulates 1,000 copies of each issue to libraries, bookstores, small presses, & interested individuals. No. 1 (August-September 1972) out of print; No. 2 (October-November 1972), 40 cents, available in limited supply; No. 3 (December 1972-January 1973) out of print; No. 4 (February-March 1973) out of print; No. 5 (April-May 1973) out of print; No. 6 (June-July 1973), 60 cents, available in limited supply; No. 7 (August-September 1973), 60 cents, available in limited supply.

Address review copies & correspondence regarding subscriptions, advertising, etc. to:

Margins
c/o Tom Montag
2912 N. Hackett
Milwaukee, WI 53211

A REVIEW OF LITTLE MAGS AND SMALL PRESS BOOKS

"Struggle Begets All" — Heraclitus

BERTOLT BRECHT wrote, upon the advent of radio, of all the people eager to say something over the radio waves, but who would have nothing to say, and of all those who would be listening eagerly but would have nothing to hear. Thus we witness the stream of endless nothings mouthed by radio, television and the "trade" publishers to fill the void, but creating only a deeper void. Consider then, the position of the small press or small magazine editor who confronts the void created by the corporate giants of American publishing. Surely the "New York" houses have twisted the old adage of 'HEAR NO EVIL, SEE NO EVIL, SPEAK NO EVIL' into an even more shapeless 'HEAR NOTHING, SEE NOTHING, and SPEAK NOTHING'. Though their stock in trade is literature and culture, they might as well be makers and sellers of soap. One can only resist this decay by setting one's self against the spirit of the age, by seeking in our lives and our art the illumination of what Ezra Pound called "the radiant gists".

The subject then is a poetry of reality as opposed to a poetry of surreality, a poetry of the Mind rather than a poetry of the Nerves. Surely the world we inhabit is no larger than our ability to speak that world. The tendency to express defeat by the real world and inhabit only a clockwork world is as deplorable among the small presses as it is in the television soap operas. Much of the poetry filling American literary magazines tittilates on the same level as the soap opera; i.e. what will happen to D'. ....or L. .... in their next appearance (the 32nd episode)? The poem, like a house made of stone, is best made when it is made to last.

True poetry does not exist without vision, a vision of the phenomenal world that grows out of experience. Another mark of the real poet as distinguished from the surreal poet: the real poet sticks in the throat like a Texas sandstorm or plunges for the heart like a hawk for a rabbit. The real poet's images ring true every step of the way like "a blade of grass as seen from the height of a walking man".

This is not to say that surreal poetry does not have its place; everything that man makes has its place in the sun. Contrast, however, the Spanish surrealists writing during and about the Spanish Civil War with the current American surrealists. The Spanish and Latin American poets have power only because the poems stick to the surface of the overwhelming reality they were undergoing. The American imitations avoid reality, in fact prefer not to undergo it; their wars are fought, in Camus' phrase, "with printer's ink but not with blood". An age of struggle is not a shameful age; rather the most shameful age is the era when ideas are swallowed whole by endless Oswalds (King Lear) who "know what party they follow". The great Russian director, Grigori Kosintzev, writes of the age of Shakespeare as an age of struggle, an age when "there were no level places, only footprints filled with blood". Who can deny our age is of equal violence, struggling to be born. The metaphor of poetry must not be a mere mirror reflecting a narcissistic self, but rather a lens that lets us see through the facade of appearances to lasting truth, to beauty that endures.

Our poetry is the weather of our days, the Northeasters that beat upon the coasts of Maine, the summer lightning that stalks the plains of Kansas, the raging waters of the Mississippi which churn to silt the myth of the invincibility of the levees. Our poetry is the ghost of the spirit of the Indian whose Manitou inhabited this land for tens of thousands of years, those who "walked dryshod from Asia". Our poetry beats with the same measure as that of the Greeks who poured down out of the steppes of the Caucasus under the boughs of the thick oaks along the Danube the length and breadth of Hellas to the sundrenched sea. Our poetry is the speech of the common man, as natural as the hand that darts the needle through the wool, as sturdy as the single—tree that swings above the plow flecked with the sweat of mules. Truly, we must struggle like mules to make it through the bogs and fens of the contemporary literary landscape. The small presses, those that are doing the work, are like "islands of the saved"; but one thing is certain, in the old parlance of the tent meetings 'no one gets to heaven alone'. Our poetry must capture the minds and hearts of our people in the same way as the sun, by stoking the fire that stirs them into life.

                                                Paul Foreman
                                                HYPERION POETRY JOURNAL
                                                2311–C Woolsey Street
                                                Berkeley, California 94705

LIFENOTES of a Small Pressman

ENCYCLOPAEDIC AND AUTOBIOGRAPHICAL, LIFENOTES IS AN EXCURSION THROUGH SPACE, TIME, STYLE AND MIND. FROM MAINE TO CALIFORNIA, THROUGH THE FIFTIES, THE SIXTIES, THE SEVENTIES, THIS IS A BIOGRAPHY OF THE SMALL PRESSES AND THE AUTOBIOGRAPHY OF LEN FULTON, WHO HAS MADE OF ALTERNATIVE PUBLISHING BOTH A LIFE AND A TIME.

LIFENOTES PRESENTS AN INTIMATE PICTURE OF THE ALTERNATIVE PUBLISHING REVOLUTION FROM THE BERKELEY FREE SPEECH MOVEMENT OF THE EARLY SIXTIES TO ITS MATURITY IN THE CURRENT SMALL PRESS CHALLENGE TO THE NEW YORK PUBLISHING MONOPOLY. FULTON'S VIEW RANGES, THE NARRATOR ON HORSEBACK. IT GIVES THE SILHOUETTE, THE ORGANIZATIONS WHICH OUTLINE THE MOVEMENT; AND THE CAMEO, PORTRAITS OF THE EDITORS, PUBLISHERS, POETS WHICH GIVE IT SUBSTANCE. AND IT HIGHLIGHTS THE LITERARY EXPLOSIONS, THE TECHNOLOGICAL STRIKES WHICH ACCOUNT FOR BOTH THE CHANGES AND THE CHOICES IN ALTERNATIVE PUBLISHING TODAY.

MUSINGS FROM THE SADDLE, CURSES FROM BEHIND THE PRESS, HOW TO GO BROKE WITH THREE NEWSPAPERS ON THE COAST OF MAINE, HOW TO PRINT, EDIT, DISTRIBUTE, POETS WHO ORGANIZE IN BERKELEY AND MAKE POSTCARDS INTO POEMS, THESE ARE THE NOTES IN LIFENOTES.

Publication Date: Jan.1, 1975 — write Dustbooks

$4.00 (paper) pre-pub
$6.50 (cloth)

LOTUS PRESS
P. O. Box 601
College Park Station
DETROIT, MICHIGAN 48221

BLACK PUBLISHERS OF POETRY

The Grassman
By Len Fulton
Illustrated by Andrew Curry

The great northwestern plains of Wyoming Territory were the last to fall before the fence, the rail, and the stock exchange. The Territory was the first to grant suffrage to women — and the first to hang one. The wind whispered names like Bridger, Phillips, and Crazy Horse down the Sundance, the Powder, and the Niobrara. White blizzard, politics and war brought it into the 20th Century, running from hell and heading for breakfast . . . .

The Grassman is Len Fulton's novel of the last moments of Wyoming's open-range cattle empires. It is the saga of the blood curse on the House of Finn: of Angus Benjamin, who ruled the Blacktail Country; of Andrew, the eastern nephew, journalist, atheist; of Holly Taft, fleeing from her father's menacing gods to a saloon of plainsmen.

And of a man named Greak, who preached, who killed, who hired out — but whose main talent was to survive.

Published by Thorp Springs Press

$2.95/paper   ISBN : 0-914476-27-0
$7.95/cloth   ISBN: 0-914476-26-2

small press review

DUSTBOOKS - Small mag/press information -- Use order blank on page 223

The SMALL PRESS REVIEW was started in 1966 as part of the skein of Dustbooks' small press trade material. It has tried to track the course of small press/mag publishing, to be a kind of running document, a moving record, a magazine which is a conscious part of the very course it examines. It contains news, reviews, features and listings related to world small presspeopleship. Rich Mangelsdorff has called it our "most venerable critical forum," in Nola Express. It also lists all books and magazines received and updates the annual Directory of Little Magazines.

The idea has been to put fact and opinion into a pragmatic mixture predicated on preserving creative enterprise, political or aesthetic theory and practice. There are no delusions as to possible or probable dominions: SPR throws in every time on the side of the little, the side of the new, the side of independent literature and thought.

It is used by libraries and universities and others as a periodic record of small press publications and activities; by booksellers as a source of saleable merchandise; by writers and small presses as a source of information and publicity, and as a yowling place.

Back issues of SPR are especially useful in characterizing the small press/magazine movement worldwide from the mid-sixties forward. All are available at $1.00 per copy, except Nos. 6-7, a turn-of-the-decade double issue, which is $2.00. No.1: an in memoriam issue for Alan Swallow; No.11: women, poetry and the small presses; No.12: small press organizations; No.15: Canadian small presses; No.16: Bukowski; No.20: African Presses; No.21: an analytic checklist of books from Something Else Press.

Published every other month starting in January. Advertising rates: $45 per full page (7" X 10"), $25 per half page (7" X 5" or 3½" X 10"), 10 cents per word Classified.

$5/year ------ $9/2 years ------ $13/3 years

ISSN No. US - 0037 - 7228

Directory of Small Magazine/Press Editors and Publishers.
5th Edition (1974-75)

A companion volume to the Directory of Little Magazines, this directory lists the editors and publishers of small magazines, presses and papers by editor's name alphabetically. It includes name and address of press or periodical which he or she edits, gives personal reading preferences, and reasons for editing.

$3.50/copy $11.00/4 yr subscription
(Back issues of Numbers 1&2 are free. Send 6x9 envelope.)

ISBN - 0 - 913218 - 28 - 6

Small Press Record of Books

This volume lists small press books and pamphlets published throughout the world. Listings are alphabetical by author and include title, publisher, height and width, number of pages, type of cover, print process, date, price and descriptive comment. Also carries a separate list of publishers and addresses.

First Edition (lists books for 1966-68) $2.00
Second Edition (1969-71) $2.50
Third Edition (1972-73) $3.50
Fourth Edition (1974) will appear early 1975 . . . . $3.50

$11.00/4 issue subscription

ISBN - 0 - 913218 - 40 - 5

NEW!

British Directory of Little Magazines and Small Presses.
1st Edition (1974-75)

This separate volume lists all British and Irish entries from the International Directory of Little Magazines and Small Presses.

$2.50/copy   ISBN - 0 - 913218 - 10 - 3

The Publish-It-Yourself Handbook:
Literary Tradition and How-To
Edited by Bill Henderson

This incredible book gives you the history of self-publishing throughout the last two centuries, tells you how to publish whatever it is you wish to publish *without* commercial or vanity publishers, and presents articles by 26 modern author publishers, including Anais Nin, Alan Swallow, Stewart Brand, Len Fulton, Leonard Woolf, Richard Kostelanetz, Dick Higgins and Alex Jackinson. It gives information on manufacturers, distributors, reviewers and promotion. ". . . no review can do justice to the variety of experiences and the wealth of information included in Henderson's book." (New York Times Book Review.) Published in 1973 by The Pushcart Book Press, there are now more than 13,000 copies of this book in print. 364 pages, illustrated.

$4.00/paper $10.00/cloth

Alternatives In Print 73-74
The Annual Catalog of Social Change Publications

A project of the Social Responsibilities Roundtable (SRRT) of the American Library Association, this third annual edition of AIP is the much-needed supplement to traditional book references such as the *Small Press Record of Books,* and *Books In Print.* From *Abortion* to *Zionism,* it is *the* comprehensive listing of alternative materials, classifying over 800 group/publishers, including fifty from Europe, and their 20,000 publications. There are four sections: 1) Thesarus of cross-referenced subject areas; 2) Subject index with groups/publishers alphabetized under each subject heading; 3) List of social change publications according to group/publisher; 4) List of all groups/publishers included in AIP. Glide Publications imprint. Introduction by Jackie Eubanks. 375 pages.

$6.95   ISBN - 912078 - 34 - 0

Bringing Forth Forms
By Andrew Curry

A poet, editor and teacher, this is Andrew Curry's philosophical memoir, essays on language, poetry, mythology, the treatment of schizophrenia, and the nature of meaning. Curry discusses many of the decade's controversies in areas as diverse as experiential and non-verbal methods of therapy, psychedelic drugs, understanding versus explanation, the use of mythology in contemporary poetry, the poetry of Hopkins and Issa in relation to psychotic experiences, and the myths of femininity. He explores the mythology of Black and White as few have done. In short, he dashes through the labyrinth and encounters the minotaur.

$3.50/paper   ISBN - 0 - 913218 - 21 - 9

Arnulfsaga *By Gary Elder*

Written from "a need to get down out of the vacuum of violence consuming us in this country," *Arnulfsaga* may be one of the most crucially important works of contemporary American poetry. With a style capable of lacing straight-talk through lyrical symphonic structures, Elder moves from sheer visionary grace through the monumental brutality born of the American experience, seeking nothing less than the comprehensive shape of that experience . . . and a great deal more. Subtitled, "Seven Fitts in The Last Days of the Nation," *Arnulfsaga* marks the commencement of a major work to come under that title.

$1.50/copy

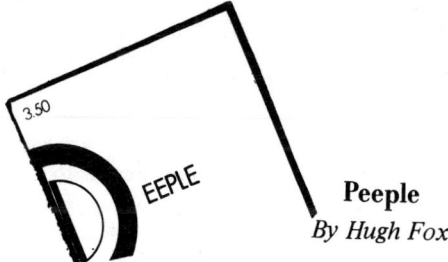

Peeple
By Hugh Fox

A series of vignettes, musings and lessons by one of the small press world's most prolific and outspoken advocates. The form is short, experimental prose. The subject is the existential human condition — in precisely eighty nine separate glances. Fox, a poet and teacher known for his Living Underground Series, gives us here his best humor, wit and wisdom.

$3.50/paper   ISBN - 0 - 913218 - 20 - 0

The Days of Tao *By Charles Baden Powell*

A BOOK OF POETRY THAT DELVES DEEPLY INTO THE PAST, THE FUTURE, THE EAST, AND THE WEST .... UNEARTHING THAT WHICH IS USEFUL TO THE PRESENT......... THE DAYS OF TAO, IS NOT A TIME .... BUT A STATE OF BEING THAT LIES WITHIN YOURSELF. IT NEVER TIRES OF WAITING ...... FOR YOUR RETURN .....

$1.50/copy ISBN - 0 - 913218 - 22 - 7

DUSTBOOKS — Use order blank on page 223

Romiossini
By Yannis Ritsos
$1.50/copy

Translation: O. Laos
Introduction: Dan Georgakas
Illustrations: Gary Elder

This is the story of the modern Greeks — the resistance movement of World War II and the betrayal of the partisans which followed. Filled with the textures of the land itself, its sights its sounds and rhythms, *Romiossini* is Ritsos' paean and lament to and for his countrymen whose tragedy and triumph he transcends as poet with the universal cry, "I love."

Conjuring A Counter-Culture *By Walt Shepperd*

If you took halting steps through the '50s, got chased through the '60s right on up against the wall of the '70s, and are trying to catch your breath, Shepperd's *Conjuring A Counter-Culture* may lend pace to your hyperventilation. In this series of poignant essays, the former publisher of the *Nickel Review* discusses Jefferson Airplane, Leary and Cleaver, the Weathermen, Henry Kissinger, and underground authors.

$3.50/paper; $5.95/cloth ISBN - 0 - 913218 - 18 - 9

The Poetry of Pop *By Joseph Bruchac*

The Doors, Dylan, Woodstock, The Beatles, The Who, The Stones, Ochs, Prine, Jethro Tull, The Impressions, The African influence — Joe Bruchac ranges over the "changeable religion" of popular music with the insight of an essayist and the vision of a poet. He contends that the lyrics of Dylan and Jagger, for example, are a poetry of the people. "Songs of certain writers brought home to me more about my own life and my culture than almost anything else I was exposed to in the way of art." An editor and prison teacher, Bruchac feels that the lyrics of popular songs have become more poetic as poetry writing itself seems to be reaching renaissance proportions. "It is time," he says, "that the lyrics of the best popular songs were looked at in the way we look at the best poems." This is what he does in *The Poetry of Pop*.

$3.50/paper ISBN - 0 - 913218 - 19 - 7

— Dustbooks, P.O. Box 1056, Paradise, CA 95969 —

DUSTBOOKS ORDER FORM

Item	Quantity
Directory/Little Magazines, Presses - paper (4.95)	
cloth (7.95)	
4 yr Subscription - paper (15.00)	
4 yr Subscription - cloth (25.00)	
Directory/Small Magazine/Press Editors - (3.50)	
4 yr Subscription - (11.00)	
Small Press Record of Books - (3.50)	
4 yr Subscription - (11.00)	
Small Press Review - 1 yr (5.00)	
2 yrs (9.00)	
3 yrs (13.00)	
Standing order (booksellers)	
The Publish-It-Yourself Handbook - paper (4.00)	
cloth (10.00)	
Alternatives In Print (6.95)	
The Grassman - paper (2.95)	
cloth (7.95)	
Conjuring a Counter-Culture - paper (3.50)	
cloth (5.95)	
Bringing Forth Forms (3.50)	
The Poetry of Pop (3.50)	
Peeple (2.00)	
Arnulfsaga (1.50)	
Romiossini (1.50)	
The Source (1.50)	
The Days of Tao (1.50)	
Once (1.50)	
Love Ode (1.00)	
Mind Dances (1.00)	
Other	

Amount enclosed _____

Name _____

Address _____

SUGGESTION BOX

THE INTERNATIONAL DIRECTORY OF LITTLE MAGAZINES AND SMALL PRESSES, now celebrating its tenth year, could not exist without the help of the editors, publishers, and writers it catalogues -- and without the readers it serves. Please use this space for complaints, comments, suggestions for improvement, or additional information you would like to see included. And above all let us know of any small magazines or presses we've missed, or new ones born after this edition. New listings will be published every two or three months in the "Updater" section of the SMALL PRESS REVIEW, and of course those new presses and mags will be sent a form for listing in next year's Directory. Thanks for the last ten years -- and on to the eleventh ....